The American Diplomatic Revolution:
a documentary history of the cold war 1941-1947

Edited by
JOSEPH M. SIRACUSA

National University Publications
KENNIKAT PRESS   //   1977
Port Washington, N. Y.   //   London

To my parents

Published and copyrighted in Australia © by Holt, Rinehart and Winston division of Holt, Saunders Pty, Ltd. United States edition published by Kennikat Press Corp.

Manufactured in the United States of America

Published by
Kennikat Press Corp.
Port Washington, N. Y./London

Library of Congress Cataloging in Publication Data
Main entry under title:

The American diplomatic revolution.

(National University publication) (Series in American studies)
      Bibliography: p.
      Includes index.
      1. World War, 1939-1945–Diplomatic history–Sources.
2. United States–Foreign relations–Russia–Sources.
3. Russia–Foreign relations–United States–Sources.
4. Atomic bomb–History–Sources. I. Siracusa, Joseph M.
D753.A76   940.53'22   76-54281
ISBN 0-8046-9174-6 (hard cover)

ISBN 0-8046-9180-0 (soft cover)

PREFACE

The purpose of this collection, which presupposes that the character of the Cold War was essentially ideological and political—a point of view generally held by the participants themselves—is twofold. First—recognizing in the words of Norman A. Graebner's pioneering study in ideas 'the significant relationship between the intellectual milieu in which a foreign policy is conducted and the foreign policy itself,[1]—it seeks to delineate the constellation of ideas, beliefs, and assumptions (both spoken and unspoken) of high level American and, to a lesser but important extent, Soviet policy makers in the period from 1941 to 1947, from Lend Lease to the Marshall Plan. Second, and equally important in the light of the present controversy over historiographical methodology[2], it seeks to provide the student of American-Soviet relations with an opportunity to confront for himself the major historical documents that have been the bases of the principal Cold War interpretations during the past thirty years. Such documents, many of which have only recently come into the public domain, have constituted the foundation of pivotal interpretations among traditional orthodox historians of the Cold War, moderate revisionists and the increasingly respectable (though anti-intellectual) New Left, whose origins and significance the editor has dealt with elsewhere.[3]

Within this general framework, the first chapter deals with Franklin D. Roosevelt's perception of the threat of totalitarianism, the Atlantic Charter controversy, and the Fulbright and Connally Resolutions—the latter consideration being a conscious effort to reintroduce the Congressional dimension to the Cold War, a dimension that in many ways determined the foreign policy parameters of the collective security debate. The second chapter deals with the growing suspicions of Ambassador Harriman, George Frost Kennan and FDR with regard to Soviet intentions in Eastern Europe in late 1944 and early 1945. The third chapter deals with the accession of Harry S. Truman to the Presidency, and suggests the extent to which he carried forward his predecessor's Russian policy. The fourth chapter deals with the hopes and expectations policy makers had of the role that the United Nations was to play in the postwar period. The fifth chapter deals with the origins and course of 'atomic diplomacy'. The sixth chapter deals with America's efforts to reconcile its own concept of national security with that of Soviet Russia's, underscoring the mutual exclusiveness of each. The seventh chapter deals with the ideas and themes that came to dominate the Cold War mentality by the end of 1946. And the eighth and final chapter deals with the nature and significance of the Truman Doctrine and its economic corollary, the Marshall Plan.

In terms of the selection made, the editor is fully aware that some may well question the wisdom either of including or excluding various documentary materials; and for this reason he frankly admits that due to the limitations of space imposed by a single volume there is no pretence of exhausting the subject matter. It is hoped, however, that the documents chosen reflect what Carl Becker used to call 'the climate of opinion'[4] or what is more fashionably known today (to borrow Thomas S. Kuhn's concept) as 'paradigm'.[5] The editor's intellectual debts, like those of any other historian of the Cold War period, are numerous and should be evident both throughout the commentary and in the bibliography that follows. More immediately, however, the editor should like to acknowledge the past scholarly assistance he has received from Professor Daniel M. Smith of the University of Colorado and Professor Robert A. Skotheim, formerly of the University of Colorado. Lastly, the editor should like to thank Mrs Mary Kooyman for her cheerful and generous cooperation in the typing of the manuscript.

St Lucia, Queensland   Joseph M. Siracusa
2 October 1974

[1] Norman A. Graebner, *Ideas and Diplomacy: Readings in the Intellectual Tradition of American Foreign Policy* (N.Y. 1964), vii.
[2] For example see Robert James Maddox, *The New Left and Origins of the Cold War* (Princeton, N.J., 1972).
[3] Joseph M. Siracusa, *New Left Diplomatic Histories and Historians: The American Revisionists* (Port Washington, N.Y., 1973).
[4] Carl Becker, 'Everyman His Own Historian,' *American Historical Review*, XXXVII (January 1932), 236.
[5] Thomas S. Kuhn, *The Structure of Scientific Revolutions* (2d ed., en1.; Chicago 1970).

Kennikat Press
National University Publications
Series in American Studies

CONTENTS

CHAPTER ONE

In Search of
a Brave New World

1   Franklin D. Roosevelt on the threat of totalitarianism and the four
     freedoms: January 6, 1941. *'Every realist knows that the democratic
     way of life is at this very moment being directly assailed in every part
     of the world . . . .'*

In his State of the Union Message to Congress on January 6 1941, shortly after his
election to an unprecedented third term of office and almost a full year before the
Japanese attack at Pearl Harbor, President Franklin D. Roosevelt carefully
combined the appeal of 'idealism' and 'realism' in requesting the American people to
resist the growing threat of totalitarian dictatorships. His speech is mainly remembered for its reference to the moral imperative of Lend Lease, the defense of the
democratic existence, and alternately the enunciation of the 'four freedoms'. President Roosevelt described in classical, realist language, the impending crisis: the
breakdown of the traditional European balance of power, the end of what has at
other times been called 'the age of free security', and the danger of allowing the vast
resources of Europe, Asia, Africa and Australia to fall into enemy hands. The two
threads of idealism and realism, which have contended with each other for the
control of American foreign policy since the early days of the Republic, were to
appear over and over again in speeches, policy statements and memoranda
throughout the wartime years and in the postwar period.

Source: *Congressional Record,* 77th Congress

I ADDRESS you, the Members of the Seventy-seventh Congress, at a moment unprecedented in the history of the Union. I use the word "unprecedented," because at no
previous time has American security been as seriously threatened from without as it is
today.

   Since the permanent formation of our Government under the Constitution, in 1789,
most of the periods of crisis in our history have related to our domestic affairs. Fortunately, only one of these—the four-year War Between the States—ever threatened our

national unity. Today, thank God, one hundred and thirty million Americans, in forty-eight States, have forgotten points of the compass in our national unity.

It is true that prior to 1914 the United States often had been disturbed by events in other Continents. We had even engaged in two wars with European nations and in a number of undeclared wars in the West Indies, in the Mediterranean and in the Pacific for the maintenance of American rights and for the principles of peaceful commerce. But in no case had a serious threat been raised against our national safety or our continued independence.

What I seek to convey is the historic truth that the United States as a nation has at all times maintained clear, definite opposition, to any attempt to lock us in behind an ancient Chinese wall while the procession of civilization went past. Today, thinking of our children and of their children, we oppose enforced isolation for ourselves or for any other part of the Americas.

That determination of ours, extending over all these years, was proved, for example, during the quarter century of wars following the French Revolution.

While the Napoleonic struggles did threaten interests of the United States because of the French foothold in the West Indies and in Louisiana, and while we engaged in the War of 1812 to vindicate our right to peaceful trade, it is nevertheless clear that neither France nor Great Britain, nor any other nation, was aiming at domination of the whole world.

In like fashion from 1815 to 1914—ninety-nine years—no single war in Europe or in Asia constituted a real threat against our future or against the future of any other American nation.

Except in the Maximilian interlude in Mexico, no foreign power sought to establish itself in this Hemisphere; and the strength of the British fleet in the Atlantic has been a friendly strength. It is still a friendly strength.

Even when the World War broke out in 1914, it seemed to contain only small threat of danger to our own American future. But, as time went on, the American people began to visualize what the downfall of democratic nations might mean to our own democracy.

We need not overemphasize imperfections in the Peace of Versailles. We need not harp on failure of the democracies to deal with problems of world reconstruction. We should remember that the Peace of 1919 was far less unjust than the kind of "pacification" which began even before Munich, and which is being carried on under the new order of tyranny that seeks to spread over every continent today. The American people have unalterably set their faces against that tyranny.

Every realist knows that the democratic way of life is at this moment being directly assailed in every part of the world—assailed either by arms, or by secret spreading of poisonous propaganda by those who seek to destroy unity and promote discord in nations that are still at peace.

During sixteen long months this assault has blotted out the whole pattern of democratic life in an appalling number of independent nations, great and small. The assailants are still on the march, threatening other nations, great and small.

Therefore, as your President, performing my constitutional duty to "give to the Congress information of the state of the Union," I find it, unhappily, necessary to report that the future and the safety of our country and of our democracy are overwhelmingly involved in events far beyond our borders.

Armed defense of democratic existence is now being gallantly waged in four continents. If that defense fails, all the population and all the resources of Europe, Asia, Africa and Australasia will be dominated by the conquerors. Let us remember that the total of those populations and their resources in those four continents greatly exceeds the sum total of the population and the resources of the whole of the Western Hemisphere—many times over.

In times like these it is immature—and incidentally, untrue—for anybody to brag that an unprepared America, single-handed, and with one hand tied behind its back, can hold off the whole world.

No realistic American can expect from a dictator's peace international generosity, or return of true independence, or world disarmament, or freedom of expression, or freedom of religion—or even good business.

Such a peace would bring no security for us or for our neighbors. "Those, who would give up essential liberty to purchase a little temporary safety, deserve neither liberty nor safety."

As a nation, we may take pride in the fact that we are soft-hearted; but we cannot afford to be soft-headed.

We must always be wary of those who with sounding brass and a tinkling cymbal preach the "ism" of appeasement.

We must especially beware of that small group of selfish men who would clip the wings of the American eagle in order to feather their own nests.

I have recently pointed out how quickly the tempo of modern warfare could bring into our very midst the physical attack which we must eventually expect if the dictator nations win this war.

There is much loose talk of our immunity from immediate and direct invasion from across the seas. Obviously, as long as the British Navy retains its power, no such danger exists. Even if there were no British Navy, it is not probable that any enemy would be stupid enough to attack us by landing troops in the United States from across thousands of miles of ocean, until it had acquired strategic bases from which to operate.

But we learn much from the lessons of the past years in Europe—particularly the lesson of Norway, whose essential seaports were captured by treachery and surprise built up over a series of years.

The first phase of the invasion of this Hemisphere would not be the landing of regular troops. The necessary strategic points would be occupied by secret agents and their dupes—and great numbers of them are already here, and in Latin America.

As long as the aggressor nations maintain the offensive, they—not we—will choose the time and the place and the method of their attack.

That is why the future of all the American Republics is today in serious danger.

That is why this Annual Message to the Congress is unique in our history.

That is why every member of the Executive Branch of the Government and every member of the Congress faces great responsibility and great accountability.

The need of the moment is that our actions and our policy should be devoted primarily—almost exclusively—to meeting this foreign peril. For all our domestic problems are now a part of the great emergency.

Just as our national policy in internal affairs has been based upon a decent respect for the rights and the dignity of all our fellow men within our gates, so our national policy in foreign affairs has been based on a decent respect for the rights and dignity of all nations, large and small. And the justice of morality must and will win in the end.

Our national policy is this:

First, by an impressive expression of the public will and without regard to partisanship, we are committed to all-inclusive national defense.

Second, by an impressive expression of the public will and without regard to partisanship, we are committed to full support of all those resolute peoples, everywhere, who are resisting aggression and are thereby keeping war away from our Hemisphere. By this support, we express our determination that the democratic cause shall prevail; and we strengthen the defense and the security of our own nation.

Third, by an impressive expression of the public will and without regard to partisanship, we are committed to the proposition that principles of morality and considerations for our own security will never permit us to acquiesce in a peace dictated by aggressors and sponsored by appeasers. We know that enduring peace cannot be bought at the cost of other people's freedom.

In the recent national election there was no substantial difference between the two great parties in respect to that national policy. No issue was fought out on this line before the American electorate. Today it is abundantly evident that American citizens everywhere are demanding and supporting speedy and complete action in recognition of obvious danger.

Therefore, the immediate need is a swift and driving increase in our armament production.

Leaders of industry and labor have responded to our summons. Goals of speed have been set. In some cases these goals are being reached ahead of time; in some cases we are on schedule; in other cases there are slight but not serious delays; and in some cases—and I am sorry to say very important cases—we are all concerned by the slowness of the accomplishment of our plans.

The Army and Navy, however, have made substantial progress during the past year. Actual experience is improving and speeding up our methods of production with every passing day. And today's best is not good enough for tomorrow.

I am not satisfied with the progress thus far made. The men in charge of the program represent the best in training, in ability, and in patriotism. They are not satisfied with the progress thus far made. None of us will be satisfied until the job is done.

No matter whether the original goal was set too high or too low, our objective is quicker and better results.

To give you two illustrations:

We are behind schedule in turning out finished airplanes; we are working day and night to solve the innumerable problems and to catch up.

We are ahead of schedule in building warships but we are working to get even further ahead of that schedule.

To change a whole nation from a basis of peacetime production of implements of peace to a basis of wartime production of implements of war is no small task. And the greatest difficulty comes at the beginning of the program, when new tools, new plant facilities, new assembly lines, and new ship ways must first be constructed before the actual materiel begins to flow steadily and speedily from them.

The Congress, of course, must rightly keep itself informed at all times of the progress of the program. However, there is certain information, as the Congress itself will readily recognize, which, in the interests of our own security and those of the nations that we are supporting, must of needs be kept in confidence.

New circumstances are constantly begetting new needs for our safety. I shall ask this Congress for greatly increased new appropriations and authorizations to carry on what we have begun.

I also ask this Congress for authority and for funds sufficient to manufacture additional munitions and war supplies of many kinds, to be turned over to those nations which are now in actual war with aggressor nations.

Our most useful and immediate role is to act as an arsenal for them as well as for ourselves. They do not need man power, but they do need billions of dollars worth of the weapons of defense.

The time is near when they will not be able to pay for them all in ready cash. We cannot, and we will not, tell them that they must surrender, merely because of present inability to pay for the weapons which we know they must have.

I do not recommend that we make them a loan of dollars with which to pay for these weapons—a loan to be repaid in dollars.

I recommend that we make it possible for those nations to continue to obtain war materials in the United States, fitting their orders into our own program. Nearly all their matériel would, if the time ever came, be useful for our own defense.

Taking counsel of expert military and naval authorities, considering what is best for our own security, we are free to decide how much should be kept here and how much should be sent abroad to our friends who by their determined and heroic resistance are giving us time in which to make ready our own defense.

For what we send abroad, we shall be repaid within a reasonable time following the close of hostilities, in similar materials, or, at our option, in other goods of many kinds, which they can produce and which we need.

Let us say to the democracies: "We Americans are vitally concerned in your defense of freedom. We are putting forth our energies, our resources and our organizing powers to give you the strength to regain and maintain a free world. We shall send you, in ever-increasing numbers, ships, planes, tanks, guns. This is our purpose and our pledge."

In fulfillment of this purpose we will not be intimidated by the threats of dictators that they will regard as a breach of international law or as an act of war our aid to the democracies which dare to resist their aggression. Such aid is not an act of war, even if a dictator should unilaterally proclaim it so to be.

When the dictators, if the dictators, are ready to make war upon us, they will not wait for an act of war on our part. They did not wait for Norway or Belgium or the Netherlands to commit an act of war.

Their only interest is in a new one-way international law, which lacks mutuality in its observance, and, therefore, becomes an instrument of oppression.

The happiness of future generations of Americans may well depend upon how effective and how immediate we can make our aid felt. No one can tell the exact character of the emergency situations that we may be called upon to meet. The Nation's hands must not be tied when the Nation's life is in danger.

We must all prepare to make the sacrifices that the emergency—almost as serious as war itself—demands. Whatever stands in the way of speed and efficiency in defense preparations must give way to the national need.

A free nation has the right to expect full cooperation from all groups. A free nation has the right to look to the leaders of business, of labor, and of agriculture to take the lead in stimulating effort, not among other groups but within their own groups.

The best way of dealing with the few slackers or trouble makers in our midst is, first, to shame them by patriotic example, and, if that fails, to use the sovereignty of Government to save Government.

As men do not live by bread alone, they do not fight by armaments alone. Those who man our defenses, and those behind them who build our defenses, must have the stamina and the courage which come from unshakable belief in the manner of life which they are defending. The mighty action that we are calling for cannot be based on a disregard of all things worth fighting for.

The Nation takes great satisfaction and much strength from the things which have been done to make its people conscious of their individual stake in the preservation of democratic life in America. Those things have toughened the fibre of our people, have renewed their faith and strengthened their devotion to the institutions we make ready to protect.

Certainly this is no time for any of us to stop thinking about the social and economic problems which are the root cause of the social revolution which is today a supreme factor in the world.

For there is nothing mysterious about the foundations of a healthy and strong democracy. The basic things expected by our people of their political and economic systems are simple. They are:

Equality of opportunity for youth and for others.

Jobs for those who can work.

Security for those who need it.

The ending of special privilege for the few.

The preservation of civil liberties for all.

The enjoyment of the fruits of scientific progress in a wider and constantly rising standard of living.

These are the simple, basic things that must never be lost sight of in the turmoil and unbelievable complexity of our modern world. The inner and abiding strength of our economic and political systems is dependent upon the degree to which they fulfill these expectations.

Many subjects connected with our social economy call for immediate improvement.

As examples:

We should bring more citizens under the coverage of old-age pensions and unemploy-ment insurance.

We should widen the opportunities for adequate medical care.

We should plan a better system by which persons deserving or needing gainful employment may obtain it.

I have called for personal sacrifice. I am assured of the willingness of almost all Americans to respond to that call.

A part of the sacrifice means the payment of more money in taxes. In my Budget Message I shall recommend that a greater portion of this great defense program be paid for from taxation than we are paying today. No person should try, or be allowed, to get rich out of this program; and the principle of tax payments in accordance with ability to pay should be constantly before our eyes to guide our legislation.

If the Congress maintains these principles, the voters, putting patriotism ahead of pocketbooks, will give you their applause.

In the future days, which we seek to make secure, we look forward to a world founded upon four essential human freedoms.

The first is freedom of speech and expression—everywhere in the world.

The second is freedom of every person to worship God in his own way—everywhere in the world.

The third is freedom from want—which, translated into world terms, means economic understandings which will secure to every nation a healthy peacetime life for its inhabitants—everywhere in the world.

The fourth is freedom from fear—which, translated into world terms, means a world-wide reduction of armaments to such a point and in such a thorough fashion that no nation will be in a position to commit an act of physical aggression against any neighbor—anywhere in the world.

That is no vision of a distant millennium. It is a definite basis for a kind of world attainable in our own time and generation. That kind of world is the very antithesis of the so-called new order of tyranny which the dictators seek to create with the crash of a bomb.

To that new order we oppose the greater conception—the moral order. A good society is able to face schemes of world domination and foreign revolutions alike without fear.

Since the beginning of our American history, we have been engaged in change—in a perpetual peaceful revolution—a revolution which goes on steadily, quietly adjusting itself to changing conditions—without the concentration camp or the quick-lime in the ditch. The world order which we seek is the cooperation of free countries, working together in a friendly, civilized society.

This nation has placed its destiny in the hands and heads and hearts of its millions of free men and women; and its faith in freedom under the guidance of God. Freedom means the supremacy of human rights everywhere. Our support goes to those who struggle to gain those rights or keep them. Our strength is our unity of purpose.

To that high concept there can be no end save victory.

2   Roosevelt, Churchill and the Atlantic Charter: August 14, 1941: '. . .
     the President of the United States of America and the Prime Minister
     . . . deem it right to make known certain common principles in the
     national policies of their respective countries on which they base
     their hopes for a better future for the world.'

In early August 1941, in Argentia Harbor of Placentia Bay in Newfoundland, President Roosevelt and Prime Minister Churchill met to discuss, among other things, the coordination of their war effort against Germany. At this time and upon consideration of what these two leaders of the Western democracies regarded as the serious

threat that German militarism posed to modern civilization, it was decided to release a joint statement of principles on which it was hoped the postwar world would be built. The impact of the message was at once profound and far-reaching. For despite the subsequent controversy over whether FDR or Churchill actually signed the document, and despite the well-known British and Soviet reservations about it, the Atlantic Charter, together with the doctrine of Unconditional Surrender announced at Casablanca by Roosevelt in January 1943, captured the public's imagination and in large measure conditioned and influenced policy makers' thinking about the role of United States foreign policy.

Source: Department of State, *Foreign Relations of the United States, Diplomatic Papers: 1941* (Wash. 1958), I, 367-69.

The following statement signed by the President of the United States and the Prime Minister of Great Britain is released for the information of the Press:

The President of the United States and the Prime Minister, Mr. Churchill, representing His Majesty's Government in the United Kingdom, have met at sea.

They have been accompanied by officials of their two Governments, including high ranking officers of their Military, Naval and Air Services.

The whole problem of the supply of munitions of war, as provided by the Lease-Lend Act, for the armed forces of the United States and for those countries actively engaged in resisting aggression has been further examined.

Lord Beaverbrook, the Minister of Supply of the British Government, has joined in these conferences. He is going to proceed to Washington to discuss further details with appropriate officials of the United States Government. These conferences will also cover the supply problems of the Soviet Union.

The President and the Prime Minister have had several conferences. They have considered the dangers to world civilization arising from the policies of military domination by conquest upon which the Hitlerite government of Germany and other governments associated therewith have embarked, and have made clear the stress which their countries are respectively taking for their safety in the face of these dangers.

They have agreed upon the following joint declaration:

Joint declaration of the President of the United States of America and the Prime Minister, Mr. Churchill, representing His Majesty's Government in the United Kingdom, being met together, deem it right to make known certain common principles in the national policies of their respective countries on which they base their hopes for a better future for the world.

First, their countries seek no aggrandizement, territorial or other;

Second, they desire to see no territorial changes that do not accord with the freely expressed wishes of the peoples concerned;

Third, they respect the right of all peoples to choose the form of government under which they will live; and they wish to see sovereign rights and self government restored to those who have been forcibly deprived of them;

Fourth, they will endeavor, with due respect for their existing obligations, to further the enjoyment by all States, great or small, victor or vanquished, of access, on equal terms, to the trade and to the raw materials of the world which are needed for their economic prosperity;

Fifth, they desire to bring about the fullest collaboration between all nations in the economic field with the object of securing, for all, improved labor standards, economic advancement and social security;

Sixth, after the final destruction of the Nazi tyranny, they hope to see established a peace which will afford to all nations the means of dwelling in safety within their own boundaries, and which will afford assurance that all the men in all the lands may live out their lives in freedom from fear and want;

Seventh, such a peace should enable all men to traverse the high seas and oceans without hindrance;

Eighth, they believe that all of the nations of the world, for realistic as well as spiritual reasons must come to the abandonment of the use of force. Since no future peace can be maintained if land, sea or air armaments continue to be employed by nations which threaten, or may threaten, aggression outside of their frontiers, they believe, pending the establishment of a wider and permanent system of general security, that the disarmament of such nations is essential. They will likewise aid and encourage all other practicable measures which will lighten for peace-loving peoples the crushing burden of armaments.

3   Policy with regard to the Soviet Union in case of the outbreak of war between the Soviet Union and Germany: June 21, 1941. *'We should steadfastly adhere to the line that the fact that the Soviet Union is fighting Germany does not mean that it is defending, struggling for, or adhering to, the principles in international relations which we are supporting.'*

Shortly before Hitler's invasion of the Soviet Union, a State Department position paper outlined a number of policies the United States should follow with respect to Russia. Of the policy recommendations made, one in particular clearly reveals the deepseated hostility towards Bolshevism that existed in pre-World War II America. This was the suggestion to steadfastly deny any connection between the principles which the United States stood for and any that might be put forward by the Kremlin in the defence against Nazi Germany.

Source: ibid, 766-67.

Reports which are coming in regarding the situation in Eastern Europe make it clear that we should not exclude the possibility of outbreak of war in the immediate future between Germany and the Soviet Union. In case war does take place we are of the opinion that our policy with regard to the Soviet Union, at least during the early stages of the conflict, should be as follows:

(1)   We should offer the Soviet Union no suggestions or advice unless the Soviet Union approaches us.

(2)   In case the Department is asked by parties other than a representative of the

Soviet Government if it intends to give aid to the Soviet Union in the event of German-Soviet conflict, the reply should be that we have as yet not been approached by the Soviet Government on this subject.

(3)   If the Soviet Government should approach us direct requesting assistance, we should so far as possible, without interfering in our aid to Great Britain and to victims of aggression or without seriously affecting our own efforts of preparedness, relax restrictions on exports to the Soviet Union, permitting it even to have such military supplies as it might need badly and which we could afford to spare.

(4)   Such economic aid as we might give the Soviet Union in the form of materials should be extended direct on the basis of mutual advantage and not in cooperation with any third power.

(5)   We should steadfastly adhere to the line that the fact that the Soviet Union is fighting Germany does not mean that it is defending, struggling for, or adhering to, the principles in international relations which we are supporting.

(6)   We should make no promises in advance to the Soviet Union with regard to the assistance which we might render in case of a German-Soviet conflict, and we should take no commitment as to what our future policy towards the Soviet Union or Russia might be. In particular we should engage in no undertaking which might make it appear that we have not acted in good faith if later we should refuse to recognize a refugee Soviet Government or cease to recognize the Soviet Ambassador in Washington as the diplomatic representative of Russia in case the Soviet Union should be defeated and the Soviet Government should be obliged to leave the country.

4   The Fulbright and Connally Resolutions—'Second Chance':
      September-November 1943

Taken together, the Fulbright Resolution (passed in the House by 360 votes to 20 on September 21, 1943) and the Connally Resolution (passed in the Senate by 85 votes to 5 on November 5, 1943) served notice to the world that the American people through their representatives in the United States Congress intended to take advantage of a 'second chance' in establishing the postwar machinery aimed at building a viable collective security system. Exhibiting a sense of guilt at having presumably abandoned Woodrow Wilson's League of Nations, Congress was determined not to repeat the mistakes of the past. Both resolutions, though seeking to safeguard American sovereignty and preserving a free hand for future Congresses, clearly foreshadowed United States participation in appropriate international machinery designed to maintain the peace against further aggression. This decision marked the beginning of a true American diplomatic revolution in the sense that, while an earlier America of Warren Harding could turn its back on the aftermath of World War I and the subsequent rampant militarism that sought to undermine the Versailles Settlement, the America of Franklin Roosevelt and later Harry S. Truman felt duty-bound to lead the resistance to what it regarded as mostly aggressive, Soviet behaviour. In the first of the readings below, then-Representative William J. Fulbright (D., Arkansas) highlighted the United States' responsibility to maintain world order, although he was under no illusions as to the dangers and difficulties that lay ahead. The following reading by Representative Walter H. Judd (R., Minnesota), a devoted friend of China who had spoken extensively during the 1930s in an attempt to arouse Americans to the menace of Japanese militarism, suggested that the only alternative to United States cooperation with other nations in the postwar world was American imperialism, a course he saw as both morally wrong and physically impracticable. The Connally Resolution, introduced by Senator Tom Connally (D., Texas), chairman of the influential Senate Foreign Relations Committee, powerfully reminded the Senate both of its past failure to realize Wilson's League of Nations and its future responsibility to unborn generations in avoiding another even more terrible world war. Critics of the Fulbright and Connally Resolutions, though numerically small, bear a striking resemblance to critics of American foreign policy during the late 1960s, mainly to the extent that each recalled definite physical limitations to what the United States could hope to accomplish in remaking the world over into its own image. Representative William Lemke (R., North Dakota), a onetime Union Party candidate for the Presidency in 1936, doubted the wisdom of signing what he believed to be a 'blank check' to involve the nation in international disputes, not to mention the cost, saying 'Uncle Sam is not going to be a perpetual Santa Claus'. The most important Senate dissenter was in many ways the prophetic Burton K. Wheeler (D., Montana), himself an unsuccessful candidate for Vice President on the ticket nominated in 1924 by the Conference for Progressive Political Action with Robert M. LaFollette. Disclaiming the title of 'isolationist' and alluding to the possible abuse of executive power, Wheeler consistently opposed as self-defeating any and all military alliances backed up by force, although he was prepared to entertain some sort of alliance system between Russia, England and the United States.

4(a)   Congressman Fulbright and the wisdom of creating international machinery adequate to establishing and maintaining a joint and lasting peace: September 20, 1943. *'I have no illusions that this resolution is the panacea for all our afflictions.'*

Source: *Congressional Record*, 78th Congress

. . . much has been said and written about the significance of this resolution. There are those who say it is too strong, that it goes too far; on the other hand, there are those who say it is innocuous and meaningless, that it is too weak. The one thing I gather from this discussion is that it must actually be about halfway between, and therefore about right.

I believe that many have become unduly suspicion of this plain and simple statement of basic principle.

I have no illusions that this resolution is the panacea for all our afflictions. It expresses what I believe the people of this country desire as the fundamental principle for our conduct toward the other nations of the world. It is simply the first small step in the process of building a policy which I hope may have better results than that which we have followed in the past. We now have, throughout the world, ample evidence of the inevitable consequences of that policy. Surely it is worth while to try a new approach to the problem of total war, even though no one can guarantee the success of our efforts. After this first step is taken, it is obvious that many more steps must be taken before an adequate policy can be achieved.

As the editor of the Washington Star said in yesterday's paper:

> What we need now is a simple expression of our determination that, having won a global war, we shall live up to our responsibilities of maintaining global peace. This resolution will not settle the future of the world. But if the House gives it united support tomorrow, the representatives of the people will have outlined the pattern of the policy we are to pursue in international collaboration after the war. What most Americans want to see is some agreement among their representatives on where we are going after this war is won. Nonpartisan endorsement of this resolution by a solid House will tell them and tell them what they want to know.

This resolution is not a grant of power to the Executive; it is simply an expression by our people, through their representatives, that we intend to participate sincerely in an effort to bring order into the world. If this resolution is adopted, the Executive can negotiate as to details with assurance that the people are willing to support any reasonable system of collective security. But, as the various components of the system are agreed upon by the different governments, they still must be approved by legislation in the nature of treaties or by joint resolution of the Senate and the House of Representatives. This is not a final acceptance now of any kind of agreements that may be evolved. Even if nothing acceptable results from these negotiations, nevertheless we will have the satisfaction of having tried and cannot in any respect be any worse off than we will be if we do nothing.

This resolution tells the world that the United States recognizes that any organization for peace must be based upon power adequate to enforce peace, and that the United States will share both in supplying that power and in the responsibility for the exercise of that power. One may say that this is a commitment that this Nation undertakes to participate with the other nations of the world in a genuine and bona fide effort to find some reasonable means to solve the international disputes by methods other than by war.

Much has been said about a provision for the use of force. The words "power adequate to establish and to maintain a just and lasting peace" not only envisage the use of some kind of force, but may also include the power, if necessary, to control the productive capacity of instruments of aggressive warfare. The traditional police force which disturbs so many people may not be nearly so important in the long run as control of strategic materials and productive capacity.

The question of relief and rehabilitation or as some call it an international W.P.A. has little to do with the formulation of a foreign policy or the creation of machinery to keep the peace. It may be that relief in the form of food or other goods has a place in military operations in occupied countries or in the settlement of this particular war. But this war is but a tragic and horrible episode which one of these days must end.

A proper foreign policy, together with the machinery to keep the peace, is continuing in its nature; it does not consist of sporadic instances of emotional altruism or niggardly selfishness. To be successful it will require the assiduous daily attention of the best brains of our country. It is brains and leadership that we must supply, and not merely gifts of bread, and milk, and money, and oil. It is not contemplated that we, the people of the United States, are to give our goods to others, that we are to raise the standards of living of the peoples of the world, or even to give them all a free and democratic government. If we can contribute leadership and our fair share of the force found necessary to make an international system of control effective, that is all the world can or should expect. As a matter of fact, if these total wars can be prevented for a reasonable length of time, most of the peoples of the world probably can work out their own economic and political salvation. I assume, of course, that our influence will always be on the side of free and democratic processes.

Participation by this Nation in a system designed to prevent war is inspired and justified primarily by the desire to preserve that integrity and freedom of the individual which is the great distinction of our Nation, and the hope of the world. It is, of course, true that in saving our own freedom we will inevitably benefit other peoples of the world. But surely we will not refuse to save ourselves simply because in doing so we may help save others.

Perhaps the most significant thing about this resolution is the fact that it originated in this House of Representatives and is a nonpartisan measure. Both are important. Our foreign policy must be consistent over the years. It must not be a partisan affair, shifting with every election. Further, since the House of Representatives is at all times more nearly reflective of the will of the people than any other body, it should play an important part in the formulation of fundamental policy. Only with congressional sanction can the other nations of the world rely with assurance upon the commitments of our Executive. The adoption of this resolution by the House and the Senate will create a precedent for the further participation by the House of Representatives in the matter of foreign policy and will give that policy stability and force. Nothing in the Constitution prohibits the participation of this House in the formulation of basic policy. If we show some intelligence and courage in expressing positively our views on these matters, I am confident they will not be ignored by our own Government or by the governments throughout the world . . . .

4(b) Walter H. Judd on the problem of learning to live together: September 21, 1943. *'Sometimes I wish we had a planet all by ourselves.'*

Source: ibid.

. . . our Nation is in the midst of the greatest crisis in her history. We have a twofold task. One is the immediate task of checking the reign of terror let loose by the Axis throughout the world. There is no possibility of there ever again being a decent, orderly, peaceful world, with security for ourselves, unless there is a complete defeat of the things that Japanese militarism and Hitlerism represent. But we can get that defeat, as we did once before, and still not get the decent world.

Victory over the enemy is prerequisite, but victory in itself does not touch the solution of our larger problem. It only gives us a chance to solve that problem.

And what is the problem? Basically, it is just this, very simple and very difficult—the peoples of the world learning to live together. That is the long-term task. We must help build new relationships between nations, and new techniques for solving their disputes, so that this sort of thing cannot happen every 25 years. To do that we must achieve with our allies a long-term collaboration and teamwork.

What kind of a world do we want? I think that if we examine our own minds and desires carefully, we will say the two things the majority of Americans wants, most of all, are prosperity and security. Can we get either of those objectives just by our own effort without regard to the rest of the world?

Let us consider first prosperity. In order to furnish food and supplies for ourselves, our men on dozens of battle fronts, our allies, and hungry millions being liberated from Axis tyranny, we have been forced to build up in America productive capacity far in excess of what we at home can consume, or at least more than we can buy and pay for. After the war we will be left with an enormously overbuilt plant, agricultural and industrial. We must then either drastically reduce our plant to what we can consume, which would mean putting millions of men and women out of work at the very time soldiers are being demobilised and we need several million more, not fewer, jobs; or, we must find new markets for our surplus productive capacity. There are only two places to develop such new markets—at home and abroad.

We must be planning now to multiply jobs by building up in every possible way new industries and markets here at home. But with all the expansion possible, the American market simply cannot be enough to keep the American farmer and manufacturer and laborer at full employment. We must, therefore, lay long-range plans to increase our markets abroad.

America can exist by herself alone, even as a farmer can exist by himself. He can grow enough grain, vegetables, chickens, hogs, sheep, and so forth, to feed and clothe himself and his family; but he cannot develop a high standard of living, he cannot secure modern conveniences, he cannot develop a satisfying social and cultural life without trade and cordial relations with his neighbors. Wealth and prosperity come from exchange of commodities on a mutually beneficial basis: and rich culture and civilization come from interchange of ideas and personalities.

But there is no possiblity of such trade and interchange between nations, and therefore no possibility of long-term economic prosperity here in America, unless there is political security throughout the world. One cannot enter into a contract with a firm in a foreign land unless there is reasonable certainty that goods can go and come, and that media of exchange will be stable, and that war or revolution will not be breaking out.

That brings us back to the other major objective—security. That is the fundamental problem—how can we get security? How can we preserve the peace after we have won it? How can we prevent these periodic outbreaks of increasingly violent, and costly, and disastrous wars?

In all history there have been but three types of security. The first was by individual armaments. Every man on our plains carried a gun on his hip. But it did not give him adequate security, because two or three others could always gang up against him.

Therefore, he went to the second stage—the stage of alliances. The cattle thieves, and horse rustlers, and highwaymen were allied in gangs. Therefore, the law-abiding citizens had to form alliances also. They were not ideal. They led at times to perversions of justice, to vigilante groups, to lynch law. But on the whole, they gave a greater degree of security than just individual armaments. It was the balance-of-power system.

Then our forefathers, as the country became more thickly settled and society became more complex, were wise enough to proceed to the third stage—that of organized security. If a man wanted to be sure that his family had a maximum of security with a minimum cost of his own time and money, the way to do it was to join with his neighbors in organizing the community to make sure there would be clean water for all, and good sewage disposal, and good schools, good highways, good public health, and a good police force.

It was not because he was more interested in his neighbor's wife than in his own that he recognized it was part of his business to see that the neighbor's wife was safe and secure. It was only because he could not be sure of his own wife's safety unless he helped build a community orderliness which would make every law-abiding person in the area reasonably secure. Only when that had been achieved could he give up carrying his gun.

We in America tried for 20 years to get along without any one of the three. We would not go into alliances with the nations whose interests were nearest to our own. We would not join with other countries in an attempt to get organized security. And then we gave up our gun. No wonder we are fighting for our lives.

We allowed ourselves to be deluded by the fact that our country, until recent decades, was able to get security by physical separation from the rest of the world. Nature gave us two wide oceans, but we ourselves destroyed them with our own inventions. It was we, not the Germans or Japanese, who invented the steamboat, the submarine, and the airplane. We ate up the cake of our physical isolation with our own inventions, and still thought we had it. We jammed ourselves into the same boat with the rest of the world, and assumed that the boat could sink, but that by some magic we remain afloat.

Sometimes I wish we had a planet all by ourselves. Wouldn't that be fine? And yet I know what we would do, being Americans. We would lie awake at night until we could think up some way to get across from that planet to this one, so we could start doing business with the people here. And then we would wonder why we no longer had the security that came from separation.

No, to try to stand alone in this jungle of a world is to be overwhelmed. How then can we get security? Only by working with other peoples of like mind to achieve in full, frank cooperation agreement as to the rules and procedures by which life and intercourse on this planet are to be conducted. They must be agreements that will be to the benefit of all parties concerned, and therefore will serve the vital interests of each. Otherwise, we cannot expect the agreements to be adhered to faithfully either by others or by ourselves.

The resolution under consideration today makes clear to the world that we of both political parties realize this situation and want to do our utmost to work out if possible such mutually beneficial rules and procedures. It recognizes fully that we in this House do not have the authority to make binding commitments in our foreign relations. It recognizes that the machinery set up in our Constitution for making treaties and binding commitments with other nations is a partnership—the Executive and the United States Senate. Any contract entered into by only one partner without the full consent of the other cannot, of course, be binding. We have not forgotten, and neither have our allies—nor our enemies—that President Wilson once made some commitments which had not been agreed upon in advance by two-thirds of the Members of the Senate and by both political parties, and which, therefore, were rejected. How can we expect a President to negotiate with other nations without handicap, or expect those nations to negotiate freely and frankly with him, if they are not sure what the other partner, the Senate, will do?

Why should anyone expect Mr. Stalin to lay his cards on the table and perhaps reach an agreement with us, when he knows that an agreement has no validity from our standpoint until ratified by the Senate? How can leaders of other nations plan intelligently with us if they have no assurance as to what the foreign policy of the United States will be after 1944?

It has been said here that we cannot make plans for the future because we do not know what Churchill's plans, or Stalin's plans, or other nations' plans are. As a matter of fact, we do know pretty well what their basic ideas are. We may not agree with some of those ideas, but they have made fairly clear what they consider their vital interests to be. We should be as frank. Until we do, we, not they, are the great question mark in the world.

Do we want to compel them to make their own plans for the post-war world without us? Does anyone believe a settlement as good for us can be reached by them without us?

Therefore, we are saying in this resolution that we in this House believe that our vital national interests require that the President and two-thirds of the Senate—and that means both political parties, too—seek to reach a basic agreement on a sound, continuing, national foreign policy. It must be neither Democratic nor Republican, but American—just as the Monroe Doctrine has always been American. The whole world has known for over a hundred years, that, no matter who was President of the United States, or what party was in power, we would not stand for any foreign nation trying to encroach on this hemisphere.

Agreement must be reached in the next few months, before we get into the heat of the Presidential campaign, before passions are stirred up over the domestic issues about which there are such vigorous and important differences of opinion.

If the Germans know now what America's position with regard to the war and the peace will be, no matter who is elected next year, they are more likely to crack up. If they think we may be disunited on this issue, or try to withdraw from cooperation with the United Nations, then our enemies are encouraged to hang on desperately, and that means more Americans boys killed every day.

I venture to warn that if our Republican leaders are willing—as I hope and believe will be the case—but the administration and Democratic leaders refuse to cooperate now in trying to work out a truly national, nonpartisan, continuing foreign policy and plans for post-war collaboration, then whatever settlement the Executive reaches in secret with other countries will be rejected by the Senate, and by the people, even though the agreements be as good as the Ten Commandments.

On the other hand, if the administration and the Democratic leaders are willing, but the Republican leaders refuse to cooperate in trying to work out now, before the campaign, such a truly national foreign policy, then the Republican Party will be rejected at the polls, and will deserve to be rejected—because it will have demonstrated it is not sufficiently constructive and forward looking and responsible to be entrusted with power in so critical a period.

This resolution both strengthens and restrains the President in his negotiations with our allies and with our enemies. It does not try to define now exactly what "appropriate international machinery with power adequate to establish and maintain a just and lasting peace" would be. But it gives no carte blanche. It makes clear that the Senate will determine at the proper time what is or is not appropriate.

I hope its passage by an overwhelming majority will encourage the members of both parties in the Senate to advise in the near future approximately how far they will go along in international collaboration to establish and maintain the peace. The Executive's hand would be enormously strengthened in his negotiations with other nations—as long as he stays within the general framework. If he should be tempted to make commitments too far outside that general framework, both he and the other nations are forewarned that such commitments are likely to be considered inappropriate, and therefore be rejected—and he is properly restrained.

Somehow we must rise above politics and partisanship to achieve a real unity and teamwork on this vital issue, so that America and the world will know that, no matter what decision Americans make in 1944 as to how they want their domestic affairs run, our foreign policy will be realistic, stable, predictable, and continuing.

It may be objected that we would be surrendering some of our sovereignty to join in a cooperative effort to maintain the peace. Well, did we have complete sovereignty? Did we have in our own hands control of the question as to whether we went to war or not? No. Japan decided for us.

Do we have absolute sovereignty now in waging the war? No. Scores of units of our fleet are fighting under the command of British admirals. Tens of thousands of British, and French, and Greeks, and Dutch, and Chinese, and Australians, and New Zealanders are fighting under the command of American generals. Americans are fighting under the command of a Chinese general. We would not hesitate to place some of our forces under Stalin's command if they were needed and he wanted them on the Russian front.

We recognise fully that there are risks in delegating, whether in war or peace, control of certain functions to the United Nations, but we do it, nevertheless, because we recognize that the risks in not working together in such a fashion are enormously greater.

America is in the valley of decision. Today and in these next few months we will be deciding, probably without realizing it, the basic attitudes and directions which are likely to determine the course of our Nation and of the world for the next half century. Four main choices are before us. First, we can try to go back to so-called isolationism. It once was possible, but that day has gone. The progress of invention, the ability of the airplane to disregard all land boundaries, and the refusal of other nations to ignore us, no matter how much we want to ignore them, make it an absolute impossibility.

Second, American imperialism. Some will say, "Well, if we can't escape the world, then we will rule it. If the world will not leave us alone, then we will get control of the key islands, and critical air bases, and main routes of trade, and fortify them until impregnable, and then build such a giant air force and navy and army that it will be certain no nation can ever attack us."

That sounds big; but let us examine, first, whether it is possible, and second, what the attempt would cost in men and money.

It is difficult for us Americans to realize that we are rapidly becoming a have – not nation in many crucial materials because of the rate at which we are exhausting our resources. If we try to police the world, the other nations certainly will gang up against us, just as we now gang up against those who would try to rule us. Those who are now helping supply us with tin, oil, rubber, copper, zinc, bauxite, tungsten, chromium, and so forth, would refuse us free access to their supplies of those resources which we never had or have used up.

Again, we will have a population of less than 140,000,000, a little tired and disillusioned, and asking only to be let alone. But there are 200,000,000 Russians and they are not tired. There are 450,000,000 Chinese, just awakening from the sleep of the centuries, and their leaders are aflame with the love of human freedom as our forefathers were in 1776. Ferment is beginning to work among 375,000,000 in India, and there are 150,000,000 in Latin America, restless and uneasy. Does anybody really think we with our limited resources and manpower can run the world or police it single-handed?

To try to do it would mean that two or three millions of our sons who are now in uniform will never get back to civilian life. Do we want them to win the war only to be permanently in uniform?

It would cost 15 to 25 billion dollars for armaments in every annual budget. Mr. Speaker, we cannot possibly contemplate such a permanent expenditure. Our taxes would have to go constantly higher. We would have less and less money for the comforts of life, the things we Americans are used to and crave. That would mean increasing dissatisfaction and discontent throughout all sections of our populace. Gradually our standard of living would go down and we would either break up into factions and go the way of France—national disintegration—or some man with a hynotic personality would come along and promise relief if we would but follow him, and the mass of people would go with him into a totalitarian system and the loss of our basic freedoms.

For America to try imperialism would be suicidal.

Third, America could try to buy the world's goodwill, by endeavoring to supply the world adequate food, clothing, medicines, and so forth, out of our own resources—the philosophy of giving people things, instead of helping them get on their feet so they can develop their own freedom-from-want. That philosophy has always been and always will be self-defeating in the long run. It destroys independence and will and initiative. Besides our Nation simply does not have the resources and money to sustain any such program.

If we cannot escape the world, or rule the world, or buy the world, is there any course left except a genuinely cooperative effort to achieve with our allies an organized security? It is not possible to settle now actual details of such organization, nor is it within the jurisdiction of the House; but if we and the other peoples of the world see, first of all that we must find some other way than war of solving our disputes, I am perfectly confident the actual appropriate machinery for doing it can be evolved.

If we are sufficiently intelligent, and wise in our own interests, to work out with our allies ways by which we can jointly win the war, then surely we are sufficiently intelligent, and wise in our own interests, to be able to work out with our allies ways by which we can jointly win the peace and jointly prevent war.

Let us, by an overwhelming vote, tell our soldiers, our people generally, our allies, and our enemies that we are dedicating ourselves today to that stern, inescapable task.

4(c)   Senator Tom Connally on the ideal of international peace: October 25, 1943: *'The ideal of international peace has long attracted the dreams and efforts of statesmen and thinkers.'*

Source: ibid.

. . . These various resolutions presented many approaches to the outstanding objective of world peace. The Committee on Foreign Relations, after long and careful study, concluded that the pending resolution most nearly interprets the sentiments of the people of the United States and that of the United States Senate than any other proposal submitted. It therefore recommends that the Senate pass the resolution without amendment or modification.

The ideal of international peace has long attracted the dreams and efforts of statesmen and thinkers. It has thrilled the imagination of men for more than a century. A great French scholar, Abbé de Saint-Pierre (1713) proposed a plan for universal peace. The great German philosopher, Immanuel Kant (1795) advanced a plan for the same objective. The .distinguished Englishman, Jeremy Bentham (1786-89) proposed his conception of a workable plan for international peace. None of these proposals met with any concrete adoption. They did, however, leave an impress on the intellect and thought of public men and scholars through succeeding generations. The League to Enforce Peace sponsored by ex-President Taft was another example. There were others.

The attainment of international peace is the logical culmination of the development of governmental and judicial processes. The primary step toward peace was begun in the establishment of agencies to settle disputes between individuals respecting personal property or personal rights within a political unit. The next step was the assumption of authority over feudal barons by the crown, or national authority, in the matter of differences between feudal lords, theretofore settled by wars between their private armies.

Possibly the most significant step in the evolution of peace was crystallized in the Constitution of the United States. Conflicts between States had rendered continuance under the Articles of Confederation intolerable. The Constitution federated the States into a Union and established the Congress to legislate for the control of the States in their relation to each other and provided a Supreme Court with authority to adjudicate disputes between the States.

In 1914 the First World War broke upon Europe in all its fury and savagery. For almost 3 years the United States was able to maintain its neutrality. However, because of repeated aggressions against American rights and the lives of American citizens, our country was reluctantly compelled to draw the sword in defense of its own safety and dignity. It is unnecessary here to catalog the sacrifices, the misery, and the tragedies that the war brought upon the humanity of the world. Millions of lives were sacrificed. Oceans of blood were loosed upon fair lands. Billions of dollars of wealth were poured into rivers of ruin and waste. The gallant and the brave were mutilated and wounded and killed in this cruel and barbaric conflict. The people of the United States and of the world suffering the horrors and miseries of that war began to fashion in their minds and hearts a desire for the establishment by international action of some agency or machinery for the settlement of the causes of war through peaceful and amicable means and therefore to prevent the recurrence of another world tragedy. The League of Nations was established by the Treaty of Versailles. The United States did not become a party to that treaty because the United States Senate failed to ratify the compact.

It is frequently said that the League of Nations was a failure. That is an unjust charge. It is granted that it was not a complete success. However, it did serve a useful purpose. Even its weaknesses and its failures have contributed to the public thought and the attitude of nations and of political leaders. It has served an additional purpose. It has demonstrated where the pitfalls may lie, and where any international organization for peace must be strengthened or buttressed. It was a new departure in international life. It was an experiment in a virgin field. It could not be expected to attain perfection. It did not spring full-panoplied with wisdom, with courage and with instrumentalities for achieving all of the ends which many hoped for and expected. The history of the League ought to lighten the pathway along which nations may travel in the years to come. Great civilized nations are now engulfed in another world war, more far-flung and involving the expenditure of greater resources and calling for more momentous sacrifices than any struggle that has ever shaken the foundations of the earth. Twice within a quarter of a century, the United States, without being guilty of aggression, without any ambitions for the lands of our neighbors, and innocent of any violation of international law, has been dragged into two world struggles that have sorrowed thousands of homes, have orphaned many thousands of children, and have wasted the national wealth, have injured our commerce and internal economy and have forced staggering sacrifices upon all of our people.

Again the people of the United States hunger for peace. Again they dream of the establishment of international authority to prevent aggression and to preserve the peace of the world.

That ambition cannot be achieved by the United States alone. It requires the cooperation of other strong and powerful nations. The United States cannot write a pattern of its own and expect all other nations to accept it in detail. The Senate of the United States cannot blueprint in advance the action of the nations whose influence, power, and arms must secure the desired results. The most that the Senate may accomplish at this time is to express to the peoples of the world and to lay before the people of the United States the attitude of the Senate with respect to this commanding problem. The Constitution of the United States provides:

> He (the President) shall have power, by and with the advice and consent of the Senate, to make treaties, provided two-thirds of the Senators present concur.

This solemn injunction places upon the Senate the high responsibility of advising the President, who must initiate treaties with respect thereto. Of course, the Senate may not ratify treaties not yet made. The present Senate may not bind the action of a future Senate. The present Senate, however, under its solemn duty may advise the President as to its sentiments and intentions with respect to any treaty which may be negotiated.

It is under this constitutional sanction that the Senate is asked by the passage of this resolution to express to the President the attitude of the Senate of the United States.

The resolution has been attacked as being general in its terms. It is broad in its terms for the reason that it is advanced as a framework within which the makers of the treaty may provide the detailed structure and the particular delimitations and affirmative provisions that may be necessary to accomplish the desired ends.

The primary condition upon which the peace of the future may be based is the necessity that the present war shall end in victory. It is therefore provided, "Resolved that the war against all our enemies be waged until complete victory is achieved." After victory shall be achieved, the next logical step is the securing of an honorable peace. Therefore it is provided, "That the United States cooperate with its comrades-in-arms in securing a just and honorable peace." When these pressing and imperative achievements shall have been accomplished the resolution then looks to the establishment and maintenance of international authority to prevent aggression and preserve the peace of the world. It is therefore provided, "That the United States, acting through its constitutional processes, join with free and sovereign nations in the establishment and maintenance of international authority with power to prevent aggression and to preserve the peace of the world." The last paragraph just quoted has been assailed because of its employment of the word "sovereign" nation. Certainly a nation would have to possess the elements of sovereignty and ability to perform its obligations and commitments under an international treaty. To the extent of the commitment assumed, the nation would, of course, be deprived of its liberty of action. It would not have, however, to surrender anything of its sovereignty. Sovereignty implies the right and the power in a nation to make its own choices and decisions. But when it assumes a treaty obligation voluntarily, it must fulfill its obligation. This is not an impairment of its sovereignty but is rather a demonstration of its sovereignty. The resolution is not suggestive of any alliance. It provides, "Join with free and sovereign nations in the establishment and maintenance of international authority."

It thus gives the widest latitude to nations that may become initially, or later, members of any organization or authority which may be created.

It has been suggested that instead of the words "international authority," the words "international organization" should be used. The word "authority" was chosen because of its breadth and comprehensiveness. It includes the employment of all existing international agencies, such as the Court at the Hague, or any other existing international organizations, as well as the creation of any new organizations.

We should not abandon what may be useful in arbitration, conciliation, the Pan American Union, the deliberations of the World Court, or the Kellogg Pact.

I was glad to see in this morning's press a statement by the distinguished Senator from Ohio [Mr. Taft] in which he suggested the utilization of the League of Nations. It indicates agreement with the general belief that the maintenance of international authority comprehends the employment of any useful agencies already in existence, and authorizes the organization and creation of any further agency or organization which might be employed, and that to confine the language to the creation of a new organization would not comprehend those very laudable purposes.

It has been suggested that the words, "with power to prevent aggression and to preserve the peace of the world" should designate the particular kind of power with which international authority may be invested. The word "power"—meaning a grant of authority—was chosen with the deliberate intent to include all forms of power necessary to prevent aggression and to preserve the peace of the world. "Power" is a term clear in its implications and any designation of particular forms of power would exclude those forms not named.

When World War No. 1 ended in victory, we hoped thereafter to live in peace with the powers of the earth. We had hoped that our heroes had not died in vain. Our great leader and Commander-in-Chief, Woodrow Wilson, with an exalted dream of peace and a noble conception of freedom from the misery of war, undertook to lead the world into the pathways of peace. We had hoped that the constructive initiative and the intelligent energies of the modern world would be devoted to the creation of useful things for the enjoyment of the peoples of the earth. We had hoped that the genius of scientists would no longer be devotèd to the manufacture of arms and murderous weapons of warfare. The United States, during the score of years following World War No. 1, made generous exertions toward peace and disarmament and arbitration. These hopes and dreams came crashing about us in ruins in 1939. The dastardly designs of megalomaniacal conquerors and the flame of the cannon's mouth shriveled them into ashes.

Today, our Nation is involved in a war that belts the globe. For 10 years Hitler was secretly arming and marching and drilling a mighty army. He planned the conquest of Europe. He hoped to master the Mediterranean and the lands which it washed. With his fantastic ambition to surpass Napoleon, he planned to subjugate Russia and extend his realm into Asia. He was to combine Napoleon and Alexander the Great and Caesar and Genghis Khan into the world's greatest military master. His ultimate ambition was to leap across the South Atlantic from Africa and challenge the independence of South America and the Monroe Doctrine.

Six thousand miles westward the crafty and treacherous Japanese for 20 years had been preparing for the hour they could strike the United States. For 5 long bloody years Japan had harried with torch and sword the territories of unoffending China. Savage and destructive war had been waged against that peaceful people. The world will long remember the dastardly and treacherous attack upon Pearl Harbor. Our soldiers and sailors were murdered without a hint of warning. While their diplomatic emissaries were standing at the door of the White House pretending to be messengers of peace, they drove the dagger of the assassin into our armed forces. With Oriental beguilement, they sought to becalm and then betray us while they planned with fiendish deviltry the barbaric attack on Pearl Harbor. We promptly declared war on Japan. Germany and Italy quickly declared war upon us, and we declared war upon them.

In this heroic struggle to save the life of free government and to preserve the liberties of the world, we fight with the United Nations as comrades-in-arms. We are fighting side by side in the cause of "collective security." If in war, concert of action is necessary, why should not we together with the United Nations and other free nations act in concert in time of peace to provide collective security to avert the horrors and miseries of brutal and unjustified aggression? Tyrants and dictators may easily make war. Their edict alone is required to declare and make war. In democratic nations constitutional requirements demand something more—the action of the people through their representatives. There is no adequate curb against the ambitions and aggressions of despots and conquerors except the joint action of peaceful nations.

We have tried "isolation"—and I say that without any desire of offense. It did not bring peace or security. Dictators planned their conquests upon the hope of "divide and conquer." Alone through cooperative action can their mad schemes be arrested. Isolation has failed. Let us try collective security.

The Senate of the United States will express the desire of the United States to join in the establishment of a world peace agency to curb international bandits and robbers and to preserve the peace of the world. Such an agency does not necessarily imply that world conditions will be frozen. It does not follow that the status quo in every particular will be preserved. The constitution of such a body could provide the necessary elasticity to meet the needs of the future. It will not be an easy task. Difficulties will be encountered. Obstacles will face us. But we need not despair. We have faced great national and international problems before. American genius and leadership and statesmanship will not be deterred by hardships and struggles. They are rather a challenge to the highest and noblest traits of national character. It will not be perfect. What human agency reaches such a goal? The Constitution of the United States has been amended, and may be amended again. The British Constitution and the structure of other powers have yielded to change. They have responded to the need of changing times. The sublime objective of world peace is worth the effort. The experiment commands our highest hopes and best aspirations.

The United States is so powerful, with such a tremendous striking power upon the sea and upon the land, that it is invincible against any single power on the globe. It is equally powerful in world councils. We gave freedom to the Philippines. We withdrew our Army from Cuba and granted it independence. The world knows that we cherish no scheme of conquest and no ambition for military rule. The hour has struck for America to instill those principles into world policy.

From our commanding point of vantage we must declare to the world that our influence and our might will be dedicated to the maintenance of world peace and the suppression of military aggression whenever it may lift its venomous head.

> 4(d) Representative William Lemke, a House dissenter: September 21, 1943. *'We are all for cooperation and collaboration, but other nations must do their share. Uncle Sam is not going to be a perpetual Santa Claus.'*

Source: ibid.

I agree with the remarks made by the gentleman from Texas [Mr. SUMNERS]. We are at war. The all important thing for us to do is to win that war. Our sons are giving their lives and limbs on foreign battlefields. This is no time for creating disunity not only of the American people but of our allies.

I also agree with the gentleman from New York [Mr. REED] that this resolution is either a blank check that will come home to plague us or it is a fraud and deception. I feel that it is both a blank check and political camouflage. It can serve no useful purpose. No one now knows what the terms of peace will be or what the "adequate power" mentioned in the resolution is to be used for.

We went into this war to protect the smaller nations against aggressor nations. Now suppose that at the end of this war that some nation should insist upon taking over these smaller nations. Is this "adequate power" to be used to keep these smaller nations under subjugation? These are problems that we can only decide after the war is won and the peace terms known.

I, too, have mingled with the people during the so-called recess. I have spoken to large crowds in several States. I have been on the trains most of the time. I have stood in trains crowded with soldiers without a seat. I know that the American people and the men in service are sick and tired of having Congress hand out blank checks for financial or political purposes to the "give-me Jimmies" of the world. These servicemen are more concerned with what is going to be done for them when they return than they are with policing the world after they have won this war.

It is so easy to deceive ourselves by wishful thinking. We all want permanent peace, but, unfortunately, mere words will not bring about that result. As I listened yesterday to the appeals of some of my colleagues I wondered whether they were placing the welfare of their Nation above their own political welfare. I do not believe that any Member of this House is foolish enough to believe that the passing of this resolution will bring about permanent peace.

Throughout the ages there has been, and will be, a desire for permanent peace. Yet the institution of war is as old as man. It had its inception when Cain arose and slew his brother Abel. The world has been cursed with it ever since. It is the hope of all that war may be ultimately abolished, but to jump from the frying pan into the fire is no solution. That will not bring about permanent peace but may bring about permanent friction and war.

There were many "one worlders" before. The idea of bringing about permanent peace by force was tried by Augustus Caesar, Alexander the Great, Charlemagne, Napoleon, and now by Hitler and lesser satellites but it always failed. The very idea of force means war. The very idea of adequate power means war. If this power had been adequate in the days of the former "one worlders" then the world perhaps would not be worth living in. It would have been subjugation and slavery by force.

The insinuation that if we had joined the League of Nations that then there would not have been another war is again the child of wishful thinking. Great Britain, China, Russia, Italy, Japan, Germany, and Austria were all members of the League of Nations. Why did they not bring about permanent peace? That was the object of the League.

When Japan wanted to grab a part of China, she resigned from the League. China's entering the League did not assure her peace or justice. The United States offered to back the League. So did Great Britain, but then shied away. Would it be too much to say that there was a falling out among the aggressors as far as the League was concerned? May we not say that history may repeat itself? Let us have the courage to act wisely and become fully informed before we blindly commit our Nation to a blind rendezvous.

A few years ago I heard a former president of the League of Nations complain about the Big Three. He told us that the Big Three were not interested in the welfare of the smaller nations, that they were selfish and grasping. He named the Big Three at that time as being composed of Great Britain, France, and Italy. He assumed that if the United States had also come into the League that then the smaller nations would have been safe. Of course, he did not know that if we had joined the League it would have been the Big Four in place of the Big Three.

I recently saw a cartoon where Uncle Sam was reading the Declaration of Independence. Miss Columbia, all dressed up and bedecked with the Stars and Stripes, was admiring her Uncle. There was a fence and a vacant lot. The vacant lot was designated "European intrigue." A little further down was "lover's lane." At the end of "lover's lane" was "super government." In the vacant lot, leaning on the fence, was an individual. He was whispering to Miss Columbia, "Are you looking for a blind date?" Is this resolution the blind date? Miss Columbia gave the cold shoulder to that individual. The American people will also give the cold shoulder to the "one worlders." They will not surrender their sovereignty. They will not sell out the future of this Nation to the "one worlders."

There is only one solution for the smaller nations of Europe—if there are any left when the peace treaty is finally signed—and that is for them to form the United States of Europe. They must abandon their religious and racial hatreds. We are all for helping them. We are all for cooperation and collaboration after the war ends, but let us win the victory first.

The other day the President gave us a picture of the war progress. We have reason to be proud of that record. It is we—the people—in action. It appears that America is doing more than her share of furnishing the manpower and material to win this war. We are glad to do this, but we are not going to accept the blind date. We are not going to surrender our sovereignty. We are not going to continue to finance the world. We are not going to continue to police it. We are all for cooperation and collaboration, but other nations must do their share. Uncle Sam is not going to be a perpetual Santa Claus.

There never was a time that the United States did not cooperate and collaborate with any nation that wanted permanent peace. We are all for peace. We hope that when this war is ended there will be a sufficient cooling off period given before the final peace and the machinery for permanent peace is established.

Let me also assure you that when the boys come back from the battle fronts they are going to have something to say about the future of this Nation and its relation with other nations. I am confident they will be favorable to cooperation and collaboration and friendship among the United Nations. They will, however, never substitute a mongrel flag for the Stars and Stripes. You can stake your life on that.

4(e)   Senator Burton Wheeler, a Senate dissenter: October 29, 1943: '. . . I do not now object, nor have I ever objected, to cooperating with other countries for world peace. I am, however, opposed to military alliances, which are backed up by force.'

Source: ibid.

I rise at this time with no idea that anything I may say will result in the defeat of the pending resolution. I know that the minds of most Senators are made up. Some Senators are going to vote for the resolution because some other Senators are against it. Some are going to vote for it because they believe it is innocuous. I do not believe the resolution is innocuous, and I do not intend to vote for it or against it because I think someone else is opposed to it or desires to amend it.

At the outset let me make it clear that this Nation hopes for better understanding among all the peoples of the world. We crave the possessions of no other people. We envy no race of men. We have no deep hatreds, and few animosities. Our fondest desire is that the Russian people, the Chinese, the British, and the French; yes, and even the enemy nations, shall go their various ways in peace and in amity toward each other and toward us. America is sick at heart over power politics. She wants no part of it. She recognizes in the course of human history the development and growth of distinct nations—each after its own type. She realizes that differing customs, ambitions, religions, and historical background make nations different. She understands that each nation contributes in its own way, through these cultural differences, to what may be called, in a general way, modern civilization. We believe in better understanding among all the nations of the world, and think that the road to such understanding lies in liberty and justice for all peoples. Toward the consummation of this aim we are willing to help.

Undoubtedly concerted common action will have to be taken to place the nations on a solid peace basis after the war is won. When that is accomplished we shall help to establish a family of nations on the basis of equity, liberty, equality, and fraternity, and in the spirit of reciprocity, fair play, and mutual aid, as distinguished from coercion on the one hand and excessive and harmful unilateral liberality on the other. But this is something that cannot be worked out overnight, and it should be emphasized that machinery alone will not establish peace. There must be a desire for peace among the different countries. Yet some internationalists would have us believe that the mere setting up of a league of nations, with an international police force, would automatically bring world peace and prosperity.

Mr. Walter Lippmann believes that there should be a military alliance between the United States, Great Britain, and Russia. Others, including the Governor of New York, believe in a military alliance between the United States and Great Britain. Hitler and Stalin had a nonaggression security alliance in August 1939, through which Russia got half of Poland and furnished Germany with material; but 22 months later they were at war, in June 1941. The Anglo-Japanese Alliance of 1902-22 is not so old as to be forgotten. Yet, Britain and Japan are now at war.

Poland had an alliance with Britain and France at the outset of the present war, a pact which pledged both to protect Polish borders. Likewise England and France had a pact with Czechoslovakia. History is strewn with more black pages than white on the subject of alliances, running all the way back to the Triple Alliance of 1688, and even the Holy Alliance of 1815; yet the world periodically came to war.

The distinguished senior Senator from Texas [Mr. CONNALLY] has said that isolationism has failed. Yet every country in the world has had, in some form or other, alliances with other countries. We ourselves joined the Kellogg-Briand Pact renouncing war forever. That was not isolationism. This country has not been isolationist, either economically, politically, socially, or in any other way.

Mr. President, I do not now object, nor have I ever objected, to cooperating with other countries for world peace. I am, however, opposed to military alliances, which are backed up by force. They never have and never will bring about lasting peace. They are essentially instruments of war . . . .

If we put our faith in alliances with other countries and not in our own strength, if we are thus deceived into a false sense of security, we start repeating the history of the disarmament conference of 1922.

George Sokolsky, a well-known authority on the Far East and a student of international relations, in the New York Sun recently stated:

> A military alliance is always aimed at an objective enemy. It is always the precursor of war. It is a design for war.

Obviously, an Anglo-American alliance could only be aimed at Soviet Russia, the only other power which at the end of this war will be capable of defending itself and making its will felt.

There are those who say we must cooperate after the war as we have during the war. Let us examine into how well we have cooperated during the war. The differences between Soviet Russia and Great Britain over the future of Iran and the Persian oil fields is nothing to laugh away. If we were a military ally, we should be required to support the British against the Russians willy-nilly. But why? How are we involved? Without an alliance we might arbitrate and help maintain peace; with an alliance we are partisans and can back up only one party.

Or, in respect to Hong Kong and Singapore and the Dutch East Indies, are we to support the British against China in her claims for Hong Kong, and are we going to support the Netherlands against the countries of Asia which may desire independence from European domination? A military alliance with Britain would require us even to fight China for Hong Kong.

While the resolution is plain so far as it is directed toward the making of military alliances, it is capable of several constructions in other respects.

It is generally conceded that lack of knowledge of how and when the war may end and of the state of affairs which will then exist precludes definite commitments at this time. The same seems to me to be true of general commitments.

The question in my mind is whether the resolution does not commit us to a general proposition which, under the rulings made by the Department of State, would be advice and consent to a treaty which the President may make and which he does not need to submit to the Senate thereafter. That is clearly the holding by the Solicitor of the Department of State. Someone has said that not much attention was paid to what the Solicitor said. The Solicitor of the Department of State, Mr. Hackworth, is a very able gentleman, who is as well versed and probably better versed in international law than any Senator. Whether Senators like him or disagree with what he has said, he is the Solicitor of the Department of State, and the one who will interpret a treaty, and if he interprets a treaty which is entered into by the President of the United States, and the President follows his interpretation, what can the Senate do about it?

It has been said that Congress can pass a law to nullify the treaty. That is true. The treaty could be abrogated by the Congress, but that could be accomplished only by passing a law through both branches of Congress. The President could veto the measure and then both Houses would have to pass it over the President's veto by a two-thirds majority . . . .

I think it is dangerous to proceed under the advice clause in advance of the making of the treaty.

Let me call attention to Prime Minister Churchill's broadcast to the British people on March 21 of this year:

> First of all, we must beware of attempts to overpersuade or even to coerce His Majesty's Government to bind themselves or their unknown successors in conditions which no one can foresee and which may be years ahead.

Let me ask Senators, to whom do they think the Prime Minister was directing that language? He was not directing it to the British people. He was directing it to the American people and to the American Government. Prime Minister Churchill continued:

> And to make them pledge themselves to particular schemes without relation to other extremely important aspects of our post-war needs.

Mr. Churchill continued:

> Nothing would be easier for me than to make any number of promises to get the immediate response of cheap cheers and glowing leading articles.

Why was the pending resolution reported by the committee? It was reported, we are told, because of the clamor of the press of the country for a resolution. Why should we pay any attention to the press of the country which wants some resolution adopted now because it fears one could not be adopted after the war is over?

I repeat Mr. Churchill's words:

> Nothing would be easier for me than to make any number of promises to get the immediate response of cheap cheers and glowing leading articles.

But, Mr. President, is that not exactly what is being done here now? I continue to read from Mr. Churchill's statement:

> However, it is our duty to peer through the mists of the future to the end of the war and to try our utmost to be prepared by ceaseless effort and forethought for the kind of situations which are likely to occur. Speaking under every reserve and not attempting to prophesy, I can imagine that sometime next year—but it may well be the year after—we might beat Hitler. By which I mean beat him and his powers of evil into death, dust, and ashes. * * * the moment when Hitler is beaten and Germany and Italy are prostrate will mark the grand climax of war and that will be the time to make a new declaration upon the task before us.

Mr. President, I find myself in complete agreement with Mr. Churchill's statement. It sets out what seems to me to be the only sensible course for the Congress of the United States to take. If this is good policy for Great Britain to follow, why is it not equally good policy for the United States to follow?

We have been told in recent days that we must do anything that Great Britain does. Well, let us follow Great Britain when she is right. Certainly the Parliament of Great Britain is not adopting any resolution of the kind now before the Senate, and certainly the British Cabinet is not proposing any such resolution.

That being so, it is difficult to see how a broad commitment, capable of several constructions, not only by this Nation but by foreign nations, should be adopted at this time.

On the contrary, it would seem that such a commitment, by reason of its very breadth, will increase the likelihood of confusion and national embarrassment from all sides at the war's end.

Furthermore, it is doubtful that any present commitment will materially affect the international complexion of things to come. It is the state of things existing at the conclusion of the war that should, and I am sure will, determine the course of action to be taken by the United States of America if the representatives of the people of this country are given a voice in passing upon it. But already we are told, and we hear the stories, that there will be no peace after the war, that there are to be only general agreements, and no peace treaties signed after the war. It would seem to follow that the passage of the present resolution would be more likely to prove harmful than helpful in the ultimate solution of the post-war problems.

Nor does the fact that this resolution is unilateral improve matters. On the contrary, it would only add to our ultimate discomfiture—and to ours alone.

Let us now examine this resolution further:

In the first paragraph we speak of waging war against "all our enemies until complete victory is achieved." In this particular war it has been difficult at times to determine who is who. Russia was our enemy. She is now our friend. Finland was our friend. She is now considered by many as our enemy. Italy, until a short time ago, was an ally of Germany. Now she is a cobelligerent of ours. Does this paragraph, then, refer to the past, the present, or the future?

And what if Russia should make a separate peace with Germany? Would this resolution automatically involve us then in war with Russia?

The second paragraph refers to our "comrades in arms." Again let me ask, "When?" A few weeks ago there was a meeting in Ottawa between Messrs. Churchill and Roosevelt, at which Russia was excluded because, as was truthfully stated at the time, Russia was not a cobelligerent against Japan. At the present time there is a meeting between the secretaries of state of Russia, England, and the United States, at which China is excluded. Suppose the war against Germany ends first, and Russia chooses to continue her present relations with Japan? What then?

The third paragraph speaks of "International authority with power to prevent aggression." Aggression when? Would we be obligated under this resolution to go to war with Russia should she intervene in the affairs of the eastern nations of Europe, absorb Finland, or take over control of the Bosporus? And what about Outer Mongolia? Are we to go to war over that? And who determines the aggressor?

These are merely some of the difficulties I have encountered in considering this resolution. Because it is susceptible of so many interpretations, it will be used at the war's end by the proponents of every varying viewpoint to sustain their ideas with respect to the method of achieving peace. How can the result be other than to add to the confusion, to hamper our representatives, and to produce the very thing it is claimed to avoid—the ultimate disillusionment of our people and a return to a form of isolationism that will make me look like an internationalist? I cannot escape the conviction, then, that this resolution, if adopted, will rise up again and again to plague us. Again I ask, "What then, is its purpose?"

I have heard Senators say on the floor of the Senate "I am not an isolationist." I do not know just what they mean; because, as I said a few moments ago, this country has never been isolationist, either economically, socially, morally, or politically. Have we not always done everything we could do to help every nation which was in trouble? Have we not gone to war twice in Europe? Have we not signed the Kellogg-Briand Pact?

Speaking commercially, do we not have our representatives all over the world, trading with every other country on the face of the globe? Do those who speak of isolationism mean by "isolationism" that one whom they call an isolationist is in favor of a tariff to protect the interests of our industries and the working people and the farmers of America? Is that what they mean by "isolationism"? What do they mean by it? Do they mean that anyone who wanted to keep this country out of war was an isolationist? If that is what they mean, then let me say that I am proud to be called an isolationist . . . .

Of course, the British Empire has always been isolationist, if one desires to apply that term. I admire the British Empire. . . wherever one goes, whether to China or to Japan or to Singapore or to Bombay or to Egypt or to Germany or to Russia or anywhere else on the face of the globe, wherever one meets an Englishman one finds that he is for Great Britain first. I admire the English for it.

Is Russia isolationist? Mr. President, today Russia is the greatest isolationist country upon the face of the globe, and has been for years.

Mr. President, socially we in the United States certainly have not been isolationists. I say that because of the fact that a number of our rich young women have gone abroad and have married all kinds of cheap dukes and broken-down princes; so socially we are not isolationists. [Laughter.]

The British Prime Minister is opposed to a resolution of this kind for Britain. Certainly the Russian Government is taking no such action, nor is the Chinese Government. Why then, I ask, single out America for special treatment?

Why is it that those who were the loudest in denouncing Stalin now are cuddling him to their bosoms? Of course, Mr. President, Senators know that I went to Russia in 1923, and spent several months there. When I returned to this country I said that the United States should recognize Russia. I did not say that because I believed in the Russian form of government, but because I felt that if the Russian people wanted to try that experiment it was none of our business, that they had a right to determine their own form of government and to have communism if they wanted it. If this country should undertake to tell every other country on the face of the globe what kind of government it should have and what kind of religion it should have, we would be constantly and continually involved in one war after another . . . .

I may be in favor of a three-power pact, which has been talked about, between Russia, England, and the United States; I may be in favor of some form of pact, but I certainly am not going to put myself on record as favoring something which will later give someone the opportunity to say, "You voted for it; you authorized the President to do it.

You advised and consented to it. He has done it, and now you are reneging on it."

What would Russia say, what would England say, and what would the other countries say if a treaty should come to the United States Senate for ratification and the Senate refused to ratify it because it provided for giving to Russia a large part of Poland? Why did England go to war? She said she went to war for the independence of Poland. We have said we want the "four freedoms" for all the countries in the world. In the face of our pledges, and in the face of our statements in the Atlantic Charter, are we going to approve a treaty which would give Russia all of Poland, and control over Europe? I do not believe we should do it. I may be wrong.

> 5   Secretary of State Cordell Hull on the hope of postwar cooperation:
>   November 18, 1943: 'At the end of the war, each of the United
>   Nations ... will have the same common interest in national
>   security, in world order under law, in peace, in the full promotion
>   of political, economic, and social welfare of their respective
>   peoples—in the principles and spirit of the Atlantic Charter and the
>   declaration by United Nations.'

Late in 1943, the long-serving Secretary of State, Cordell Hull, an inveterate Wilsonian with a relatively minor impact on the overall direction of Rooseveltian foreign policy, travelled to Moscow to assist in preparing the groundwork of a postwar collective security system. At this conference, which also created the European Advisory Commission and the Advisory Council for Italy, Hull totally identified the policies and principles of the United States, and especially the Atlantic Charter, with the policies and principles of Great Britain and the Soviet Union. Such a decision, which for Hull foreshadowed the end of secret agreements, spheres of influence, and balance of power politics, clearly contradicted the earlier recommendation of the State Department to disassociate American from Soviet principles in the struggle against Nazi militarism, not to mention the unilateral British and Russian reservations to the Charter. Nonetheless, the conference's four-nation declaration (with China acceding to it), which supposedly recognized 'the necessity of establishing at the earliest practicable date a general international organization, based on the principle of the sovereign equality of all peaceloving states', set up an illusion of continued American-Soviet cooperation that would soon be rudely shattered.

Source: *ibid*

I am immensely gratified to be back in these Legislative Halls and again meet numerous friends, old and new, and especially former colleagues in the two Houses, for each of whom I have long entertained sentiments of great respect and genuine affection. I appreciate deeply the high compliment of being invited to meet with you today. But I appreciate even more the fact that, by your invitation, you have emphasized your profound interest in the principles and policies for which the Moscow Conference stood, and in the progress made by the participating governments in carrying them forward.

In the minds of all of us here present, and of the millions of Americans all over the country, and at battle stations across the seas, there is and there can be, at this moment, but one consuming thought—to defeat the enemy as speedily as possible. We have reached a stage in the war in which the United Nations are on the offensive in every part of the world. Our enemies are suffering defeat after defeat. The time will come when their desperate movement to destroy the world will be utterly crushed. But there are in store for us still enormous hardships and vast sacrifices. The attainment of victory will be hastened only in proportion as all of us, in this country and in all of the United Nations, continue to exert all possible effort to press home our advantage without the slightest relaxation or deviation.

The glorious successes which have already attended our arms and the confidence which we all feel today in assured, though still immensely difficult, victory would have been impossible if this country and Great Britain and the Soviet Union and China and the other victims of aggression had not each risen as a unit in defense of its liberty and independence. They would have been equally impossible if all these nations had not come together in a brotherhood of self-preservation.

While we are thus engaged in the task of winning the war, all of us are acutely conscious of the fact that the fruits of our victory can easily be lost unless there is among us wholehearted acceptance of those basic principles and policies which will render impossible a repetition of our present tragedy, and unless there is promptly created machinery of action necessary to carry out these principles and policies. The Moscow Conference is believed to have been an important step in the direction both of shortening the war and of making provision for the future.

The convocation of the conference was the result of a profound conviction on the part of President Roosevelt, Prime Minister Churchill, and Marshal Stalin that, at this state of the war, frank and friendly exchanges of views between responsible representatives of their three Governments on problems of post-war, as well as war, collaboration were a matter of great urgency. Up to that time such exchanges of views had taken place on several occasions between our Government and that of Great Britain. But the exigencies of war had been obstacles to the participation of the Soviet Government in similar exchanges to the same extent. With the acceleration of the tempo of war against Germany, the necessity became daily more and more apparent for more far-reaching discussions and decisions by the three Governments than had occurred theretofore.

I went to Moscow, by direction of President Roosevelt, to discuss with the representatives of Great Britain and the Soviet Union some basic problems of international relations in the light of principles to which our country, under the President's leadership, has come to give widespread adherence. It has never been my fortune to attend an international conference at which there was greater determination on the part of all the participants to move forward in a spirit of mutual understanding and confidence.

The conference met against the background of a rapidly changing military situation. From the east and from the south, the Nazi armies were being steadily hammered back into narrower and narrower confines. From the west, the Allied air forces were relentlessly and systematically destroying the nerve centers of German industrial and military power.

Formidable as the war task still is, it has been increasingly clear that the time is nearing when more and more of the territory held by the enemy will be wrested from his grasp, and when Germany and its remaining satellites will have to go the way of Fascist Italy. In these circumstances, new problems arise which require concerted action by the Allies—to hasten the end of the war, to plan for its immediate aftermath, and to lay the foundation for the post-war world. Our discussions in Moscow were concerned with many of these problems. Important agreements were reached; but there were no secret agreements, and none was suggested.

Of the military discussions which took place it can be stated that they were in the direction of facilitating closer cooperation between the three countries in the prosecution of the war against the common enemy. I am glad to say that there is now in Moscow a highly competent United States Military Mission, headed by Maj. Gen. John R. Deane.

The attention of the conference was centered upon the task of making sure that the nations, upon whose armed forces and civilian efforts rests the main responsibility for defeating the enemy, will, along with other peacefully minded nations, continue to perform their full part in solving the numerous and vexatious problems of the future. From the outset, the dominant thought at the conference was that, after the attainment of victory, cooperation among peace-loving nations in support of certain paramount mutual interests will be almost as compelling in importance and necessity as it is today in support of the war effort.

At the end of the war, each of the United Nations and each of the nations associated with them, will have the same common interest in national security, in world order under law, in peace, in the full promotion of the political, economic, and social welfare of their respective peoples—in the principles and spirit of the Atlantic Charter and the declaration by United Nations. The future of these indispensable common interests depends absolutely upon international cooperation. Hence, each nation's own primary interest requires it to cooperate with the others.

These considerations led the Moscow Conference to adopt the four-nation declaration, with which you are all familiar. I should like to comment briefly on its main provisions.

In that document it was jointly declared by the United States, Great Britain, the Soviet Union, and China "that their united action, pledged for the prosecution of the war against their common enemies, will be continued for the organization and maintenance of peace and security."

To this end, the four governments declared that they "recognize the necessity of establishing at the earliest practicable date a general international organization, based on the principle of the sovereign equality of all peace-loving states and open to membership by all such states, large and small." I should like to lay particular stress on this provision of the declaration. The principle of sovereign equality of all peace-loving states, irrespective of size and strength, as partners in a future system of general security will be the foundation stone upon which the future international organization will be constructed.

The adoption of this principle was particularly welcome to us. Nowhere has the conception of sovereign equality been applied more widely in recent years than in the American family of nations, whose contribution to the common effort in wartime will now be followed by representation in building the institutions of peace.

The four governments further agreed that, pending the inauguration in this manner of a permanent system of general security, "they will consult with one another and as occasion requires with other members of the United Nations with a view to joint action on behalf of the community of nations" whenever such action may be necessary for the purpose of maintaining international peace and security.

Finally, as an important self-denying ordinance, they declared "that after the termination of hostilities they will not employ their forces within the territories of other states except for the purposes envisaged in this declaration and after joint consultation."

Through this declaration, the Soviet Union, Great Britain, the United States, and China have laid the foundation for cooperative effort in the post-war world toward enabling all peace-loving nations, large and small, to live in peace and security, to preserve the liberties and rights of civilized existence, and to enjoy expanded opportunities and facilities for economic, social, and spiritual progress. No other important nations anywhere have more in common in the present war or in the peace that is to follow victory over the Axis Powers. No one, no two of them can be most effective without the others, in war or in peace.

Each of them had, in the past, relied in varying degrees upon policies of detachment and aloofness. In Moscow, their four governments pledged themselves to carry forward to its fullest development a broad and progressive program of international cooperation. This action was of world-wide importance.

As the provisions of the four-nation declaration are carried into effect, there will no longer be need for spheres of influence, for alliances, for balance of power, or any other of the special arrangements through which, in the unhappy past, the nations strove to safeguard their security or to promote their interests.

The conference faced many political problems growing out of the military activities in Europe. It was foreseen that problems of common interest to our three governments will continue to arise as our joint military efforts hasten the defeat of the enemy. It is impracticable for several governments to come to complete and rapid understanding on such matters through the ordinary channels of diplomatic communication. The conference accordingly decided to set up a European Advisory Commission with its seat in London. This Commission will not of itself have executive powers. Its sole function will be to advise the Governments of the United States, Great Britain, and the Soviet Union. It is to deal with nonmilitary problems relating to enemy territories and with such other problems as may be referred to it by the participating governments. It will provide a useful instrument for continuing study and formulation of recommendations concerning questions connected with the termination of hostilities.

For the purpose of dealing with problems arising from the execution of the terms of surrender of Italy and with related matters growing out of the developing situation in that country, the conference established an advisory council for Italy. This council will consist of representatives of the Governments of the United States, Great Britain, and the Soviet Union, of the French Committee of National Liberation, and of the Governments of Yugoslavia and Greece, as early as practicable. The members of the council will advise the Allied commander in chief and will make recommendations to the respective governments and to the French committee concerning nonmilitary problems relating to Italy.

It was clearly understood that the setting up of these two agencies was not intended to supersede the usual diplomatic channels of communication between the three Governments. On the contrary, arrangements were made for expeditious and effective handling of questions of concern to the three Governments through tripartite diplomatic conversations in any one of the three capitals.

In a declaration on Italy, the conference set forth a number of principles on the basis of which democratic restoration of that country's internal political structure should take place. These principles—including freedom of religion, of speech, of the press, and of assembly, and the right of the people ultimately to choose their own form of government—are among the most basic human rights in civilized society.

In a declaration on Austria, the forcible annexation of that unhappy country was pronounced null and void. It was further declared that Austria is to be given an opportunity to become re-established as a free and independent state, although the Austrians were put on notice that in final analysis the treatment to be accorded them will depend upon the contribution which they will make toward the defeat of Germany and the liberation of their country.

The Conference also served as an occasion for a solemn public declaration by the heads of the three governments with regard to the perpetrators of the bestial and abominable crimes committed by the Nazi leaders against the harassed and persecuted inhabitants of occupied territories—against people of all races and religions, among whom Hitler has reserved for the Jews his most brutal wrath. Due punishment will be administered for all these crimes.

Finally, the Conference gave preliminary attention to a number of other specific problems relating to the eventual transition from war to peace. A fruitful exchange of views took place on such questions as the treatment of Germany and its satellites, the various phases of economic relations, the promotion of social welfare, and the assurance of general security and peace.

These were among the outstanding developments at the Moscow Conference. The intensive discussion, lasting 2 weeks, did not and was not intended to bring about the solution of all the problems that are before us. Much less could we anticipate the problems that are bound to arise from day to day and from year to year. There were other problems, such, for example, as questions relating to boundaries, which must, by their very nature, be left in abeyance until the termination of hostilities. This is in accordance with the position maintained for some time by our Government.

Of supreme importance is the fact that at the Conference, the whole spirit of international cooperation, now and after the war, was revitalized and given practical expression. The Conference thus launched a forward movement which, I am firmly convinced, will steadily extend in scope and effectiveness. Within the framework of that movement, in the atmosphere of mutual understanding and confidence which made possible its beginning in Moscow, many of the problems which are difficult today will, as time goes on, undoubtedly become more possible of satisfactory solution through frank and friendly discussion.

I am happy on this occasion to pay personal tribute to those with whom it was my privilege to confer in Moscow. Mr. Molotov arranged for the business of the conference in a most efficient manner. Both as chairman and participant, he manifested throughout the highest order of ability and a profound grasp of international affairs. Mr. Eden, with his exceptional wisdom and experience, exhibited the finest qualities of states-

manship. I found in Marshal Stalin a remarkable personality, cne of the great statesmen and leaders of this age.

I was deeply impressed by the people of Russia and by the epic quality of their
patriotic fervor. A people who will fight against ruthless aggression, in utter contempt
of death, as the men and women of the Soviet Union are fighting, merit the admiration
and good will of the peoples of all countries.

We of today shall be judged in the future by the manner in which we meet the unprecedented responsibilities that rest upon us—not alone in winning the war, but also in
making certain that the opportunities for future peace and security shall not be lost. As
an American, I am proud of the breadth and height of the vision and statesmanship
which has moved you, ladies and gentlemen, in each House of the Congress, to adopt,
by overwhelming nonpartisan majorities, resolutions in favor of our country's participation with other sovereign nations in an effective system of international cooperation
for the maintenance of peace and security.

Only by carrying forward such a program with common determination and united
national support, can we expect, in the long range of the future, to avoid becoming
victims of destructive forces of international anarchy which in the absence of organized
international relations will rule the world. By the procedure of cooperation with other
nations likewise intent upon security, we can and will remain masters of our own fate.

6   Senator Vandenberg: the conversion of a former noninterven-
     tionist: January 10, 1945: '. . . there are critical moments in the life
     of every nation which call for the straightest, the plainest, and the
     most courageous thinking of which we are capable. We confront
     such a moment now.'

On January 10, 1945, Senator Arthur H. Vandenberg, the Republican leader in the
Senate and former member of the non-interventionist bloc in Congress, reminded
President Roosevelt of the necessity of recapturing 'the original spirit of the Atlantic
Charter' before the wartime Allies set about making the peace on a unilateral basis.
Alluding to Stalin's proposed partition of Poland, which presumably included surrounding Russia with 'friendly' buffer states, Vandenberg suggested that there
should be no obstacle to the United States immediately concluding a treaty with her
major Allies designed to demilitarize Germany and Japan indefinitely. In the
absence of such action, Vandenberg correctly predicted postwar Soviet
expansionism as the only Russian alternative to the possible rebirth of German
militarism. For many of Roosevelt's foreign policy critics this was the golden opportunity to reassure the Soviets of American intentions to help guard the peace in
Eastern Europe; for, it was reasoned, after the advent of the atomic bomb, that the
Soviets could never again bring themselves to trust American motives
unquestioningly.

Source: *Congressional Record*, 79th Congress

I shall detain the Senate less than 30 minutes. I desire to speak about some phases of foreign policy. Because of the solemnity of the subject itself I ask the indulgence of my colleagues that I be permitted at least to make my preliminary statement without interruption.

Mr. President, there are critical moments in the life of every nation which call for the straightest, the plainest, and the most courageous thinking of which we are capable. We confront such a moment now. It is not only desperately important to America. It is important to the world. It is important not only to this generation which lives in blood. It is important to future generations if they shall live in peace.

No man in his right senses will be dogmatic in his viewpoint at such an hour. A global conflict which uproots the earth is not calculated to submit itself to the dominion of any finite mind. The clashes of rival foreign interests, which have motivated wars for countless centuries, are not likely suddenly to surrender to some simple man-made formula, no matter how nobly meditated. Each of us can only speak according to his little lights—and pray for a composite wisdom that shall lead us to high, safe ground. It is only in this spirit of anxious humility that I speak today. Politics, in any such connection, would be as obnoxious at home as they are in manipulations abroad.

Mr. President, we still have two major wars to win. I said "We." That does not mean America alone. It means the continued and total battle fraternity of the United Nations. It must mean one for all and all for one; and it will mean this, unless somewhere in this grand alliance the stupid and sinister folly of ulterior ambitions shall invite the enemy to postpone our victory through our own rivalries and our own confusion. The United Nations, in even greater unity of military action than heretofore, must never, for any cause, permit this military unity to fall apart. If it does, we shall count the cost in mortal anguish, even though we stumble on to a belated, though inevitable victory. And, getting down to what Mr. Churchill would call the bare bones of the matter, this is an obligation which rests no less upon our allies than upon us, and no less upon us than upon our allies. First things must come first. History will not deal lightly with any who undermine this aim ere it is achieved. Destiny will one day balance any such ghastly accounts.

We not only have two wars to win, we also have yet to achieve such a peace as will justify this appalling cost. Here again an even more difficult unity is indispensable. Otherwise we shall look back upon a futile, sanguinary shambles and—God save the mark—we shall be able to look forward only to the curse of World War No. 3.

Unfortunately, Mr. President, the morale of unity in war is often threatened by sharply clashing and often disillusioning disclosures which threaten this unity in peace. The two considerations cannot be dissociated. President Roosevelt correctly said in his annual message that "the nearer we come to vanquishing our enemies the more we become inevitably conscious of differences among the victors." He also correctly said that "nations like individuals do not always see alike or think alike, and international cooperation and progress are not helped by any nation assuming that it has a monopoly of wisdom or of virtue." That applies to us. It applies to each of our allies. But when "differences among the victors"—to use the White House phrase—when "differences among the victors," before they have clinched their victory, threaten both the victory and the peace, the hour cannot much longer be postponed when any such trends shall be reversed. We shall not reverse them by our silence upon the issues that are clearly involved; nor, and I say it with great respect, shall we reverse them merely by a generalized restatement of the high aspirations revoiced in the recent Presidential message. Certainly we shall not reverse them by a snarling process of international recrimination in which every United Nation's capital tries to outdo the other in bitter back-talk about the infirmities of each. Such bickering is dangerous—over there or over here. It is water on the Axis wheel. Again I agree wholeheartedly with President Roosevelt when he says:

> We must not let such differences divide us and blind us to our more important common and continuing interests in winning the war and building the peace.

On the other hand, I hold the deep belief that honest candor, devoid of prejudice or ire, is our greatest hope and our greatest necessity; and that the Government of the United States, above all others, is called at long last to exercise this honest candor not only with its allies but also with its own faithful people.

I hesitate, even now, to say these things, Mr. President, because a great American illusion seems to have been built up—wittingly or otherwise—that we, in the United States, dare not publicly discuss these subjects lest we contribute to international dissension and thus encourage the very thing we all need to cure. But I frankly confess that I do not know why we must be the only silent partner in his grand alliance. There seems to be no fear of disunity, no hesitation in Moscow, when Moscow wants to assert unilateral war and peace aims which collide with ours. There seems to be no fear of disunity, no hesitation in London, when Mr. Churchill proceeds upon his unilateral way to make decisions often repugnant to our ideas and our ideals. Perhaps our allies will plead that their actions are not unilateral; that our President, as Bevin said, has initialed this or that at one of the famous Big Three conferences; that our President, as Churchill said, has been kept constantly "aware of everything that has happened"; in other words, that by our silence we have acquiesced. But that hypothesis would only make a bad matter worse. It would be the final indictment of our silence—the final obituary for open covenants. We, of course, accept no conception that our contribution to unity must be silence, while others say and do what they please, and that our only role in this global tragedy is to fight and die and pay, and that unity for us shall only be the unity which Jonah enjoyed when he was swallowed by the whale.

I hasten to say that any such intolerable conception would be angrily repudiated by every American—from the President down to the last citizen among us. It has not been and is not true. Yet it cannot be denied that our Government has not spoken out—to our own people or to our allies—in any such specific fashion as have the others. It cannot be denied, as a result, that too often a grave melancholy settles upon some sectors of our people. It cannot be denied that citizens, in increasing numbers, are crying: "What are we fighting for?" It cannot be denied that our silence—at least our public and official silence—has multiplied confusion at home and abroad. It cannot be denied that this confusion threatens our unity—yes, Mr. President, and already hangs like a cloud over Dumbarton Oaks. So I venture to repeat, with all the earnestness at my command, that a new rule of honest candor in Washington—as a substitute for mystifying silence or for classical generalities—honest candor on the high plane of great ideals—is the greatest contribution we can make to the realities of unity at this moment when enlightened civilization is our common stake.

Let us not mistake the meaning of unity. Unity does not require universal and peremptory agreement about everything. It does not demand a meeting of all minds now in respect to all the minutiae of a post-war world which will take years to stabilize. The President is wholly right in pleading for tolerance upon this score and in warning that we must not expect what he calls perfectionism overnight. Here in the Senate we do not have perpetual agreement between the two sides of the aisle, but we have never failed to have basic unity when crisis calls. The unity I discuss is the over-all tie which must continue to bind the United Nations together in respect to paramount fundamentals. We had it once in the original spirit of the Atlantic Charter, and we must get it back again before it is too late.

When Mr. Churchill spoke in the British Parliament last December 15, defending his own current course in Greece and Mr. Stalin's proposed partition of Poland, he said:

> There is no doubt that when the time comes the United States will make its own pronouncement upon these matters, bearing in mind, as it will, the practical aspects which these matters assume and also how much failure on the part of the three greatest powers to work together would damage all our hopes for the future structure of a world government which, whatever else it might fail to do, will at any rate be equipped with all powers necessary to prevent outbreak of future war.

I do not like one of the implications in this quotation. It seems to say that unless we acquiesce in these self-serving unilateral arrangements now being made by great European powers, we shall be the scapegoats to be made responsible for the next war. I would respond categorically to any such abortive thesis by saying that, regardless of the future structure of a world government, an unjust peace, built upon the age-old frictions of international power politics, is the most fatal of all threats which our hopes for the future can possibly confront. But that is not the reason I use the quotation at this point. Of even greater importance is the other implication—namely, that the United States has not spoken; that her official attitude is not dependably recorded; and that, until she does speak, the world cannot find its bearings.

There is no doubt—

Says Mr. Churchill—

that when the time comes the United States will make its own pronouncement.

When the time comes. Mr. President, is the time not here right now?

If it is, Mr. President, what shall we say that we have not already said in the Connally resolution in the Senate and the Fulbright resolution in the House and in the Presidential utterances?

It seems to me, Mr. President, that the first thing we must say, beyond misunderstanding, is that we have not altered our original commitments; that we have not lowered our sights; that we have not diluted our dedications; that we are not fighting to pull ancient chestnuts out of alien fires; that the smell of victory is not an anaesthetic which puts our earlier zeals to sleep. We still propose to win this war, come what may. We are fighting to defend America. We still propose to help create the post-war world on a basis which shall stop aggressors for keeps and, so far as humanly possible, substitute justice for force among freemen. We propose to do it primarily for our own sake. We still propose also, to substitute justice for force—if we can—in writing the peace which terminates this war when we deal with the victims of Axis tyranny. That is the road to permanent peace. We still propose that none of the United Nations shall seek aggrandizement, territorial, or otherwise—though conceding that all change is not necessarily aggrandizement. We still propose, outside the Axis, that there shall be no territorial changes which do not accord with the freely expressed wishes of the people concerned. Similarly we still propose to respect the right of all peoples to choose the form of government under which they will live. We still propose to see sovereign rights and self-government restored to those who have been forcibly deprived of them, if it lies within our power.

In a word, Mr. President, it seems to me that the first thing we must do is to reassert, in high places, our American faith in these particular elemental objectives of the so-called Atlantic Charter, which was officially issued as a signed document by the State Department on August 14, 1941; which was officially communicated to the Congress as a signed document by the President of the United States in his message of August 21, 1941; which was embodied in a joint resolution of all the United Nations on January 1, 1942; which was commemorated by the President on August 14, 1943 in a proclamation on the second anniversary of its "signing"—his word—which had a tragic sinking spell when its formal authenticity was amazingly depreciated in a White House press conference a fortnight ago, but which the President re-embraced in his message of January 6, 1945.

I am sure the President did not anticipate the shocking results of his recent almost jocular, and even cynical, dismissal of the Atlantic Charter as a mere collection of fragmentary notes. It jarred America to its very hearthstones. It seemed to make a mere pretense out of what has been an inspiringly accepted fact. It seemed almost to sanction alien contempts. It seemed to suggest that we have put too much emphasis upon a fighting creed which did not deserve the solemnity which we have been taught to ascribe to it. Coming at a particularly critical moment when these pledges seemed to be at least partially paralyzed in Moscow—and when even Mr. Churchill's memory about the charter was proving to be admittedly fickle—the President's statement was utterly devastating in its impact. He has since sought to repair this damage. I hope he has succeeded. With justification he reminds us in his annual message that there are no rules of easy application—of the charter—to each and every one of this war-torn world's tangled situations. He now says correctly and bravely, "We shall not hesitate to use our influence—and use it now—to secure so far as is humanly possible the fulfillment of these principles." That is the indispensable point. These basic pledges cannot now be dismissed as a mere nautical nimbus. They march with our armies. They sail with our fleets. They fly with our eagles. They sleep with our martyred dead. The first requisite of honest candor, Mr. President, I respectfully suggest, is to relight this torch.

The next thing we need to do, Mr. President, if I may be so bold, in this spirit of honest candor, is to appeal to our allies, in the name of reason, to frankly face the post-war alternatives which are available to them and to us as a means to preserve tomorrow's peace for them and for us. There are two ways to do it. One way is by exclusive individual action in which each of us tries to look out for himself. The other way is by joint action in which we undertake to look out for each other. The first way is the old way which has twice taken us to Europe's interminable battlefields within a quarter century. The second way is the new way in which our present fraternity of war becomes a new fraternity of peace. I do not believe that either we or our allies can have it both ways. They serve to cancel out each other. We cannot tolerate unilateral privilege in a multilateral peace. Yet, that seems to be the fatalistic trend today. I think we must make our choice. I think we must make it wholly plain to our major allies that they, too, must make their choice.

I hasten to make my own personal viewpoint clear. I have always been frankly one of those who has believed in our own self-reliance. I still believe that we can never again—regardless of collaborations—allow our national defense to deteriorate to anything like a point of impotence. But I do not believe that any nation hereafter can immunize itself by its own exclusive action. Since Pearl Harbor, World War No. 2 has put the gory science of mass murder into new and sinister perspective. Our oceans have ceased to be moats which automatically protect our ramparts. Flesh and blood now compete unequally with winged steel. War has become an all-consuming juggernaut. If World War No. 3 ever unhappily arrives, it will open new laboratories of death too horrible to contemplate. I propose to do everything within my power to keep those laboratories closed for keeps. I want maximum American cooperation, consistent with legitimate American self-interest, with constitutional process and with collateral events which warrant it, to make the basic idea of Dumbarton Oaks succeed. I want a new dignity and a new authority for international law. I think American self-interest requires it. But, Mr. President, this also requires whole-hearted reciprocity. In honest candor I think we should tell other nations that this glorious thing we contemplate is not and cannot be one-sided. I think we must say again that unshared idealism is a menace which we could not undertake to underwrite in the post-war world.

Now, I am not so impractical as to expect any country to act on any final motive other than self-interest. I know of no reason why it should. That is what nations are for. I certainly intend that intelligent and loyal American self-interest shall be just as vigilantly and vigorously guarded as is amply obvious, from time to time, in their own behalf by the actions of our allies. The real question always becomes just this: Where does real self-interest lie?

Here, Mr. President, we reach the core of the immediate problem. Without remotely wanting to be invidious, I use one of many available examples. I would not presume, even under these circumstances, to use it except that it ultimately involves us. Russia's unilateral plan appears to contemplate the engulfment, directly or indirectly, of a surrounding circle of buffer States, contrary to our conception of what we thought we were fighting for in respect to the rights of small nations and a just peace. Russia's announced reason is her insistent purpose never again to be at the mercy of another German tyranny. That is a perfectly understandable reason. The alternative is collective security. Now, which is better, in the long view? That is the question I pose. Which is better, in the long view, from a purely selfish Russian standpoint: To forcefully surround herself with a cordon of unwillingly controlled or partitioned states, thus affronting the opinions of mankind, as a means of post-war protection against a renaissance of German aggression, or to win the priceless asset of world confidence in her by embracing the alternative, namely, full and wholehearted cooperation with and reliance on a vital international organization in which all of us shall honorably participate to guarantee that Axis aggression shall never rise again? Well—at that point, Russia, or others like her, in equally honest candor, has a perfect right to reply, "Where is there any such alternative reliance until we know what the United States will do? How can you expect us to rely on an enigma?"

Now we are getting somewhere. Fear of reborn German aggression in years to come is at the base of most of our contemporary frictions. It is a perfectly human and understandable fear on the part of all neighboring nations which German militarism has twice driven to the valley of the shadow within one generation. Fear of reborn German aggression in years to come is the cause assigned to unilateral plans for Russian post-war expansion. Fear of reborn German aggression is the reason assigned to the proposed partition of Poland. Fear of reborn German aggression gave birth to the Anglo-Soviet agreement of 1942, the Soviet-Czechoslovak agreement of 1943, the Franco-Soviet Treaty of 1944, and to similar unilateral and bilateral actions inevitably yet to come. Fear of reborn German aggression is our apple of discord. This second World War plagues the earth chiefly because France and Britain did not keep Germany disarmed, according to contract, after World War No. 1. In other words, when we deal with Europe's fear—her justified fear—of another rebirth of German military tyranny in some future post-war era, we are at the heart of the immediate problem which bedevils our Allied relationships.

I propose that we meet this problem conclusively and at once. There is no reason to wait. America has this same self-interest in permanently, conclusively, and effectively disarming Germany and Japan. It is simply unthinkable that America, or any other member of the United Nations, would allow this Axis calamity to reproduce itself again. Whether we Americans do or do not agree upon all the powers that shall reside in all ultimate international council to call upon us for joint military action in behalf of collective security, surely we can agree that we do not ever want an instant's hesitation or doubt about our military cooperation in the peremptory use of force, if needed, to keep Germany and Japan demilitarized. Such a crisis would be the lengthened shadow of the present war. It would be a direct epilog to the present war. It should be handled as this present war is handled. There should be no more need to refer any such action back to Congress than that Congress should expect to pass upon battle plans today. The Commander in Chief should have instant power to act, and he should act. I know of no reason why a hard-and-fast treaty between the major allies should not be signed today to achieve this dependable end. We need not await the determination of our other post-war relationships. This problem—this menace—stands apart by itself. Regardless of what our later decision may be in respect to the power that shall be delegated to the President to join our military force with others in a new peace league—no matter what limitations may commend themselves to our ultimate judgments in this regard, I am sure we can agree that there should be no limitations when it comes to keeping the Axis out of piracy for keeps. I respectfully urge that we meet this problem now. From it stem many of today's confusions, doubts, and frustrations. I think we should immediately put it behind us by conclusive action. Having done so, most of the reasons given for controversial unilateral and bilateral actions by our allies will have disappeared; and then we shall be able, at least, to judge accurately whether we have found and cured the real hazard to our relationships. We shall have closed ranks. We shall have returned infinitely closer to basic unity.

Then, in honest candor, Mr. President, I think we have the duty and the right to demand that whatever immediate unilateral decisions have to be made in consequence of military need—and there will be such even in civil affairs—they shall all be temporary and subject to final revision in the objective light of the post-war world and the post-war peace league as they shall ultimately develop. As President Roosevelt put it in his annual message:

> During the interim period, until conditions permit a genuine expression of the peoples' will, we and our allies have a duty, which we cannot ignore, to use our influence to the end that no temporary or provisional authorities in the liberated countries block the eventual exercise of the peoples' right freely to choose the government and institutions under which, as free men, they are to live.

I agree to that. Indeed, I would go further. I would write it in the bond. If Dumbarton Oaks should specifically authorize the ultimate international organization to review protested injustices in the peace itself, it would at least partially nullify the argument that we are to be asked to put a blank-check warrant behind a future status quo which is unknown to us and which we might be unwilling to defend.

We are standing by our guns with epic heroism. I know of no reason why we should not stand by our ideals. If they vanish under ultimate pressures, we shall at least have kept the record straight; we shall have kept faith with our soldier sons; and we then shall clearly be free agents, unhampered by tragic misunderstandings, in determining our own course when Berlin and Tokyo are in Allied hands. Let me put it this way for myself: I am prepared, by effective international cooperation, to do our full part in charting happier and safer tomorrows. But I am not prepared to guarantee permanently the spoils of an unjust peace. It will not work.

Mr. President, we need honest candor even with our foes. Without any remote suggestion of appeasement—indeed, it seems to me that it is exactly the contrary—I wish we might give these Axis peoples some incentive to desert their own tottering tyrannies by at least indicating to them that the quicker they unconditionally surrender the cheaper will be unconditional surrender's price. Here again we need plain speaking which has been too conspicuous by its absence, and, upon at least one calamitous occasion, by its error.

Mr. President, I conclude as I began. We must win these wars with maximum speed and minimum loss. Therefore we must have maximum Allied cooperation and minimum Allied frictions. We have fabulously earned the right to be heard in respect to the basis of this unity. We need the earliest possible clarification of our relations with our brave allies. We need this clarification not only for the sake of total Allied cooperation in the winning of the war but also in behalf of a truly compensatory peace. We cannot drift to victory. We must have maximum united effort on all fronts. We must have maximum united effort in our councils. And we must deserve the continued united effort of our own people.

I realize, Mr. President, in such momentous problems how much easier it is to be critical than to be correct. I do not wish to meddle. I want only to help. I want to do my duty. It is in this spirit that I ask for honest candor in respect to our ideals, our dedications, and our commitments, as the greatest contribution which government can now make to the only kind of realistic unity which will most swiftly bring our victorious sons back home, and which will best validate our aspirations, our sacrifices, and our dreams.

7   FDR reports on the Crimean Conference: March 1, 1945: *'I think the Crimean Conference was a successful effort by the three leading nations to find a common ground for peace. It spells—and it ought to spell—the end of the system of unilateral action, exclusive alliances, and spheres of influence, and balances of power, and all the other expedients which have been tried for centuries and have always failed.'*

In his report to Congress on the results of the Crimean Conference and in the public communique issued at the end of the conference, President Roosevelt gave the nation what, in retrospect, could only be regarded as a false sense of the unity of the Allies. Pressed by one *fait accompli* after another, and none more troublesome than the Soviet Union's support of the so-called Lublin Government of Poland consisting mainly of fellow travellers, Roosevelt did what most American Presidents have done when faced with an insoluble problem—i.e. devised a ceremonial solution.

In this case, the ceremonial solution took the form of allegedly reorganizing the Soviet-supported provincial government of Poland by broadening its base, thereby allowing some London Poles to enter into a coalition. The truth of the matter is that Stalin was steadfast in his refusal to allow the Lublin Government to become anything other than his own creature. Again, critics of Roosevelt's foreign policy, 'Realists' and New Left revisionist historians alike, have questioned the wisdom of American foreign policy in resisting Soviet demands in Poland, given the large loss of Russian lives as well as Russia's significant role in conquering the Nazi war machine in this territory. While the President's private morality might have permitted such a development, his public morality stand, including the large Polish voting bloc, remained officially committed to a peace 'based on the sound and just principles of the Atlantic Charter'. In any case, FDR's overly optimistic remarks regarding the solidarity of Allied war and peace aims failed to cushion the blow of the rapid deterioration of Soviet-American relations (before the President's death in April 1945) and the subsequent public disclosure of the secret terms of the Yalta Accords (especially the provisions that allowed Stalin to re-obtain Chinese territories and special privileges lost to Japan in the Russo-Japanese War of 1904).

Source: ibid.

. . . First of all, I want to say, it is good to be home.

It has been a long journey. I hope you will also agree that it has been, so far, a fruitful one.

Speaking in all frankness, the question of whether it is entirely fruitful or not lies to a great extent in your hands. For unless you here in the halls of the American Congress—with the support of the American people—concur in the general conclusions reached at Yalta, and give them your active support, the meeting will not have produced lasting results.

That is why I have come before you at the earliest hour I could after my return. I want to make a personal report to you—and, at the same time, to the people of the country. Many months of earnest work are ahead of us all, and I should like to feel that when the last stone is laid on the structure of international peace, it will be an achievement for which all of us in America have worked steadfastly and unselfishly—together.

I am returning from this trip—that took me so far—refreshed and inspired. I was well the entire time. I was not ill for a second, until I arrived back in Washington, and there I heard all of the rumors which had occurred in my absence. I returned from the trip refreshed and inspired. The Roosevelts are not, as you may suspect, averse to travel. We seem to thrive on it!

Far away as I was, I was kept constantly informed of affairs in the United States. The modern miracles of rapid communication have made this world very small. We must always bear in mind that fact, when we speak or think of international relations. I received a steady stream of messages from Washington—I might say from not only the executive branch with all its departments, but also from the legislative branch—and except where radio silence was necessary for security purposes, I could continuously send messages any place in the world. And of course, in a grave emergency, we would have even risked the breaking of the security rule.

I come from the Crimea Conference with a firm belief that we have made a good start on the road to a world of peace.

There were two main purposes in this Crimea Conference. The first was to bring defeat to Germany with the greatest possible speed, and the smallest possible loss of Allied men. That purpose is now being carried out in great force. The German Army, and the German people, are feeling the ever-increasing might of our fighting men and of the Allied armies. Every hour gives us added pride in the heroic advance of our troops in Germany—on German soil—toward a meeting with the gallant Red Army.

The second purpose was to continue to build the foundation for an international accord that would bring order and security after the chaos of the war, that would give some assurance of lasting peace among the Nations of the world.

Toward that goal also, a tremendous stride was made.

At Teheran, a little over a year ago, there were long-range military plans laid by the Chiefs of Staff of the three most powerful Nations. Among the civilian leaders at Teheran, however, at that time, there were only exchanges of views and expressions of opinion. No political arrangements were made—and none was attempted.

At the Crimea Conference, however, the time had come for getting down to specific cases in the political field.

There was on all sides at this Conference an enthusiastic effort to reach an agreement. Since the time of Teheran, a year ago, there had developed among all of us a—what shall I call it?—a greater facility in negotiating with each other, that augurs well for the peace of the world. We know each other better.

I have never for an instant wavered in my belief that an agreement to insure world peace and security can be reached.

There were a number of things that we did that were concrete—that were definite. For instance, the lapse of time between Teheran and Yalta without conferences of civilian representatives of the three major powers has proved to be too long—fourteen months. During that long period, local problems were permitted to become acute in places like Poland and Greece and Italy and Yugoslavia.

Therefore, we decided at Yalta that, even if circumstances made it impossible for the heads of the three Governments to meet more often in the future, we would make sure that there would be more frequent personal contacts for the exchange of views, between the Secretaries of State and the Foreign Ministers of these three powers.

We arranged for periodic meetings at intervals of three or four months. I feel very confident that under this arrangement there will be no recurrences of the incidents which this winter disturbed the friends of world-wide cooperation and collaboration.

When we met at Yalta, in addition to laying our strategic and tactical plans for the complete and final military victory over Germany, there were other problems of vital political consequence.

For instance, first, there were the problems of the occupation and control of Germany—after victory—the complete destruction of her military power, and the assurance that neither the Nazis nor Prussian militarism could again be revived to threaten the peace and the civilization of the world.

Second—again for example—there was the settlement of the few differences that remained among us with respect to the International Security Organization after the Dumbarton Oaks Conference. As you remember, at that time, I said that we had agreed ninety percent. Well, that's a pretty good percentage. I think the other ten percent was ironed out at Yalta.

Third, there were the general political and economic problems common to all of the areas which had been or would be liberated from the Nazi yoke. This is a very special problem. We over here find it difficult to understand the ramifications of many of these problems in foreign lands, but we are trying to.

Fourth, there were the special problems created by a few instances such as Poland and Yugoslavia.

Days were spent in discussing these momentous matters and we argued freely and frankly across the table. But at the end, on every point, unanimous agreement was reached. And more important even that the agreement of words, I may say we achieved a unity of thought and a way of getting along together.

Of course, we know that it was Hitler's hope—and the German war lords'—that we would not agree—that some slight crack might appear in the solid wall of Allied unity, a crack that would give him and his fellow gangsters one last hope of escaping their just doom. That is the objective for which his propaganda machine has been working for many months.

But Hitler has failed.

Never before have the major Allies been more closely united—not only in their war aims but also in their peace aims. And they are determined to continue to be united with each other—and with all peace-loving Nations—so that the ideal of lasting peace will become a reality.

The Soviet, British, and United States Chiefs of Staff held daily meetings with each other. They conferred frequently with Marshal Stalin, and with Prime Minister Churchill and with me, on the problem of coordinating the strategic and tactical efforts of the Allied powers. They completed their plans for the final knock-out blows to Germany.

At the time of the Teheran Conference, the Russian front was removed so far from the American and British fronts that, while certain long-range strategic cooperation was possible, there could be no tactical, day-by-day coordination. They were too far apart. But Russian troops have now crossed Poland. They are fighting on the Eastern soil of Germany herself; British and American troops are now on German soil close to the Rhine River in the West. It is a different situation today from what it was fourteen months ago; a closer tactical liaison has become possible for the first time in Europe—and, in the Crimea Conference, that was something else that was accomplished.

Provision was made for daily exchange of information between the armies under the command of General Eisenhower on the western front, and those armies under the command of the Soviet marshals on that long eastern front, and also with our armies in Italy—without the necessity of going through the Chiefs of Staff in Washington or London as in the past.

You have seen one result of this exchange of information in the recent bombings by American and English aircraft of points which are directly related to the Russian advance on Berlin.

From now on, American and British heavy bombers will be used—in the day-by-day tactics of the war—and we have begun to realize, I think, that there is all the difference in the world between tactics on the one side, and strategy on the other—day-by-day tactics of the war in direct support of the Soviet armies, as well as in the support of our own on the western front.

They are now engaged in bombing and strafing in order to hamper the movement of German reserves and materials to the eastern and western fronts from other parts of Germany or from Italy.

Arrangements have been made for the most effective distribution of all available material and transportation to the places where they can best be used in the combined war effort—American, British, and Russian.

Details of these plans and arrangements are military secrets, of course; but this tying of things in together is going to hasten the day of the final collapse of Germany. The Nazis are learning about some of them already, to their sorrow. And I think all three of us at the Conference felt that they will learn more about them tomorrow and the next day—and the day after that!

There will be no respite for them. We will not desist for one moment until unconditional surrender.

You know, I've always felt that common sense prevails in the long run—quiet, overnight thinking. I think that is true in Germany, just as much as it is here.

The German people, as well as the German soldiers must realize that the sooner they give up and surrender by groups or as individuals, the sooner their present agony will be over. They must realize that only with complete surrender can they begin to reestablish themselves as people whom the world might accept as decent neighbors.

We made it clear again at Yalta, and I now repeat that unconditional surrender does not mean the destruction or enslavement of the German people. The Nazi leaders have deliberately withheld that part of the Yalta declaration from the German press and radio. They seek to convince the people of Germany that the Yalta declaration does mean slavery and destruction for them—they are working at it day and night for that is how the Nazis hope to save their own skins, and deceive their people into continued and useless resistance.

We did, however, make it clear at the Conference just what unconditional surrender does mean for Germany.

It means the temporary control of Germany by Great Britain, Russia, France, and the United States. Each of these Nations will occupy and control a separate zone of Germany—and the administration of the four zones will be coordinated in Berlin by a Control Council composed of representatives of the four Nations.

Unconditional surrender means something else. It means the end of Nazism. It means the end of the Nazi Party—and of all its barbaric laws and institutions.

It means the termination of all militaristic influence in the public, private, and cultural life of Germany.

It means for the Nazi war criminals a punishment that is speedy and just—and severe.

It means the complete disarmament of Germany; the destruction of its militarism and its military equipment; the end of its production of armament; the dispersal of all its armed forces; the permanent dismemberment of the German General Staff which has so often shattered the peace of the world.

It means that Germany will have to make reparations in kind for the damage which has been done to the innocent victims of its aggression.

By compelling reparations in kind—in plants, in machinery, in rolling stock, and in raw materials—we shall avoid the mistake that we and other Nations made after the last war, the demanding of reparations in the form of money which Germany could never pay.

We do not want the German people to starve, or to become a burden on the rest of the world.

Our objective in handling Germany is simple—it is to secure the peace of the rest of the world now and in the future. Too much experience has shown that that objective is impossible if Germany is allowed to retain any ability to wage aggressive warfare.

These objectives will not hurt the German people. On the contrary, they will protect them from a repetition of the fate which the General Staff and Kaiserism imposed on them before, and which Hitlerism is now imposing upon them again a hundredfold. It will be removing a cancer from the German body politic which for generations has produced only misery and only pain to the whole world.

During my stay in Yalta, I saw the kind of reckless, senseless fury, the terrible destruction that comes out of German militarism. Yalta, on the Black Sea, had no military significance of any kind. It had no defenses.

Before the last war, it had been a resort for people like the Czars and princes and for the aristocracy of Russia—and the hangers-on. However, after the Red Revolution, and until the attack on the Soviet Union by Hitler, the palaces and the villas of Yalta had been used as a rest and recreation center by the Russian people.

The Nazi officers took these former palaces and villas—took them over for their own use. The only reason that the so-called former palace of the Czar was still habitable, when we got there, was that it had been given—or he thought it had been given— to a German general for his own property and his own use. And when Yalta was so destroyed, he kept soldiers there to protect what he thought would become his own, nice villa. It was a useful rest and recreation center for hundreds of thousands of Russian workers, farmers, and their families, up to the time that it was taken again by the Germans. The Nazi officers took these places for their own use, and when the Red Army forced the Nazis out of the Crimea—almost just a year ago—all of these villas were looted by the Nazis, and then nearly all of them were destroyed by bombs placed on the inside. And even the humblest of the homes of Yalta were not spared.

There was little left of it except blank walls—ruins—destruction and desolation.

Sevastopol—that was a fortified port, about forty or fifty miles away—there again was a scene of utter destruction—a large city with great navy yards and fortifications—I think less than a dozen buildings were left intact in the entire city.

I had read about Warsaw and Lidice and Rotterdam and Coventry—but I *saw* Sevastopol and Yalta! And I know that there is not room enough on earth for both German militarism and Christian decency.

Of equal importance with the military arrangements at the Crimea Conference were the agreements reached with respect to a general international organization for lasting world peace. The foundations were laid at Dumbarton Oaks. There was one point, however, on which agreement was not reached at Dumbarton Oaks. It involved the procedure of voting in the Security Council. I want to try to make it clear by making it simple. It took me hours and hours to get the thing straight in my own mind—and many conferences.

At the Crimea Conference, the Americans made a proposal on this subject which, after full discussion was, I am glad to say, unanimously adopted by the other two Nations.

It is not yet possible to announce the terms of that agreement publicly, but it will be in a very short time.

When the conclusions reached with respect to voting in the Security Council are made known, I think and I hope that you will find them a fair solution of this complicated and difficult problem. They are founded in justice, and will go far to assure international cooperation in the maintenance of peace.

A conference of all the United Nations of the world will meet in San Francisco on April 25, 1945. There, we all hope, and confidently expect, to execute a definite charter of organization under which the peace of the world will be preserved and the forces of aggression permanently outlawed.

This time we are not making the mistake of waiting until the end of the war to set up the machinery of peace. This time, as we fight together to win the war finally, we work together to keep it from happening again.

I—as you know—have always been a believer in the document called the Constitution of the United States. And I spent a good deal of time in educating two other

Nations of the world in regard to the Constitution of the United States. The charter has to be—and should be—approved by the Senate of the United States, under the Constitution. I think the other Nations all know it now. I am aware of that fact, and now all the other Nations are. And we hope that the Senate will approve of what is set forth as the Charter of the United Nations when they all come together in San Francisco next month.

The Senate of the United States, through its appropriate representatives, has been kept continuously advised of the program of this Government in the creation of the International Security Organization.

The Senate and the House of Representatives will both be represented at the San Francisco Conference. The Congressional delegates to the San Francisco Conference will consist of an equal number of Republican and Democratic members. The American Delegation is—in every sense of the word—bipartisan.

World peace is not a party question. I think that Republicans want peace just as much as Democrats. It is not a party question—any more than is military victory—the winning of the war.

When the Republic was threatened, first by the Nazi clutch for world conquest back in 1940 and then by the Japanese treachery in 1941, partisanship and politics were laid aside by nearly every American; and every resource was dedicated to our common safety. The same consecration to the cause of peace will be expected, I think, by every patriotic American, and by every human soul overseas.

The structure of world peace cannot be the work of one man, or one party, or one Nation. It cannot be just an American peace, or a British peace, or a Russian, a French, or a Chinese peace. It cannot be a peace of large Nations—or of small Nations. It must be a peace which rests on the cooperative effort of the whole world.

It cannot be a structure of complete perfection at first. But it can be a peace—and it will be a peace—based on the sound and just principles of the Atlantic Charter—on the concept of the dignity of the human being—and on the guarantees of tolerance and freedom of religious worship.

As the Allied armies have marched to military victory, they have liberated people whose liberties had been crushed by the Nazis for four long years, whose economy has been reduced to ruin by Nazi despoilers.

There have been instances of political confusion and unrest in these liberated areas—that is not unexpected—as in Greece or in Poland or in Yugoslavia, and there may be more. Worse than that, there actually began to grow up in some of these places queer ideas of, for instance, "spheres of influence" that were incompatible with the basic principles of international collaboration. If allowed to go on unchecked, these developments might have had tragic results in time.

It is fruitless to try to place the blame for this situation on one particular Nation or on another. It is the kind of development that is almost inevitable unless the major powers of the world continue without interruption to work together and to assume joint responsibility for the solution of problems that may arise to endanger the peace of the world.

We met in the Crimea, determined to settle this matter of liberated areas. Things that might happen that we cannot foresee at this moment might happen suddenly—unexpectedly—next week or next month. And I am happy to confirm to the

Congress that we did arrive at a settlement—and, incidentally, a unanimous settlement.

The three most powerful Nations have agreed that the political and economic problems of any area liberated from Nazi conquest, or of any former Axis satellite, are a joint responsibility of all three Governments. They will join together, during the temporary period of instability—after hostilities—to help the people of any liberated area, or of any former satellite state, to solve their own problems through firmly established democratic processes.

They will endeavor to see to it that the people who carry on the interim government between occupation of Germany and true independence, will be as representative as possible of all democratic elements in the population, and that free elections are held as soon as possible thereafter.

Responsibility for political conditions thousands of miles away can no longer be avoided by this great Nation. Certainly, I do not want to live to see another war. As I have said, the world is smaller—smaller every year. The United States now exerts a tremendous influence in the cause of peace throughout all the world. What we people over here are thinking and talking about is in the interest of peace, because it is known all over the world. The slightest remark in either House of the Congress is known all over the world the following day. We will continue to exert that influence, only if we are willing to continue to share in the responsibility for keeping the peace. It will be our own tragic loss, I think, if we were to shirk that responsibility.

The final decisions in these areas are going to be made jointly; and therefore they will often be a result of give-and-take compromise. The United States will not always have its way a hundred percent—nor will Russia nor Great Britain. We shall not always have ideal answers—solutions to complicated international problems, even though we are determined continuously to strive toward that ideal. But I am sure that under the agree-ments reached at Yalta, there will be a more stable political Europe than ever before.

Of course, once there has been a free expression of the people's will in any country, our immediate responsibility ends—with the exception only of such action as may be agreed on in the International Security Organization that we hope to set up.

The United Nations must also soon begin to help these liberated areas adequately to reconstruct their economy so that they are ready to resume their places in the world. The Nazi war machine has stripped them of raw materials and machine tools and trucks and locomotives. They have left the industry of these places stagnant and much of the agricultural areas are unproductive. The Nazis have left a ruin in their wake.

To start the wheels running again is not a mere matter of relief. It is to the national interest that all of us see to it that these liberated areas are again made self-supporting and productive so that they do not need continuous relief from us. I should say that was an argument based on plain common sense.

One outstanding example of joint action by the three major Allied powers in the liberated areas was the solution reached on Poland. The whole Polish question was a potential source of trouble in postwar Europe—as it has been sometimes before—and we came to the Conference determined to find a common ground for its solution. And we did—even though everybody does not agree with us, obviously.

Our objective was to help to create a strong, independent, and prosperous Nation. That is the thing we must always remember, those words, agreed to by Russia, by Britain, and by the United States: the objective of making Poland a strong, independent, and prosperous Nation, with a government ultimately to be selected by the Polish people themselves.

To achieve that objective, it was necessary to provide for the formation of a new government much more representative than had been possible while Poland was enslaved. There were, as you know, two governments—one in London, one in Lublin—practically in Russia. Accordingly, steps were taken at Yalta to reorganize the existing Provisional Government in Poland on a broader democratic basis, so as to include democratic leaders now in Poland and those abroad. This new, reorganized government will be recognized by all of us as the temporary government of Poland. Poland needs a temporary government in the worst way—an ad interim government, I think is another way of putting it.

However, the new Polish Provisional Government of National Unity will be pledged to holding a free election as soon as possible on the basis of universal suffrage and a secret ballot.

Throughout history, Poland has been the corridor through which attacks on Russia have been made. Twice in this generation, Germany has struck at Russia through this corridor. To insure European security and world peace, a strong and independent Poland is necessary to prevent that from happening again.

The decision with respect to the boundaries of Poland was, frankly, a compromise. I did not agree with all of it, by any means, but we did not go as far as Britain wanted, in certain areas; we did not go so far as Russia wanted, in certain areas; and we did not go so far as I wanted, in certain areas. It *was* a compromise. The decision is one, however, under which the Poles will receive compensation in territory in the North and West in exchange for what they lose by the Curzon Line in the East. The limits of the western border will be permanently fixed in the final Peace Conference. We know, roughly, that it will include—in the new, strong Poland—quite a large slice of what now is called Germany. And it was agreed, also, that the new Poland will have a large and long coast line, and many new harbors. Also, that most of East Prussia will go to Poland. A corner of it will go to Russia. Also, that the anomaly of the Free State of Danzig will come to an end; I think Danzig would be a lot better it if were Polish.

It is well known that the people east of the Curzon Line—just for example, here is why I compromised—are predominantly white Russian and Ukrainian—they are not Polish; and a very great majority of the people west of the line are predominantly Polish, except in that part of East Prussia and eastern Germany, which will go to the new Poland. As far back as 1919, representatives of the Allies agreed that the Curzon Line represented a fair boundary between the two peoples. And you must remember, also, that there had not been any Polish government before 1919 for a great many generations.

I am convinced that the agreement on Poland, under the circumstances, is the most hopeful agreement possible for a free, independent, and prosperous Polish state.

The Crimea Conference was a meeting of the three major military powers on whose shoulders rested chief responsibility and burden of the war. Although, for this reason, France was not a participant in the Conference, no one should detract from the recognition that was accorded there of her role in the future of Europe and the future of the world.

France has been invited to accept a zone of control in Germany, and to participate as a fourth member of the Allied Control Council of Germany.

She has been invited to join as a sponsor of the International Conference at San Francisco next month.

She will be a permanent member of the International Security Council together with the other four major powers.

And, finally, we have asked that France be associated with us in our joint responsibility over all the liberated areas of Europe.

Agreement was reached on Yugoslavia, as announced in the communiqué; and we hope that it is in process of fulfillment. But, not only there but in some other places, we have to remember that there are a great many prima donnas in the world. All of them wish to be heard before anything becomes final, so we may have a little delay while we listen to more prima donnas.

Quite naturally, this Conference concerned itself only with the European war and with the political problems of Europe—and not with the Pacific war.

In Malta, however, our combined British and American staffs made their plans to increase the attack against Japan.

The Japanese war lords know that they are not being overlooked. They have felt the force of our B-29's, and our carrier planes; they have felt the naval might of the United States, and do not appear very anxious to come out and try it again.

The Japs now know what it means to hear that "The United States Marines have landed." And I think I can add that, having Iwo Jima in mind, "The situation is well in hand."

They also know what is in store for the homeland of Japan now that General MacArthur has completed his magnificent march back to Manila and now that Admiral Nimitz is establishing air bases right in the back yard of Japan itself—in Iwo Jima.

But, lest somebody else start to stop work in the United States, I repeat what I have so often said—in one short sentence—even in my sleep: "We haven't won the *wars* yet"—with an *s* on "wars".

It is still a long, tough road to Tokyo. It is longer to go to Tokyo than it is to Berlin, in every sense of the word. The defeat of Germany will not mean the end of the war against Japan. On the contrary, we must be prepared for a long and costly struggle in the Pacific.

But the unconditional surrender of Japan is as essential as the defeat of Germany. I say that advisedly, with the thought in mind that that is especially true if our plans for world peace are to succeed. For Japanese militarism must be wiped out as thoroughly as German militarism.

On the way back from the Crimea, I made arrangements to meet personally King Farouk of Egypt, Haile Selassie, the Emperor of Ethiopia, and King Ibn Saud of Saudi Arabia. Our conversations had to do with matters of common interest. They will be of great mutual advantage because they gave me, and a good many of us, an opportunity of meeting and talking face to face, and of exchanging views in personal conversation instead of formal correspondence.

For instance, on the problem of Arabia, I learned more about that whole problem—the Moselm problem, the Jewish problem—by talking with Ibn Saud for five minutes, than I could have learned in the exchange of two or three dozen letters.

On my voyage, I had the benefit of seeing the Army and Navy and the Air Force at work.

All Americans, I think, would feel as proud of our armed forces as I am, if they could see and hear what I saw and heard.

Against the most efficient professional soldiers and sailors and airmen of all history, our men stood and fought—and won.

This is our chance to see to it that the sons and the grandsons of these gallant fighting men do not have to do it all over again in a few years.

The Conference in the Crimea was a turning point—I hope in our history and therefore in the history of the world. There will soon be presented to the Senate of the United States and to the American people a great decision that will determine the fate of the United States—and of the world—for generations to come.

There can be no middle ground here. We shall have to take the responsibility for world collaboration, or we shall have to bear the responsibility for another world conflict.

I know that the word "planning" is not looked upon with favor in some circles. In domestic affairs, tragic mistakes have been made by reason of lack of planning; and, on the other hand, many great improvements in living, and many benefits to the human race, have been accomplished as a result of adequate, intelligent planning—reclamation of desert areas, developments of whole river valleys, and provision for adequate housing.

The same will be true in relations between Nations. For the second time in the lives of most of us this generation is face to face with the objective of preventing wars. To meet that objective, the Nations of the world will either have a plan or they will not. The groundwork of a plan has now been furnished, and has been submitted to humanity for discussion and decision.

No plan is perfect. Whatever is adopted at San Francisco will doubtless have to be amended time and again over the years, just as our own Constitution has been.

No one can say exactly how long any plan will last. Peace can endure only so long as humanity really insists upon it, and is willing to work for it—and sacrifice for it.

Twenty-five years ago, American fighting men looked to the statesmen of the world to finish the work of peace for which they fought and suffered. We failed them then. We cannot fail them again, and expect the world again to survive.

The Crimea Conference was a successful effort by the three leading Nations to find a common ground for peace. It ought to spell the end of the system of unilateral action, the exclusive alliances, the spheres of influence, the balances of power, and all the other expedients that have been tried for centuries—and have always failed.

We propose to substitute for all these, a universal organization in which all peace-loving Nations will finally have a chance to join.

I am confident that the Congress and the American people will accept the results of this Conference as the beginnings of a permanent structure of peace upon which we can begin to build, under God, that better world in which our children and grandchildren—yours and mine, the children and grandchildren of the whole world—must live, and can live.

And that, my friends, is the principal message I can give you. But I feel it very deeply, as I know that all of you are feeling it today, and are going to feel it in the future.

CHAPTER TWO

Suspicions About the Future of Soviet Intentions

8   Ambassador Harriman sounds the alarm from Moscow: September 1944.

Ambassador W. Averell Harriman was early persuaded that the Bolshevik Revolution was in every sense antipathetical to American ideas and practices. Convinced of the necessity for Russian cooperation in defeating Nazi Germany, he was also the originator of the plan of adopting 'a firm but friendly *quid pro quo* attitude' toward Stalin and the Kremlin, and he is therefore the key to understanding the Roosevelt administration's shift in Soviet policy in late 1944. Historically, the motives behind American policy in this regard are located in two of Harriman's cables from Moscow in September 1944. The first cable, which Harriman recalled in his brief reminiscences, *America and Russia in a Changing World* (1971), was directed to Harry Hopkins, the President's Special Assistant, on September 10. In this particular telegram Harriman urgently conveyed to Hopkins the impression that the Soviets had misinterpreted American generosity toward them both as a sign of Western weakness and acquiescence of their policies in Eastern Europe. The corrective to this misunderstanding, reasoned Harriman, should not take the form of a drastic action but rather a firm and friendly *quid pro quo* attitude. Shortly afterwards and in response to a request from Secretary of State Cordell Hull, who together with his advisers seemed to detect a reversal of the Russian policy of cooperation, Ambassador Harriman warned that although Stalin did not appear to reverse his previous policy of cooperation, there appeared to be much confusion over the concept of what the Soviets understood to have been reached in the past. At this stage the greatest problem confronting Soviet-American relations revolved around the question of noninterference in the internal affairs of other countries. Simply stated, Stalin sought what he regarded as 'friendly' nations on Russia's border; and the Americans sought to safeguard the political liberties and independence of those 'friendly' nations against Russian hegemony—principles for which the American people believed they had gone to war in the first place, and in no place more important than in relation to Poland. Despite the obvious difficulties, Harriman hoped for the best and formulated what he regarded as a reasonable response to Soviet unilateralism: 'In general we should be understanding of their [Soviet] sensitivity, meet them more than half way, encourage them and support them wherever we can, and yet oppose them promptly with the greatest of firmness where we see them go wrong.'

8(a) Ambassador Harriman to Harry L. Hopkins on the Soviet change of attitude: September 10, 1944: 'Now that the end of the war is in sight our relations with the Soviets have taken a startling turn evident during the last 2 months.'

Source: Department of State, *Foreign Relations of the United States, Diplomatic Papers: 1944* (Wash. 1966), IV, 988-90.

I feel that I should report to the President at the earliest convenient time and place. Now that the end of the war is in sight our relations with the Soviets have taken a startling turn evident during the last 2 months. They have held up our requests with complete indifference to our interests and have shown an unwillingness even to discuss pressing problems.

We started the proposal for winter program for FRANTIC[1] at the end of June and formally presented it to the Foreign Office in early July. No acknowledgement even of my letters or numerous talks has been received. All requests for PR[2] unit have been unacted upon for the last several weeks. Prior to that time they were operating several a day. No answer or permission to transport trucks to our Air Forces in China has been received. There has been no reply to our request presented a week ago followed by urgent conversation with Mototov to allow General Eaker's[3] bombing appraisal party to visit Ploesti.[4] The Soviets indifference to world opinion regarding their unbending policy toward Poland and ruthless attitude toward the uprising in Warsaw are best described by Molotov's statement that the Soviets would judge their friends by those that accept the Soviet position. In spite of Stalin's promises no action has been taken on major future planning. These are only a few examples.

I have been conscious since early in the year of a division among Stalin's advisors on the question of cooperation with us. It is now my feeling that those who oppose the kind of cooperation we expect have recently been getting their way and the policy appears to be crystallizing to force us and the British to accept all Soviet policies backed by the strength and prestige of Red Army.

Demands on us are becoming insistent. You have seen a part of it in the negotiations over financial terms of the Protocol in Washington. We have other examples here. The general attitude seems to be that it is our obligation to help Russia and accept her policies because she has won the war for us.

I am convinced that we can divert this trend but only if we materially change our policy toward the Soviet Government. I have evidence that they have misinterpreted our generous attitude toward them as a sign of weakness, and acceptance of their policies.

Time has come when we must make clear what we expect of them as the price of our good will. Unless we take issue with the present policy there is every indication the Soviet Union will become a world bully wherever their interests are involved. This policy will reach into China and the Pacific as well when they can turn their attention in that direction. No written agreement[s] can be of any value unless they are carried out in a spirit of give and take and recognition of the interests of other people.

I am disappointed but not discouraged. The job of getting the Soviet Government to play a decent role in international affairs is however going to be more difficult than we had hoped. The favorable factors are still the same. Ninety percent of the Russian people want friendship with us and it is much to the interest of the Soviet Government to develop it. It is our problem to strengthen the hand of those around Stalin who want to play the game along our lines and to show Stalin that the advice of the counselors of a tough policy is leading him into difficulties.

I realize I cannot in a cable convey to you a fully comprehensible picture of the perplexing developments. However what I say is fully endorsed by General Deane, the Air Officers here and the Embassy Officers.

The relation of Deane and our other Officers with the Red Air Force are good. The Soviet Officers have shown embarrassment at the attitude expressed through the Foreign Office. The influences that I speak of are as unpopular with this group as with us. When it comes to the question of what we should do in dealing with the situation I am not going to propose any drastic action but a firm but friendly *quid pro quo* attitude. In some cases where it has been possible for us to show a firm hand we have been making definite progress.

I feel that I should urgently report personally to the President these recent developments and my recommendations. I would appreciate your discussing this message with the President and advising me.

1 The code name for England-to-the-Soviet Union air-shuttle bombing operations.
2 Photographic Reconnaissance Aircraft.
3 Lt. Gen. Ira C. Eaker, Commander in Chief, Mediterranean Allied Air Forces.
4 The oil fields around Ploesti had been bombed by airplanes of the 15th Army Air Force on June 6, 9, and 13, 1944.

8(b) Ambassador Harriman to Secretary of State Cordell Hull: September 20, 1944. *'I believe the time has come to develop a more definitive policy toward them than has been possible up to now.'*

Source: ibid., 992-98.

I do not believe that Stalin and the Kremlin have determined to reverse their policy of cooperation decided upon by them at Moscow and Tehran. The difficult thing for us to understand is precisely their concept of the understanding that was reached at these conferences. Molotov has on a number of occasions indicated to me that he considered that after they had put us on notice of a Soviet policy or plan and we did not at that time object, we had acquiesced in and accepted the Soviet position. Point 1 of my cable of yesterday referred to above is a case in point. I believe the Soviets consider that we accept at Moscow their position that although they would keep us informed they had the right to settle their problems with their western neighbors unilaterally. Then too, words have a different connotation to the Soviets than they have to us. When they speak of insisting on "friendly governments" in their neighboring countries, they have in mind something quite different from what we would mean. With Czechoslovakia they have insisted upon a military alliance. Although they guaranteed Czechoslovakia noninterference in internal affairs, they insisted that Benes[1] should agree to give a prominent position in his national government to the Communist Party. As they appeared satisfied with the attitude of Benes' government, these were the only conditions imposed. In the case of Poland, however, where there is not the same political stability and where greater suspicion of Soviet good intents exists, they are insisting on a hand picked government which will insure Soviet domination. It is too early to judge how far this policy will be carried in other neighboring countries or how far they will insist in the future on subservience to the Moscow will. In terms that we would understand I believe that it is their intention to have a positive sphere of influence over their western neighbors in the Balkans. It is also too early to judge how far they expect to extend Soviet practices in these states on such questions as secret police (thereby eliminating personal freedom), control of the press, and controlled education. It can be argued that American interests need not be concerned over the affairs of this area. What frightens me however is that when a country begins to extend its influence by strong arm methods beyond its borders under the guise of security it is difficult to see how a line can be drawn. If the policy is accepted that the Soviet Union has a right to penetrate her immediate neighbors for security, penetration of the next immediate neighbors becomes at a certain time equally logical. In my talks with Molotov about Poland he has given me the impression that he does not understand why we and particularly the British are unwilling to support their demand for a friendly government, and all arguments that I have used regarding our policy of non-interference in the internal affairs of a country appear not to have impressed him.

It seems to me that we have a basic issue with the Soviet Government on the definition of the term "friendly governments". I am not optimistic that we can in the near future arrive at an understanding with the Soviet Government on this matter. At the present time I believe they certainly expect us to give them a free hand with their western neighbors. They are therefore most suspicious that this policy will be affected if they agree to refrain from voting on disputes in which the Soviet Government is involved.

Before discussing the problem as it relates to world organization it is my strong feeling that the only way we can eventually come to an understanding with the Soviet Union on the question of non-interference in the internal affairs of other countries is for us to take a definite interest in the solution of the problems of each individual country as they arise. If we give them a free hand with any one country the precedent will be established, whereas if through our influence we can temper Soviet domination in each situation, I believe we have a chance to lead them to a behavior in international affairs that is compatible to our concepts. Specifically I have in mind not only the

Polish situation but now also the former enemy satellites Rumania and Bulgaria. In the case of Rumania I strongly recommend that we appoint an experienced political representative on the Control Commission and insist that he shall have freedom of contact with the Rumanian Government and freedom to obtain information outside of the Allied (Soviet) High Command. Wherever we find that Soviet behavior offends our standards we should call it forcibly to the attention of the Soviet Government. I recognize that this will lead to unpleasant situations but for reasons which I will explain later I am satisfied that the Soviets will accede at least to a reasonable degree to our insistent demands. I have particularly in mind objection to the institution of secret police who may become involved in the persecution of persons of truly democratic convictions who may not be willing to conform to Soviet methods, and also to suppression, under the pretence of military requirements, of public information not only in Rumania but in the outside world. I refer to the interpretation which the Soviets will, I am afraid, place on their powers under articles I, V and XVI of the Rumanian Armistice Agreement. I believe it was not an incident of drafting but design which motivated the Soviet Government in insisting upon the words "in particular to the Soviet Union" in article XV. The same principles should be applied in my opinion to Bulgaria. I hope I have made it plain that I am not reccommending interference in Rumanian affairs but quite the reverse, insisting that the Soviets do not unduly interfere in exercising their responsibilities as the occupying power.

The Polish question is of course far more complicated. I consider it so partly because of my lack of sympathy with the attitude of a number of the men in the Polish Government in London. I refer of course particularly to General Sosnkowski[2] and Messrs. Kot[3] and Kukiel.[4] I cannot help but agree with the insistent demands of the Soviet Government that these men play no part in Poland's future. I feel their objection is equally well founded as is ours against Colonel Farrell[5] in Argentina. But when it comes to forcing on the Poles with the support of the Red Army the handful of individuals making up the Polish Committee of Liberation[6] I don't see how we can afford to stand aside without registering the strongest of objections.

2. In attempting to answer the questions you raise in the last two sentences of the second paragraph of your cable I can first say with confidence that the meeting of the two Allies at Quebec without Soviet participation has not affected the Soviet attitude expressed at Dumbarton Oaks. It is however more difficult to put one's finger on the causes for the change in Soviet attitude toward the United States and Great Britain. I am not certain that there is a change in fundamental policy or attitude. It might well be that the change in developments has brought to the surface the underlying attitude. A clearer understanding on their part however of our and the British attitude on different problems may well have had an influence on the Soviet attitude.

As to their attitude toward us as distinct from the British, it is my feeling, without being entirely clear, that when the Soviets saw victory in sight they began to put into practice policies they intend to follow in peace. In order to get our cooperation during the war they have to a small degree at least bent their policies to foster our cooperation. True it has been meager in comparison with what we considered we were entitled to but this policy did permit the approval of granting to U.S. the use of bases for shuttle-bombing and in other ways giving our people certain consideration and information. It would seem that their post-war policy will be to have the Soviet Government and its officials participate in world affairs, but to protect the Russian people from almost all contact with and influence of Western civilization and ideas. There is evidence that the NKVD[7] and the Party never liked the idea of our troops coming into Russian bases. Influence was perhaps brought to bear from these sources to close them down as soon as possible. On the other hand, although we have had less consideration of the many matters that we have taken up with the Soviet Government in which our interests are involved, we have frequently had the quickest of action on the part of the Soviet Government on matters in which they consider their interests are affected. I mention as an example the quick response which was obtained when I was instructed to inform the Soviet Government that Mr. Morgenthau[8] would announce the report of the experts on monetary matters without Soviet participation unless word was received the same day. Within 3 hours of leaving my meeting with the Commissar of Finance,[9] Molotov called me over to give me the Soviet *aide-mémoire*. Although this case is somewhat more dramatic than others it is not the only case. The Soviet Government, as we well know, is not handicapped by the need to be consistent and when it found that it was up against a stone wall of British opinion in regard to aid to the insurgents in Warsaw, backed up by our own representations, the Soviet Government gave in, with bad grace it is true, but the fact remains that it did give way. This incident is the most encouraging we have experienced and I will refer to it again later.

As to the British there is no doubt that the Soviet attitude is less friendly to and more suspicious of them than U.S. However I do not feel we should place too much importance on this. This is due no doubt not only to the historic clashes but also to the greater insistence of the British in their demands. For example, the British have been more aggressive in opposing the Soviet policy vis-a-vis Poland and you are familiar with the difficulties that the Prime Minister had with Molotov in April over Rumania. They are also suspicious of the British moves in Turkey, Greece, et cetera. The Soviets also do not feel that they have as much to look forward to in aid from Britain in reconstruction as they have from us and have been somewhat more careful not to offend us. I believe they have the feeling also that we are not going to oppose their policies in Europe to the same degree as the British. However as I have explained above our long term interests may compel us to take issue with Soviet policy in Europe as it unfolds. When it comes to the Far East, we may also find ourselves in conflict with the Soviet policy at various points.

3. On the constructive side I desire to make the following brief comments. In spite of what I have said in this cable and in my background cable of yesterday referred to, it is my conviction that Stalin and his principal advisers place the greatest importance and reliance on the newly won relationship with the British and ourselves and desire above all else to take a leading role in international affairs. We must realize that very few of them have ever been abroad and those who have for any extended period of time are suspect in the minds of the others. Thus, they, the group as a whole, have little understanding of the real concept of Western civilization. They are fearful of the antagonism of the world against them. They are always conscious of the fact that they are a backward country materially and culturally. Now they take great pride in the strength of the Red Army. All of this makes them unduly sensitive and suspicious of our motives and

actions. With it all they are realists and have developed a fairly clear idea of what they want. I believe the time has come to develop a more definitive policy toward them than has been possible up to now. In general we should be understanding of their sensitivity, meet them much more than half way, encourage them and support them wherever we can, and yet oppose them promptly with the greatest of firmness where we see them going wrong. In the latter there can be no compromise or indecision if we are to build a sound foundation for future relations with this strange country. When we oppose them we must be certain that we are right and be clear in advance how far we are ready to go. In minor matters, the registering of our objection may be sufficient but in these cases we must make it plain that we do not intend to take further action. When it comes to matters of greater importance, we should make it plain that their failure to conform to our concepts will affect our willingness to cooperate with them, for example, in material assistance for reconstruction. They should be made promptly to feel specific results from our displeasure. Lastly on matters that are vital to us and on which we can find no compromise (as I understand from what you say is the case in connection with the voting of the four powers) I believe we should make them understand patiently but firmly that we cannot accept their point of view and that we are prepared to take the consequences if they adhere to their position. In such cases, I am satisfied that in the last analysis Stalin will back down. We have seen him reverse his decision in connection with aid to the insurgents in Warsaw.

We should bear in mind always in connection with the Soviets that many of Stalin's counselors see things to a degree at least as we do, whereas others are opposed. The Soviet Government is not one mind. Through our actions we should attempt to encourage his confidence in the advice of the former group and make him realize that the others get him into trouble when he follows their advice. There is no doubt that the overwhelming majority of the Russian people want friendship with us, and my contacts in Moscow lead me to feel that the principal men in the Government hold the same view.

If a general policy of the kind that I have outlined is adopted and consistently pursued by all branches of our Government, I have confidence that in time we can find common ground with these people.

[1] Edward Benes, President of the Czechoslovak National Committee in London, 1930-1945, recognized as President of Czechoslovakia by the Allied Powers after July 1940.
[2] Gen. Kazimierz Sosnkowski, who had been relieved as successor-designate to the presidency of Poland in June 1944, and who was dismissed on September 30 as Commander in Chief of the Polish Army.
[3] Stanislaw Kot, former Polish Ambassador to the Soviet Union, 1941-1942, and Minister of Information in the Cabinet of Prime Minister Stanislaw Mikolajezyk, 1943-1944.
[4] Lt. Gen. Marjan Kukiel, Minister of National Defence in the Cabinets of Mikolajezyk and Tomasz Arciszewski, 1944-1945.
[5] Gen. Edelmiro S. Farrell, Acting President, then President of Argentina from March 10, 1944, following the failure of a coup d'etat.
[6] The Communist-sponsored and Soviet-supported Polish Committee of National Liberation was established by decree of the National People's Council of Poland on July 21, 1944. It originally met in Kholm (Chelm), but early in August transferred to Lublin, After which it was frequently called the Lublin Committee.
[7] The Soviet People's Commissariat for Internal Affairs.
[8] Henry Morgenthau, Jr., Secretary of the Treasury.
[9] Arseny Grigoryevich Zveryev.

9   George Frost Kennan—'Russia—seven years later': September 1944:
     'People at home would find Soviet words and actions easier to
     understand if they would bear in mind the character of Russian aims
     in eastern and central Europe. Russian efforts in this area are
     directed to only one goal: power.'

With his appointment as minister-counselor to the American embassy at Moscow in 1944 after an absence of seven years, George Frost Kennan became at the age of forty the senior member of the diplomatic corps in length of service in Russia. For a long time he had been an exponent of the view that United States policy towards the Soviet Union was based on a grievous misunderstanding of Russian society. Although it was understood that he was to have no political responsibility in shaping policy at this time, Kennan worked up an analysis of the Soviet system of government that was to become the basis of his famous 'X' article in *Foreign Affairs* in 1947. Kennan, as he observed in his *Memoirs, 1925-1950* (1967), was forced by conscience 'to attempt to reduce to words on paper the views I held on the nature of the Soviet leaders and of the situation in which they found themselves as they entered upon the final phase of the war, and to make this statement at least available to those who had responsibility for the formulation of American policy,—although it was not until many years later that he learned that Ambassador Harriman had forwarded his analysis to Washington. The significance of 'Russia—Seven Years Later' lay in the fact not only that it foreshadowed what would become the standard conception of the working of Soviet society but also that for its time it was a 'minority' opinion. What transformed the minority into a majority was the Western response to Stalin's attempt to seek Soviet hegemony over Eastern Europe, a movement that both sought to erect 'friendly' nations on Russia's borders—which many conceded as the price of Nazi Germany's destruction—and the elimination of the possibility of permitting political self-determination to the 'liberated' countries of Europe, which were traditionally anti-Russian.

Source: ibid., 902-14.

It is characteristic of the contradictory quality of all Russian reality that one can argue whether it is more presumptuous to write about Russia after a long presence or after a long absence. Each doubtless has its values. Each also has its risks. It is the latter than I propose to undertake in this paper; and in justification of it I can cite only the sublety of all change in a country where the relationship between public feeling and official policy, between motive and action, between cause and effect, is a jealously guarded secret of state. This subtlety often makes invisible to the permanent resident of Moscow the movement of the society in which he lives. He himself moves with the stream; everything that he sees moves with him; and like the navigator at sea he has no subjective perception of the current upon which he is borne. This is why it is sometimes easier for someone who leaves and returns to estimate the speed and direction of movement, to seize and fix the subtelities of trend. And this, incidentally, is why no foreign observer should ever be asked to spend more than a year in Russia without going out into the outside world for the recovery of perspective. . . .

If political conditions are quiet internally, the same cannot be said for foreign policy. Ever since the conclusion of the purges and the establishment of Stalin's power beyond question in the internal political life of the country, the political effort of the Kremlin has concentrated in increasing measure on relations of Russia to the outside world.

It is depressing to reflect how many volumes could be filled with the speculation that has appeared in the foreign press during the past two years on Russia's foreign political aims. The questions involved have been repeated with a monotony that almost discourages the attempt to answer. Has Russian policy changed? Does Russia want to "communize" other countries? Does Russia propose to "cooperate"? Etc., etc.

These questions are one which, in the Soviet view, are very elementary. The reader must, therefore, not take it amiss if the answers are the same.

Soviet leaders have never forgotten the weak and vulnerable position in which the Soviet regime found itself in the early days of its power. The treaty of Brest-Litovsk, the intervention of Allied forces in various parts of Russia, the repulse of the Red Army from the Baltic States, the invasion of the Western provinces in the Polish-Russian war of 1920; all these left in Soviet minds an indelible and undoubtedly exaggerated impression of the dangers which threatened Soviet power from without. Fed by the traditional Russian mistrust of the stranger, and reinforced by the continual reverses suffered in the early attempts to increase Russian power through communization, this feeling of fear and insecurity lived and flourished and came to underlie almost all Soviet thought about the outside world.

In the early years of communism it was still officially held, and widely believed, that Russia could and would be saved from what was felt to be its perilous predicament by the growing conflicts between the imperialist powers and by the world revolution which was bound to ensue. Orders given to foreign communist parties to direct their efforts to the earliest possible achievement of social and political revolution were therefore considered to serve the cause of Soviet military security as well as the broader purposes of communist ideology. To Stalin's own sense of realism must go the credit for the gradual appreciation that not only were there no real chances for the success of this world revolutionary undertaking, but that the communist parties operating under such instructions were actually of less practical advantage to the Soviet Union than the groups of bourgeois-liberal enthusiasts for whom—somewhere to Moscow's own surprise—the Soviet Union soon came to have so powerful an attraction. Soviet policy thus began with time to lay less stress on the immediate bringing about of revolution in other countries and began to concentrate on using all foreign sympathizers, communist and otherwise, as vehicles for a purely nationalistic Soviet foreign policy. That was indeed a change, and an important change. But it did not alter the basic conception of Soviet policy, which was to increase in every way and with all possible speed the relative strength of the Soviet Union in world affairs, and to exploit to the utmost for this purpose the rivalries and differences between other powers.

During the years just preceding Hitler's rise to power in Germany the Kremlin, enamoured of its role as the innocent object of evil designs, began—like Shakespeare's lady—to protest too much. It fussed and fumed about the dangers of capitalistic encirclement and about the plans for "intervention" on the part of the "Anglo-French imperialists". It held propaganda trials to impress the population with the proximity of these dangers. All realists knew that the substance behind these fears was not great and that the value of this constant beating of the alarm lay rather in the stimulus as it might bring to the domestic efforts of the Russian population than in the meeting of any real need for national defense. But it served its purpose in large measure, and the Soviet leaders succeeded in convincing many people, themselves included, that mortal danger was at hand.

With Hitler's rise to power, the Kremlin—having cried "wolf" largely out of ulterior motives for a number of years—suddenly found a real wolf at the door. What had once been declamation now became grim reality. During the years from 1933 to 1938, it was well understood in Moscow that the Soviet Union did not have the strength to sustain alone, without aid from outside, a German attack. It seemed to Russian minds, there-fore, that the best chance of safety lay in inducing somebody else to fight Hitler before his plans for aggression in the east could develop. Had not Lenin himself said that the "contradictions between the imperialist powers" should always be ruthlessly exploited in the interests of communism? Perhaps this was not only Russia's mortal danger but also Russia's golden opportunity, depending on how it was played.

The result was a sudden enthusiasm for collective security. The Soviet press developed marked solicitude for the precarious position of the western democracies in the face of the Nazi menace. The Soviet Union joined the League of Nations. Litvinov went to Geneva, spoke eloquently of the dangers of aggression, of the indivisibility of peace and of the hopelessness of supposing that war, once begun, would not become universal. The western powers, he argued, should agree to fight at the first sign of German aggression anywhere. He advanced one legalistic formula after another designed to assure that there could be no German aggression which would not involve the western powers. He was generous in his offers to join anyone and everyone in pacts of mutual assistance.

In all of this, there was no real evidence that Moscow had any serious intention of undertaking major military activities on anyone else's behalf. Traditional Russian pre-occupation with the *interpretation* rather than the *letter* of an agreement quickly suggested to the Russian mind that there could be little danger in incurring obliga-tions which Russia herself would be able to interpret unilaterally when the time came to deliver. The main thing was to assure that Germany could not fight in the east without fighting in the west. Once military complications in that theatre were assured, Russia could take care of herself.

This, incidentally, is the answer to the Russian attitude at the time of Munich. Russia, on the precedent of the Spanish War, would have been glad to give token military assistance to Czechoslovakia—particularly in the air. There was no will—and, as the Germans well knew, no possibility—for the despatch of any sizeable ground force to Czechoslovakia at that time.

Litvinov's efforts tided over a difficult period, during which both German and Russian armaments were built up. But they did not succeed in drawing the western powers into obligations which would compel them to fight Hitler if the latter embarked on a policy of expansion; and the chances of accomplishing this looked progressively dimmer as Nazi power increased and western appeasement continued.

If Russia could not rely on the western nations to save her, it then seemed to Russian minds that the alternative lay not only in the utmost development of Russian military power within the 1938 borders, but also in new territorial acquisitions designed to strengthen Russia's strategic and political position, and in the creation of a sphere of influence even beyond these limits. In drawing up this expansionist program, Soviet planners leaned heavily on the latter-day traditions of tsarist diplomacy.

The experience of Munich, at which moment the nightmare of an isolated German-Russian war seemed close to becoming reality, finally dispelled all serious hopes in the prospects of inducing the western world to fight Hitler except in direct self-defense, and the stage reached at that moment in the military industrialization of Russia lent justification to the final junking of Litvinov's tenuous program. The road was now open for a policy of open territorial expansion, designed if possible to forestall attack on Russia, but at any rate to soften the shock of the attack when it came. In this way it came about that the Kremlin, in the summer of 1939, rejected the advances of the western powers, who had neither the will nor the strength to hand over whole sections of the eastern Europe to the Soviet Union, and accepted the advances of the Germans, in whom neither this will nor this strength were lacking.

It would be useful to the western world to realize that despite all the vicissitudes by which Russia has been afflicted since August 1939, the men in the Kremlin have never abandoned their faith in that program of territorial and political expansion which had once commended itself so strongly to Tsarist diplomatists, and which underlay the German-Russian non-aggression pact of 1939. The program meant the re-establishment of Russian power in Finland and the Baltic states, in eastern Poland, in the northern Bukovina, and in Bessarabia. It meant a protectorate over western Poland, and an access to the sea for the Russian empire somewhere in East Prussia. It meant the establishment of dominant Russian influence over all the Slavs of central Europe and the Balkans, and, if possible, the creation of a corridor from the western to the southern Slavs somewhere along the border between Austria and Hungary. Finally, it meant Russian control of the Dardanelles through the establishment of Russian bases at that point. This program was intended not only to increase the physical military strength of Russia. It was intended to prevent the formation in central and eastern Europe of any power or coalition of powers capable of challenging Russian security.

It was considered in Moscow in 1939 that if a portion of this program could be realized by an agreement with the Germans such as was actually concluded, an agreement which would at the same time turn the point of German weapons toward the west, this would be a handsome achievement. While it was recognized that it would hardly prevent the growth of a power in central Europe dangerous to Russia, it did seem to assure that that power would first exhaust itself against the western nations, and would in any event not be turned against Russia alone.

The course of the war proved a bitter disappointment to this line of Russian thought. The west collapsed rapidly, without having brought any serious exhaustion to German military power. Hitler turned out to be in a position to turn a large portion of German strength against Russia in a period of quiescence of military activity in the west. And the territorial gains of the non-aggression pact proved to have little real military value. The Russians lost their eastern half of Poland more rapidly, when the time came, than the Poles had lost their western half in 1939. What minor strategic advantages the newly acquired territories might have brought were at least partially balanced off by the ruin of the national armies they had once supported. If still in existence, these armies might have taken up at least some of the shock of the German attack. Their disappearance, to which Russia herself had so largely contributed, left the Red Army face to face with the Reichswehr.

But all these reversals failed to shake Russian confidence in the ultimate efficacy of this policy of expansion. It was rather that it had not been carried far enough. When, after the first war winter, the prospects of victory began to grow on the horizon, Russian minds saw the possibility of completing successfully in 1945 what had been unsuccessfully begun in 1939. This time there would be no powerful Germany to be reckoned with. An exhausted and war-torn eastern Europe would provide a plastic and yielding mass from which the objectives of Russian statesmanship could easily be moulded.

Until June 1944, however, all such Russian aims had to await the exertion of a real military effort by the western powers. Without that effort, not even Russian victory was assured. The second front was a paramount requirement of all Russian policy. The suspicious Russian mind naturally exaggerated the danger of Russia's being left in the lurch by her western Allies. To offset this danger the Kremlin was prepared to go a long way to meet the requirements and the prejudices of the western world.

Western conceptions of future collective security and international collaboration seemed naive and unreal to the Moscow eye. But if talking in unreal terms was the price of victory, why not? If the western world needed Russian assurances of future collaboration as a condition of military support, why not? Once satisfied of the establishment of her power in eastern and central Europe (and who, after all, would be able to prevent the establishment of that power when the day of German collapse arrived?) Russia would presumably not find too much difficulty in going through whatever motions were required for conformity with these strange western schemes for collaboration in the preservation of peace. What dangers could collaboration bring to a country which already held in its hand the tangible guarantees of its own security? On the contrary, if it were properly exploited, participation in arrangements for world security might even be made into a form of re-insurance for the protection of Russia's interests. Considerations of prestige, furthermore, would demand that Russia not be missing from any of the counsels of the world powers.

In this way, thoughts of international collaboration settled down only too easily beside dreams of empire in minds schooled from infancy to think and deal in even sharper contradictions than these. As long as no second front existed, expediency suggested that the idea of collaboration be kept rather to the fore, the idea of spheres of interest rather in the background. But when the second front became reality, there was no longer any need for excessive delicacy. The resultant bluntness of Soviet policy has caused some surprise and questioning in the west.

People at home would find Soviet words and actions easier to understand if they would bear in mind the character of Russian aims in eastern and central Europe. Russian efforts in this area are directed to only one goal: power. The form this power takes, the methods by which it is achieved: these are secondary questions. It is a matter of indifference to Moscow whether a given area is "communistic" or not. All things being equal, Moscow might prefer to see it communized, although even that is debatable. But the main thing is that it should be amenable to Moscow influence, and if possible to ˙Moscow authority. If this can be achieved inconspicuously, with the acquiescence of most of the inhabitants and through a concealed form, so much the better. If not, it will be achieved by other means. For the smaller countries of eastern and central Europe, the issue is not one of communism or capitalism. It is one of the independence of national life or of domination by a big power which has never shown itself adept at making any permanent compromises with rival power groups. Neither the behavior of Red Army occupying forces nor the degree of "communization" of the country is any criterion of the eventual outcome of this issue. It is not a question of boundaries or of constitutions or of formal independence. It is a question of real power relationships, more often than not carefully masked or concealed. As such—and in no other way—should it be judged.

Today, in the autumn of 1944, the Kremlin finds itself committed by its own inclination to the concrete task of becoming the dominant power of eastern and central Europe. At the same time, it also finds itself committed by past promises and by world opinion to a vague program which western statesmen—always so fond of quaint terms agreeable to their electorates—call collaboration.

The first of these programs implies taking. The second implies giving. No one can stop Russia from doing the taking, if she is determined to go through with it. No one can force Russia to do the giving, if she is determined not to go through with it. In these circumstances, others may worry. The Kremlin chimes, never silent since those turbulent days when Lenin had them repaired and set in motion, now peal out the hours of night with a ring of self-assurance and of confidence in the future. And the sleep of those who lie within the Kremlin walls is sound and undisturbed. . . .

The men I have mentioned[1] are all men prominently connected with Russia's formal diplomatic relations with the western world. They are men who have contact with foreigners in their work and presumably access to the foreign press and foreign literature. Possibly this has indeed widened their horizons to some extent. But what about those other leading figures in the regime whose voice in the inner councils of state is obviously greater than the voice of any of these four, except possibly Molotov? What about such men as Beriya, Zhdanov, Shcherbakov, Andreyev, Kaganovich, etc? What advice do these men give to Stalin about foreign policy?

These prominent Soviet leaders know little of the outside world. They have no personal knowledge of foreign statesmen. To them, the vast pattern of international life, political and economic, can provide no associations, can hold no significance, except in what they conceive to be its bearing on the problems of Russian security and Russian internal life. It is possible that the conceptions of these men might occasionally achieve a rough approximation to reality, and their judgments a similar approximation to fairness; but it is not likely. Independence of judgment has never been a strong quality of leading Communist figures. There is evidence that they are as often as not the victims of their own slogans, the slaves of their own propaganda. To keep a level head in the welter of propaganda and autosuggestion with which Russia has faced the world for the past twenty years would tax the best efforts of a cosmopolitan scholar and philosopher. These men are anything but that. God knows what strange images and impressions are created in their minds by what they hear of life beyond Russia's borders. God knows what conclusions they draw from all this, and what recommendations they make on the basis of those conclusions.

There is serious evidence for the hypothesis that there are influences in the Kremlin which place the preservation of a rigid police regime in Russia far ahead of the happy development of Russia's foreign relations, and which are therefore strongly opposed to any association of Russia with foreign powers except on Russia's own terms. These terms would include the rigid preservation of the conspiratorial nature of the Communist Party, of the secrecy of the working of the Soviet state, of the isolation of the population from external influences, of feelings of mistrust of the outside world and dependence on the Soviet regime among the population, of the extreme restriction of all activities of foreigners in the Soviet Union, and the use of every means to conceal Soviet reality from world opinion.

There is reason to believe that these influences have a certain measure of control over the information and advice that reach Stalin. Certainly there has been no appreciable relaxation, as compared with seven years ago, in the restrictions on association between foreigners and Russians; and representatives of Russia's allies continue to be treated today with no less suspicion than was shown to German representatives in the days of the most violent anti-fascist press polemics, prior to the conclusion of the Non-Aggression Pact. Fortunately, however, there is as yet no reason to conclude that this issue is finally decided and that the isolationists have entirely won the day. The overwhelming sentiment of the country is against them, so much so that this may become a serious internal issue in the aftermath of the war. So is the pressure of events in international life. They are undoubtedly balanced off by many men who have a healthier, a saner, and a more worthy conception of Russia's mission in the world. But that this xenophobian group exists and that it speaks with a powerful voice in the secret councils of the Kremlin is evident. And that it is in no way accessible to the pleas or arguments of responsible people in the outside world is no less clear.

As long as this situation endures, the great nations of the west will unavoidably be in a precarious position in their relations with Russia. They will never be able to be sure when, unbeknownst to them, people of whom they have no knowledge, acting on motives utterly obscure, will go to Stalin with misleading information and with arguments to be used to their disadvantage—information which they cannot correct and arguments which they have no opportunity to rebut. As long as this possibility exists, as long as it is not corrected by a freer atmosphere for the forming of acquaintances and the exchange of views, it is questionable whether even the friendliest of relations could be considered sound and dependable.

Those men of good will, among the foreign representatives in Moscow, for whom the relations of Russia with the world at large have become one of the great experiences and hopes of contemporary life, may go on with their patient work of unraveling the never-ending tangle of misunderstandings and difficulties which lie across the path of Russia's foreign relations. They will continue to be borne up in this trial of patience by their unanimous faith in the greatness of the Russian people and by their knowledge of the need of the world for Russia's talents. But at heart they all know that until the Chinese wall of the spirit has been broken down, as the actual Chinese wall of Moscow's business district was recently broken—until new avenues of contact and of vision are opened up between the Kremlin and the world around it—they can have no guarantee that their efforts will meet with success and that the vast creative abilities of Russia will not lead to the tragedy, rather than to the rescue, of western civilization.

Russia remains today, more than ever, an enigma for the western world. Simple American minds imagine that this is because "we don't know the truth about it." They are wrong. It is not our lack of knowledge which causes us to be puzzled by Russia. It is that we are incapable of understanding the truth about Russia when we see it.

We are incapable, in the first place, of understanding the role of contradiction in Russian life. The Anglo-Saxon instinct is to attempt to smooth away contradictions, to reconcile opposing elements, to achieve something in the nature of an acceptable middle-ground as a basis for life. The Russian tends to deal only in extremes, and he is not particularly concerned to reconcile them. To him, contradiction is a familiar thing. It is the essence of Russia. West and east, Pacific and Atlantic, arctic and tropics, extreme cold and extreme heat, prolonged sloth and sudden feats of energy, exaggerated cruelty and exaggerated kindness, ostentatious wealth and dismal squalor, violent xenophobia and uncontrollable yearning for contact with the foreign world, vast power and the most abject slavery, simultaneous love and hate for the same objects: these are only some of the contradictions which dominate the life of the Russian people. The Russian does not reject these contradictions. He has learned to live with them, and in them. To him, they are the spice of life. He likes to dangle them before him, to play with them philosophically. He feels competent to handle them, to profit from them. Perhaps he even expects, at some time in the dim future, to lead them out into a synthesis more tremendous than anything the world has yet seen. But for the moment, he is content to move in them with that same sense of adventure and experience which supports a young person in the first contradictions of love.

The American mind will not apprehend Russia until it is prepared philosophically to accept the validity of contradiction. It must accept the possibility that just because a proposition is true, the opposite of that proposition is not false. It must agree never to entertain a proposition about the Russian world without seeking, and placing in apposition to it, its inevitable and indispensable opposite. Then it must agree to regard both as legitimate, valid conceptions. It must learn to understand that Russian life at any given moment is not the common expression of harmonious, integrated elements, but a precarious and ever shifting equilibrium between numbers of conflicting forces.

But there is a second, and even more daring, *tour de force* which the American mind must make if it is to try to find Russian life comprehensible. It will have to understand that for Russia, at any rate, there are no objective criteria of right and wrong. There are not even any objective criteria of reality and unreality.

What do we mean by this? We mean that right and wrong, reality and unreality, are determined in Russia not by any God, not by any innate nature of things, but simply by men themselves. Here men determine what is true and what is false.

The reader should not smile. This is a serious fact. It is the gateway to the comprehension of much that is mysterious in Russia. Bolshevism has proved some strange and disturbing things about human nature. It has proved that what is important for people is not what is there but what they conceive to be there. It has shown that with unlimited control over people's minds—and that implies not only the ability to feed them your own propaganda but also to see that no other fellow feeds them any of his—it is possible to make them feel and believe practically anything. And it makes no difference whether that "anything" is true, in our conception of the word. For the people who believe it, it becomes true. It attains validity, and all the powers of truth. Men can enthuse over it, fight for it, die for it—if they are led to believe that it is something worthy. They can abhor it, oppose it, combat it with unspeakable cruelty—if they are led to believe that it is something reprehensible. Moreover, it becomes true (and this is one of the most vital apprehensions) not only for those to whom it is addressed, but for those who invent it as well. The power of autosuggestion plays a tremendous part in Soviet life.

Let not the brash American think that he personally stands above these disturbing phenomena of the Russian world. Unless he is a man of great mental obtuseness or of great mental strength, he too, upon the first contact with Russian life, will begin to react strongly to these man-made currents, the reality of which he would have contemptuously rejected from a distance. He will soon take them as real forces, as real threats or as real promises. In that, he will be right. But he will not know what he is doing. He will remain the tool, rather than the master, of the material he is seeking to understand.

Soberly viewed, there is little possibility that enough Americans will ever accomplish these philosophical evolutions to permit of any general understanding of Russia on the part of our Government or our people. It would imply a measure of intellectual humility and a readiness to reserve judgment about ourselves and our institutions, of which few of us would be capable. For the foreseeable future the American, individually and collectively, will continue to wander about in the maze of contradiction and the confusion which is Russia, with feelings not dissimilar to those of Alice in Wonderland, and with scarcely greater effectiveness. He will be alternately repelled or attracted by one astonishing phenomenon after another, until he finally succumbs to one or the other of the forces involved or until, dimly apprehending the depth of his confusion, he flees the field in horror.

Distance, necessity, self-interest, and common-sense may enable us, thank God, to continue that precarious and troubled but peaceful co-existence which we have managed to lead with the Russians up to this time. But if so, it will not be due to any understanding on our part of the elements involved. Forces beyond our vision will be guiding our footsteps and shaping our relations with Russia. There will be much talk about the necessity for "understanding Russia"; but there will be no place for the American who is really willing to undertake this disturbing task. The apprehension of what is valid in the Russian world is unsettling and displeasing to the American mind. He who would undertake this apprehension will not find his satisfaction in the achievement of anything practical for his people, still less in any official or public appreciation for his efforts. The best he can look forward to is the lonely pleasure of one who stands at long last on a chilly and inhospitable mountain top where few have been before, where few can follow, and where few will consent to believe that he has been.

---

[1] In the omitted portion of document the author had commented upon the powerful position of Iosif Vissarionovich Stalin, and these men in particular who were prominently engaged in diplomatic relations with Western Powers and who presumably gave advice to Stalin on foreign policy: Vyacheslav Mikhailovich Molotov, People's Commissar for Foreign Affairs; Andrey Yanuaryevich Vyshinsky, First Assistant People's Commissar for Foreign Affairs, formerly Chief Prosecutor of the Soviet Union; Solomon Abramovich Lozovsky, Assistant People's Commissar for Foreign Affairs, formerly Secretary General of the Red International of Trade Unions (Profintern); and Dmitry Zakharovich Manuilsky, People's Commissar for Foreign Affairs of the Ukrainian Soviet Socialist Republic, formerly a leading member of the Presidium of the Executive Committee of the III (Communist) International (Comintern).

10   President Roosevelt expresses concern over Soviet activity in Rumania to Prime Minister Churchill: March 11, 1945. ' . . . *Rumania is not a good place for a test case.*'

Despite President Roosevelt's optimistic report to Congress on the Yalta Conference, there can be little doubt that both he and Churchill entertained serious reservations about Soviet intentions to live up to their agreements. On March 11, 1945, approximately a month before he died, FDR expressed his concern to Churchill over Stalin's decision to sponsor a minority government in Rumania, an act which boded ill for the future. It is interesting to note the President's decision at this time was *not* to make Rumania a 'test case'—the implication being, of course, that he presaged a showdown with Stalin in the near future. Because Gar Alperovitz's *Atomic Diplomacy* (1945) builds much of its case against Truman on the basis of his administration's policy to pursue either a strategy of 'immediate' versus 'delayed' showdown, supposedly in contrast to FDR's policy of cooperation with the Russians, it is interesting that Roosevelt himself seemed to be maneuvering into a showdown strategy, an eventuality that would perforce have given a marked continuity between the Russian policies of Roosevelt and Truman.

Source: Department of State, *Foreign Relations of the United States, Diplomatic Papers: 1945* (Wash. 1967), 509-10.

I have of course had very much in mind the considerations in regard to Rumania and to the Polish question . . . and share your concern over these developments. I am fully determined, as I know you are, not to let the good decisions we reached at the Crimea slip through our hands and will certainly do everything I can to hold Stalin to their honest fulfillment. In regard to the Rumanian situation Averell has taken up and is taking up again the whole question with Molotov invoking the Declaration on Liberated Europe and has proposed tripartite discussions to carry out these responsibilities. It is obvious that the Russians have installed a minority government of their own choosing, but apart from the reasons you mentioned in your message, Rumania is not a good place for a test case. The Russians have been in undisputed control from the beginning and with Rumania lying athwart the Russian lines of communications it is moreover difficult to contest the plea of military necessity and security which they are using to justify their action. We shall certainly do everything we can, however, and of course will count on your support.

11   FDR, Churchill and the Polish imbroglio: March 29, 1945. *'Our peoples and indeed those of the whole world are watching with anxious hope the extent to which the decisions we reached at the Crimea are being honestly carried forward.'*

President Roosevelt's message to Churchill in late March 1945 left no doubt in the leaders' minds that if Rumania was unsuitable for a test case of Stalin's willingness to cooperate, Poland was not. Although he understood that the Polish compromise reached at Yalta 'tilted' slightly in favor of the Communist-controlled Lublin Government, FDR was adamant in defending his 'right to call for consultation a group of Polish leaders that are truly representative .... ' Further, and more ominously, the President reiterated to Churchill that he intended to shirk no responsibility which he had assumed under the Yalta accords.

Source: ibid, 189-90.

. . . I have likewise been watching with anxiety and concern the development of Soviet attitude since the Crimea Conference. I am acutely aware of the dangers inherent in the present course of events not only for the immediate issues involved and our decisions at the Crimea but also for the San Francisco Conference and future world cooperation. Our peoples and indeed those of the whole world are watching with anxious hope the extent to which the decisions we reached at the Crimea are being honestly carried forward. For our part (and I know for yours) we intend to shirk no responsibility which we have assumed under those decisions. I agree with you that we should not neglect any step calculated to demonstrate to the Soviet Government the vital importance of their doing likewise. It is for this reason and because of the magnitude of the issues involved that I consider it essential to base ourselves squarely on the Crimea decisions themselves and not allow any other considerations, no matter how important, to cloud the issue at this time. I have this particularly in mind with respect to the Polish negotiations.

You will recall that the agreement on Poland at Yalta was a compromise between the Soviet position that the Lublin Government should merely be "enlarged" and our contention that we should start with a clean slate and assist in the formation of an entirely new Polish Government. The wording of the resulting agreement reflects this compromise but if we attempt to evade the fact that we placed, as clearly shown in the agreement, somewhat more emphasis on the Lublin Poles than on the other two groups from which the new Government is to be drawn I feel we will expose ourselves to the charge that we are attempting to go back on the Crimean decision. It by no means follows, however, and on this we must be adamant, that because of this advantage the Lublin group can in any way arrogate to itself the right to determine what Poles from the other two groups are to be brought in for consultation. For the foregoing reasons I feel strongly that we should first of all bring the matter to a head on the question that falls clearly within the Yalta agreement, namely, our right to call for consultation a group of Polish leaders that are truly representative and that it is for the Commission and the Commission alone to decide which Poles are representative. Our Ambassadors in Moscow appear to be in agreement that we should proceed on the basis of their redraft, designed to reconcile our basic instructions with the points put forward by Molotov. They will at the same time make it absolutely clear that we have not receded in the slightest from the other points in our instructions of March 19 and shall revert to them at a later stage.

I do feel the other questions of procedure and the proper time for reopening the other points can be safely left to our Ambassadors. They know exactly what we think and feel on the entire question and I am personally completely confident that under no circumstances will they take any step or agree to anything which would impair the objectives we both seek. For example, I believe that if we can get Soviet agreement to the principle that the Commission and the Commission alone shall determine what Poles shall be invited for consultation and a definite list is drawn up and invitations issued then consultation with the Lublin Poles first might even afford certain advantages. They could be told how we interpret the Yalta decision and thus avoid the danger of having the question of interpretation become a matter of dispute between the Polish groups themselves. I feel subject to your approval that our Ambassadors should proceed along this line to bring our differences with Molotov into sharp focus without waiting for us to concert our messages to Stalin. Averell is ready to go ahead on this basis if we can obtain you concurrence which I earnestly hope you will give.

I agree with you, however, that the time has come to take up directly with Stalin the broader aspects of the Soviet attitude (with particular reference to Poland) and my immediate following telegram will contain the text of the message I propose to send.

I hope you will let me have your reaction as soon as possible.

12   President Roosevelt appeals directly to Joseph Stalin to clarify the Polish situation: April 1, 1945. *'I cannot conceal from you the concern with which I view the development of events of mutual interest since our fruitful meeting at Yalta.'*

On April 1, 1945, President Roosevelt made it perfectly clear to Marshal Stalin that a thinly disguised continuance of the Warsaw regime or Lublin Government could not be tolerated. In addition to pointing out what he regarded as the Soviet Government's inexplicable misreading of the Polish compromise reached at Yalta, FDR underscored the resolution of this problem as a prerequisite to continued Soviet-American cooperation in the postwar period. He also lectured Stalin on the role of American public opinion and the extent to which he was powerless to overrule it. This was Roosevelt's last message to Stalin on the matter.

Source: ibid, 194-96.

I cannot conceal from you the concern with which I view the development of events of mutual interest since our fruitful meeting at Yalta. The decisions we reached there were good ones and have for the most part been welcomed with enthusiasm by the peoples of the world who saw in our ability to find a common basis of understanding the best pledge for a secure and peaceful world after the war. Precisely because of the hopes and expectations that these decisions raised, their fulfillment is being followed with the closest attention. We have no right to let them be disappointed. So far there has been a discouraging lack of progress made in the carrying out, which the world expects, of the political decisions which we reached at the Conference particularly those relating to the Polish question. I am frankly puzzled as to why this should be and must tell you that I do not fully understand in many respects the apparent indifferent attitude of your Government. Having understood each other so well at Yalta I am convinced that the three of us can and will clear away any obstacles which have developed since then. I intend, therefore, in this message to lay before you with complete frankness the problem as I see it.

Although I have in mind primarily the difficulties which the Polish negotiations have encountered, I must make a brief mention of our agreement embodied in the declaration on liberated Europe. I frankly cannot understand why the recent developments in Rumania should be regarded as not falling within the terms of that agreement. I hope you will find time personally to examine the correspondence between our Governments on this subject.

However, the part of our agreements at Yalta which has aroused the greatest popular interest and is the most urgent relates to the Polish question. You are aware of course that the Commission which we set up has made no progress. I feel this is due to the interpretation which your Government is placing upon the Crimean decisions. In order that there shall be no misunderstanding I set forth below my interpretation of the points of the agreement which are pertinent to the difficulties encountered by the Commission in Moscow.

In the discussions that have taken place so far your Government appears to take the position that the new Polish Provisional Government of National Unity which we agreed should be formed should be little more than a continuation of the present Warsaw Government. I cannot reconcile this either with our agreement or our discussions. While it is true that the Lublin Government is to be reorganized and its members play a prominent role it is to be done in such a fashion as to bring into being a new Government. This point is clearly brought out in several places in the text of the agreement. I must make it quite plain to you that any such solution which would result in a thinly disguised continuance of the present Warsaw regime would be unacceptable and would cause the people of the United States to regard the Yalta agreement as having failed. It is equally apparent that for the same reason the Warsaw Government cannot under the agreement claim the right to select or reject what Poles are to be brought to Moscow by the Commission for consultation. Can we not agree that it is up to the Commission to select the Polish leaders to come to Moscow to consult in the first instance and invitations be sent out accordingly. If this could be done I see no great objection to having the Lublin group come first in order that they may be fully acquainted with the agreed interpretation of the Yalta decisions on this point. It is of course understood that if the Lublin group comes first no arrangements would be made independently with them before the arrival of the other Polish leaders called for consultation. In order to facilitate the agreement the Commission might first of all select a small but representative group of Polish leaders who could suggest other names for the consideration of the Commission. We have not and would not bar or veto any candidate for consultation which Mr. Molotov might propose being confident that he would not suggest any Poles who would be inimical to the intent of the Crimean decision. I feel that it is not too much to ask that my Ambassador be accorded the same confidence and that any candidate for consultation presented by any one of the Commission be accepted by the others in good faith. It is obvious to me that if the right of the Commission to select these Poles is limited or shared with the Warsaw Government the very foundation on which our agreement rests would be destroyed. While the foregoing are the immediate obstacles which in my opinion have prevented the Commission from making any progress in this vital matter there are two other suggestions which were not in the agreement but nevertheless have a very important bearing on the result we all seek. Neither of these suggestions has been as yet accepted by your Government. I refer to (1) that there should be the maximum of political tranquility in Poland and that dissident groups should cease any measures and counter-measures against each other. That we should respectively use our influence to that end seems to me so eminently reasonable. (2) It would also seem entirely natural in view of the responsibilities placed upon them by the agreement that representatives of the American and British members of the Commission should be permitted to visit Poland. As you will recall Mr. Molotov himself suggested this at an early meeting of the Commission and only subsequently withdrew it.

I wish I could convey to you how important it is for the successful development of our program of international collaboration that this Polish question be settled fairly and speedily. If this is not done all of the difficulties and dangers to Allied unity which we had so much in mind in reaching our decision at the Crimea will face us in an even more acute form. You are, I am sure, aware that genuine popular support in the United States is required to carry out any Government policy foreign or domestic. The American people make up their own mind and no Government action can change it. I mention this fact because the last sentence of your message about Mr. Molotov's attendance at San Francisco made me wonder whether you give full weight to this factor.

13   Stalin replies: April 7, 1945. 'The Polish question has indeed reached an impasse.'

Unconcerned with the pressures of public opinion as such, Stalin firmly replied to Roosevelt's objections. Beginning with the observation that 'the Polish question has reached an impasse', Stalin countercharged that the representatives of the United States and Britain in Moscow sought to reverse the decisions of the Big Three at Yalta to recognize the Lublin Government as the 'core' of the new government to be reconstructed. Instead, the Western Powers had ignored the Polish Provincial Government, paid little heed to it, and, worst of all, placed the troublesome London Poles (the initially-recognized Polish Government in exile) on an equal footing with the Lublin Poles. Moreover, continued Stalin in a manner that made it obvious what he expected from any Polish government, the Soviet Government's Polish policy rested on the two simple assumptions: first, that 'those invited for consultation should be in the first instance Polish leaders who recognize the decisions of the Crimea Conference, including the one on the Curzon Line and, secondly, who actually want friendly relations between Poland and the Soviet Union.' What constituted 'friendly', however, left little to the imagination. With the impasse on Poland, and before Roosevelt's death, it may safely be argued that the Cold War began.

Source: *Correspondence between the Chairman of the Council of Ministers of the U.S.S.R. and the Presidents of the U.S.A. and the Prime Ministers of Great Britain during the Great Patriotic War of 1941-1945* (Moscow, 1957(, 11,211-13. (Hereafter this source will be referred to as *Soviet Correspondence*.)

With reference to your message of April 1st I think I must make the following comments on the Polish question.

The Polish question has indeed reached an impasse.

What is the reason?

The reason is that the U.S. and British Ambassadors in Moscow—members of the Moscow Commission—have departed from the instructions of the Crimea Conference, introducing new elements not provided for by the Crimea Conference.

Namely:

(a) At the Crimea Conference the three of us regarded the Polish Provisional Government as the government now functioning in Poland and subject to reconstruction as the government that should be the core of a new Government of National Unity. The U.S. and British Ambassadors in Moscow, however, have departed from that thesis; they ignore the Polish Provisional Government, pay no heed to it and at best place individuals in Poland and London on a par with the Provisional Government. Furthermore, they hold that reconstruction of the Provisional Government should be understood in terms of its abolition and the establishment of an entirely new government. Things have gone so far that Mr Harriman declared in the Moscow Commission that it might be that not a single member of the Provisional Government would be included in the Polish Government of National Unity.

Obviously this thesis of the U.S. and British Ambassadors cannot but be strongly resented by the Polish Provisional Government. As regards the Soviet Union, it certainly cannot accept a thesis that is tantamount to direct violation of the Crimea Conference decisions.

(b) At the Crimea Conference the three of us held that five people should be invited for consultation from Poland and three from London, not more. But the U.S. and British Ambassadors have abandoned that position and insist that each member of the Moscow Commission be entitled to invite an unlimited number from Poland and from London.

Clearly the Soviet Government could not agree to that, because, according to the Crimea decision, invitations should be sent not by individual members of the Commission, but by the Commission as a whole, as a body. The demand for no limit to the number invited for consultation runs counter to what was envisaged at the Crimea Conference.

(c) The Soviet Government proceeds from the assumption that, by virtue of the Crimea decisions, those invited for consultation should be in the first instance Polish leaders who recognise the decisions of the Crimea Conference, including the one on the Curzon Line and, secondly, who actually want friendly relations between Poland and the Soviet Union. The Soviet Government insists on this because the blood of Soviet soldiers, so freely shed in liberating Poland, and the fact that in the past 30 years the territory of Poland has twice been used by an enemy for invading Russia, oblige the Soviet Government to ensure friendly relations between the Soviet Union and Poland.

The U.S. and British Ambassadors in Moscow, however, ignore this and want to invite Polish leaders for consultation regardless of their attitude to the Crimea decisions and to the Soviet Union.

Such, to my mind, are the factors hindering a settlement of the Polish problem through mutual agreement.

In order to break the deadlock and reach an agreed decision, the following steps should, I think, be taken:

(1)   Affirm that reconstruction of the Polish Provisional Government implies, not its abolition, but its reconstruction by enlarging it, it being understood that the Provisional Government shall form the core of the future Polish Government of National Unity.

(2)   Return to the provisions of the Crimea Conference and restrict the number of Polish leaders to be invited to eight persons, of whom five should be from Poland and three from London.

(3)   Affirm that the representatives of the Polish Provisional Government shall be consulted in all circumstances, that they be consulted in the first place, since the Provisional Government is much stronger in Poland compared with the individuals to be invited from London and Poland whose influence among the population in no way compares with the tremendous prestige of the Provisional Government.

I draw your attention to this because, to my mind, any other decision on the point might be regarded in Poland as an affront to the people and as an attempt to impose a government without regard to Polish public opinion.

(4)   Only those leaders should be summoned for consultation from Poland and from London who recognise the decisions of the Crimea Conference on Poland and who in practice want friendly relations between Poland the Soviet Union.

(5)   Reconstruction of the Provisional Government to be effected by replacing a number of Ministers of the Provisional Government by nominees among the Polish leaders who are not members of the Provisional Government.

As to the ratio of old and new Ministers in the Government of National Unity, it might be established more or less on the same lines as was done in the case of the Yugoslav Government.

I think if these comments are taken into consideration the Polish question can be settled in a short time.

CHAPTER THREE

President Truman and the Intensification of the Polish Question

14   A meeting with Ambassador Harriman and what to do with the Soviets: April 20, 1945. *'Ambassador Harriman said that in effect what we were faced with was a "barbarian invasion of Europe", that Soviet control over any foreign country did not mean merely influence on their foreign relations but the extension of the Soviet system . . . .'*

Generally uninformed of the contents of his predecessor's Russian policy, relatively inexperienced in the field of foreign affairs, and forced to rely for much of his advice on Roosevelt's political and military advisers, Harry S. Truman was, for all his limitations, a man of his times. An active supporter of collective security, President Truman was at once determined to continue the policies of the Roosevelt Administration and to be President in his own right. Truman, together with Churchill, whom he greatly respected, responded to Stalin's message of April 7 by saying, 'The real issue between us is whether or not the Warsaw Government has the right to veto individual candidates for consultation.' For Truman, as was increasingly the case with FDR, the Polish issue—mainly the American demand that the base of the Lublin Government be broadened to accommodate more democratic elements—became a roadblock to improved Soviet-American relations. Or, as Truman himself recalled, 'in its larger aspects the Polish question had become for our people the symbol of the future development of our international relations.' Disturbed by the news from Moscow that a Russo-Polish treaty of mutual assistance was on the verge of being concluded, President Truman prepared for his forthcoming meeting with Soviet Foreign Minister Molotov in Washington in late April by conferring first with Ambassador Harriman. After outlining what he regarded as Stalin's attempt to pursue a simultaneous policy of cooperation with the Western Powers on the one hand and extending Soviet control over Eastern Europe on the other, Harriman warned Truman (in the words of a memorandum of that conversation prepared by Charles E. Bohlen, assistant to the Secretary of State), 'that in effect what we were faced with was a "barbarian invasion of Europe", that Soviet control over any foreign country did nòt mean merely influence on their foreign relations but the extension of the Soviet system with secret police, extinction of the freedom of press, etc., and that we had to decide what should be our attitude in the face of these unpleasant facts.' That Truman understood the import of his words, Harriman had no doubts. For, as he later recorded, 'Truman grasped the importance of the Polish problem and took the opportunity of Molotov's call on him to impress on him bluntly, perhaps too bluntly, the United States' insistence that the Yalta agreements be carried out.'

Source: Department of State, *Foreign Relations of the United States, Diplomatic Papers: 1945* (Wash. 1967), V, 231-34.

After the Secretary presented Ambassador Harriman to the President the latter said that he wished to thank the Ambassador for the great service he had done for him in connection with Molotov's coming to the San Francisco Conference. He said that he deeply appreciated this and he wished to congratulate the Ambassador and to express the hope that he would return to Moscow and continue his excellent work. Ambassador Harriman said that he had felt that that was the most appropriate suggestion he could make when Marshal Stalin had indicated his desire to make some gesture. He said that he had not felt it possible to do anything abouth the Polish question since Stalin was merely speaking of a gesture.

At the President's request Ambassador Harriman then made a brief report on his opinion of the present problems facing the United States in relation to the Soviet Union. He said that he thought the Soviet Union had two policies which they thought they could successfully pursue at the same time—one, the policy of cooperation with the United States and Great Britain, and the other, the extension of Soviet control over neighboring states through unilateral action. He said that he thought our generosity and desire to cooperate was being misinterpreted in Moscow by certain elements around Stalin as an indication that the Soviet Government could do anything that it wished without having any trouble with the United States. He said that he thought the Soviet Government did not wish to break with the United States since they needed our help in order to reduce the burden of reconstruction and that he felt we had nothing to lose by standing firm on issues that were of real importance to us. The Ambassador then outlined a number of the specific difficulties which he had recently encountered in Moscow and described the deterioration of the Soviet attitude since the Yalta Conference. The President said that he was not in any sense afraid of the Russians and that he intended to be firm but fair since in his opinion the Soviet Union needed us more than we needed them. Ambassador Harriman said that he believed that some quarters in Moscow believed erroneously that American business needed as a matter of life and death the development of exports to Russia. Mr. Harriman said that this was of course not true but that a number of Russian officials believed it. The President again repeated that he intended to be firm with the Russians and make no concessions from American principles or traditions for the fact of winning their favor. He said he felt that only on a give and take basis could any relations be established.

Ambassador Harriman said that in effect what we were faced with was a "barbarian invasion of Europe", that Soviet control over any foreign country did not mean merely influence on their foreign relations but the extension of the Soviet system with secret police, extinction of freedom of speech, etc., and that we had to decide what should be our attitude in the face of these unpleasant facts. He added that he was not pessimistic and felt that we could arrive at a workable basis with the Russians but that this would require a reconsideration of our policy and the abandonment of the illusion that for the immediate future the Soviet Government was going to act in accordance with the principles which the rest of the world held to in international affairs. He said that obviously certain concessions in the give and take of negotiation would have to be made. The President said that he thoroughly understood this and said that we could not, of course, expect to get 100 percent of what we wanted but that on important matters he felt that we should be able to get 85 percent.

The Ambassador then outlined briefly the issues involved in the Polish question explaining his belief that Stalin had discovered from the Lublin Poles that an honest execution of the Crimean decision would mean the end of Soviet-backed Lublin control over Poland since any real democratic leader such as Mikolajczyk would serve as a rallying point for 80 or 90 percent of the Polish people against the Lublin Communists. He said it was important for us to consider what we should do in the event that Stalin rejected the proposals contained in the joint message from the President and the Prime Minister and if Molotov proved adamant in the negotiations here in Washington.

He said he would like to inquire in this connection of the President how important he felt the Polish question was in relation to the San Francisco Conference and American participation in the world organization. The President replied immediately and decisively that in his considered opinion unless settlement of the Polish question was achieved along the lines of the Crimean decision that the treaty of American adherence to a world organization would not get through the Senate. He added that he intended to tell Molotov just this in words of one syllable.

The Secretary inquired whether if Molotov was so late in arriving in Washington there would not be sufficient time for any real discussion between the Foreign Ministers, if the President would desire that the conversations on Poland be continued in San Francisco. The President replied that he thought that was a good idea.

Ambassador Harriman inquired whether or not we would be disposed to go ahead with the world organization plans even if Russia dropped out as he had understood from the Secretary. The President said that the truth of the matter was that without Russia there would not be much of a world organization.

In concluding the interview the President stated that he fully realized that he was not up on all details of foreign affairs and would rely on the Secretary of State and his Ambassadors to help him in this matter but that he did intend to be firm in his dealings with the Soviet Government. He said he hoped to see the Secretary and Ambassador Harriman again before Molotov arrived.

15   Preparing for Mr Molotov's visit: April 23, 1945, 2 pm. *'He [President Truman] . . . felt that our agreements with the Soviet Union so far had been a one way street and that could not continue: it was now or never. He intended to go on with the plans for San Francisco and if the Russians did not wish to join us they could go to hell.'*

After formally receiving Molotov on the Sunday evening, of April 22, 1945, at Blair House, President Truman continued preparations for his next encounter with the Soviet Foreign Minister by calling a meeting of his major advisers the following day. At this gathering (again recorded in a memorandum prepared by Bohlen) the most important men in the administration had an opportunity to voice their views on what course America's Russian policy should take. Secretary of State Edward Stetinnius opened the discussion by saying that at a late Sunday evening meeting of Foreign Ministers, Molotov proved increasingly intractable on the Polish question and that it appeared obvious to the Secretary of State 'that the Soviet Government intended to try to enforce upon the United States and British Governments this puppet government of Poland.' Others, including the Secretary of the Navy James V. Forrestal, were inclined to take a hard line attitude with Stalin over Poland. Although Truman made it clear that while the Russians 'could go to hell' on the issue of joining the United Nations, 'he had no intention of delivering an ultimatum to Mr. Molotov . . . ' Secretary of War Henry L. Stimson, considered by many historians as a consumate realist, cautioned his colleagues to appreciate the Russian position in Poland more fully before deciding on a course of action. It is interesting to note that a supposedly thorough-going realist, who showed an amazing lack of understanding both of Polish history and sensitivity, should in part buttress his case on the ground 'that their ideas of independence and democracy in areas that they regarded as vital to the Soviet Union are different from ours.' Such reasoning suggests that perhaps the idealism of the so-called 'realists' has played a larger role than first imagined.

Source: ibid, 252-55.

THE SECRETARY OF STATE told the meeting that Mr. Molotov had arrived in good spirits yesterday and had had a good talk with the President yesterday evening but that at the Foreign Ministers meeting later great difficulties had developed over the Polish question. The continuance of the meeting this morning had produced no improvement and a complete deadlock had been reached on the subject of the carrying out of the Yalta agreement on Poland. The Secretary said that the truth of the matter was the Lublin or Warsaw Government was not representative of the Polish people and that it was now clear that the Soviet Government intended to try to enforce upon the United States and British Governments this puppet government of Poland and obtain its acceptance as the legal government of Poland. He said that as they all recalled at Yalta an agreement had been reached regarding the formation of a new Polish Government representative of the people by means of the reorganization of the present provisional government in consultation with other Polish democratic leaders. He said it had been made plain to Mr. Molotov how seriously the United States Government regarded this matter and how much public confidence would be shaken by our failure to carry out the Crimean decision.

THE PRESIDENT said that he had told Mr. Molotov last night that he intended fully to carry out all the agreements reached by President Roosevelt at the Crimea. He added that he felt our agreements with the Soviet Union so far had been a one way street and that could not continue: it was now or never. He intended to go with the plans for San Francisco and if the Russians did not wish to join us they could go to hell. The President then asked in rotation the officials present for their view.

MR. STIMSON said that this whole difficulty with the Russians over Poland was new to him and he felt it was important to find out what the Russians were driving at. He said in the big military matters the Soviet Government had kept their word and that the military authorities of the United States had come to count on it. In fact he said that they had often been better than their promise. He said it was important to find out what motives they had in mind in regard to these border countries and that their ideas of independence and democracy in areas that they regarded as vital to the Soviet Union are different from ours. Mr. Stimson remarked that they had a good deal of trouble on minor military matters and it was necessary in these cases to teach them manners. In this case he said that without fully understanding how seriously the Russians took this Polish question we might be heading into very dangerous water. He remarked that 25 years ago virtually all of Poland had been Russian.

MR. FORRESTAL said that he felt that this difficulty over Poland could not be treated as an isolated incident, that there had been many evidences of the Soviet desire to dominate adjacent countries and to disregard the wishes of her allies. He said he had felt that for some time the Russians had considered that we would not object if they took over all of Eastern Europe into their power. He said it was his profound conviction that if the Russians were to be rigid in their attitude we had better have a show down with them now than later.

AMBASSADOR HARRIMAN said that in regard to Mr. Stimson's question as to the issues and the motives he felt that when Stalin and Molotov had returned to Moscow after Yalta they had been informed by Bierut (the present head of the provisional government) concerning the situation in Poland and had realized that the provisional government was in a shaky condition and that the introduction of any genuine Polish leader such as Mikolajczyk would probably mean the elimination of the Soviet hand-picked group. He remarked that the real issue was whether we were to be a party to a program of Soviet domination of Poland. He said obviously we were faced with a possibility of a real break with the Russians but he felt that if properly handled it might be avoided. The President said that he had no intention of delivering an ultimatum to Mr. Molotov but merely to make clear the position of this Government.

MR. STIMSON observed that he would like to know how far the Russian reaction to a strong position on Poland would go. He said he thought that the Russians perhaps were being more realistic than we were in regard to their own security.

ADMIRAL LEAHY said that he had left Yalta with the impression that the Soviet

Government had no intention of permitting a free government to operate in Poland and that he would have been surprised had the Soviet Government behaved any differently than it had. In his opinion the Yalta agreement was susceptible to two interpretations. He added that he felt that it was a serious matter to break with the Russians but that we should tell them that we stood for a free and independent Poland.

THE SECRETARY OF STATE then read the part of the Yalta decision relating to the formation of the new Government and the holding of free elections and said he felt that this was susceptible of only one interpretation.

GENERAL MARSHALL said he was not familiar with the Polish issue and its political aspects. He said from the military point of view the situation in Europe was secure but that they hoped for Soviet participation in the war against Japan at a time when it would be useful to us. The Russians had it within their power to delay their entry into the Far Eastern war until we had done all the dirty work. He said the difficulties with the Russians such as in the case of CROSS-WORD usually straightened out. He was inclined to agree with Mr. Stimson that possibility of a break with Russia was very serious.

MR. STIMSON observed that he agreed with General Marshall and that he felt that the Russians would not yield on the Polish question. He said we must understand that outside the United States with the exception of Great Britain there was no country that understood free elections; that the party in power always ran the election as he well knew from his experience in Nicaragua.[1]

ADMIRAL KING inquired whether the issue was the invitation to the Lublin Government to San Francisco. The President informed him that that was a settled matter and not the issue. The issue was the execution of agreements entered into between this Government and the Soviet Union. He said he intended to tell Mr. Molotov that we expected Russia to carry out the Yalta decision as we were prepared to do for our part.

AMBASSADOR HARRIMAN then remarked that while it was true that the Soviet Union had kept its big agreements on military matters that those were decisions which it had already reached by itself but that on other military matters it was impossible to say they had lived up to their commitments. He said for example over a year ago they had agreed to start on preparations for collaboration in the Far Eastern war but that none of these had been carried out. He asked General Deane to express his opinion.

GENERAL DEANE said that he felt that the Soviet Union would enter the Pacific war as soon as it was able irrespective of what happened in other fields. He felt that the Russians must do this because they could not afford too long a period of let down for their people who were tired, there was only a short season in which offensive action against Manchuria was possible and that they would not dare attempt a Bulgarian gambit in the Far East. He said he was convinced after his experiences in Moscow that if we were afraid of the Russians we would get nowhere and he felt that we should be firm when we were right.

THE PRESIDENT then thanked the military representation and said that he felt that he had their point of view well in mind and would ask the Secretary of State and his advisers to stay behind to work out the details of his forthcoming talk with Mr. Molotov.

The President then said that he was satisfied that from a military point of view there was no reason why we should fail to stand up to our understanding of the Crimean agreements and he requested the Secretary of State to prepare for him (1) a statement to be handed to Mr. Molotov for communication to Marshal Stalin, (2) a list of points he might mention orally to Mr. Molotov and (3) a draft of a statement to the press. He said he would be prepared to receive the Secretary of State and his advisers just as soon as this could be done and afterwards he would see Mr. Molotov. The Secretary agreed and said he would have the drafts in the President's hands by 5:00 o'clock.

¹ In the spring of 1927, Mr. Stimson served as a special emissary to Nicaragua for President Coolidge.

16   The confrontation: April 23, 1945.

Several hours after meeting with his advisers, President Truman, who daily grew in his determination to stand firm on the principles involved in the Polish issue, confronted Molotov with the observation that 'an agreement had been reached on Poland and that it only required carrying out by the Soviet Government.' Truman's undeniably rough handling of the Soviet Foreign Minister has constituted for critics of the Truman Administration ample proof that FDR's successor had completely reversed, in the embittered judgment of D.F. Fleming, 'the entire Roosevelt-Hull approach to Russia and inaugurated an era of toughness in our dealings with Russia.' Although such a thesis overlooks the evidence that Roosevelt himself was moving in the same direction before his untimely death, there can be little doubt to the truth in Molotov's reaction that he had never been talked to like that in his life. For, as Charles E. Bohlen put it in his *Witness to History, 1929-1969* (1973), these were 'probably the first sharp words uttered during the war by an American President to a high Soviet official.' The attached message merely reiterated the joint Truman-Churchill statement to Stalin of April 18.

16(a) Truman gets tough with Molotov: April 23, 1945. *'The President replied with great firmness that an agreement had been reached on Poland and that it only remained for Marshall Stalin to carry it out in accordance with his word.'*

Source: ibid, 256-58.

After greeting Mr. Molotov the President said that he had been sorry to learn that no progress had been made towards a solution of the Polish question. Mr. Molotov said that he also regretted that. The President then stated that the proposals contained in the joint message from himself and the Prime Minister were eminently fair and reasonable and that we go as far as we can to meet the desires of the Soviet Government as expressed in the message which Marshal Stalin sent on April 7. He emphasized that the United

States Government could not agree to be a party to the formation of a Polish Government which was not representative of all Polish democratic elements. He added that the United States Government was deeply disappointed that the Soviet Government had not found it possible to carry out the consultation with representatives of the Polish Government other than those who were not officials of the Warsaw regime. He said that the United States Government is determined together with other members of the United Nations to go ahead with plans for the world organization no matter what difficulties or differences may arise with regard to other matters. He felt nevertheless that the failure of the three principal allies who had borne the brunt of the war to carry out the Crimea decision with regard to Poland will cast serious doubt upon our unity of purpose in regard to postwar collaboration. He mentioned that in his last message to Marshal Stalin on April 1 President Roosevelt had made it plain that no policy in the United States whether foreign or domestic could succeed unless it enjoyed public confidence and support. He said that this applied of necessity to economic collaboration as well as political. The President added that legislative appropriation was required for any economic measures in the foreign field and that he could not hope to get these measures through Congress unless there was public support for them. He concluded by expressing the sincere hope that the Soviet Government would keep these factors in mind in considering the request that the British and American proposals in the joint message from himself and the Prime Minister on Poland be accepted and that Mr. Molotov be authorized to continue the discussions in San Francisco on that basis. He then handed to Mr. Molotov with the request that it be transmitted immediately to Marshal Stalin the attached message.

Mr. Molotov asked if he could make a few observations. Mr. Molotov said that he hoped he expressed the views of the Soviet Government in stating that they wished to cooperate with the United States and Great Britain as before. The President said he agreed; otherwise, they would not be talking today. Mr. Molotov continued that he had been authorized to set forth the point of view of the Soviet Government. The basis of collaboration had been established and that although inevitable difficulties had arisen the three Governments had been able to find a common language and that on this basis they had been settling these differences. He said the three Governments had dealt as equal parties and there had been no case where one or two of the three had attempted to impose their will on another. He said this was the basis of cooperation and the only one acceptable to the Soviet Government.

The President agreed and said that all we were asking was that the Soviet Government carry out the Crimean decision on Poland.

Mr. Molotov said that as an advocate of the Crimean decisions his Government stood by them and that it was a matter of honour for them; that his Government felt that the good base which existed was the result of former work and offered even brighter prospects for the future. He said that the Soviet Government was convinced that all difficulties could be overcome.

The President replied with great firmness that an agreement had been reached on Poland and that it only remained for Marshal Stalin to carry it out in accordance with his word.

Mr. Molotov replied that Marshal Stalin in his message of April 7 had given his views on the agreement and he personally could not understand why if the three Governments could reach an agreement on the question of the composition of the Yugoslav Government the same formula could not be applied in the case of Poland. The President replied sharply that an agreement had been reached on Poland and that it only required carrying out by the Soviet Government. Mr. Molotov said that his Government supported the Crimean decisions and then said that he could not agree that an abrogation of those decisions by others could be considered as a violation by the Soviet Government. He added that surely the Polish question involving a neighboring country was of very great interest to the Soviet Government.

The President repeated that as he had said last night the United States Government was prepared to carry out loyally all the agreements reached at the Crimea and he only asked that the Soviet Government do the same. The President said that he desired the friendship of the Soviet Government, but that he felt it could only be on the basis of mutual observation of agreements and not on the basis of a one way street. In conclusion he arose and handed to Mr. Molotov the press release which he stated he intended to release to the press this evening. Mr. Molotov read the release and thanked the President for the information.

16(b) President Truman to Marshal Stalin: April 23, 1945. *'The Soviet Government must realize that the failure to go forward at this time with the implementation of the Crimean decision on Poland would seriously shake confidence in the unity of the three Governments and their determination to continue the collaboration in the future as they have in the past.'*

Source: ibid, 259-60.

There was an agreement at Yalta in which President Roosevelt participated for the United States Government to reorganize the Provisional Government now functioning in Warsaw in order to establish a new Government of National Unity in Poland by means of previous consultation between representatives of the Provisional Polish Government of Warsaw and other Polish democratic leaders from Poland and from abroad.

In the opinion of the United States Government the Crimean decision on Poland can only be carried out if a group of genuinely representative democratic Polish leaders are invited to Moscow for consultation. The United States Government cannot be party to any method of consultation with Polish leaders which would not result in the establishment of a new Provisional Government of National Unity genuinely representative of the democratic elements of the Polish people. The United States and British Governments have gone as far as they can to meet the situation and carry out the intent of the Crimean decisions in their joint message delivered to Marshal Stalin on April 18th.

The United States Government earnestly requests that the Soviet Government accept the proposals set forth in the joint message of the President and Prime Minister to Marshal Stalin. And that Mr. Molotov continue the conversations with the Secretary of State and Mr. Eden in San Francisco on that basis.

The Soviet Government must realize that the failure to go forward at this time with the implementation of the Crimean decision on Poland would seriously shake confidence in the unity of the three Governments and their determination to continue the collaboration in the future as they have in the past.

17   Marshal Stalin replies: April 24, 1945. *'I cannot understand why in discussing Poland no attempt is made to consider the interests of the Soviet Union in terms of security as well.'*

Probably for both strategic and ideological considerations, Stalin, like Truman, continued to grow firm in his determination to resist what he conceived to be unnecessary Western meddling in matters that were of vital concern to the national security of Soviet Russia. In a brief and pointed geography lesson, he reminded Truman that 'Poland borders on the Soviet Union which cannot be said about Great Britain or the U.S.A.' Furthermore, ran the argument, Stalin suggested he could not abide by the West's attempts to impose its will on his own nation, for in allowing such a thing to happen, he in effect would be renouncing the interests of the security of the Soviet Union. Stalin, as is well known, held his ground, and in the months ahead the West was compelled to accept the *fait accompli* of the Russian domination of the hapless Poles. Nonetheless, the acrimony generated by the Polish question continued to poison Soviet-American relations for many years to come.

Source: *Soviet Correspondence*, II,219-20.

I have received from you and Prime Minister Churchill the joint message of April 18 and the message transmitted to me through V. M. Molotov on April 24.

The messages indicate that you still regard the Polish Provisional Government, not as the core of a future Polish Government of National Unity, but merely as a group on a par with any other group of Poles. It would be hard to reconcile this concept of the position of the Provisional Government and this attitude towards it with the Crimea decision on Poland. At the Crimea Conference the three of us, including President Roosevelt, based ourselves on the assumption that the Polish Provisional Government, as the Government now functioning in Poland and enjoying the trust and support of the majority of the Polish people, should be the core, that is, the main part of a new, reconstructed Polish Government of National Unity.

You apparently disagree with this understanding of the issue. By turning down the Yugoslav example as a model for Poland, you confirm that the Polish Provisional Government cannot be regarded as a basis for, and the core of, a future Government of National Unity.

2.   Another circumstance that should be borne in mind is that Poland borders on the

Soviet Union, which cannot be said about Great Britain or the U.S.A.

Poland is to the security of the Soviet Union what Belgium and Greece are to the security of Great Britain.

You evidently do not agree that the Soviet Union is entitled to seek in Poland a Government that would be friendly to it, that the Soviet Government cannot agree to the existence in Poland of a Government hostile to it. This is rendered imperative, among other things, by the Soviet people's blood freely shed on the fields of Poland for the liberation of that country. I do not know whether a genuinely representative Government has been established in Greece, or whether the Belgian Government is a genuinely democratic one. The Soviet Union was not consulted when those Governments were being formed, nor did it claim the right to interfere in those matters, because it realises how important Belgium and Greece are to the security of Great Britain.

I cannot understand why in discussing Poland no attempt is made to consider the interests of the Soviet Union in terms of security as well.

3.   One cannot but recognise as unusual a situation in which two Governments—those of the United States and Great Britain—reach agreement beforehand on Poland, a country in which the U.S.S.R is interested first of all and most of all, and place its representatives in an intolerable position, trying to dictate to it.

I say that this situation cannot contribute to agreed settlement of the Polish problem.

4.   I am ready to accede to your request and to do all in my power to reach an agreed settlement. But you are asking too much. To put it plainly, you want me to renounce the interests of the security of the Soviet Union; but I cannot proceed against the interests of my country.

I think there is only one way out of the present situation and that is to accept the Yugoslav precedent as a model for Poland. That, I believe, might enable us to arrive at agreed settlement.

18   Sumner Welles on departing from FDR's policy of accommodation towards the Russians—the beginning of the great debate: May 22, 1945. *'In five short weeks since the death of President Roosevelt the policy which he had so painstakingly carried on has been changed. Our Government now appears to the Russians as the spearhead of an apparent bloc of the western nations opposed to the Soviet Union.'*

As all historiographical debates are rooted in the record of the past, it is not surprising that exponents of the thesis that Truman first departed from and then reversed Roosevelt's policy of cooperation with the Soviets should find comfort in Sumner Welles' remarks to the same effect. Welles, a former State Department official and a Wilsonian to the core, charged that 'In five short weeks since the death of President Roosevelt the policy which he so painstakingly carried on has been changed.' Conceding that 'the Russian concept of legitimate postwar security differs very materially from the ideas which the western powers hold on that point', Welles contended that Roosevelt clearly understood 'the United States has never had any basic causes for hostility towards the Soviet Union.' Much like Stimson, whose sense of idealism informed his own 'realistic' approach to external affairs, Welles' sense of the realistic prospects for peace in the near future informed his own 'idealism' with regard to the chances of the newly-founded United Nations.

Source: *Congressional Record,* 78th Congress, Appendix, May 25, 1945.

It would be far more agreeable for me tonight to limit myself to telling you of the nature of the progress which has this week been made at the Conference at San Francisco.

On one critical issue, which has up to now been a major stumbling block, a solution has been found. The Soviet delegation, after some delay, has agreed with the delegations of the other major powers as to the way in which regional systems of collective security will be enabled to function under the authority of the world organization. This formula is acceptable to most of the other American republics which have been insistent that the inter-American security system should not be prevented by the world organization from operating if some country of the new world is attacked.

The solution of this difficulty makes it now seem probable that the conference can complete its work by June 9, and that all of the United Nations will then agree upon the final charter for a new international organization.

But there is nothing more dangerous than for an enlightened democracy, such as ours, to shut its eyes to facts and to think that, because the charter of the new international organization will be agreed upon at San Francisco, we can, as soon as our victory over Japan is won, sit back and enjoy the blessings of a peaceful world. For there is little use in concentrating upon the progress that is being made at San Francisco, and less than any use in believing that that alone implies an end to future wars and the security of our own country, so long as the present tension between the Soviet Union and ourselves becomes constantly more serious.

For while a charter for international organization will be agreed upon at San Francisco, it can neither function effectively, nor even perhaps be prevented from breaking down completely, unless this country of ours is able with vigor and determination to establish in the immediate future a wholly different relationship between the Soviet Union and the United States than that which, unfortunately exists today.

When the final history of these times is written, I believe it will be realized that one of the greatest contributions which President Roosevelt made to the future interest of this country was his effort to establish a working agreement between our Government and Moscow. For President Roosevelt saw clearly that no world organization can operate successfully in the first years after the war unless it is based on understanding and cooperation between Russia and the United States. He knew that cooperation between the United States and Great Britain, whatever temporary difficulties might arise, could always be achieved. He knew that in the long run cooperation between our country and France or China would be possible.

But in the case of the Soviet Union, he always had in mind these facts.

Russia has been isolated from the rest of the world for a quarter of a century. For this reason, and because of the policies of the great powers during the years between the two great wars, deep-rooted suspicions of the western powers are imbedded in the minds of Russian leaders and of the Russian people.

Because of the stupendous victories which the Russian armies have won against Germany, the Russian Government, the Russian military leaders and the Russian people have today a feeling of almost unlimited physical power in their part of the globe.

The Russian concept of legitimate postwar security differs very materially from the ideas which the western powers hold on that point.

Present and traditional reasons for rivalry and antagonism between Russia and Great Britain are very deep indeed.

For all of these reasons, and for reasons of ideology as well, the President foresaw that the establishment of any true understanding between the United States and the Soviet Union would prove to be one of the most difficult tasks which our Government was going to confront.

On the other hand, the President remembered that during the whole of our independent history the United States has never had any basic causes for hostility towards the Soviet Union. He knew that there are neither geographic, political or economic reasons for rivalry or for antagonism between the Russian people and the people of the United States.

He saw that in its own interest and in the highest interests of world peace, the United States should undertake a patient, constructive and continuing attempt to serve as moderator when difficulties arose between the Soviet Union and the other great powers and particularly between Great Britain and the Soviet Union.

He never had the faintest idea of permitting the United Stated to be used as a cat's-paw either by the Soviet Union or by Great Britain. But he did believe that when disputes arose between those two countries, as he knew they would arise, the United States could act as a mediating and conciliating influence, and by refraining from serving the individual interests of either nation, undertake to serve the highest interest of the world.

In five short weeks since the death of President Roosevelt the policy which he had so painstakingly carried on has been changed. Our Government now appears to the Russians as the spearhead of an apparent bloc of the western nations opposed to the Soviet Union.

At the present moment there are four outstanding causes for friction between the Soviet Union and the United States.

These are the bitter controversy over what kind of a democratic government of Poland is to be set up under the agreement of Yalta: the action of the Soviet Government in establishing a government of Austria without the knowledge or consent of the United States or of Great Britain: the action of the Moscow-dominated government of Yugoslavia in occupying Trieste and the Istrian Peninsula and regions to southern Austria; and the persistent refusal of the Soviet authorities to give the western powers any real knowledge of what is going on in such countries as Poland, Hungary, Rumania, and Bulgaria, all occupied by the Soviet, as well as in that sector of Germany which is occupied by Russian troops. To these grounds for dissension there may well be added the inexplicable policy pursued by the Russian armies with regard to American and British prisoners of war who were liberated by the Russian forces from German prison camps.

Now, in my judgment, the policy pursued by the Soviet Union in regard to every one of these issues is wholly unjustifiable. What will do more harm, perhaps, in the long run is the failure of the Soviet Government to explain clearly to public opinion in the United States its own reasons for what it has done. There are few instances in modern times where the policy of a great nation has been so ineptly presented to public opinion in other parts of the world as in this instance.

The result has been that a certain section of the American press which thrives on its effort to create ill will between the American people and the people of certain other countries has been able to seize the opportunity to fan the flames of resentment. This element of the American press has been helped by many powerful groups within the United States which hate the Soviet Government. Every shred of alleged evidence which could be presented to foster prejudice and suspicion here has been utilized. Blind passion is rapidly rising.

And at the same time the Russian press appears to have given quite as biased a picture of American policy and of American intentions to Russian public opinion.

But if we here in the United States intend to be fair in our analysis of the reasons for the present situation, we will have to confess that the Russian press has been able to cite many evidences of American policy which can understandably stimulate popular misunderstanding and resentment in the Soviet Union.

At the very moment when the Russian armies and the American armies have as allies won their bloody victory against the common enemy, Germany, the people of Russia are informed of the increasingly bitter attacks which are daily being made in the United States against the Soviet Union.

They are told to their amazement of the extraordinarily cordial treatment accorded to leading Nazi criminals by the American armies which have captured them. They learn of Mr. Churchill's official announcement that German authorities will be permitted to administer Germany because it will be too much trouble for authorities of the United Nations to undertake the task. They learn that no contrary view has as yet been expressed by the Government of the United States.

To the average Russian such reports as these are quite as incomprehensible and quite as infuriating as the reports which we Americans receive with regard to those recent actions of the Soviet Government which I recited a few moments ago.

And what are in reality the chief causes for the present situation?

First of all, there is no committee, or council, of high-ranking authorities of the major powers through which political disputes such as those which now exist, can be threshed out, and settled. If Russia enters the war against Japan, such machinery would be all the more necessary.

There is no agreement between the United States and the Soviet Union on postwar policy toward Germany.

There is no agreement as to the treatment to be given German war criminals.

There is no agreement whatever upon a joint policy toward Poland, toward Hungary, toward Rumania, Yugoslavia, or Bulgaria, toward Austria, or with regard to the major economic questions, such as reparations, which have to be decided promptly if the situation in Europe is not to degenerate into a state of open anarchy, and if relations between the Soviet Union and the United States are not to deteriorate into open and bitter hostility.

There exists as yet no basis for that kind of cooperation between the two greatest powers of the world which is indispensable if world order is to be restored.

If this situation continues in the powder keg which is Europe, almost anything can happen.

There are two immediate remedies which can be tried.

The first is for President Truman, Prime Minister Churchill, and Marshal Stalin to meet without further delay in order to seek equitable and constructive solutions for the difficulties which have already arisen, and in order to set up adequate intergovernmental peace machinery capable of working out precise agreements upon every one of the settlements which must be had if a real peace is to be restored to Europe.

And the second step is for us here in the United States to refuse to be stampeded into that blind popular hostility toward the Soviet Union, into which many powerful and some sinister forces in this country—and by no means least among them those German propagandists who are in our midst—are endeavoring to drive us.

Of one thing we can be everlastingly certain, and that is that, unless the United States and the Soviet Union find the means of constructing a relationship of cooperation so that we can work together in solving the innumerable problems with which we will all be faced during the years to come, not only will the international organization to be founded in San Francisco prove to be ineffective, but chaos throughout the world may well become inevitable.

CHAPTER FOUR

The United Nations Debate: Avoiding the Mistakes of the Past

19   Soviet Foreign Minister Molotov at the opening of the United
      Nations Conference in San Francisco: April 26, 1945. *'If the sad
      lessons of the League of Nations have to be recalled here, it is only
      that the errors of the past may be avoided in the future . . . .'*

Almost immediately after his confrontation with Truman, Molotov travelled to San Francisco to attend the United Nations Conference. Molotov, like most of the statesmen present, appealed to his colleagues' sense of history as a guide to avoiding the mistakes of the past in the creation of a postwar collective security system. In his opening remarks to the conference, the Soviet Foreign Minister reminded the gathering both of the enormity of the deeds of Nazi Germany and what he regarded as the utter failure of the League of Nations to prevent them. Implicit in Molotov's address—which, it should be recalled, was delivered several months before the American detonation of the atomic bomb over Hiroshima—was the boast that Soviet Russia could take care of herself whatever the results of the conference.

Source:V.M. Molotov, *Problems of Foreign Policy: Speeches and Statements* (Moscow 1949), 13-20. (Hereafter this source will be referred to as *Molotov Speeches.*)

. . . .The Soviet Government attaches great importance to the International Conference in San Francisco. The end of the war has drawn near—at least in Europe. The rout of Hitler Germany, the principal aggressor in this war, has become a fact. The time has come to take care of the postwar period—of the future.

This conference is called upon to consider the problem of setting up an organization to protect the general peace and security of nations after the war. Hence the responsibility resting upon this conference is very great indeed.

Today as on many other occasions we must recall once again the great name of President Franklin Roosevelt. His services in the struggle for the achievement of lasting peace and in the preparation of this historic conference have been widely acknowledged among all peace-loving nations.

The second world war by far surpassed the first world war in the scope of military operations and in the size of the armies involved, in the number of casualties, in the immeasurable destruction, and in the unprecedentedly severe consequences for the life of many peoples. Hitler Germany which unleashed this war shrank from no crimes in the attempt to impose her domination on Europe and to pave the way for the world supremacy of German imperialism. The mass murders of children, women and old men; the extermination of entire nationalities; the wholesale destruction of peaceful civilians who were not to the liking of the fascists; the barbaric destruction of culture and of unsubmissive cultural leaders; the destruction of many thousands of towns and villages; the collapse of the economic life of entire nations, and other incalculable losses— all these are things that must not be forgotten ....

German fascism not only openly prepared its armies and armaments for piratical attack on peaceful countries; Hitlerism cynically geared the mentality of many millions of people in its country to the aim of establishing domination over foreign nations. This too was the purpose of the illiterate misanthropic theory of "the German master race," which other nations supposedly had to serve.

Long before it directly attacked its neighbours Hitlerism had openly prepared for a criminal war, which it unloosed at a moment of its own choice. We know that Hitlerism found unscrupulous abettors and sanguinary accomplices. We also know that when German fascism, which until then had freely promenaded through Europe, invaded the Soviet Union it encountered an unflinching adversary. The Soviet country, which in bloody battles against German fascism saved European civilization, has now every reason to remind the governments of their responsibility for the future of the peace-loving nations after the termination of this war. This is all the more necessary because before this war the warning voice of the Soviet Republic was not heeded with due attention.

This is not the time to go at length into the reasons for this. It cannot be proved that there was no desire to prevent war. But it has been fully proved that the governments which once claimed a leading part in Europe manifested their inability, if not their reluctance, to prevent this war, whose consequences it will be not so easy to undo.

This conference is called upon to found the organization of the future security of nations. This is a great problem, which it has hitherto been impossible to solve successfully. Everybody knows that the League of Nations did not cope with this problem in the least. It betrayed the hopes of those who believed in it. Obviously, no one now wishes to restore a League of Nations which had no rights or power, which did not hinder any aggressor in hatching war against peace-loving nations, and which sometimes even positively lulled the vigilance of the peoples with regard to impending aggression. The prestige of the League of Nations was especially undermined when unceremonious attempts were made to turn it into a tool of reactionary forces and privileged Powers. If the sad lessons of the League of Nations have to be recalled here, it is only so that the errors of the past may be avoided in future; these errors must not be allowed to be committed again, even under the mask of new florid promises. But one should not count indefinitely on the patience of the peoples, if the governments again betray an inability to set up an international organization to safeguard the peaceful life of people, their lands and their younger generations against the horrors and calamities of new piratical imperialist wars.

The Soviet Government is a sincere and firm advocate of the establishment of a strong international security organization. Whatever may depend upon it and its efforts in the common cause of creating such a postwar organization for protecting the peace and security of nations, the Soviet Government will readily do. We will fully cooperate in the solution of this great problem with all other governments which are genuinely devoted to this noble cause. We are confident that, in spite of all the obstacles, this historic goal will be achieved by the joint effort of the peace-loving nations.

A big contribution to this cause was the work done at Dumbarton Oaks last year, with which we are all familiar. There the representatives of the United States of America, Great Britain, China and the Soviet Union worked out principles for an international security organization that constitute an important basis for an international organization of a new type. Quite recently at the suggestion of the great American President, Franklin Roosevelt, the Crimea conference adopted important supplements to this draft. As a result, this conference has a sound basis for successful work.

Quite naturally, the new international security organization will be built on the foundation laid by the United Nations in this war.

We know that in the strenuous struggle against the common enemy a great coalition of democratic Powers came into being in Europe. The formation of the Anglo-Soviet-American coalition ensured the demolition of German fascism and its abettors. The other nations of Europe fought or are fighting for their liberation led by this coalition. The coalition of great Powers, with their inflexible will to defend their national rights, as well as to promote the liberation of all other nations which fell victim to sanguinary aggression, is consummating the defeat of the enemy—the foe of all the United Nations. It has been able to do this both because it was conscious of its historical responsibility and because it possessed immense manpower and material resources, which were unswervingly employed in the way demanded by the struggle against the common enemy. But we must always bear in mind that the prestige won may be easily squandered, if certain elementary things are forgotten, such as the lessons of the League of Nations, or the lessons of this war, in which the democratic nations united against an imperialist Power which fancied itself the master of Europe and which wanted to impose its will well-nigh on the whole world.

This coalition was forged in the fire of struggle, and has already rendered great service to the cause of the United Nations. It must be admitted that the presence in this coalition of such a country as the Soviet Union, where the problem of relations between big peoples and small has been consistently solved on a basis of equality and true democracy, is of extreme and fundamental importance. Nor is it possible to overrate the active part played in this coalition by the United States of America, which formerly remained aloof from the problems of an international organization, but which is now contributing to this cause its initiative and its enormous international prestige. This coalition would have been simply impossible without Great Britain, which holds a prominent place in the international association of democratic countries. China in Asia and France in Europe are the great countries which strengthen this coalition as a powerful factor in the postwar world too.

If the leading democratic countries demonstrate their ability to act in harmony in the postwar period as well, this will mean that the peace and security of nations have at last found their most effective bulwark and defence. But this is not enough. Are other peace-loving nations ready to rally around these leading Powers and create an effective international security organization?—this is the question which must be settled at this conference in the interest of the future peace and security of nations.

The question is one of creating an international organization endowed with definite powers to safeguard the general peace. This organization must also have certain means necessary for the military protection of the security of nations.

Only if such conditions are created as will guarantee that no violation of the peace, or threat of such violation, will go unpunished, and that the necessary punitive measures are not too belated, will the security organization be able to shoulder responsibility for the cause of peace. Thus the question is to create an effective organization to safeguard the general peace and security of nations, for which all sincere partisans of the peaceful development of nations have long been yearning, but which has always had many irreconcilable enemies in the camp of the more aggressive imperialists.

After the countless sacrifices of this war, after the sufferings and hardships of these past years the longing of the peoples for such an organization has become particularly poignant. But the opponents of such an international organization have not laid down their arms. They are carrying on their subversive activities even now, though in most cases in veiled and camouflaged form. For this purpose they frequently use ostensibly the most democratic watchwords and arguments, even going so far as to verbally uphold the interests of small nations or the principles of justice and equality of nations. But, when all is said and done, it is not what reasons or pretexts will have been used to sabotage the establishment of an effective security organization of nations that matters. If this time, too, no such effective organization is created to protect the postwar peace, this will be one more indication of inability to cope with this great problem with the given forces. But it will be no proof that the need for such an organization is not ripe, or that such an organization will not be set up ultimately.

We must not minimize the difficulties of creating an international security organization. We shall not find the right road with our eyes closed. We must give warning of these difficulties in order to overcome them and, avoiding illusions, to find at last a reliable road for our march towards this noble objective.

As far as the Soviet Union is concerned, I should like to assure this conference that the entire people of our country are brought up in a spirit of faith in, and devotion to, the cause of creating a firm organization of international security. I should also like to assure this conference that the Soviet people will lend a responsive ear to the voices, wishes and suggestions of all sincere friends of this great cause among the nations of the world.

You know that in the Soviet Union there are millions of people capable of defending their country arms in hand to the last. At the same time, let it be marked, the people of our Soviet country are devoted heart and soul to the cause of lasting general peace and are ready to support with all their strength the efforts of other nations to create a reliable organization for the peace and security of nations. You should definitely know that in the matter of safeguarding the peace and security of nations, the Soviet Union can be relied upon. This great cause is resolutely backed by our peace-loving people, by the Soviet Government and the Red Army, and by our great Marshal Stalin. To voice these sentiments and thoughts of the Soviet people is one of the cardinal tasks of the delegation of the Soviet Government.

I shall conclude my statement by expressing the fervent wish that our joint work at this conference may be crowned with success.

20 President Truman's address in San Francisco at the closing session of the United Nations: June 26, 1945. *'By this Charter, you have given reality to the ideal of that great statesman of a generation ago — Woodrow Wilson.'*

During the final plenary session of the United Nations Conference, held on 26 June, 1945, representatives of the fifty nations assembled in San Francisco signed the Charter of the United Nations. On this historic occasion President Truman took the opportunity to congratulate the delegates for building a solid structure on which the peace of the world could be built, although he fully recognized the practical difficulties that lay ahead. For Truman the Charter signified nothing less than the realization of the Wilsonian ideal writ large, and it uniquely offered the world the second and 'supreme chance to establish a world-wide rule of reason—to create an enduring peace under the guidance of God.'

Source: *Public Papers of the Presidents of the United States: Harry S. Truman, 1945* (Wash. 1961),I,138-45. (Hereafter this source will be referred to as *Presidential Papers*.)

I deeply regret that the press of circumstances when this Conference opened made it impossible for me to be here to greet you in person. I have asked for the privilege of coming today, to express on behalf of the people of the United States our thanks for what you have done here, and to wish you Godspeed on your journeys home.

Somewhere in this broad country, every one of you can find some of our citizens who are sons and daughters, or descendants in some degree, of your own native land. All our people are glad and proud that this historic meeting and its accomplishments have taken place in our country. And that includes the millions of loyal and patriotic Americans who stem from the countries not represented at this Conference.

We are grateful to you for coming. We hope you have enjoyed your stay, and that you will come again.

You assembled in San Francisco nine weeks ago with the high hope and confidence of peace-loving people the world over.

Their confidence in you has been justified.

Their hope for your success has been fulfilled.

The Charter of the United Nations which you have just signed is a solid structure upon which we can build a better world. History will honor you for it. Between the victory in Europe and the final victory in Japan, in this most destructive of all wars, you have won a victory against war itself.

It was the hope of such a Charter that helped sustain the courage of stricken peoples through the darkest days of the war. For it is a declaration of great faith by the nations of the earth—faith that war is not inevitable, faith that peace can be maintained.

If we had had this Charter a few years ago—and above all, the will to use it—millions now dead would be alive. If we should falter in the future in our will to use it, millions now living will surely die.

It has already been said by many that this is only a first step to a lasting peace. That is true. The important thing is that all our thinking and all our actions be based on the realization that it is in fact only a first step. Let us all have it firmly in mind that we start today from a good beginning and, with our eye always on the final objective, let us march forward.

The Constitution of my own country came from a Convention which—like this one—was made up of delegates with many different views. Like this Charter, our Constitution came from a free and sometimes bitter exchange of conflicting opinions. When it was adopted, no one regarded it as a perfect document. But it grew and developed and expanded. And upon it there was built a bigger, a better, a more perfect union.

This charter, like our own Constitution, will be expanded and improved as time goes on. No one claims that it is now a final or a perfect instrument. It has not been poured into any fixed mold. Changing world conditions will require readjustments—but they will be the readjustments of peace and not of war.

That we now have this Charter at all is a great wonder. It is also a cause for profound thanksgiving to Almighty God, who has brought us so far in our search for peace through world organization.

There were many who doubted that agreement could ever be reached by these fifty countries differing so much in race and religion, in language and culture. But these differences were all forgotten in one unshakable unity of determination—to find a way to end wars.

Out of all the arguments and disputes, and different points of view, a way was found to agree. Here is the spotlight of full publicity, in the tradition of liberty-loving people, opinions were expressed openly and freely. The faith and the hope of fifty peaceful nations were laid before this world forum. Differences were overcome. This Charter was not the work of any single nation or group of nations, large or small. It was the result of a spirit of give-and-take, of tolerance for the views and interests of others.

It was proof that nations, like men, can state their differences, can face them, and then can find common ground on which to stand. That is the essence of democracy; that is the essence of keeping the peace in the future. By your agreement, the way was shown toward future agreement in the years to come.

This Conference owes its success largely to the fact that you have kept your minds firmly on the main objective. You had the single job of writing a constitution—a charter for peace. And you stayed on that job.

In spite of the many distractions which came to you in the form of daily problems and disputes about such matters as new boundaries, control of Germany, peace settlements, reparations, war criminals, the form of government of some of the European countries—in spite of all these, you continued in the task of framing this document.

Those problems and scores of others, which will arise, are all difficult. They are complicated. They are controversial and dangerous.

But with united spirit we met and solved even more difficult problems during the war. And with the same spirit, if we keep to our principles and never forsake our objectives, the problems we now face and those to come will also be solved.

We have tested the principle of cooperation in this war and have found that it works. Through the pooling of resources, through joint and combined military command, through constant staff meetings, we have shown what united strength can do in war. That united strength forced Germany to surrender. United strength will force Japan to surrender.

The United Nations have also had experience, even while the fighting was still going on, in reaching economic agreements for times of peace. What was done on the subject of relief at Atlantic City, food at Hot Springs, finance at Bretton Woods, aviation at Chicago, was a fair test of what can be done by nations determined to live cooperatively in a world where they cannot live peacefully any other way.

What you have accomplished in San Francisco shows how well these lessons of military and economic cooperation have been learned. You have created a great instrument for peace and security and human progress in the world.

The world must now use it!

If we fail to use it, we shall betray all those who have died in order that we might meet here in freedom and safety to create it.

If we seek to use it selfishly—for the advantage of any one nation or any small group of nations—we shall be equally guilty of that betrayal.

The successful use of this instrument will require the united will and firm determination of the free peoples who have created it. The job will tax the moral strength and fibre of us all.

We all have to recognize—no matter how great our strength—that we must deny ourselves the license to do always as we please. No one nation, no regional group, can or should expect, any special privilege which harms any other nation. If any nation would keep security for itself, it must be ready and willing to share security with all. That is the price which each nation will have to pay for world peace. Unless we are all willing to pay that price, no organization for world peace can accomplish its purpose.

And what a reasonable price that is!

Out of this conflict have come powerful military nations, now fully trained and equipped for war. But they have no right to dominate the world. It is rather the duty of these powerful nations to assume the responsibility for leadership toward a world of peace. That is why we have here resolved that power and strength shall be used not to wage war, but to keep the world at peace, and free from the fear of war.

By their own example the strong nations of the world should lead the way to international justice. That principle of justice is the foundation stone of this Charter. That principle is the guiding spirit by which it must be carried out—not by words alone but by continued concrete acts of good will.

There is a time for making plans—and there is a time for action. The time for action is now! Let us, therefore, each in his own nation and according to its own way, seek immediate approval of this Charter—and make it a living thing.

I shall send this Charter to the United States Senate at once. I am sure that the overwhelming sentiment of the people of my country and of their representatives in the Senate is in favor of immediate ratification.

A just and lasting peace cannot be attained by diplomatic agreement alone, or by military cooperation alone. Experience has shown how deeply the seeds of war are planted by economic rivalry and by social injustice. The Charter recognizes this fact for it has provided for economic and social cooperation as well. It has provided for this cooperation as part of the very heart of the entire compact.

It has set up machinery of international cooperation which men and nations of good will can use to help correct economic and social causes for conflict.

Artificial and uneconomic trade barriers should be removed—to the end that the standard of living of as many people as possible throughout the world may be raised. For Freedom from Want is one of the basic Four Freedoms toward which we all strive. The large and powerful nations of the world must assume leadership in this economic field as in all others.

Under this document we have good reason to expect the framing of an international bill of rights, acceptable to all the nations involved. That bill of rights will be as much a part of international life as our own Bill of Rights is a part of our Constitution. The Charter is dedicated to the achievement and observance of human rights and fundamental freedoms. Unless we can attain those objectives for all men and women everywhere—without regard to race, language or religion—we cannot have permanent peace and security.

With this charter the world can begin to look forward to the time when all worthy human beings may be permitted to live decently as free people.

The world has learned again that nations, like individuals, must know the truth if they would be free—must read and hear the truth, learn and teach the truth.

We must set up an effective agency for constant and thorough interchange of thought and ideas. For there lies the road to a better and more tolerant understanding among nations and among peoples.

All Fascism did not die with Mussolini. Hitler is finished—but the seeds spread by his disordered mind have firm root in too many fanatical brains. It is easier to remove tyrants and destroy concentration camps than it is to kill the ideas which gave them birth and strength. Victory on the battlefield was essential, but it was not enough. For a good peace, a lasting peace, the decent peoples of the earth must remain determined to strike down the evil spirit which has hung over the world for the last decade.

The forces of reaction and tyranny all over the world will try to keep the United Nations from remaining united. Even while the military machine of the Axis was being destroyed in Europe—even down to its very end—they still tried to divide us.

They failed. But they will try again.

They are trying even now. To divide and conquer was—and still is—their plan. They still try to make one Ally suspect the other, hate the other, desert the other.

But I know I speak for every one of you when I say that the United Nations will remain united. They will not be divided by propaganda either before the Japanese surrender—or after.

This occasion shows again the continunity of history.

By this Charter, you have given reality to the ideal of that great statesman of a generation ago—Woodrow Wilson.

By this Charter, you have moved toward the goal for which that gallant leader in this second world struggle worked and fought and gave his life—Franklin D. Roosevelt.

By this Charter, you have realized the objectives of many men of vision in your own countries who have devoted their lives to the cause of world organization for peace.

Upon all of us, in all our countries, is now laid the duty of transforming into action these words which you have written. Upon our decisive action rests the hope of those who have fallen, those now living, those yet unborn—the hope for a world of free countries—with decent standards of living—which will work and cooperate in a friendly civilized community of nations.

This new structure of peace is rising upon strong foundations.

Let us not fail to grasp this supreme chance to establish a world-wide rule of reason— to create an enduring peace under the guidance of God.

21   Senator Connally appeals to the past in opening the debate on whether or not the United States Senate should ratify the United Nations Charter: July 23, 1945. *'Can you not see upon the walls the marks here in the [Senate] Chamber where the League of Nations was done to death?'*

In the course of his introductory remarks at the opening of the Senate ratification debate of the United Nations Charter on July 23, 1945, Senator Tom Connally (the author of the Connally Resolution discussed in Chapter I) reiterated a number of themes that had come to dominate Congressional and public opinion attitudes towards external affairs since Pearl Harbor. Noting the participation of the United States in World Wars I and II, despite the many efforts of the country to abstain from them, taking account of the national blood and treasure in prosecuting these conflicts, and focussing on the impossibility of remaining aloof from such involvement in a technologically-shrinking world in the twentieth century, Connally persuasively alluded both to the mistakes of the past and the responsibilities of the future. In his concluding remarks, appealing to his fellow Senators to make America the first nation to ratify the Charter as an example to the world, Connally called on the ghost of Wilson's League of Nations to drive home the necessity of the Senate's obligation to atone for its past sins. 'Can you not still see', he said, 'the blood on the floor? Can you not see upon the walls the marks of the conflict that raged here in the Chamber where the League of Nations was done to death?' Connally need not have worried about the outcome. For, according to Robert A. Divine's *Second Chance* (1967): 'By June of 1945 the internationalists had created such overwhelming public support that Senate approval of the United Nations Charter was a certainty.'

Source: *Congressional Record*, 79th Congress.

. . . in conclusion, permit me to say that ever since World War I there has been among the people of the United States and, I think, among the people of the world a feeling, growing over the years, that the statesmen of the world were challenged and that civilization was being challenged by our failure to erect some kind of international machinery for the cooperation of the peoples of the earth who do not want war, to bring about situations which would at least minimize the danger of war and advance the cause of peace.

We all know that the United States did not want to become involved in the First World War or in the present World War. We did not want to send our sons to foreign territory, there to be sacrificed upon the bloody altars of war. We did not want to pour out our treasure in destructive activities. However, we did just that. We were drawn into the First World War. During the Second World War we were ruthlessly and treacheorously attacked at Pearl Harbor, and the allies of Japan, namely Hitler, Mussolini, and others, declared war upon the United States before we drew the sword.

So, Mr. President, in this modern time when the tides of war are running high, it is almost impossible for the United States to keep itself out of involvement. We know the price which we are now paying. That price consists of more than a million casualties, some of them bearing on their bodies the marks of their courage all the way to the tomb. We have suffered more than a million casualties of the finest young manhood of this Republic. Billions upon billions of dollars of treasure have been poured out in order to advance the cause of the war. There will be repercussions of a postwar character which will perhaps dislocate our economic life, and disrupt a return to civilian life of the soldiers and sailors who have fought so gallantly. That is a stupendous price to pay for war. We want no more of it. Therefore, the growing sentiment against war has resulted in the United States in the proposal of measures of various kinds. I refer to the resolution of the Foreign Relations Committee, the Fulbright resolution adopted by the House, the Dumbarton Oaks Conference, and recently, the charter which was agreed to at San Francisco, and which is now before the Senate.

Mr. President, I may advise Senators that the Foreign Relations Committee arranged for the printing and publication of the hearings, and undertook each morning to place in the office of each Senator copies of the hearing which were held on the day previous. There is also available to the Senate the very exhaustive report of the former Secretary of State to the President of the United States, consisting of approximately 150 pages. In addition to copies of the extensive hearings, the report of the committee itself is available. The testimony of Mr. Stettinius, which covered the entire charter, is available. I commend to Senators the testimony of Dr. Leo Pasvolsky who followed Mr. Stettinius in testifying at the hearings. Dr. Pasvolsky is a technician of great ability and a man of long experience. He went over the charter at the hearings chapter by chapter, paragraph by paragraph, and answered every question which was propounded to him, and explained every phase and aspect of the Charter.

Mr. President, the longings to which I have referred for an organization for world peace have brought about the Charter which was agreed to at San Francisco. We advance it not as a magical instrument which will guarantee that there shall be no more wars. We realize that any instrumentality will have its imperfections and weaknesses. This charter is not an absolute guaranty that there shall never be another war. However, Mr. President, it is an advance over the ground where we now stand. It is an approach. It brings into contact the nations of the world. It brings them into contact in the General Assembly where they may freely discuss international questions, and do so with no restrictions being placed upon them. More than that, in the Security Council the great nations of the earth are brought into contact with each other, such as nations who today possess military and material resources, armies and navies, and air forces which are capable of making war, and are therefore capable of keeping peace. The Security Council brings together great nations who, by appending their signatures to the Charter, made solemn pledges with each other to settle their disputes by peaceful means, to support the Charter, and to undertake to bring their influences and resources to the execution of the policies and doctrines of the charter. Mr. President, if the charter does no more than to assemble in solemn conferences the representatives of the 50 nations who will make up the assembly, and the representatives of those same nations in the Security Council, to discuss and express their views respecting international questions which are fraught with the danger of war, it represents a great advance of the forces of peace out yonder into the territory of darkness and danger in which we have groped in the past.

But it does more than that, Mr. President. It establishes agencies for the settlement of disputes. It establishes a World Court to which may be referred justiciable questions. It sets up an assembly where matters may be freely discussed by the humblest, smallest, and weakest nation, as well as by the mightiest nation. It will be one place where the equality of all nations will be recognized.

The Charter also establishes a Security Council. It places upon the Security Council and the great nations which possess powerful military, naval and material resources, the primary obligation of preserving the peace. It is so written in the bond. It is denominated in the charter that the primary responsibility for preserving the peace of the world rests upon the Security Council. When a dispute is submitted to the Security Council it may be discussed, considered freely, and debated. If the Security Council takes jurisdiction of the matter, there are set forth in the Charter a number of steps which may be taken to bring about a settlement of the dispute. First, in order to preserve peace, and in order to bring about peaceful settlements, the Security Council suggests to the disputants, "Submit your case, Settle it between yourselves if you can do so. If you cannot settle it by diplomatic action, try arbitration or negotiation, and endeavor to adjust your dispute by peaceful means. If you cannot adjust your differences by peaceful means, the Security Council will have to adopt its own program." That program, Mr. President, may be a suggestion to the parties as to how the dispute should be settled. It would be merely a suggestion, however. There would be no exercise of compulsion. There is no jurisdiction or authority in the Security Council to compel the disputants to accept the formula which may be submitted. If all these measures fail, and as a result thereof violence is threatened, the Security Council may, as a last resort, and as a final effort to preserve peace, employ armed forces to prevent aggressions and preserve the peace.

Mr. President, I regard this document as a great instrument in the history of the world, a great instrument in the field of international relations. To my mind it is the greatest document of its kind that has ever been formulated. It is far superior to the League of Nations. The League of Nations did much good. The League of Nations, even through its failures and its weaknesses helped light the way to future international negotiations and to the construction of this Charter itself. The League of Nations carried the matter of agreement further than the pending Charter. Under the League there had to be unanimity of agreement as to every member of the Council, and when they agreed, while the League could persuade and could beg, it had no compulsive powers whatever; it could not enforce a peace; it could not prevent armed aggression; it had no authority and no power in those respects.

So, Mr. President, we do not advance this instrument as embodying perfection. I dare say that ingenious Senators can take any statute that we pass here and find many things in it they do not like and which, if they were writing it, they would change. So I venture to say that if now the rewriting of this entire Charter were committed to individual Senators, when they got through, instead of having 1 charter, we would have 95 charters, and, if there were not a vacancy in the Senate, we would have 96 charters. Somewhere along the line every Senator would deviate from his colleagues, perhaps not on fundamental principles, but when it came to details there would be disagreement. So we have got to accept this Charter on the over-all picture, on its entirety.

Think about the 50 nations that met at San Francisco, many of which had divergent views. Many of them did not like certain things in the Charter, but they tried to look ahead, they tried to look down the vista of the years, they tried to envision what the future would hold, and finally they came to say, "Regardless of our objections to the voting procedure and to the Security Council, regardless of our views about the Assembly, we think the Charter is the best hope for peace and world security, and we will vote to ratify it."

Mr. President, you would have been stirred, I am sure, had you been on the steering committee representing all 50 of the nations, when the roll was called and every nation responded "yea." It was a historic event, it was a stirring event, when the vote was recorded and it was announced that 50 nations had recorded their views that the Charter ought to be ratified.

Mr President, do not misunderstand me. Those who expect an automatic piece of machinery which it is necessary only to set up and then they can go ahead about their business and it will preserve the peace and stop war, will not have their expectations met by this Charter. This Charter is going to require the constant support and assistance of those who love peace, the nations who love peace and the peoples who love peace, if it is to be successful and if it is to achieve the high objectives for which it is designed.

Those who want to join a league that is magic, that requires no care, that requires no fuel, that requires no sacrifice on our part, that requires the sending of no troops by us if it comes to that point, are doomed to disappointment. There is no such league; there never has been such a league, and there never will be such a league. There has got to be constant cooperation of the nations of the earth in support of the spirit as well as the letter of the Charter and the high purposes which it envisions.

Mr. President, these are the general principles upon which we base our appeal for the ratification of this charter. Let me say in closing that ratification of the Charter by the Senate may well give a tremendous impulse to its ratification by the other nations of the earth. It will mean that we shall be the first of the great powers to ratify the treaty. Strange as it may seem, in view of the practical unanimity of the people of the United States in support of the Charter, many representatives of foreign nations are still doubtful as to what the vote on the charter will be here in the Senate. They remember 1919. They know how the League of Nations was slaughtered here on the floor. Can you not still see the blood on the floor? Can you not see upon the walls the marks of the conflict that raged here in the Chamber where the League of Nations was done to death? They fear that that same sentiment may keep the United States from ratifying this Charter. Our ratification of it will instill hope into the hearts of the peoples of the earth. We heard it constantly at San Francisco. Not publicly in debate but privately delegates would approach us and inquire what we thought about the prospects of the ratification of the charter. So I trust that the Senate, after such debate as it sees fit to indulge upon the subject, will ratify this Charter by a vote so overwhelming as to carry the conviction over the earth that the United States expects to assume its obligations for the purpose of keeping them, for the purpose of living up to them, for the purpose of supporting a world organization for peace with all our spirit and with all our hearts.

Mr. President, we have not been afraid to go to war. We have had the courage to fight on the battlefields. Shall we lack the courage now to assume the responsibility of this organization? Shall we be afraid that we cannot do our part? Shall we say, "Oh, no; we cannot do that; the United States must not send a soldier, its representative must not vote on any question unless it comes back here to the Senate." Can we not have the same courage and fortitude with which we faced the enemy upon the battlefield in behalf of war, in behalf of destruction, in behalf of the taking of human life? Can we not show some of that same courage in the cause of peace and accept the obligations which we assume and fulfill them and live up to them and make a contribution to the history of civilization and to the cause of peace that has never been rivaled in all the centuries that have rolled over the head of Mother Earth.

Mr. President, I hope we may ratify this Charter by a vote that will resound round the earth. Yonder at Concord Bridge was fired the shot heard round the world. The verse of Ralph Waldo Emerson in the Concord Hymn comes to mind:

> By the rude bridge that arched the flood,
> Their flag to April's breeze unfurled,
> Here once the embattled farmers stood,
> And fired the shot heard round the world.

Mr. President, by this vote let us fire a shot in behalf of peace that will be heard round the world. [Applause.]

22   Senator Wheeler urges caution: July 24, 1945. *'Can it be that this [United States Charter] fatuous marriage of idealism with a neo-realism based on pure and unadulterated might and violence which our propaganda peddlers have sold to the American people is not the cause for the pathological state of mind that holds this country in its grip?'*

Although he ultimately voted in favor of Senate ratification of the Charter (in his words, 'in the faint hope that it will do some good',), Senator Burton Wheeler delivered a scathing and in many ways effective critique of United States participation in the United Nations. Wheeler contended that with Europe in ruins and the threat of totalitarianism everywhere rampant, America ran the risk of corrupting its own ideals and liberties by associating itself with the hegemonial policy of Stalin's Russia, which in any case threatened to fill 'the gaping emptiness that yawns like a deep abyss ... from the Ukraine to Bordeau, and from the Scandinavian Peninsula to the Mediterranean.' Wheeler's idealistically-inspired realist critique of the internationalists' position, together with the cautionary tone of Connally's remarks in the preceding reading, suggest the basic idealism of the realists as well as, conversely, the basic realism of the idealists, a theme that has in large measure been overlooked by students of the period who have at times tended to be heavily engaged in scoring points. The Senate voted overwhelmingly in favor of the Charter by a vote 89 to 2 on July 28, 1945; and the world was given notice that America intended to play its part.

Source: ibid.

. . . Sir Edward Grey warned the world just before the First World War broke out, "The lights are going out all over Euorpe, and we shall not see them relighted again in our time."

Even now, 31 years later, the problems of peace following on the heels of a Second World War, loom momentarily against an ever-darkening sky. Of one thing we can be certain, namely, the problems we faced following the last war were child's play compared to the chaos with which we are now confronted. We can be certain that while our statesmen breathe an air of confident expectancy or of casual tolerance toward the future, the terrible truth of the matter is they are whistling in the dark. At this very moment fear grips the hearts and minds of all men who honestly face the magnitude and complexity of the consequences of this war, which already threatens to overwhelm us.

The chaos in Europe is tragic beyond description. The threat of a rampant totalitarian tyranny everywhere raises its ugly head. The resurgence of a brutal and fanatical fascism lurks in every flooded cellar, behind every shattered tree, and beneath every ugly ruin in Europe. An almost inevitable triumph of disease, starvation, and frustration already challenges the sanity of men. Yet in spite of these horrible conditions, tragic as they are, my greatest fear for the future is that the light of reason is being extinguished here at home.

Mr. President, I never believed I should live to see the time when Americans— to say nothing of foreign countries and foreign people—would not be able or willing to sit down and reason together. Yet today any man who dares to speak his deepest convictions, even in what he conceives to be the highest service of his country, not only does not get a hearing, but he is reviled and smeared, his intentions publicly slandered and his reputation broken on a twisted rack of interventionist lies.

The fact that he is only pleading for a hearing for the priceless lessons of the past, the fact that he is attempting to champion America's traditional principles and the basic liberties and rights and dignity of human character, serves only to intensify the viciousness and the bitterness of his attackers.

Mr. President, in February 1941 I stood on the floor of the Senate and pleaded in vain against the deliberate involvement of America in the ancient feuds and the endless cycle of crises of the Old World, which the passage of the Lend-Lease Act would guarantee. I was only following the dictates of my conscience in a complete consistency of action. It was not politically an expedient thing to do. All the propaganda was in favor of it. I had bitterly opposed every step which this country was compelled to take against its will by the executive branch of this Government down the tortuous trail to war. From the "Quarantine" speech of 1937 on, I warned this country that each one of the administration's manufactured inevitabilites was taking us to war. The repeal of the Neutrality Act, the cash-and-carry provisions, the destroyer-bases deal, the Selective Service Act in peacetime, the convoys-to-Britain slogan, and then lend-lease—each, I charged, mean only one thing, namely, involvement in a catastrophic war, the end of which no man could see.

At that time I warned the American people.

We stand today at the crossroads. So far as it is given ordinary mortals the power to see, both roads which stretch ahead of us are fraught with danger. There is no sure road to safety. But if we take one road—the road for which this bill before us is a signpost—what lies ahead is clearly obvious. Down that road lies involvement in Europe's wars, eventual commitments to help bring order out of chaos in all the world, the shouldering of a back-breaking debt for all our people, possibly, if not probably, death in some foreign land for the flower of our young men, the end of democracy and civil liberties certainly not only for the duration but perhaps for generations.

And today, Mr. President, the America in which I live is no longer afraid of totalitarian tyranny. It openly embraces what President Roosevelt declared to be a dictatorship as absolute as any in the world. We gaze fondly upon it and proudly arrogate to ourselves the right to join such select company.

Mr. President, all I have to say to the American people is that if, as our contemporary wolf pack of propagandists is attempting to prove by its yapping, the simple statement of historical facts and American principles and ideals is divisive, destructive, or subversive to American interests, then America as a nation of free peoples is already blindly groping toward her doom. . . .

By the provisions of this Charter the people of all eastern Europe are denied the principles and the rights embodied in the Atlantic Charter. And as between the victor powers, there is not a single international convention, covenant, or principle in common among them to which the people of eastern or central Europe can appeal, or by which any decision, agreement, or compromise among the Big Three must be bound.

Mr. President, at this point I desire to state again what I said on the Senate floor on February 28, 1941:

> I despise totalitarianism and all that it symbolizes. I hate Hitler and Hitlerism, Mussolini and fascism, Stalin and communism. I abhor intolerance or bigotry whether it be predicated upon color, race, or religion. I oppose and denounce political control by a financial oligarchy whether it be the Thyssens and Krupps in Germany or international bankers in the United States. I believe fervently in civil liberties—and I would do more than render mere lip service for freedom of assemblage, freedom of religious worship, freedom of the press, and all our other precious civil rights. Mr. President, I speak of these things because I love them, because they are America—and because I sincerely believe that we are about to lose them all.

Mr. President, I speak of these things because they are American and because I sincerely believe that we are about to lose them. I have not changed my mind one iota as so many of my colleagues now seem to have done. I hate totalitarian tyranny, brutal violence, and despotism of every kind, shape, degree, and description. What I have said about Germany is just a simple statement of fact which bodes ill for the future. It may be a kind of poetic justice that Germans should today be sitting in the rubble and ruin of the destructive fury of war. It is poetic justice that they should now fear the imposition of the institution and techniques of slave labor which they helped to extend throughout Europe. But I am not thinking of the effect upon the Germans, but what it will do to put our stamp of approval upon human slavery and savagery in Europe even if it be upon those who themselves have practiced it. Certainly the fact that we ourselves fought a terrible civil war in order to set the colored race free ought to shock us into a realization of the consequences which would follow on our legalizing the reinstitution of slavery over the white race. America can no more stoop to the brutal and savage practices of tyranny and get away with it than Hitler or Tojo or Mussolini. For there is one certain lesson which both history and psychology teach; that the practice of brutality brutalizes.

Mr. President, I want earnestly to emphasize with all the strength at my command that the facts I am discussing and the inevitable consequences of the present trend in power politics which I am predicting are based on concrete historical evidence. The facts which I am pointing out are not the ranting reveries of an obstructionist, an isolationist, or of a perfectionist. These facts form the basic substance of the realism to which the charter's proponents attribute its genius, if I understand them correctly. Furthermore, what I am about to say concerns facts the recognition of which may mean a matter of life or death for the whole of cultured and christianized humanity.

Mr. President, the outcome of this war has left a gaping vacuum in the heart of

Europe. We have won an overwhelming military victory, but it is a victory which has left in its wake the destruction of every political, economic, social, and geographical structure in Europe. Where thirty-odd independent nations once stood, there is not a single stable government left. The realism of this fact to which I am referring is found in the simple observation that of all these social, economic, military, political, and geographical systems, the only stable government left is Russia. It is stable only because of the tremendous military and police power of the state.

Thus, the question at the very outset is how Russia can help but be sucked into this maelstrom of madness when such a terribly complete vacuum keeps tugging at Stalin's shirt sleeves. How can Russia keep from being drawn into the gaping emptiness that yawns like a deep abyss before her every step from the Ukraine to Bordeaux, and from the Scandinavian Peninsula to the Mediterranean?

Mr. President, a year ago last May when I talked with one of the very high ranking officers of this country, I asked him, "How are you going to keep Europe from going Communist?" He replied that he did not believe Stalin wanted to take over Europe. I said, "It is not a question of Stalin taking over Europe. It is a question of whether or not Europe will fall into his lap."

Today every student of European history, and every person who has visited Europe believes and feels that that is one of the things which may take place in the near future.

Mr. President, if we are to be honest with ourselves, and with the facts of history, we confront not only this physical circumstance, we also confront the fact of Russia's attack on Finland, her annexation of Latvia, Estonia, and Lithuania, her treacherous attack on Poland, and the long series of unilateral acts from the Baltics to the Balkans, which have followed on the turn of the battle at Stalingrad, which have continued right through all the solemn deliberations of the Dumbarton Oaks Conference, and which now have been carried on right into the social propaganda and diplomatic attacks on Sweden, Turkey, and Switzerland.

It is a matter of record that even while all these solemn deliberations have been going on at San Francisco, Russia has been determined to make political hay while a non-Anglo-American-military-intervention sun was shining ...

There are however, two startling differences between the years 1918 and 1945. In 1918 the problems we confronted were largely confined to Europe and they were settled on the base of an attempt to free the peoples of Europe from the threat and scourge of famine, war, and chaos, by guaranteeing the political and territorial integrity of some twenty-odd seperate states. At least the concept of individuality was preserved even in the artificial and arbitrary division of territory, minorities, and resources of Europe that comprised the Versailles settlements.

But in the year 1945 the problems we confront have not only been magnified a thousand times; they now extend to Africa and Asia. The settlement of these problems is not being left this time, however, to individual states, but to the division of the world into three tremendous spheres, one of which is determined that these problems and the destiny of hundreds of millions of human beings shall be left to the mercy of an ever-expanding collective state and totalitarian political tyranny. Does anyone challenge that statement?

Mr. President, I want at this point earnestly to assert that I am speaking out of my deep concern for the future. The fate of my native land and the principles of democracy, of a constitutional representative republic, and all the glorious traditions and liberties with which this native land of mine has been blessed are all at stake.

I believe in President Truman and have confidence in his determination to steer our ship of state through the stormy seas ahead as best he knows how. What I have to say further is moved only by my concern to strengthen his hand and to shoulder my own responsibility for salvaging America from the tragic consequences of war-provoking policies and commitments and acts which I have wholeheartedly and bitterly opposed. We confront a new responsibility as a Nation. We in America, together with all the other peoples on earth, as distinguished from the rulers of some countries, are determined that so far as lies within our power, war shall not again lay its heavy curse upon us. But, Mr. President, we must deal with the trying problems which now tax the combined resources of the human mind and heart by rising to the challenge of the unprecedented future we confront. If by some great tragedy of misguided fervor we should in our haste perpetuate the very policies and practices which have brought this war upon us, not even the Almighty could save us from ourselves. Ours is the challenge of a broken and despairing humanity to find some heroically intelligent and creative solution to the threat of a third world war which is already rooted and growing in conflict between western civilization and the Communist totalitarian tyranny in the East.

What I am saying is that a failure on our part to meet this challenge will boomerang against everything we still hold sacred. If we are to participate in this proposed new world organization as a convert to power politics, with all its attendant evils of imperialistic expansion and militarism, we shall sign our own death warrant as a Nation when this charter is ratified unless, Mr. President, we go in determined that certain principles shall be enunciated by the five great powers, or the three great powers. I say "the three great powers," because every one recognizes the fact that only three great powers are going to determine what this organization is to do . . .

The trouble with so many idealistic Americans is that they judge all the other countries on the face of the earth by the same high ideals and principles which we have here in the United States. They do not realize that the people of many of the countries in Europe and Asia do not even know what democracy means, because they have never understood it. They have been ruled by an iron hand. Democracy means, one thing to a Chinaman or a Russian, and it means quite a different thing to the people of the United States.

What other power on earth is going to sacrifice itself to guarantee the strengthening and perpetuation of our way of life if not America?

Mr. President, what I am saying is simply this: This charter expresses the maximum of agreement possible among the great victor powers in this war. I assume that to be correct. It has been heralded across the world as the great beginning of a new and warless world. It is, we have been told, a seed which must be watered and nourished that a great tree of peace and security may some day shelter the international hens and lambs together beneath its shade.

But, Mr. President, the facts which I have herein documented point to another and wholly different conclusion. If this is the beginning of genuine international cooperation and good faith, it is also the end. Does any sane man in his right mind think that the horror that has been loosed upon a suffering and broken humanity has furthered the possibility of peace and security—or the guarantee of the "four freedoms"? Does anyone imagine that the chaos, famine, disease, immorality, suffering, and the stinking desert of conflict that has been made of Europe and that is fast being spread over the Orient, is fertile ground in which the roots of democracy can flourish? Are the proponents of this Charter attempting to tell the American people that the catastrophic consequences of this most hideous struggle of all time are conducive to the development of stable governments and societies in which the lessons of the past are so integrated into the social, legal, and diplomatic structure of nations that we may look now toward reliance upon a new reign of law and not to a reversion to trust in brute force? Any man who holds out such an ethereal dream as a prospective reality to the Americal people is simply deluding himself.

Can it be possible that America has not yet learned her lesson? Can it be that this fatuous marriage of idealism with a neo-realism based on pure and unadulterated might and violence which our propaganda peddlers have sold to the American people is not the cause for the present pathological state of mind that holds this country in its grip? Are we such fools that we are pointing to the outcome of this war as a gracious and unprecedented blessing to American hopes and dreams, to American security and to American society in the years ahead?

CHAPTER FIVE

Enter The Bomb:
Origins of 'Atomic Diplomacy'

23   President Truman's statement announcing the use of the atomic
bomb at Hiroshima: August 6, 1945. *'Sixteen hours ago an
American airplane dropped one bomb on Hiroshima . . .'*

The dropping of the American atomic bombs on Hiroshima and Nagasaki in early
August 1945 not only hastened the Japanese decision to surrender but also
accelerated the American-Soviet rivalry that had originated over the composition of
Poland's postwar government. For, adumbrating New Left criticism of 'atomic
diplomacy' by almost twenty years, British physicist P.M.S. Blackett concluded that
'the dropping of the atomic bomb was not so much the last military act of the Second
World War, as the first act of the cold diplomatic war with Russia in progress.'
American historians have generally held two views on the subject. Traditional
historians such as Herbert Feis held that, despite the regrettable misery visited on
the Japanese people, the primary aim of the atomic bomb was to shock the
Japanese Government into submission and thereby obviate the necessity of an
American invasion of the home islands, an invasion which was calculated to cost
one million American casualties. And in this sense Feis and others corroborated
President Truman's contention that he 'regarded the bomb as a military weapon and
never had any doubt that it should be used.' In contrast, critics of the traditional
interpretation, led by Gar Alperovitz, argued that the decision to employ the atomic
bomb in Japan did not derive solely from military considerations to defeat the
already beaten Japanese, but rather derived from the majority judgment of
Truman's advisers that 'a combat demonstration was needed to convince the
Russians to accept the American plan for a stable peace.' This interpretation lends
itself more readily to the Russian position, which according to the first volume of the
projected official twelve-volume work titled *History of the Second World War, 1939-
1945* (1973), suggested that the United States bombing of Hiroshima and Nagasaki
was a 'criminal act aimed at threatening the peoples of the globe—above all the

Soviet Union.' President Truman's statement below was the first official announcement of that fateful August day in Hiroshima.

Source: *Presidential Papers: Harry S. Truman, 1945*, I, 197-200.

Sixteen hours ago an American airplane dropped one bomb on Hiroshima, an important Japanese Army base. That bomb had more power than 20,000 tons of T.N.T. It had more than two thousand times the blast power of the British "Grand Slam" which is the largest bomb ever yet used in the history of warfare.

The Japanese began the war from the air at Pearl Harbor. They have been repaid many fold. And the end is not yet. With this bomb we have now added a new and revolutionary increase in destruction to supplement the growing power of our armed forces. In their present form these bombs are now in production and even more powerful forms are in development.

It is an atomic bomb. It is a harnessing of the basic power of the universe. The force from which the sun draws its power has been loosed against those who brought war to the Far East.

Before 1939, it was the accepted belief of scientists that it was theoretically possible to release atomic energy. But no one knew any practical method of doing it. By 1942, however, we knew that the Germans were working feverishly to find a way to add atomic energy to the other engines of war with which they hoped to enslave the world. But they failed. We may be grateful to Providence that the Germans got the V-1's and V-2's late and in limited quantities and even more grateful that they did not get the atomic bomb at all.

The battle of the laboratories held fateful risks for us as well as the battles of the air, land and sea, and we have now won the battle of the laboratories as we have won the other battles.

Beginning in 1940, before Pearl Harbor, scientific knowledge useful in war was pooled between the United States and Great Britain, and many priceless helps to our victories have come from that arrangement. Under that general policy the research on the atomic bomb was begun. With American and British scientists working together we entered the race of discovery against the Germans.

The United States had available the large number of scientists of distinction in the many needed areas of knowledge. It had the tremendous industrial and financial resources necessary for the project and they could be devoted to it without undue impairment of other vital war work. In the United States the laboratory work and the production plants, on which a substantial start had already been made, would be out of reach of enemy bombing, while at that time Britain was exposed to constant air attack and was still threatened with the possibility of invasion. For these reasons Prime Minister Churchill and President Roosevelt agreed that it was wise to carry on the project here. We now have two great plants and many lesser works devoted to the production of atomic power. Employment during peak construction numbered 125,000 and over 65,000 individuals are even now engaged in operating the plants. Many have worked there for two and a half years. Few know what they have been producing. They see great quantities of material going in and they see nothing coming out of these plants, for the physical size of the explosive charge is exceedingly small. We have spent two billion dollars on the greatest scientific gamble in history—and won.

But the greatest marvel is not the size of the enterprise, its secrecy, nor its cost, but the achievement of scientific brains in putting together infinitely complex pieces of knowledge held by many men in different fields of science into a workable plan. And hardly less marvelous has been the capacity of industry to design, and of labor to operate, the machines and methods to do things never done before so that the brain child of many minds came forth in physical shape and performed as it was supposed to do. Both science and industry worked under the direction of the United States Army, which achieved a unique success in managing so diverse a problem in the advancement of knowledge in an amazingly short time. It is doubtful if such another combination could be got together in the world. What has been done is the greatest achievement of organized science in history. It was done under high pressure and without failure.

We are now prepared to obliterate more rapidly and completely every productive enterprise the Japanese have above ground in any city. We shall destroy their docks, their factories, and their communications. Let there be no mistake; we shall completely destroy Japan's power to make war.

It was to spare the Japanese people from utter destruction that the ultimatum of July 26 was issued at Potsdam. Their leaders promptly rejected that ultimatum. If they do not now accept our terms they may expect a rain of ruin from the air, the like of which has never been seen on this earth. Behind this air attack will follow sea and land forces in such numbers and power as they have not yet seen and with the fighting skill of which they are already well aware.

The Secretary of War, who has kept in personal touch with all phases of the project, will immediately make public a statement giving further details.

His statement will give facts concerning the sites at Oak Ridge near Knoxville, Tennessee, and at Richland near Pasco, Washington, and an installation near Santa Fe, New Mexico. Although the workers at the sites have been making materials to be used in producing the greatest destructive force in history they have not themselves been in danger beyond that of many other occupations. for the utmost care has been taken of their safety.

The fact that we can release atomic energy ushers in a new era in man's understanding of nature's forces. Atomic energy may in the future supplement the power that now comes from coal, oil, and falling water, but at present it cannot be produced on a basis to compete with them commercially. Before that comes there must be a long period of intensive research.

It has never been the habit of the scientists of this country or the policy of this Government to withhold from the world scientific knowledge. Normally, therefore, everything about the work with atomic energy would be made public.

But under present circumstances it is not intended to divulge the technical processes of production or all the military applications, pending further examination of possible methods of protecting us and the rest of the world from the danger of sudden destruction.

I shall recommend that the Congress of the United States consider promptly the establishment of an appropriate commission to control the production and use of atomic power within the United States. I shall give further consideration and make further recommendations to the Congress as to how atomic power can become a powerful and forceful influence towards the maintenance of world peace.

NOTE: This statement was released in Washington. It was drafted before the President left Germany, and Secretary of War Stimson was authorized to release it when the bomb was delivered. On August 6, while returning from the Potsdam Conference aboard the U.S.S. *Augusta*, the President was handed a message from Secretary Stimson informing him that the bomb had been dropped at 7:15 p.m. on August 5.

24   President Truman's special message to Congress on atomic energy: October 3, 1945. *'Never in history has society been confronted with a power so full of potential danger and at the same time so full of promise for the future of man and for the peace of the World.'*

The introduction of atomic weaponry into the American arsenal together with the implied peacetime use of the atom posed a number of serious problems for the Truman administration. Fully recognizing the revolutionary nature of harnessing atomic energy, though perhaps underestimating the relative ability of other nations to translate its theoretical knowledge into practical application, President Truman approached his task from the domestic and international level. At the domestic level he requested Congress to enact legislation aimed at the creation of an Atomic Energy Commission 'for the control, use and development of atomic energy within the United States.' At the international level the President sought to initiate a dialogue first with Great Britain and Canada and then other powers 'in an effort to effect agreement on the conditions under which cooperation might replace rivalry in the field of atomic power.'

Source: ibid, 362-66.

Almost two months have passed since the atomic bomb was used against Japan. That bomb did not win the war, but it certainly shortened the war. We know that it saved the lives of untold thousands of American and Allied soldiers who would otherwise have been killed in battle.

The discovery of the means of releasing atomic energy began a new era in the history of civilization. The scientific and industrial knowledge on which this discovery rests does not relate merely to another weapon. It may some day prove to be more revolutionary in the development of human society than the invention of the wheel, the use of metals, or the steam or internal combustion engine.

Never in history has society been confronted with a power so full of potential danger and at the same time so full of promise for the future of man and for the peace of the world. I think I can express the faith of the American people when I say that we can use the knowledge we have won, not for the devastation of war, but for the future welfare of humanity.

To accomplish that objective we must proceed along two fronts— the domestic and the international.

The first and most urgent step is the determination of our domestic policy for the control, use and development of atomic energy within the United States.

We cannot postpone decisions in this field. The enormous investment which we made to produce the bomb has given us the two vast industrial plants in Washington and Tennessee, and the many associated works throughout the country. It has brought together a vast organization of scientists, executives, industrial engineers and skilled workers—a national asset of inestimable value.

The powers which the Congress wisely gave to the Government to wage war were adequate to permit the creation and development of this enterprise as a war project. Now that our enemies have surrendered, we should take immediate action to provide for the future use of this huge investment in brains and plant. I am informed that many of the people on whom depend the continued successful operation of the plants and the further development of atomic knowledge, are getting ready to return to their normal pursuits. In many cases these people are considering leaving the project largely because of uncertainty concerning future national policy in this field. Prompt action to establish national policy will go a long way towards keeping a strong organization intact.

It is equally necessary to direct future research and to establish control of the basic raw materials essential to the development of this power whether it is to be used for purposes of peace or war. Atomic force in ignorant or evil hands could inflict untold disaster upon the nation and the world. Society cannot hope even to protect itself—much less to realize the benefits of the discovery—unless prompt action is taken to guard against the hazards of misuse.

I therefore urge, as a first measure in a program of utilizing our knowledge for the benefit of society, that the Congress enact legislation to fix a policy with respect to our existing plants, and to control all sources of atomic energy and all activities connected with its development and use in the United States.

The legislation should give jurisdiction for these purposes to an Atomic Energy Commission with members appointed by the President with the advice and consent of the Senate.

The Congress should lay down the basic principles for all the activities of the Commission, the objectives of which should be the promotion of the national welfare, securing the national defense, safeguarding world peace and the acquisition of further knowledge concerning atomic energy

The people of the United States know that the overwhelming power we have developed in this war is due in large measure to American science and American industry, consisting of management and labor. We believe that our science and industry owe their strength to the spirit of free inquiry and the spirit of free enterprise that characterize our country. The Commission, therefore, in carrying out its functions should interfere as little as possible with private research and private enterprise, and should use as much as possible existing institutions and agencies. The observance of this policy is our best guarantee of maintaining the pre-eminence in science and industry upon which our national well-being depends.

All land and mineral deposits owned by the United States which constitute sources of atomic energy, and all stock piles of materials from which such energy may be derived, and all plants or other property of the United States connected with its development and use should be transferred to the supervision and control of the Commission.

The Commission should be authorized to acquire at a fair price, by purchase or by condemnation, any minerals or other materials from which the sources of atomic energy can be derived, and also any land containing such minerals or materials, which are not already owned by the United States.

The power to purchase should include real and personal property outside the limits of the United States.

The Commission should also be authorized to conduct all necessary research, experimentation, and operations for the further development and use of atomic energy for military, industrial, scientific, or medical purposes. In these activities it should, of course, use existing private and public institutions and agencies to the fullest practicable extent.

Under appropriate safeguards, the Commission should also be permitted to license any property available to the Commission for research, development and exploitation in the field of atomic energy. Among other things such licensing should be conditioned of course upon a policy of widespread distribution of peacetime products on equitable terms which will prevent monopoly.

In order to establish effective control and security, it should be declared unlawful to produce or use the substances comprising the sources of atomic energy or to import or export them except under conditions prescribed by the Commission.

Finally, the Commission should be authorized to establish security regulations governing the handling of all information, material and equipment under its jurisdiction. Suitable penalties should be prescribed for violating the security regulations of the Commission or any of the other terms of the Act.

The measures which I have suggested may seem drastic and far-reaching. But the discovery with which we are dealing involves forces of nature too dangerous to fit into any of our usual concepts.

The other phase of the problem is the question of the international control and development of this newly discovered energy.

In international relations as in domestic affairs, the release of atomic energy constitutes a new force too revolutionary to consider in the framework of old ideas. We can no longer rely on the slow progress of time to develop a program of control among nations. Civilization demands that we shall reach at the earliest possible date a satisfactory arrangement for the control of this discovery in order that it may become a powerful and forceful influence towards the maintenance of world peace instead of an instrument of destruction.

Scientific opinion appears to be practically unanimous that the essential theoretical knowledge upon which the discovery is based is already widely known. There is also substantial agreement that foreign research can come abreast of our present theoretical knowledge in time.

The hope of civilization lies in international arrangements looking, if possible, to the renunciation of the use and development of the atomic bomb, and directing and encouraging the use of atomic energy and all future scientific information toward peaceful and humanitarian ends. The difficulties in working out such arrangements are great. The alternative to overcoming these difficulties, however, may be a desperate armament race which might well end in disaster. Discussion of the international problem cannot be safely delayed until the United Nations Organization is functioning and in a position adequately to deal with it.

I therefore propose to initiate discussions, first with our associates in this discovery, Great Britain and Canada, and then with other nations, in an effort to effect agreement on the conditions under which cooperation might replace rivalry in the field of atomic power.

I desire to emphasize that these discussions will not be concerned with disclosures relating to the manufacturing processes leading to the production of the atomic bomb itself. They will constitute an effort to work out arrangements covering the terms under which international collaboration and exchange of scientific information might safely proceed.

The outcome of the discussions will be reported to the Congress as soon as possible, and any resulting agreements requiring Congressional action will be submitted to the Congress.

But regardless of the course of discussions in the international field, I believe it is essential that legislation along the lines I have indicated be adopted as promptly as possible to insure the necessary research in, and development and control of, the production and use of atomic energy.

25   The Soviet reaction—through British eyes: December 3, 1945. *'Then plump came the Atomic Bomb.'*

One of the most thoughtful analyses of the character of the Soviet reaction to the American monopoly of atomic weapons is contained in a memorandum originally prepared by the British Ambassador at Moscow, Clark Kerr, for the British Secretary of State for Foreign Affairs. It was written shortly after the United States, Great Britain and Canada had agreed in November 1945 not to share information regarding the practical application of atomic energy before devising effective safeguards (Washington statement reference). Ambassador Kerr dwelled on the Soviet leadership's search for security since the time of the Bolshevik Revolution: civil war, foreign intervention, internal purges and the invasion of Nazi Germany all reinforced Russian fears; later, the exaltation that came after the defeat of Hitler could hardly be enjoyed before the long-sought security was once again shattered—this time by the West's acquisition of the atomic bomb and its apparent determination to monopolize it. Kerr perceived that in these circumstances Anglo-American leaders should not expect much cooperation with Soviet Russia in the United Nations on the matter without first attempting to repair the damage that presumably resulted from the West's early failure to share its atomic data. Revisionist critics such as Martin J. Sherwin and Barton J. Bernstein have elaborated on this theme and argued that because of the failure to take Stalin into its confidence, the West had only itself to blame for the atomic arms race that grew out of Cold War conditions.

Source: Department of State, *Foreign Relations of the United States, Diplomatic Papers: 1945* (Wash. 1967), 82-84. (The above copy was transmitted to the Department under cover of a note from the British Chargé (Balfour), dated December 6, which stated that this document was forwarded at the suggestion of Mr. Bevin, who felt it might be of interest to Mr. Byrnes in view of the forthcoming meeting in Moscow.)

1.   Perhaps it might be useful if I were to try to describe present state of mind in Moscow as we see it here, towards the Atomic Bomb in general which may well govern the Russians' approach to the question and misshape their judgment.

2.   For this purpose I should probably reach back a longish way in order to draw in a little of the psychological background of the people upon whose minds the bomb exploded last August. For years they have been toiling after something like security for their country, their system and their own bodies. Nearly all of those who now govern Russia and mould opinion have led hunted lives since their early manhood when they were chased from pillar to post by the Tsarist police. Then came the immense and dangerous gamble of the Revolution followed by the perils and the ups and downs of intervention and civil war. Independence and even ostracism may have brought some passing relief to their country but not to the survival of their system or to their bodies whose safety remained as precarious as ever. Witness the prolonged and internecine struggle that came after the death of Lenin and the years of the purges when their system was wobbling and no one of them knew today whether he would be alive tomorrow. Admission to the League of Nations which synchronised with the turning of the economic corner may have given some slight respite. But this was fugitive and it may be said that through all these years they trembled for the safety of their country and their system as they trembled for their own. Meanwhile, they worked feverishly and by means of a kind of terror till they dragooned an idle and slipshod people without regard for its suffering into building up a machine that might promise the kind of security they rightly felt they needed. The German invasion caught them still unready and swept them to what looked like the brink of defeat. Then came the turn of the tide and with it first the hope and then a growing belief that the immense benison of national security was at last within their reach. As the Red Army moved westwards belief became confidence and the final defeat of Germany made confidence conviction.

3.   There was a great exaltation. Russia could be made safe at last. She could put her house in order and more than this from behind her matchless three hundred divisions she could stretch out her hand and take most of what she needed and perhaps more. It was an exquisite moment, all the more so because this resounding success under their guidance justified at last their faith in the permanence of their system.

4.   I have reviewed all this in order to recall to you the uncommon, and at times almost unbearable, tension that has strained these people's lives (it explains perhaps some of their abnormalities): and has hung over the whole history of the movement they have led, and in order also to suggest the measure of relief that must have come to them with the end of Nazism it would be hard to over-estimate.

5.   Then plump came the Atomic Bomb. At a blow the balance which had now seemed set and steady was rudely shaken. Russia was balked by the west when everything seemed to be within her grasp. The three hundred divisions were shorn of much of their value. About all this the Kremlin was silent but such was the common talk of the people. But their disappointment was tempered by the belief inspired by such echoes of foreign press as were allowed to reach them that their Western comrades in

arms would surely share the bomb with them. That some such expectation as this was shared by the Kremlin became evident in due course. But as time went on and no move came from the West, disappointment turned into irritation and, when the bomb seemed to them to become an instrument of policy, into spleen. It was clear that the West did not trust them. This seemed to justify and it quickened all their old suspicions. It was a humiliation also and the thought of this stirred up memories of the past. We may assume that all these emotions were fully shared by the Kremlin. (Molotov's speech of the 6th of November and the disturbing absence of any reply to the advance notice of Washington statement).

6.   If my interpretation of the state of mind of the Russians is anything like right we may I think expect them to approach the proposal to discuss Atomic Energy in the first instance in the open forum of the General Assembly with all the prickliness of which they are capable.

7.   We cannot indeed rule out the possibility of a refusal to discuss it at all. It seems to me therefore that if we are to secure the Russians' cooperation we must go about things in a different way. I mean that before the Assembly gathers we and the Americans must have preliminary and private talks with Molotov who though unlikely in any circumstances to be willing to sponsor the Washington statements, might then be persuaded to treat the whole matter with goodwill and reason. It would not be enough to approach him through the diplomatic channel.

26   Bernard M. Baruch's proposals for an Atomic Development Authority: June 14, 1946. '. . . the matter of punishment lies at the very heart of our present security system.'

In an address delivered at the opening session of the United Nations Atomic Energy Commission, held in New York on June 14, 1945, United States representative Bernard M. Baruch outlined a program of atomic energy controls that immediately became known as the 'Baruch Plan'. The Baruch Plan was relatively easy for the general public to grasp. Baruch approached the subject from what has often been referred to as the legalistic-moralistic level of international problem solving, which postulated the indivisibility of peace and the necessity of punishing the lawbreaker. He proposed the creation of an International Atomic Development Authority whose duty it would be to oversee all phases of the development and uses of atomic energy. The key to the successful operation of such an agency would be its effectiveness in controlling and inspecting atomic energy activities—for then, and only then, would the United States be prepared both to cease the manufacture of atomic bombs and dispose of its stockpile. Needless to say, such a proposal, which seems to the modern reader naive in the extreme, would have little appeal to the traditionally xenophobic Soviets.

Source: Department of State, *Bulletin*, XIV (June 23, 1946), 1057-62.

We are here to make a choice between the quick and the dead.

That is our business.

Behind the black portent of the new atomic age lies a hope which, seized upon with faith, can work our salvation. If we fail, then we have damned every man to be the slave of Fear. Let us not deceive ourselves: We must elect World Peace or World Destruction.

Science has torn from nature a secret so vast in its potentialities that our minds cower from the terror it creates. Yet terror is not enough to inhibit the use of the atomic bomb. The terror created by weapons has never stopped man from employing them. For each new weapon a defense has been produced, in time. But now we face a condition in which adequate defense does not exist.

Science, which gave use this dread power, shows that it *can* be made a giant help to humanity, but science does *not* show us how to prevent its baleful use. So we have been appointed to obviate that peril by finding a meeting of the minds and the hearts of our peoples. Only in the will of mankind lies the answer.

It is to express this will and make it effective that we have been assembled. We must provide the mechanism to assure that atomic energy is used for peaceful purposes and preclude its use in war. To that end, we must provide immediate, swift, and sure punishment of those who violate the agreements that are reached by the nations. Penalization is essential if peace is to be more than a feverish interlude between wars. And, too, the United Nations can prescribe individual responsibility and punishment on the principles applied at Nürnberg by the Union of Soviet Socialist Republics, the United Kingdom, France, and the United States—a formula certain to benefit the world's future.

In this crisis, we represent not only our governments but, in a larger way, we represent the peoples of the world. We must remember that the peoples do not belong to the governments but that the governments belong to the peoples. We must answer their demands; we must answer the world's longing for peace and security.

In that desire the United States shares ardently and hopefully. The search of science for the absolute weapon has reached fruition in this country. But she stands ready to proscribe and destroy this instrument—to lift its use from death to life—if the world will join in a pact to that end.

In our success lies the promise of a new life, freed from the heart-stopping fears that now beset the world. The beginning of victory for the great ideals for which millions have bled and died lies in building a workable plan. Now we approach fulfilment of the aspirations of mankind. At the end of the road lies the fairer, better, surer life we crave and mean to have.

Only by a lasting peace are liberties and democracies strengthened and deepened. War is their enemy. And it will not do to believe that any of us can escape war's devastation. Victor, vanquished, and neutrals alike are affected physically, economically, and morally.

Against the degradation of war we can erect a safeguard. That is the guerdon for which we reach. Within the scope of the formula we outline here there will be found, to those who seek it, the essential elements of our purpose. Others will see only emptiness.

Each of us carries his own mirror in which is reflected hope—or determined desperation—courage or cowardice.

There is a famine throughout the world today. It starves men's bodies. But there is a greater famine—the hunger of men's spirit. That starvation can be cured by the conquest of fear, and the substitution of hope, from which springs faith—faith in each other, faith that we want to work together tóward salvation, and determination that those who threaten the peace and safety shall be punished.

The peoples of these democracies gathered here have a particular concern with our answer, for their peoples hate war. They will have a heavy exaction to make of those who fail to provide an escape. They are not afraid of an internationalism that protects; they are unwilling to be fobbed off by mouthings about narrow sovereignty, which is today's phrase for yesterday's isolation.

The basis of a sound foreign policy, in this new age, for all the nations here gathered, is that anything that happens, no matter where or how, which menaces the peace of the world, or the economic stability, concerns each and all of us.

That, roughly, may be said to be the central theme of the United Nations. It is with that thought we begin consideration of the most important subject that can engage mankind—life itself.

Let there be no quibbling about the duty and the responsibility of this group and of the governments we represent. I was moved, in the afternoon of my life, to add my effort to gain the world's quest, by the broad mandate under which we were created. The resolution of the General Assembly, passed January 24, 1946 in London, reads:

"Section V. Terms of Reference of the Commission

"The Commission shall proceed with the utmost despatch and enquire into all phases of the problems, and make such recommendations from time to time with respect to them as it finds possible. In particular the Commission shall make specific proposals:

"(*a*) For extending between all nations the exchange of basic scientific information for peaceful ends;

"(*b*) For control of atomic energy to the extent necessary to ensure its use only for peaceful purposes;

"(*c*) For the elimination from national armaments of atomic weapons and of all other major weapons adaptable to mass destruction;

"(*d*) For effective safeguards by way of inspection and other means to protect complying States against the hazards of violations and evasions.

"The work of the Commission should proceed by separate stages, the successful completion of each of which will develop the necessary confidence of the world before the next stage is undertaken . . . ."

Our mandate rests, in text and in spirit, upon the outcome of the Conference in Moscow of Messrs. Molotov of the Union of Soviet Socialist Republics, Bevin of the United Kingdom, and Byrnes of the United States of America. The three Foreign Ministers on December 27, 1945 proposed the establishment of this body.

Their action was animated by a preceding conference in Washington on November 15, 1945, when the President of the United States, associated with Mr. Attlee, Prime

Minister of the United Kingdom, and Mr. Mackenzie King, Prime Minister of Canada, stated that international control of the whole field of atomic energy was immediately essential. They proposed the formation of this body. In examining that source, the Agreed Declaration, it will be found that the fathers of the concept recognized the final means of world salvation—the abolition of war. Solemnly they wrote:

"We are aware that the only complete protection for the civilized world from the destructive use of scientific knowledge lies in the prevention of war. No system of safeguards that can be devised will of itself provide an effective guarantee against production of atomic weapons by a nation bent on aggression. Nor can we ignore the possibility of the development of other weapons, or of new methods of warfare, which may constitute as great a threat to civilization as the military use of atomic energy."

Through the historical approach I have outlined, we find ourselves here to test if man can produce, through his will and faith, the miracle of peace, just as he has, through science and skill, the miracle of the atom.

The United States proposes the creation of an International Atomic Development Authority, to which should be entrusted all phases of the development and use of atomic energy, starting with the raw material and including—

1. Managerial control or ownership of all atomic-energy activities potentially dangerous to world security.

2. Power to control, inspect, and license all other atomic activities.

3. The duty of fostering the beneficial uses of atomic energy.

4. Research and development responsibilities of an affirmative character intended to put the Authority in the forefront of atomic knowledge and thus to enable it to comprehend, and therefor to detect, misuse of atomic energy. To be effective, the Authority must itself be the world's leader in the field of atomic knowledge and development and thus supplement its legal authority with the great power inherent in possession of leadership in knowledge.

I offer this as a basis for beginning our discussion.

But I think the peoples we serve would not believe—and without faith nothing counts—that a treaty, merely outlawing possession or use of the atomic bomb, constitutes effective fulfilment of the instructions to this Commission. Previous failures have been recorded in trying the method of simple renunciation, unsupported by effective guaranties of security and armament limitation. No one would have faith in that approach alone.

Now, if ever, is the time to act for the common good. Public opinion supports a world movement toward security. If I read the signs aright, the peoples want a program not composed merely of pious thoughts but of enforceable sanctions—an international law with teeth in it.

We of this nation, desirous of helping to bring peace to the world and realizing the heavy obligations upon us arising from our possession of the means of producing the bomb and from the fact that it is part of our armament, are prepared to make our full contribution toward effective control of atomic energy.

When an adequate system for control of atomic energy, including the renunciation of the bomb as a weapon, has been agreed upon and put into effective operation and condign punishments set up for violations of the rules of control which are to be stigmatized as international crimes, we propose that—

1. Manufacture of atomic bombs shall stop;
2. Existing bombs shall be disposed of pursuant to the terms of the treaty; and
3. The Authority shall be in possession of full information as to the know-how for the production of atomic energy.

Let me repeat, so as to avoid misunderstanding: My country is ready to make its full contribution toward the end we seek, subject of course to our constitutional processes and to an adequate system of control becoming fully effective, as we finally work it out.

Now as to violations: In the agreement, penalties of as serious a nature as the nations may wish and as immediate and certain in their execution as possible should be fixed for—

1. Illegal possession or use of an atomic bomb;
2. Illegal possession, or separation, of atomic material suitable for use in an atomic bomb;
3. Seizure of any plant or other property belonging to or licensed by the Authority;
4. Wilful interference with the activities of the Authority;
5. Creation or operation of dangerous projects in a manner contrary to, or in the absence of, a license granted by the international control body.

It would be a deception, to which I am unwilling to lend myself, were I not to say to you and to our peoples that the matter of punishment lies at the very heart of our present security system. It might as well be admitted, here and now, that the subject goes straight to the veto power contained in the Charter of the United Nations so far as it relates to the field of atomic energy. The Charter permits penalization only by concurrence of each of the five great powers—the Union of Soviet Socialist Republics, the United Kingdom, China, France, and the United States.

I want to make very plain that I am concerned here with the veto power only as it affects this particular problem. There must be no veto to protect those who violate their solemn agreements not to develop or use atomic energy for destructive purposes.

The bomb does not wait upon debate. To delay may be to die. The time between violation and preventive action or punishment would be all too short for extended discussion as to the course to be followed.

As matters now stand several years may be necessary for another country to produce a bomb, *de novo*. However, once the basic information is generally known, and the Authority has established producing plants for peaceful purposes in the several countries, an illegal seizure of such a plant might permit a malevolent nation to produce a bomb in 12 months, and if preceded by secret preparation and necessary facilities perhaps even in a much shorter time. The time required—the advance warning given of the possible use of a bomb—can only be generally estimated but obviously will depend upon many factors, including the success with which the Authority has been able to introduce elements of safety in the design of its plants and the degree to which illegal and. secret preparation for the military use of atomic energy will have been eliminated. Presumably no nation would think of starting a war with only one bomb.

This shows how imperative speed is in detecting and penalizing violations.

The process of prevention and penalization—a problem of profound statecraft—is, as I read it, implicit in the Moscow statement, signed by the Union of Soviet Socialist Republics, the United States, and the United Kingdom a few months ago.

But before a country is ready to relinquish any winning weapons it must have more than words to reassure it. It must have a guarantee of safety, not only against the offenders in the atomic area but against the illegal users of other weapons—bacteriological, biological, gas—perhaps—why not?—against war itself.

In the elimination of war lies our solution, for only then will nations cease to compete with one another in the production and use of dread "secret" weapons which are evaluated solely by their capacity to kill. This devilish program takes us back not merely to the Dark Ages but from cosmos to chaos. If we succeed in finding a suitable way to control atomic weapons, it is reasonable to hope that we may also preclude the use of other weapons adaptable to mass destruction. When a man learns to say "A" he can, if he chooses, learn the rest of the alphabet too.

Let this be anchored in our minds:

Peace is never long preserved by weight of metal or by an armament race. Peace can be made tranquil and secure only by understanding and agreement fortified by sanctions. We must embrace international cooperation or international disintegration.

Science has taught us how to put the atom to work. But to make it work for good instead of for evil lies in the domain dealing with the principles of human duty. We are now facing a problem more of ethics than of physics.

The solution will require apparent sacrifice in pride and in postion, but better pain as the price of peace than death as the price of war.

I now submit the following measures as representing the fundamental features of a plan which would give effect to certain of the conclusions which I have epitomized.

1. **General.** The Authority should set up a thorough plan for control of the field of atomic energy, through various forms of ownership, dominion, licenses, operation, inspection, research, and management by competent personnel. After this is provided for, there should be as little interference as may be with the economic plans and the present private, corporate, and state relationships in the several countries involved.

2. **Raw Materials.** The Authority should have as one of its earliest purposes to obtain and maintain complete and accurate information on world supplies of uranium and thorium and to bring them under its dominion. The precise pattern of control for various types of deposits of such materials will have to depend upon the geological, mining, refining, and economic facts involved in different situations.

The Authority should conduct continuous surveys so that it will have the most complete knowledge of the world geology of uranium and thorium. Only after all current information on world sources of uranium and thorium is known to us all can equitable plans be made for their production, refining, and distribution.

3. **Primary Production Plants.** The Authority should exercise complete managerial control of the production of fissionable materials. This means that it should control and operate all plants producing fissionable materials in dangerous quantities and must own and control the product of these plants.

4. **Atomic Explosives.** The authority should be given sole and exclusive right to conduct research in the field of atomic explosives. Research activities in the field of atomic explosives are essential in order that the Authority may keep in the forefront of knowledge in the field of atomic energy and fulfil the objective of preventing illicit manufacture of bombs. Only by maintaining its position as the best-informed agency will the Authority be able to determine the line between intrinsically dangerous and non-dangerous activities.

5. **Strategic Distribution of Activities and Materials.** The activities entrusted exclusively to the Authority because they are intrinsically dangerous to security should be distributed throughout the world. Similarly, stockpiles of raw materials and fissionable materials should not be centralized.

6. **Non-Dangerous Activities.** A function of the Authority should be promotion of the peacetime benefits of atomic energy.

Atomic research (except in explosives), the use of research reactors, the production of radio-active tracers by means of non-dangerous reactors, the use of such tracers, and to some extent the production of power should be open to nations and their citizens under reasonable licensing arrangements from the Authority. Denatured materials, whose use we know also requires suitable safeguards, should be furnished for such purposes by the Authority under lease or other arrangement. Denaturing seems to have been overestimated by the public as a safety measure.

7. **Definition of Dangerous and Non-Dangerous Activities.** Although a reasonable dividing line can be drawn between dangerous and non-dangerous activities, it is not hard and fast. Provision should, therefore, be made to assure constant reexamination of the questions and to permit revision of the dividing line as changing conditions and new discoveries may require.

8. **Operations of Dangerous Activities.** Any plant dealing with uranium or thorium after it once reaches the potential of dangerous use must be not only subject to the most rigorous and competent inspection by the Authority, but its actual operation shall be under the management, supervision, and control of the authority.

9. **Inspection.** By assigning intrinsically dangerous activities exclusively to the Authority, the difficulties of inspection are reduced. If the Authority is the only agency which may lawfully conduct dangerous activities, then visible operation by others than the Authority will constitute an unambiguous danger signal. Inspection will also occur in connection with the licensing functions of the Authority.

10. **Freedom of Access.** Adequate ingress and egress for all qualified representatives of the Authority must be assured. Many of the inspection activities of the Authority should grow out of, and be incidental to, its other functions. Important measures of inspection will be associated with the tight control of raw materials, for this is a keystone of the plan. The continuing activities of prospecting, survey, and research in relation to raw materials will be designed not only to serve the affirmative development functions of the Authority but also to assure that no surreptitious operations are conducted in the raw-materials field by nations or their citizens.

11. **Personnel.** The personnel of the Authority should be recruited on a basis of proven competence but also so far as possible on an international basis.

12. **Progress by Stages.** A primary step in the creation of the system of control is the

setting forth, in comprehensive terms, of the functions, responsibilities, powers, and limitations of the Authority. Once a charter for the Authority has been adopted, the Authority and the system of control for which it will be responsible will require time to become fully organized and effective. The plan of control will, therefore, have to come into effect in successive stages. These should be specifically fixed in the charter or means should be otherwise set forth in the charter for transitions from one stage to another, as contemplated in the resolution of the United Nations Assembly which created this Commission.

13. **Disclosures.** In the deliberations of the United Nations Commission on Atomic Energy, the United States is prepared to make available the information essential to a reasonable understanding of the proposals which it advocates. Further disclosures must be dependent, in the interests of all, upon the effective ratification of the treaty. When the Authority is actually created, the United States will join the other nations in making available the further information essential to that organization for the performance of its functions. As the successive stages of international control are reached, the United States will be prepared to yield, to the extent required by each stage, national control of activities in this field to the Authority.

14. **International Control.** There will be questions about the extent of control to be allowed to national bodies, when the Authority is established. Purely national authorities for control and development of atomic energy should to the extent necessary for the effective operation of the Authority be subordinate to it. This is neither an endorsement nor a disapproval of the creation of national authorities. The Commission should evolve a clear demarcation of the scope of duties and responsibilities of such national authorities.

And now I end. I have submitted an outline for present discussion. Our consideration will be broadened by the criticism of the United States proposals and by the plans of the other nations, which, it is to be hoped, will be submitted at their early convenience. I and my associates of the United States Delegation will make available to each member of this body books and pamphlets, including the Acheson-Lilienthal report, recently made by the United States Department of State, and the McMahon Committee Monograph No. 1 entitled "Essential Information on Atomic Energy" relating to the McMahon bill recently passed by the United States Senate, which may prove of value in assessing the situation.

All of us are consecrated to making an end of gloom and hopelessness. It will not be an easy job. The way is long and thorny, but supremely worth traveling. All of us want to stand erect, with our faces to the sun, instead of being forced to burrow into the earth, like rats.

The pattern of salvation must be worked out by all for all.

The light at the end of the tunnel is dim, but our path seems to grow brighter as we actually begin our journey. We cannot yet light the way to the end. However, we hope the suggestions of my Government will be illuminating.

Let us keep in mind the exhortation of Abraham Lincoln, whose words, uttered at a moment of shattering national peril, form a complete text for our deliberation. I quote, paraphrasing slightly:

"We cannot escape history. We of this meeting will be remembered in spite of ourselves. No personal significance or insignificance can spare one or another of us. The fiery trial through which we are passing will light us down in honor or dishonor to the latest generation.

"We say we are for Peace. The world will not forget that we say this. We know how to save Peace. The world knows that we do. We, even we here, hold the power and have the responsibility.

"We shall nobly save, or meanly lose, the last, best hope of earth. The way is plain, peaceful, generous, just—a way which, if followed, the world will forever applaud."

My thanks for your attention.

27   Address by Soviet representative Gromyko to the United Nations Atomic. Energy Commission: June 19, 1946. ' . . . to continue the use of this discovery for the production of [atomic] weapons of mass destruction is likely to intensify mistrust between States and to keep the peoples of the world in a continual anxiety and uncertainty.'

The Russian response to the Baruch Plan came five days later in an address delivered by Soviet representative Gromyko. Sidestepping the American position of first initiating safeguards and erecting an adequate control system as a prerequisite to discussing the disposition of current stocks, Gromyko called for an international convention aimed at the immediate prohibition, production and destruction of atomic weapons. Like the Baruch Plan, the Gromyko Plan was easy to grasp. What was not so easy to grasp, at least from the negotiative point of view, was the mutual incompatibility of the essential points of both plans, each in its own way reflecting the basic needs and requirements of the foreign policies of their respective societies.

Source: Department of State, *Documents on Disarmament, 1945-1956* (Wash. 1960), 17-24.

The Atomic Energy Commission created in accordance with the resolution of the Moscow Conference of the Foreign Ministers of the Three Powers and with the resolution of the first session of the General Assembly, must proceed to the practical realization of the tasks set before it. The significance of these tasks and, consequently, of the activities of the Commission, is determined by the importance of the very discovery of methods of using atomic energy, which led to the creation of this Commission. Scientific efforts have produced a result, the significance of which is hard to appraise. That which is already known regarding the significance of this discovery and which, undoubtedly, is merely the preliminary to still greater conquests of science in this field in the future, emphasizes how important are the tasks and activities of the Commission.

As the result of the definite course of events during the last few years the circumstances were combined in such a way that one of the greatest discoveries of mankind found its first material application in the form of a particular weapon—the atomic bomb. However, although up to the present time this use of atomic energy is the only known form of its practical application, it is the general opinion that humanity stands at the threshold of a wide application of atomic energy for peaceful purposes for the benefit of the peoples, for promoting their welfare and raising their standard of living and for the development of science and culture.

There are thus two possible ways in which this discovery can be used. One way is to use it for the purpose of producing the means of mass destruction. The other way is to use it for the benefit of mankind.

The paradox of the situation lies in the fact that it is the first way that has been more studied and more effectively mastered in practice. The second way has been less studied and effectively mastered in practice. However, this circumstance not only does not diminish the importance of the tasks that lie before the Atomic Commission but, on the contrary, emphasizes to an even greater degree the significance of these tasks for all that concerns the strengthening of peace between the nations.

There can be no active and effective system of peace if the discovery of the means of using atomic energy is not placed in the service of humanity and is not applied to peaceful purposes only. The use of this discovery only for the purpose of promoting the welfare of the peoples and widening their scientific and cultural horizons will help to strengthen confidence between the countries and friendly relations between them.

On the other hand, to continue the use of this discovery for the production of weapons of mass destruction is likely to intensify mistrust between States and to keep the peoples of the world in a continual anxiety and uncertainty. Such a position is contrary to the aspirations of the peace-loving peoples, who long for the establishment of enduring peace and are making every effort in order that these aspirations may be transformed into reality.

As one of the primary measures for the fulfilment of the resolution of the General Assembly of 24 January 1946, the Soviet delegation proposes that consideration be given to the question of concluding an international convention prohibiting the production and employment of weapons based on the use of atomic energy for the purpose of mass destruction. The object of such a convention should be the prohibition of the production and employment of atomic weapons, the destruction of existing stocks of atomic weapons and the condemnation of all activities undertaken in violation of this convention. The elaboration and conclusion of a convention of this kind would be, in the opinion of the Soviet delegation, only one of the primary measures to be taken to prevent the use of atomic energy to the detriment of mankind. This act should be followed by other measures aiming at the establishment of methods to ensure the strict observance of the terms and obligations contained in the above-mentioned convention, the establishment of a system of control over the observance of the convention and the taking of decisions regarding the sanctions to be applied against the unlawful use of atomic energy. The public opinion of the whole civilized world has already rightly condemned the use in warfare of asphyxiating, poisonous and other similar gases, as well as all similar liquids and substances, and likewise bacteriological means, by concluding corresponding agreements for the prohibition of their use.

In view of this, the necessity of concluding a convention prohibiting the production and employment of atomic weapons is even more obvious. Such a convention would correspond in an even greater degree to the aspirations of the peoples of the whole world.

The conclusion of such a convention and the elaboration of a system of measures providing for the strict fulfilment of its terms, the establishment of control over the observance of the obligations imposed by the convention, and the establishment of sanctions to be applied against violators of the convention will, in the opinion of the Soviet delegation, be a serious step forward on the way towards the fulfilment of the tasks that lie before the Atomic Energy Commission, and fully corresponds to the aspirations and conscience of the whole of progressive humanity.

The necessity for the States to assume the obligation not to produce or employ atomic weapons is also dictated by the fact that the character of this weapon is such, that its employment brings untold misery above all to the peaceful population. The results of its employment are incompatible with the generally accepted standards and ideas riveted in the consciousness of humanity in the course of many centuries to the effect that the rules of warfare must not allow the extermination of innocent civilian populations.

The situation existing at the present time, which has been brought about by the discovery of the means of applying atomic energy and using them for the production of atomic weapons, precludes the possibility of normal scientific co-operation between the States of the world. At the very basis of the present situation, which is characterized by the absence of any limitation in regard to the production and employment of atomic weapons, there are reasons which can only increase the suspicion of some countries in regard to others and give rise to political instability. It is clear that the continuation of such a situation is likely to bring only negative results in regard to peace.

Moreover, the continuation of the present situation means that the latest scientific attainments in this field will not be a basis for joint scientific efforts among the countries for the object of discovering ways of using atomic energy for peaceful purposes. Hence there follows only one correct conclusion, namely, the necessity of an exchange of scientific information between countries and the necessity of joint scientific efforts directed toward a broadening of the possibilities of the use of atomic energy only in the interests of promoting the material welfare of the peoples and developing science and culture. The success of the work of the Commission will be determined in a large measure by the extent to which it succeeds in solving this important task.

The proposal for a wide exchange of scientific information is timely because such a scientific discovery, as the discovery of methods of using atomic energy, cannot remain for an indefinite time the property of only one country or small group of countries. It is bound to become the property of a number of countries. This confirms the necessity of a wide exchange of scientific information on the problem in question, and the necessity of drawing up corresponding measures in this field, including measures of organization. . . .

28   Molotov on 'Atomic Diplomacy'—a Soviet Perception: October 29, 1946. *'And now, as we know, there is already talk of "atomic diplomacy" as well.'*

The fundamental issues that separated the Baruch Plan and the Gromyko Plan, as seen from the Soviet perspective, were clearly drawn by Soviet Foreign Minister Molotov in a speech before the UN General Assembly in late December 1946. After observing that 'there is already talk of "atomic diplomacy" ', Molotov maintained that the Baruch Plan was little more than a thinly-veiled cover, in his words, 'to secure for the United States of America the monopolistic possession of the atomic bomb'. Such a desire, continued Molotov, based itself on the illusion that the secret of atomic weaponry—or more precisely the practical application of atomic energy to the means of warfare—could be held indefinitely, a proposition Soviet leaders refused to accept. The only alternative to an arms race, then, lay in adopting Russia's counterproposal of immediately prohibiting the production and use of atomic weapons. Rebuffed at this time, the Soviet Union, which in any case had for several years been working on the problem of atomic arms, exploded its first atomic device in 1949. And with this particular challenge to the American monopoly there then appeared the prospect that the Cold War rivalry between the United States and the Soviet Union, together with their respective allies, could turn very hot.

Source: United Nations, *Plenary Meetings of the General Assembly: October 23-December 16, 1946* (Flushing Meadows, N.Y., 1946), 841-45.

. . . We know that there are quite a number of ways in which the stronger Powers can bring pressure to bear on other States. We know that squadrons of warships and military aeroplanes sometimes appear on seas and in the sky where they had not been before, when this is considered necessary in order to achieve greater success in diplomatic negotiations. We also know that dollars and pounds sterling do not always stay at home, especially when it is necessary to set "dollar diplomacy" to work, if only, let us say, for the purpose of securing due respect for "dollar democracy". And now, as we know, there is already talk of "atomic diplomacy" as well.

It is an open secret that these and other means, in various combinations, are not infrequently resorted to for the purpose of influencing other countries, and the small ones in particular. But there are people and whole influential groups who are not content with all this; for them, it would be worth while to remove all barriers, including the liquidation of the principle of unanimity of the great Powers within the United Nations, thus paving the way for the operations of those persons and groups who will not content themselves with anything less than the submission of all peoples to their dictate and to their money bags!

To counteract such insatiable appetites and strivings for world domination is the most important task of the United Nations. Only when it has proved, in fact, its ability to act in this direction will the United Nations be able to give the necessary reply to the question whether we are following the right path.

In this connexion it is necessary to dwell on the question of the atomic bomb, which now plays such an important part in the political calculations of certain circles.

Only recently, Joseph Stalin, the head of the Soviet Government, clarified, in a convincing manner, the views of the Soviet Union on this subject. He particularly emphasized that the atomic bomb "cannot decide the outcome of war since atomic bombs are by no means sufficient for this purpose", and he said also that, if one is to speak of threats to peace, "certainly monopolistic possession of the secret of the atomic bomb does create a threat" against which "at least two remedies exist: (a)   Monopolistic possession of the atomic bomb cannot last long, and (b)   The use of the atomic bomb will be prohibited". There should be a due appreciation of these authoritative statements, which echoed throughout of the world and met with a sympathetic response in the hearts of many millions of people.

As we know, there are two different plans regarding the use of atomic energy. I have in mind the plan of the United States of America, on the one hand, and the plan of the Soviet Union, on the other.

The United States plan, the so-called "Baruch plan," unfortunately suffers from a certain amount of egoism. It proceeds from the desire to secure for the United States of America the monopolistic possession of the atomic bomb. At the same time, it calls for the earliest possible establishment of control over the production of atomic energy in all countries, giving to this control an international character in outward appearance, but in fact attempting to protect, in a veiled form, the monopolistic position of the United States in this field. It is obvious that projects of this kind are unacceptable, since they are based on a narrow conception of the interests of one country and on the inadmissible negation of the equal rights of States and of their legitimate interests.

This plan, moreover, suffers from certain illusions.

Even in the field of atomic energy, the monopolistic position of any single country should not be counted on. Science and scientists cannot be shut up in a box and kept under lock and key. It is time that illusions on this score were discarded. The expectations that the atomic bomb will have a decisive effect in time of war are likewise illusions.

It is common knowledge that the atomic bomb was used against such towns as Nagasaki and Hiroshima. The populations of these Japanese towns experienced the cruel effect of the atomic bomb. But the atomic bomb has not yet been used anywhere for action against troops. And this is not fortuitous. If, however, there are plans to use atomic bombs against the civilian population of towns and, moreover, to use them on a large scale, as certain newspapers babble, one should not foster any illusions with regard to the international effect which would result from the carrying out of atrocious plans of this kind. Justified indignation would sweep over honest people in all countries, and the sanguine hopes regarding the decisive importance of the atomic bomb in a future war may lead to political consequences which will mean the greatest disillusionment, above all for the authors of these plans.

Lastly, it should not be forgotten that atomic bombs used by one side may be opposed by atomic bombs and something else from the other side, and then the final collapse of all the present-day calculations of certain conceited but short-sighted people will become only too obvious. Illusions in serious matters are always dangerous, as both Mr. Baruch and his partners will probably have to recognize.

All this goes to show that truth and justice are not on the side of the United States plan, not to mention even the fact that the carrying out of this plan is in contradiction to the unanimously adopted decisions of the United Nations. It suffices to say that, to carry out this plan, it is necessary to break the United Nations Charter, to abandon the principle of unanimity of the great Powers in the Security Council, where the question of the atomic bomb is being decided. Is it not because there is a desire to give a free hand to the admirers of the atomic bomb that someone is raising such a hubbub over the veto?

All this goes to show that the Baruch plan, both in its substance and in its form, fails to meet the interests of the United Nations.

There is a different plan for the atomic bomb, the plan proposed by the Soviet Union. This plan is based on an altogether different policy.

We, the Soviet people, do not tie up our calculations for the future with the use of the atomic bomb. Please remember also that the General Assembly has already declared itself for the exclusion of atomic weapons from national armaments. Therefore, there is no reason to postpone the adoption of the international convention proposed by the Soviet Union prohibiting the production and use of atomic weapons. Only by taking such a decision shall we create suitable conditions for a free and fruitful examination of the questions relating to the establishment of control over atomic energy in all countries.

After the first World War, already, the nations agreed to prohibit the use for military purposes of poisonous gases, bacteriological preparations and other inhuman means of warfare. It is all the more necessary to prohibit the use for military purposes of atomic bombs as well as any other means for the mass extermination of people, which in this case means the wholesale destruction of the inhabitants of towns and civilians in general, since a merciless blow will fall mainly on children, women, sick persons and old men.

Those who yesterday fought against the aggressors and those who are really opposed to aggression should consider it their sacred duty to outlaw the use of atomic bombs and to see that the use of the newly discovered atomic energy is directed exclusively towards peaceful purposes. Only such use of atomic energy will be acknowledged by humanity as a just cause. The honour and conscience of the freedom-loving peoples demand that the atomic bomb be outlawed, for the United Nations will never assume the responsibility for any plans to use atomic energy for the purpose of destroying people wholesale and, in general, to use it to the detriment of mankind.

Our disputes in this case were probably inevitable owing to the novelty of the question. But, here too, we must avoid splitting up into two camps: the militant atomists, on the one hand, and the advocates of the use of atomic energy exclusively for peaceful purposes on the other. We must hope, therefore, that the exchange of views which has begun on this subject will lead in the long run to a unanimous opinion among the United Nations, including the United States of America.

Otherwise, what would people think and what should we reply to their perplexed questions?

The other day you may have read in the New York newspapers the speech delivered by Mr. Baruch, who was fairly outspoken in his views on peace and war. On 12 October, at the College of the City of New York, he stated: "Peace seems beautiful during the savagery of war, but it becomes almost hateful when war is over." Late in his reflections, Mr. Baruch was not sparing of words in expressing his love for "freedom." But it is easy to see that his idea of freedom is far removed from the real aspirations of the common people for freedom, well-being and lasting peace. He would like to see all people satisfied with the freedom under which only the lucky ones can enjoy the benefits of life, not only in the days of peace but also during a raging war. Mr. Baruch's sentiments are far removed from those of the people who have to sweat in heavy daily toil or who defend the freedom and the future of their native land with their own hands and at the cost of their lives. If that were not so, public men of his class would also have to agree that the so-called "common people" are nowadays mostly concerned that their Governments and their politicians should regard it as their main task to defend the peace and security of the nations because, after all the trials of the second World War, the longing for security and lasting peace is the innermost sentiment of the common people, men and women, throughout the world.

Far-reaching plans connected with the atomic bomb are perhaps dictated by the very same philosophy which is expressed in the words: "Peace becomes almost hateful when war is over." If this gloomy philosophy is followed, then naturally, the relevant political conclusions should be drawn, namely, to inflate military budgets, to increase the size of armies and try to be ahead of others in the armaments race, including the atomic bomb. This militant philosophy can only lead to preparations for a new aggression, which the United Nations have been so unanimous in condemning. But it is easy to see through the vicious arguments concerning "almost hateful peace." Those who hold this philosophy can scarcely hide their deep lack of faith in the peaceful development of their own country, and a pessimistic lack of confidence in their own strength, insofar as the prospect of peaceful competition between States and social systems is concerned. On the other hand, in this philosophy there is striking evidence of an irresistible yearning for expansion and undivided domination of the world.

We cannot believe that the majority of Americans are partisans of a philosophy of this kind. We suppose that, even after the successes they achieved during the second World War, the Americans, like all the other peace-loving nations, are anxious, above all, that peace should be as stable as possible and that the security of the peoples should be the main concern of the Governments of the United Nations. These sentiments of the common people of the Soviet Union and of the United States unite them to each other and to all the other United Nations.

The Soviet Union emerged from the recent war as a country which had experienced the hateful occupation by the enemy of a considerable part of its territory. For many years to come our people will not be able to forget their great sacrifices and the devastated towns and villages, which they are now engaged in restoring with their utmost exertions. These and other gigantic tasks already form part of our new Stalin Five-Year Plan which we have begun to put into effect this year. We are full of confidence that the time is not far off when our industry and agriculture, our transport system and cultural institutions, our towns and villages will fully recover from the consequences of war, will flourish again and will thus show other nations the might and the great possibilities of a liberated people and of the workers' State created by them.

There is no lack of faith among our people in the peaceful paths of progress and there is none of the uncertainty which appears in countries with unstable economic and political conditions, for we stand firmly on the positions won by the people. There is a great desire among our people to take part in the peaceful rivalry of States and social systems, a rivalry in which individual peoples would be able not only to reveal their internal possibilities but also to bring about closer co-operation with each other and in a greater variety of ways.

Our people long for lasting peace and believe that only in peace conditions can economic well-being and real prosperity be guaranteed for many years to come, together with the free life of the common people and of all mankind. The Soviet Union is alien to the strivings of those strong Powers and of influential groups in other countries which are infected by imperialistic dreams of world domination. The Soviet Union sees its best friends in the truly peace-loving States. We regard the strengthening of international co-operation on behalf of peace and progress as our most important task.

. . .

CHAPTER SIX

The Problem of National Security

29   President Truman's report to the American people on the Potsdam
Conference: August 9, 1945. *'No one nation can expect to get
everything it wants. It is a question of give and take — of being
willing to meet your neighbor half-way.'*

Upon his return from the Potsdam Conference—which was held near Berlin from
July 17 to August 2, 1945, and which concerned itself with laying plans for the
occupation and control of Germany and with initiating procedures for the drafting of
peace treaties with former enemy countries—President Truman continued publicly
to emphasize Allied unity. Like Roosevelt, Truman said he found it easy to get along
in mutual understanding and friendship with Generalissimo Stalin. Furthermore, he
continued, 'there was a fundamental accord and agreement upon the objectives
ahead of us—an assertion that hardly reflected the deep-seated American-Soviet
differences over such matters as reparations and occupation policies in Germany
and Austria. Thus, while on the surface relations between the erstwhile rivals
appeared tranquil enough, policy makers at the highest levels had moved well along
in the direction of locating and identifying the Soviet Union as the most serious
threat to world peace.

Source: *Presidential Papers: Harry S. Truman, 1945*, 203-14.

I have just returned from Berlin, the city from which the Germans intended to rule the
world. It is a ghost city. The buildings are in ruins, its economy and its people are in
ruins.

Our party also visited what is left of Frankfurt and Darmstadt. We flew over the
remains of Kassel, Magdeburg, and other devastated cities. German women and
children and old men were wandering over the highways, returning to bombed-out
homes or leaving bombed-out cities, searching for food and shelter.

War has indeed come home to Germany and to the German people. It has come home
in all the frightfulness with which the German leaders started and waged it.

The German people are beginning to atone for the crimes of the gangsters whom they placed in power and whom they wholeheartedly approved and obediently followed.

We also saw some of the terrific destruction which the war had brought to the occupied countries of Western Europe and to England.

How glad I am to be home again! And how grateful to Almighty God that this land of ours has been spared!

We must do all we can to spare her from the ravages of any future breach of the peace. That is why, though the United States wants no territory or profit or selfish advantage out of this war, we are going to maintain the military bases necessary for the complete protection of our interests and of world peace. Bases which our military experts deem to be essential for our protection, and which are not now in our possession, we will acquire. We will acquire them by arrangements consistent with the United Nations Charter.

No one can foresee what another war would mean to our own cities and our own people. What we are doing to Japan now—even with the new atomic bomb—is only a small fraction of what would happen to the world in a third World War.

That is why the United Nations are determined that there shall be no next war.

That is why the United Nations are determined to remain united and strong. We can never permit any aggressor in the future to be clever enough to divide us or strong enough to defeat us.

That was the guiding spirit in the conference at San Francisco.

That was the guiding spirit in the conference of Berlin.

That will be the guiding spirit in the peace settlements to come.

In the conference of Berlin, it was easy for me to get along in mutual understanding and friendship with Generalissimo Stalin, with Prime Minister Churchill, and later with Prime Minister Attlee.

Strong foundations of good will and cooperation had been laid by President Roosevelt. And it was clear that those foundations rested upon much more than the personal friendships of three individuals. There was a fundamental accord and agreement upon the objectives ahead of us.

Two of the three conferees of Teheran and Yalta were missing by the end of this conference. Each of them was sorely missed. Each had done his work toward winning this war. Each had made a great contribution toward establishing and maintaining a lasting world peace. Each of them seems to have been ordained to lead his country in its hour of greatest need. And so thoroughly had they done their jobs that we were able to carry on and to reach many agreements essential to the future peace and security of the world.

The results of the Berlin conference have been published. There were no secret agreements or commitments—apart from current military arrangements.

And it was made perfectly plain to my colleagues at the conference that, under our Constitution, the President has no power to make any treaties without ratification by the Senate of the United States.

I want to express my thanks for the excellent services which were rendered at this conference by Secretary of State Byrnes, and which were highly commended by the leaders of the other two powers. I am thankful also to the other members of the American delegation—Admiral Leahy and Ambassadors Harriman, Davies, and Pauley—and to the entire American staff. Without their hard work and sound advice the conference would have been unable to accomplish as much as it did.

The conference was concerned with many political and economic questions. But there was one strictly military matter uppermost in the minds of the American delegates. It was the winning of the war against Japan. On our program, that was the most important item.

The military arrangements made at Berlin were of course secret. One of those secrets was revealed yesterday, when the Soviet Union declared war on Japan.

The Soviet Union, before she had been informed of our new weapon, agreed to enter the war in the Pacific. We gladly welcome into this struggle against the last of the Axis aggressors our gallant and victorious ally against the Nazis.

The Japs will soon learn some more of the other military secrets agreed upon at Berlin. They will learn them firsthand—and they will not like them.

Before we met at Berlin, the United States Government had sent to the Soviet and British Governments our ideas of what should be taken up at the conference. At the first meeting our delegation submitted these proposals for discussion. Subjects were added by the Soviet and British Governments, but in the main the conference was occupied with the American proposals.

Our first nonmilitary agreement in Berlin was the establishment of the Council of Foreign Ministers.

The Council is going to be the continuous meeting ground of the five principal governments, on which to reach common understanding regarding the peace settlements. This does not mean that the five governments are going to try to dictate to , or dominate, other nations. It will be their duty to apply, so far as possible, the fundamental principles of justice underlying the Charter adopted at San Francisco.

Just as the meeting at Dumbarton Oaks drew up the proposals to be placed before the conference at San Francisco, so this Council of Foreign Ministers will lay the groundwork for future peace settlements. This preparation by the Council will make possible speedier, more orderly, more efficient, and more cooperative peace settlements than could otherwise be obtained.

One of the first tasks of the Council of Foreign Ministers is to draft proposed treaties of peace with former enemy countries—Italy, Rumania, Bulgaria, Hungary, and Finland.

These treaties, of course, will have to be passed upon by all the nations concerned. In our own country the Senate will have to ratify them. But we shall begin at once the necessary preparatory work. Adequate study now may avoid the planting of the seeds of future wars.

I am sure that the American people will agree with me that this Council of Foreign Ministers will be effective in hastening the day of peace and reconstruction.

We are anxious to settle the future of Italy first among the former enemy countries. Italy was the first to break away from the Axis. She helped materially in the final defeat of Germany. She has now joined us in the war against Japan. She is making real progress toward democracy.

A peace treaty with a democratic Italian government will make it possible for us to receive Italy as a member of the United Nations.

The Council of Foreign Ministers will also have to start the preparatory work for a German peace settlement. But its final acceptance will have to wait until Germany has developed a government with which a peace treaty can be made. In the meantime, the conference of Berlin laid down the specific political and economic principles under which Germany will be governed by the occupying powers.

Those principles have been published. I hope that all of you will read them.

They seek to rid Germany of the forces which have made her so long feared and hated, and which have now brought her to complete disaster. They are intended to eliminate Nazism, armaments, war industries, the German General Staff and all its military tradition. They seek to rebuild democracy by control of German education, by reorganizing local government and the judiciary, by encouraging free speech, free press, freedom of religion, and the right of labor to organize.

German industry is to be decentralized in order to do away with concentration of economic power in cartels and monopolies. Chief emphasis is to be on agriculture and peaceful industry. German economic power to make war is to be eliminated. The Germans are not to have a higher standard of living than their former victims, the people of the defeated and occupied countries of Europe.

We are going to do what we can to make Germany over into a decent nation, so that it may eventually work its way from the economic chaos it has brought upon itself, back into a place in the civilized world.

The economic action taken against Germany at the Berlin conference included another most important item—reparations.

We do not intend again to make the mistake of exacting reparations in money and then lending Germany the money with which to pay. Reparations this time are to be paid in physical assets from those resources of Germany which are not required for her peacetime subsistence.

The first purpose of reparations is to take out of Germany everything with which she can prepare for another war. Its second purpose is to help the devastated countries to bring about their own recovery by means of the equipment and material taken from Germany.

At the Crimea conference a basis for fixing reparations had been proposed for initial discussion and study by the Reparations Commission. That basis was a total amount of reparations of twenty billions of dollars. Of this sum, one half was to go to Russia, which had suffered more heavily in the loss of life and property than any other country.

But at Berlin the idea of attempting to fix a dollar value on the property to be removed from Germany was dropped. To fix a dollar value on the share of each nation would be a sort of guarantee of the amount each nation would get—a guarantee which might not be fulfilled.

Therefore, it was decided to divide the property by percentages of the total amount available. We still generally agreed that Russia should get approximately half of the total for herself and Poland, and that the remainder should be divided among all the other nations entitled to reparations.

Under our agreement at Berlin, the reparations claims of the Soviet Union and

Poland are to be met from the property located in the zone of Germany occupied by the Soviet Union, and from the German assets in Bulgaria, Finland, Hungary, Rumania and East Austria. The reparations claims of all the other countries are to be met from property located in the western zones of occupation in Germany, and from the German assets in all other countries. The Soviet waives all claim to gold captured by the Allied troops in Germany.

This formula of taking reparations by zones will lead to less friction among the Allies than the tentative basis originally proposed for study at Yalta.

The difficulty with this formula, however, is that the industrial capital equipment not necessary for German peace economy is not evenly divided among the zones of occupation. The western zones have a much higher percentage than the eastern zone, which is mostly devoted to agriculture and to the production of raw materials. In order to equalize the distribution and to give Russia and Poland their fair share of approximately 50 percent, it was decided that they should receive, without any reimbursement, 10 percent of the capital equipment in the western zones available for reparations.

As you will note from the communique, a further 15 percent of the capital equipment in the western zones not necessary for Germany's peace economy is also to be turned over to Russia and Poland. But this is not free. For this property, Poland and Russia will give to the western zones an equal amount in value in food, coal, and other raw materials. This 15 percent, therefore, is not additional reparations for Russia and Poland. It is a means of maintaining a balanced economy in Germany and providing the usual exchange of goods between the eastern part and the western part.

It was agreed at Berlin that the payment of reparations, from whatever zones taken, should always leave enough resources to enable the German people to subsist without sustained support from other nations.

The question of Poland was a most difficult one. Certain compromises about Poland had already been agreed upon at the Crimea conference. They obviously were binding upon us at Berlin.

By the time of the Berlin conference, the Polish Provisional Government of National Unity had already been formed; and it had been recognized by all of us. The new Polish Government had agreed to hold free and unfettered elections as soon as possible, on the basis of universal suffrage and the secret ballot.

In acceptance—in accordance with the Crimea agreement, we did seek the opinion of the Polish Provisional Government of National Unity with respect to its western and northern boundaries.

They agreed, as did we all, that the final determination of the borders could not be accomplished at Berlin, but must await the peace settlement. However, a considerable portion of what was the Russian zone of occupation in Germany was turned over to Poland at the Berlin conference for administrative purposes until the final determination of the peace settlement.

Nearly every international agreement has in it the element of compromise. The agreement on Poland is no exception. No one nation can expect to get everything that it wants. It is a question of give and take—of being willing to meet your neighbor half-way.

In this instance, there is much to justify the action taken. The agreement on some line—even provisionally—was necessary to enable the new Poland to organize itself, and to permit the speedier withdrawal of the armed forces which had liberated her from the Germans. In the area east of the Curzon line there are over 3,000,000 Poles who are to be returned to Poland. They need room, room to settle. The new area in the West was formerly populated by Germans. But most of them have already left in the face of the invading Soviet Army. We were informed that there were only about a million and a half left.

The territory the Poles are to administer will enable Poland better to support its population. It will provide a short and more easily defensible frontier between Poland and Germany. Settled by Poles, it will provide a more homogeneous nation.

The Three Powers also agreed to help bring about the earliest possible return to Poland of all Poles who wish to return, including soldiers, with the assurance that they would have all the rights of other Polish citizens.

The action taken at Berlin will help carry out the basic policy of the United Nations toward Poland—to create a strong, independent, and prosperous nation with a government to be selected by the people themselves.

It was agreed to recommend that in the peace settlement a portion of East Prussia should be turned over to Russia. That, too, was agreed upon at Yalta. It will provide the Soviet Union, which did so much to bring about victory in Europe, with an ice-free port at the expense of Germany.

At Yalta it was agreed, you will recall, that the three governments would assume a common responsibility in helping to reestablish in the liberated and satellite nations of Europe governments broadly representative of democratic elements in the population. That responsibility still stands. We all recognize it as a joint responsibility of the three governments.

It was reaffirmed in the Berlin Declarations on Rumania, Bulgaria, and Hungary. These nations are not to be spheres of influence of any one power. They are now governed by Allied control commissions composed of representatives of the three governments which met at Yalta and Berlin. These control commissions, it is true, have not been functioning completely to our satisfaction; but improved procedures were agreed upon at Berlin. Until these states are reestablished as members of the international family, they are the joint concern of all of us.

The American delegation was much disturbed over the inability of the representatives of a free press to get information out of the former German satellite nations. The three governments agreed at Berlin that the Allied press would enjoy full freedom from now on to report to the world upon all developments in Rumania, Bulgaria, Hungary, and Finland. The same agreement was reaffirmed also as to Poland.

One of the persistent causes for wars in Europe in the last two centuries has been the selfish control of the waterways of Europe. I mean the Danube, the Black Sea Straits, the Rhine, the Kiel Canal, and all the inland waterways of Europe which border upon two or more states.

The United States proposed at Berlin that there be free and unrestricted navigation of these inland waterways. We think this is important to the future peace and security of the world. We proposed that regulations for such navigation be provided by international authorities.

The function of the agencies would be to develop the use of the waterways and assure equal treatment on them for all nations. Membership on the agencies would include the United States, Great Britain, the Soviet Union, and France, plus those states which border on the waterways.

Our proposal was considered by the conference and was referred to the Council of Ministers. There, the United States intends to press for its adoption.

Any man who sees Europe now must realize that victory in a great war is not something you win once and for all, like victory in a ball game. Victory in a great war is something that must be won and kept won. It can be lost after you have won it—if you are careless or negligent or indifferent.

Europe today is hungry. I am not talking about Germans. I am talking about the people of the countries which were overrun and devastated by the Germans, and particularly about the people of Western Europe. Many of them lack clothes and fuel and tools and shelter and raw materials. They lack the means to restore their cities and their factories.

As the winter comes on, the distress will increase. Unless we do what we can to help, we may lose next winter what we won at such terrible cost last spring. Desperate men are liable to destroy the structure of their society to find in the wreckage some substitute for hope. If we let Europe go cold and hungry, we may lose some of the foundations of order on which the hope for worldwide peace must rest.

We must help to the limits of our strength. And we will.

Our meeting at Berlin was the first meeting of the great Allies since victory was won in Europe. Naturally our thoughts now turn to the day of victory in Japan.

The British, Chinese, and United States Governments have given the Japanese people adequate warning of what is in store for them. We have laid down the general terms on which they can surrender. Our warning went unheeded; our terms were rejected. Since then the Japanese have seen what our atomic bomb can do. They can foresee what it will do in the future.

The world will note that the first atomic bomb was dropped on Hiroshima, a military base. That was because we wished in this first attack to avoid, insofar as possible, the killing of civilians. But that attack is only a warning of things to come. If Japan does not surrender, bombs will have to be dropped on her war industries and, unfortunately, thousands of civilian lives will be lost. I urge Japanese civilians to leave industrial cities immediately, and save themselves from destruction.

I realize the tragic significance of the atomic bomb.

Its production and its use were not lightly undertaken by this Government. But we knew that our enemies were on the search for it. We know now how close they were to finding it. And we knew the disaster which would come to this Nation, and to all peace-loving nations, to all civilization, if they had found it first.

That is why we felt compelled to undertake the long and uncertain and costly labor of discovery and production.

We won the race of discovery against the Germans.

Having found the bomb we have used it. We have used it against those who attacked us without warning at Pearl Harbor, against those who have starved and beaten and executed American prisoners of war, against those who have abandoned all pretense of obeying international laws of warfare. We have used it in order to shorten the agony of war, in order to save the lives of thousands and thousands of young Americans.

We shall continue to use it until we completely destroy Japan's power to make war. Only a Japanese surrender will stop us.

The atomic bomb is too dangerous to be loose in a lawless world. That is why Great Britain, Canada, and the United States, who have the secret of its production, do not intend to reveal that secret until means have been found to control the bomb so as to protect ourselves and the rest of the world from the danger of total destruction.

As far back as last May, Secretary of War Stimson, at my suggestion, appointed a committee upon which Secretary of State Byrnes served as my personal representative, to prepare plans for the future control of this bomb. I shall ask the Congress to cooperate to the end that its production and use be controlled, and that its power be made an overwhelming influence towards world peace.

We must constitute ourselves trustees of this new force—to prevent its misuse, and to turn it into the channels of service to mankind.

It is an awful responsibility which has come to us.

We thank God that it has come to us, instead of to our enemies; and we pray that He may guide us to use it in His ways and for His purposes.

Our victory in Europe was more than a victory of arms.

It was a victory of one way of life over another. It was a victory of an ideal founded on the rights of the common man, on the dignity of the human being, on the conception of the State as the servant—and not the master—of its people.

A free people showed that it was able to defeat professional soldiers whose only moral arms were obedience and the worship of force.

We tell ourselves that we have emerged from this war the most powerful nation in the world—the most powerful nation, perhaps, in all history. That is true, but not in the sense some of us believe it to be true.

The war has shown us that we have tremendous resources to make all the materials for war. It has shown us that we have skillful workers and managers and able generals, and a brave people capable of bearing arms.

All these things we knew before.

The new thing—the thing which we had not known—the thing we have learned now and should never forget, is this: that a society of self-governing men is more powerful, more enduring, more creative than any other kind of society, however disciplined, however centralized.

We know now that the basic proposition of the worth and dignity of man is not a sentimental aspiration or a vain hope or a piece of rhetoric. It is the strongest, most creative force now present in this world.

Now let us use that force and all our resources and all our skills in the great cause of a just and lasting peace!

The Three Great Powers are now more closely than ever bound together in determination to achieve that kind of peace. From Teheran, and the Crimea, from San Francisco and Berlin—we shall continue to march together to a lasting peace and a happy world!

30   A top secret memorandum prepared by the Joint Chiefs of Staff
September 19, 1945: *'Any nation, which in the future may attempt
to dominate the world, may be expected to make her major effort
against the United States . . . .'*

An important, if perhaps extreme, reflection of the growing concern of the United States with Soviet foreign policy was the suggestion by the Joint Chiefs of Staff (JCS) in a memorandum which had in all its essentials been approved as early as September 19, 1945, that the end of Allied cooperation seemed imminent. 'In the last analysis the maintenance of ... world peace', remarked this recently declassified top secret document, 'will depend upon mutual cooperation among Britain, Russia and the United States. The possibility of a breakdown in the relations between these major powers and the resulting necessity to exercise individual or collective self-defense requires for our preservation, that we be so prepared that if necessary we can maintain our security without immediate or substantial assistance from other nations.' With the unmistakable implication that Russia constituted the only real threat to America, the memorandum went on to argue that future confrontation would most certainly become World War III, and that the primary objective of enemy aggression would be the United States. Finally, recognizing that technological improvement in weaponry had greatly reduced invulnerability from a first attack, the JCS concluded that the United States must perforce maintain a superior military posture so as to make it 'unwise' for any hostile power to initiate a major thrust against the nation.

Source: Department of State, *Foreign Relations of the United States, Diplomatic Papers: 1946* (Wash. 1972), I, 1160-65.

1.   The basic purpose for maintaining United States armed forces is to provide for our security and to uphold and advance our national policies, foreign and domestic. The essentials of our military policy are determined by our national policies.

2.   The major national policies which determine our military policy are:

a.   Maintenance of the territorial integrity and security of the United States, its territories, possessions, leased areas and trust territories.

b.   Advancing the political, economic and social well-being of the United States.

c.   Maintenance of the territorial integrity and the sovereignty or political independence of other American states, and regional collaboration with them in the maintenance of international peace and security in the Western Hemisphere.

d.   Maintenance of the territorial integrity, security and, when it becomes effective, the political independence of the Philippine Islands.

e.   Participation in and full support of the United Nations Organization.

f.   Enforcement, in collaboration with our Allies, of terms imposed upon the defeated enemy states.

g.   Maintenance of the United States in the best possible relative position with respect to potential enemy powers, ready when necessary to take military action abroad to maintain the security and integrity of the United States.

3.   These policies in the aggregate are directed toward the maintenance of world peace, under conditions which insure the security, well-being and advancement of our country.

4.   In the last analysis the maintenance of such a world peace will depend upon mutual cooperation among Britain, Russia and the United States. The possibility of a breakdown in the relation between these major powers and the resulting necessity to exercise individual or collective self-defense requires, for our own preservation, that we be so prepared that if necessary we can maintain our security without immediate or substantial assistance from other nations. Such an eventuality presents the maximum problem from the military point of view. A military policy that will maintain the security of the United States, standing alone, would meet all other military requirements. Any future conflict between major foreign powers will almost certainly precipitate a third world war, in which we could not hope to escape being involved. Any nation, which in the future may attempt to dominate the world, may be expected to make her major effort against the United States and before we can mobilize our forces and productive capacity. The power, range and prospective development of modern weapons are such as to favor such an attack. As a result, there will be a marked reduction in the degree of invulnerability to ready attack that has been provided in the past by our geographical position.

5.   It is to be borne in mind, however, that, in correspondingly equal degree, we will possess the means for retaliatory or punitive attack against other powers who may threaten the United States or the international peace structure in general. The means for preserving peace under the United Nations are both tacit and explicit. They are primarily tacit with regard to the major powers in that, whereas the existence of effective military power must be real, its implementation or assertion must be avoided, if possible. If the stability of the international structure is to be maintained, unbalanced power factors or stresses must be guarded against. From the point of view of the United States, this means that our country, if she is to play her proper part toward the maintenance of international peace, must have sufficient military power to make it unwise for any major aggressor nation to initiate a major war against the opposition of the United States. The relative military power required for fulfilling the potential role of this international sanction should not exceed that required for national security purposes, as set forth in the preceding paragraph. It would not be maintained for, nor used in any way as, an international threat, nor for purposes of asserting world domination.

6.   More explicit is the maintenance of an international security force. The United Nations Charter provides for the use, if required, of certain armed forces made available to the Security Council, by previous agreement, to maintain international peace and security. Under its terms concerted military action by the United Nations can be taken only when all five of the permanent members of the Security Council, plus two non-permanent members, agree that other means are inadequate to maintain or restore international peace and security. It may therefore be assumed that the total requirement of the Security Council for armed forces will be small, and consequently, that the United States commitment will be only a small part of the military forces which will be required in any event for national security against the in no way remote possibility of a

breakdown in the relation of major powers.

7.   The other definite military commitment, and the one that is most immediate, is to provide the necessary forces for the occupation and demilitarization of Germany and Japan, and the prevention of their resurgence as aggressor nations.

8.   It is recognized that the maintenance of overwhelmingly strong forces in time of peace is politically and economically unacceptable to the people of the United States. However, they should accept as requirements essential to their security:

a.   The maintenance of sufficient active forces to afford assurance of the security of the United States, its territories and possessions during the initial period of mobilization of national means—manpower, resources and industry.

b.   Readiness and determination to take prompt and effective military action abroad to anticipate and prevent attack.

c.   An intelligence system which would assure this government information concerning military, political, economic and technological developments abroad and hence provide the necessary forewarning of hostile intent and capability.

d.   A national organization which will promote and coordinate civilian and military activities in technical research and development.

c.   Maintenance of an adequate system of overseas bases.

9.   It may be assumed that the United States, relative to other great powers, will maintain in peace time as armed forces only a minimum percentage of its war time potential. It is imperative therefore that these forces be the best trained in the world, and equipped with superior matériel and so disposed strategically that they can be brought to bear at the source of enemy military power, or in other critical areas in time to thwart attack by a potential aggressor. These forces must be supported by an adequate system of bases and machinery for the rapid mobilization of our national resources. Plans and preparations must be kept abreast of developments of new weapons and counter-measures against them and provide for exploitation of our superior mechanical and industrial capabilities. When it becomes evident that forces of aggression are being arrayed against us by a potential enemy, we cannot afford, through any misguided and perilous idea of avoiding an aggressive attitude to permit the first blow to be struck against us. Our government, under such conditions, should press the issue to a prompt political decision, while making all preparations to strike the first blow if necessary.

10.   In view of the above, the United States military policy may be stated as follows:

STATEMENT OF UNITED STATES MILITARY POLICY

11.   *Basic Military Policy.*   To insure the security of the United States and to uphold and advance its national interests by military readiness to support its national policies and international commitments.

12.   *General Military Policy.*   To be prepared to take prompt and effective military action wherever necessary with the armed forces of the United States:

a.   To maintain the security of the United States, its territories, possessions, leased areas, trust territories and the Philippine Islands.

b.   To secure and to maintain international peace within the Western Hemisphere, acting collectively with other American states, but if necessary acting alone.

c.   To fulfill our military commitments in the maintenance of international peace and security as a member of the United Nations.

d.   To fulfill our military commitments in the enforcement, in cooperation with our Allies, of the terms imposed upon defeated enemy states.

e.   To maintain the United States in the best possible relative position with respect to potential enemy powers.

13.   *Principal Supporting Military Policies:*

a.   To maintain mobile striking forces in strength, composition and state of readiness for prompt and adequate action and to provide necessary fixed and mobile logistic support for such forces.

b.   To maintain adequate forces required by our commitments for the enforcement of terms imposed on defeated enemy states.

c.   To provide security for vital areas in the United States, its territories, possessions, leased areas and trust territories against possible enemy attacks, including attacks with newly developed weapons.

d.   To maintain an adequate reserve of appropriate composition, both as to personnel and matériel, which is capable of rapid mobilization.

e.   To develop and maintain an adequate system of supporting establishments within the continental United States for our operating forces, capable of rapid expansion.

f.   To develop and maintain a system of outlying bases, adequately equipped and defended, for the support of our mobile forces, and capable of rapid expansion.

g.   To develop and maintain an intelligence system which would assure adequate information concerning military, political, economic and technological developments abroad and provide the necessary warning of hostile intent and capability.

h.   To promote research, development and provision of new weapons, processes, matériel and countermeasures, and in so far as possible and desirable to deny such knowledge and capacity to possible enemy states.

i.   To provide for the rapid mobilization in an emergency, of national means— manpower, resources and industry—by supporting:

(1)   Universal military training.

(2)   Maintenance of a large United States Merchant Marine, both active and reserve.

(3)   Development and maintenance of United States domestic and international commercial air transport systems.

(4)   Plans and preparations for the mobilization of manpower, resources and industry.

(5)   Maintenance of industries essential to the national war effort so designed and located as to give maximum insurance against destruction by enemy attack.

(6)   Stockpiling of critical strategic materials.

j.   To develop and maintain close coordination and mutual understanding between the State, War and Navy Departments, and those other agencies of government and industry which contribute to the national war effort.

k. To maintain liaison with and to support the development and training of the armed forces of the American republics, the Dominion of Canada, the Philippine Islands, and other nations which contribute to the security of the United States, its territories, possessions, leased areas, trust territories, and the Western Hemisphere.

l. In concert with political and economic measures taken by the other departments of the government, to maintain the United States in the best possible military position with respect to potential enemy powers.

31   Secretary of State Byrne's report on the first session of the Council of Foreign Ministers: October 5, 1945. *'It [the issue] is whether the peace shall be made by three or even five nations to the exclusion of other nations vitally concerned in the maintenance and enforcement of the peace which is being prepared.'*

On October 5, 1945, in a radio broadcast originating from Washington, D.C., Secretary of State James E. Byrnes announced to the American people that the first session of the Council of Foreign Ministers, which met in London in September 1945, had closed in a stalemate. The underlying tensions that had undermined American-Soviet diplomacy since the last days of Franklin Roosevelt's Administration now threatened to erupt to the surface. The London Conference, which was in session from September 11 to October 2, 1945, broke up essentially over the unexpected Soviet refusal to allow China and France to participate in the drafting of peace treaties with Italy, Bulgaria, Hungary and Rumania, the objection being that only nations signatory to surrender documents had the right to speak on the subject at this time. Other difficulties included the joint Anglo-American refusal to recognize the pro-Soviet governments of Bulgaria and Rumania. The Americans based their refusal squarely on the ideological ground that freedom of speech and assembly were still being denied to the Bulgarian and Rumanian people, and that these were basic rights without which political self-determination could not hope to be realized.

Source: Department of State, *Bulletin,* XIII (October 7, 1945), 507-12.

The first session of the Council of Foreign Ministers closed in a stalemate. But that need not, and should not, deprive us of a second and better chance to get on with the peace.

In the past I have been both criticized and commended for being a compromiser. I confess that I do believe that peace and political progress in international affairs as in domestic affairs depend upon intelligent compromise. The United States Delegation acted in that spirit at Berlin: We acted in that spirit at London. And we shall continue to act in that spirit at future conferences.

That spirit is essential in international conferences where action can be taken only by unanimous agreement. When any one member can prevent agreement, compromise is a necessity. Men and women who have served on a jury can appreciate that.

Compromise, however, does not mean surrender, and compromise unlike surrender requires the assent of more than one party.

The difficulties encountered at the London conference will, I hope, impress upon the peoples of all countries, including our own people, the hard reality that none of us can expect to write the peace in our own way. If this hard reality is accepted by statesmen and peoples at an early stage of the peacemaking process, it may at later stages save us and save the peace of the world from the disastrous effects of disillusionment and intransigences.

Regardless of how Americans may differ as to domestic policies, they desire unity in our foreign policies. This unity will be essential in the days ahead of us when we may expect differences in views by various governments as to peace settlements. However, the political party in power cannot expect this unity unless it freely consults representatives of the opposing political party.

Believing this, I requested Mr. John Foster Dulles, one of the best-informed Americans in the field of foreign relations and a loyal Republican, to accompany me to London in an advisory capacity. He has been more than an adviser; he has been a partner. Between us there have been no secrets. At the Council table and in private conference he has participated in the making of all decisions. Our accord serves to show that in foreign affairs Republicans and Democrats can work together and that in vital matters of foreign policy we Americans are united.

When it was agreed at Berlin to establish the Council of Foreign Ministers I think we all had in mind the precedent of the Dumbarton Oaks Conference. There, representatives of Great Britain, the Soviet Union, China, and the United States worked together to prepare draft proposals for the United Nations Charter as a basis for discussion with other nations. France was not present at Dumbarton Oaks only because France had not yet been liberated. Her right to permanent membership on the United Nations Security Council was not questioned.

Experience reveals that a certain degree of understanding among the major powers is essential to secure general agreement among many nations. When understanding among the great powers is not achieved in advance of a conference participated in by many nations, it usually has to be secured informally during the conference.

At the Versailles Conference, for example, it took the Big Three and the Big Five so long to agree among themselves that the complaint was made that the smaller powers had little more time to consider the treaty than was given to the Germans.

The Berlin agreement envisaged the naming of highranking deputies who could carry on the work of the Council in the absence of their chiefs, the Foreign Secretaries. The Council, as President Truman and I understood it, was to be a sort of combined staff to explore the problems and prepare proposals for the final peace settlements.

At Berlin it certainly was never intended that the three powers present or the five powers constituting the Council should take unto themselves the making of the final peace. The Berlin declaration setting up the Council begins with the statement "The Conference reached the following agreement for the establishment of a Council of Foreign Ministers to do the necessary preparatory work for the peace settlements."

The Council was not to make the peace settlements but to do the necessary preparatory work for the peace settlements. It certainly was not my intention to agree to any final treaty without first getting the views of the Foreign Relations Committee of the Senate which must pass upon all treaties before ratification.

The first session of the Council, so far as the personal participation of the Foreign Ministers was concerned, was intended to provide directives for the deputies in the preparation of treaties for Italy, Rumania, Bulgaria, Hungary, and Finland.

This work was exploratory—to find out on what points we were in agreement, on what points we differed, and on what points further study and data were required. It is a little naive to suppose that when really vital differences emerge, one nation or another is likely to abandon its position on the first interchange of views.

At this stage it is as important to know and understand wherein we and our Allies differ as wherein we agree. We must understand our points of difference before we can intelligently consider means of reconciling them.

So far as the Italian treaty was concerned I think we made very good progress toward agreement on directives to govern the work of our deputies.

There was ready acceptance of our proposal that Italy should undertake to maintain a bill of rights which will secure the freedoms of speech, religious worship, political belief, and public meeting envisaged for Italy in the Moscow declaration of November 1943 and which will confirm the human rights and fundamental freedoms set forth in the Charter of the United Nations.

There was some difference among the conferees at the start as to providing for the limitation of armaments. But it was our feeling that Italy should rely on the United Nations for protection against aggression and should not engage in competition in armaments when all her resources are badly needed to restore her civilian economy. And this view gained general acceptance.

While the very controversial boundary dispute between Yugoslavia and Italy was not settled, it was encouraging to find that it was possible to agree that the line should in the main be governed by ethnic considerations and that regardless of its sovereignty there should be a free port at Trieste under international control.

The Council was in general agreement that the Dodecanese Islands should go to Greece although the assent of one member was qualified pending the study of certain questions by his government.

There was general agreement that the Italian colonies should come under the trusteeship provisions of the United Nations Charter. Various views were expressed as to the preferred form of trusteeship for the colonies.

The American Delegation was particularly gratified that the directive to the deputies, while not restricting their studies, called for special consideration of the American proposal for a truly international administration directly responsible to the United Nations with a view to the attainment of the greatest degree of independence of the inhabitants of two of the colonies at the end of ten years and independence for the people of a third colony at as early a date as possible.

This proposal was presented by the American Delegation when the Italian treaty first was taken up and was consistently adhered to.

It is our view that the object of a trusteeship should be to promote the self-government of the people of a colony and not to enrich a trustee or increase its economic or military power.

It was also agreed that Italian sovereignty should be restored on the conclusion of the treaty so that foreign troops may be withdrawn and, except as specially provided in the treaty, foreign controls within Italy terminated.

There was no definite understanding on reparations. The United States took the position that Italy could not pay anything like $600,000,000. Apart from certain foreign assets, she should be required to pay as reparations only such factory and tool equipment designed for the manufacture of war implements which are not required for the limited military establishment permitted to her and which cannot be readily converted to peaceful purposes. If she is stripped of more, then her economy cannot be restored.

We have contributed several hundred million dollars for the relief of the Italian people. Their condition is deplorable. We must continue to help them. But we cannot contribute more millions, if those millions are to be used to enable Italy to pay reparations to other governments. We did that for Germany after the last war. We shall not do it again.

Substantial progress was also made on the directives for the preparatory work on the Finnish treaty and the treaties with Rumania and Bulgaria. The principles suggested by the American Delegation and accepted for the Italian treaty for the safeguarding of human rights and fundamental freedoms are also to be incorporated in these treaties.

The directives concerning the limitation of armament for Rumania and Bulgaria are expected to follow the same general line as those accepted for Italy.

Before work could be commenced upon the directives for the Hungarian treaty the Soviet Delegation announced they felt obliged to withdraw their assent to the procedure previously accepted by the Council for dealing with peace treaties.

Before taking up these procedural difficulties I should say a few words about the Soviet Delegation's disappointment with the failure of Great Britain and the United States to recognize the Bulgarian and Rumanian Governments.

The thought apparently exists in their mind that our government objects to these governments because they are friendly to the Soviet Union and that our unwillingness to recognize these governments is a manifestation of unfriendliness to the Soviet Union.

There could be no greater misconception of our attitude. I was at Yalta. The Yalta declaration on the liberated and ex-satellite countries was based on a proposal submitted by President Roosevelt. Under it the Allied Powers, including the Soviet Union, assumed the responsibility of concerting their policies to assist in the establishment of interim governments broadly representative of all important democratic elements in the population and pledged to the earliest possible establishment through free elections of governments responsive to the will of the people. That pledge cannot be fulfilled in countries where freedom of speech and of assembly are denied.

That policy sponsored by President Roosevelt was America's policy and remains America's policy.

We are well aware that no government is perfect and that the representative character of any provisional government will always be subject to debate. We do not demand perfection where perfection is unobtainable.

In an effort to concert our policies with our Allies we have tried to show a spirit of conciliation. Certainly we did not make unduly exacting the requirements we set before we recognized the Provisional Polish Government or the conditions which we have proposed as a basis for the recognition of the Provisional Hungarian Government.

And I hope that as the result of efforts now being made by the Provisional Austrian Government to broaden its representation, we may soon be able to recognize that Government.

At Berlin we stated we would examine in the near future, in the light of prevailing conditions, the question of recognition of Rumania and Bulgaria. We have investigated and we shall continue to investigate. But we cannot know whether conditions justify recognition unless our political representatives are fully informed and unless our news correspondents are permitted freely to enter countries and freely to send their stories uncensored.

We do not seek to dictate the internal affairs of any people. We only reserve for ourselves the right to refuse to recognize governments if after investigation we conclude they have not given to the people the rights pledged to them in the Yalta agreement and in the Atlantic Charter.

The peace of Europe depends upon the existence of friendly relations between the Soviet Union and its European neighbors, and two wars in one generation have convinced the American people that they have a very vital interest in the maintenance of peace in Europe.

The American Government shares the desire of the Soviet Union to have governments friendly to the Soviet Union in eastern and central Europe.

But lasting peace depends not only upon friendship between governments but upon friendship between peoples.

Had it not been for the difficulties experienced by the Allied governments in agreeing upon a common policy in regard to the recognition of the governments of Rumania and Bulgaria a more conciliatory spirit might possibly have prevailed and might greatly have helped to overcome the procedural difficulties of the Council.

No one present at the Council on September 11 questioned the decision taken by the Council that day inviting all five members to be present at all meeetings.

Directives for the Italian treaty were under discussion for several days with China, not a party to the surrender terms, present, participating in the discussion, but not voting. No one objected.

Directives for the Finnish treaty were then considered, with the United States, France, and China present but not voting. No one objected.

Directives for the Rumanian treaty and then for the Bulgarian treaty were considered, with France and China present but not voting. No one objected.

It was only on September 22 that the Soviet Delegation took the position that the decision of the Council on September 11 violated the Berlin agreement.

It will be recalled that the Berlin agreement set up a Council of the Soviet Union, Great Britain, France, China, and the United States to undertake the necessary preparatory work for the peace settlements. It provided that the Council should draw up with a view to their submission to the United Nations peace treaties with Italy, Rumania, Bulgaria, Hungary, and Finland.

It provided that in the discharge of these tasks the Council will be composed of members representing those states which were signatory to the terms of surrender imposed upon the enemy state concerned, and for the purpose of the Italian settlement

France should be regarded as signatory to the surrender terms.

The Berlin agreement further provided that other members of the Council will be invited to participate when matters directly concerning them are under discussion.

This distinction between members of the Council who were parties to the surrender terms and those who were not, was not part of the original American proposal and was reluctantly accepted by us. We were fully aware that a member would not have the right to vote if not a party to the surrender terms, but we understood from the exchange of views at the table that all members would be allowed to participate in all discussions in the Council.

It certainly never occurred to President Truman or myself that any of the five members of the Council who are also the five permanent members of the United Nations Security Council, which is charged with the responsibility for maintaining the peace which the Council of Foreign Ministers is preparing, would not be invited to be present during the discussions of the treaties.

Such exclusion of two permanent members of the Security Council would not promote the harmonious relations essential to the success of the United Nations Organization.

The Soviet Delegation's position was not simply that they wished to withdraw the invitation to China and France to participate without right to vote. Their position was that it was beyond the authority of the States signatory to the surrender terms to extend the invitation.

Although this construction of the Berlin agreement did not accord with the understanding of the American Delegation or the British Delegation or the President of the United States or the Prime Minister of Great Britain, the Soviet Delegation insisted that they could no longer discuss treaty matters in the presence of members who were not parties to the surrender terms.

Thereafter the meetings of the Council for a number of days were confined to the discussion of other items on the agenda such as international inland waterways, the Ruhr, acceleration of German reparations, restitution, repatriation of Allied nationals, and the Austrian food supply.

When the general items on the agenda were exhausted, agreement had not been reached for solving the procedural obstacles which, in the view of the Soviet Delegation, made further discussion of treaty matters impossible until the decision of September 11 should be rescinded.

Since it had always been my view that the Berlin agreement contemplated a broadening out of the participants before the final conclusion of a peace treaty, I sought to find a compromise along that line.

The Berlin agreement expressly provided in section 4 of the article establishing the Council that the Council may adapt its procedures to the particular problems under discussion; that in some cases it may hold its own discussions prior to the participation of other interested states; and in other cases it may convoke a formal conference of states interested in particular problems.

I therefore proposed, with considerable reluctance, that we ask our French and Chinese colleagues to accept the position of the Soviet Delegation that the preparatory and exploratory work of the Council for the peace settlements be confined to the signatories of the surrender terms in question, provided that at the same time it should be agreed that a truly representative peace conference should be convoked before the end of the year. To ensure the calling of such a conference we thought that France and China, in the interest of peace, might make even this sacrifice.

This conference would be convoked for the purpose of considering the peace treaties with Italy, Rumania, Bulgaria, Hungary, and Finland. To the conference would be invited:

(1) The five members of the Council of Foreign Ministers which are also the five permanent members of the United Nations Security Council;
(2) All European members of the United Nations;
(3) All non-European members of the United Nations which supplied substantial military contingents in the war against the European members of the Axis.

The American Delegation took the position that, in an interdependent, democratic world, peace cannot be the exclusive concern of a few presently powerful states; that unless we were to revert to a world of isolationism none of the states which we wanted invited to the peace conference could be said to be not directly concerned in the peace.

We urged that those states, both large and small, which had fought and suffered in the war must make the peace. This has been a peoples' war and it must be a peoples' peace.

The Soviet Delegation stated, however, that they could not agree to the American proposal for a peace conference until they had returned to Moscow and had personal consultations with their Government.

It therefore became obvious that there could be no agreement unless the other delegations were prepared to yield their views and convictions to those of the Soviet Delegation. This none of the other delegations was prepared to do.

The United States is willing to dictate terms of peace to an enemy but is not willing to dictate terms of peace to its Allies.

Our task then became one of arranging an adjournment until the Soviet Delegation could return to Moscow. It is customary before adjournment to adopt and have all conferees to sign a protocol containing a record of the agreed decisions of a conference. The Soviet Delegation would not agree to the inclusion in the protocol of the decision of September 11 that the five members should participate in all meetings, even though it included a statement of the action taken by the Soviet Delegation on September 22 to withdraw their assent to that decision.

On the last day of the session the Soviet Delegation announced it would offer a compromise proposal. The proposal was that there should be four separate protocols without recording in any of them the decision of September 11 which had been agreed to by them but which they later wished to rescind. This was the same position that they had urged for days. The only thing new about it was the suggestion that on the following day they would discuss unsettled questions including the American proposal for a peace conference and the disputed September 11 decision.

In answer to a question the Soviet Foreign Minister stated that while he could discuss the proposal for a peace conference, he still was without authority to act upon it. The proposal had been discussed for a week. Further discussion without action was futile.

It was also obvious that once the four protocols were signed, it would be useless on the following day to discuss the question of inserting in the protocols the decision of September 11. An objection by the Soviet Delegation would prevent its insertion.

The Soviet Delegation also reiterated their position that they would not discuss the treaties in the presence of members they now believed to be ineligible. This would have excluded China from the consideration of all treaties and France from the consideration of all but one, without any assurance of participation in a peace conference.

It became apparent that agreement was impossible and further meetings were useless. The Chinese Foreign Minister, who was presiding when the Council adjourned and at whose instance the Council had remained in session from Sunday until Tuesday, stated that under the circumstances he could not ask the Council to continue in session longer.

As the record stands the Foreign Minister of the Soviet Union has not rejected our proposal for a peace conference. During the discussions he admitted it was correct in principle. My hope is that, after he has conferred with his government, his government will agree that the nations that fought the war—the World War—shall have a chance to make the world peace.

The matter that caused the suspension of our work is no trivial or technical question. It presented an issue that had to be met. It is whether the peace shall be made by three or even five nations to the exclusion of other nations vitally concerned in the maintenance and enforcement of the peace which is being prepared.

The issue goes even deeper. The Council of Foreign Ministers acts under the unanimity rule just as the Security Council of the United Nations must act in many important matters, but in the Security Council no nation has the veto power in procedural matters while in the Council of Foreign Ministers one nation can veto all action.

The veto power is a great power and should not be lightly exercised. We are willing to make many concessions but the United States does not believe in agreement at any price.

The power of veto in procedural matters should not be used by the United States or any other nation to coerce the judgment and conscience of fellow nations.

Peace must be based upon mutual understanding and mutual respect. It can not be secured by procedural maneuverings which obscure from the people the real and vital issues upon which their peace depends.

Undeterred by temporary set-backs and ever willing to accord to others that tolerant understanding that we wish others to accord to us, we must not relax in our efforts to achieve a just and lasting peace for ourselves and all nations. "With firmness in the right as God gives to see the right, let us strive on to finish the work we are in."

32   President Truman's restatement of United States foreign policy: October 27, 1945. *'We seek to use our military strength solely to preserve the peace of the world.'*

In a hard-hitting address delivered in New York City's Central Park on October 27, 1945, in connection with the celebration of Navy Day, President Truman warned the Soviet Union that while his nation still hoped for continued cooperation, the United States was determined to play a fundamental role in keeping the international peace. Nonetheless, he was still hopeful that some sort of *modus vivendi* could be worked out. For, according to America's tough-minded (and tough-talking) leader from Missouri, 'There are no conflicts of interest among the victorious powers so deeply-rooted that they can not be resolved.' Finally, in a speech that also noted the necessity of the United States to adopt universal military training, the President restated in a manner that appealed directly to the common man what he regarded as the basic ideas and ideals of American foreign policy. Probably no single document of the period better illustrates the hold that the nation's historical past had on Presidential thinking.

Source: ibid, XIII (October 28, 1945), 653-56.

MAYOR LAGUARDIA, LADIES AND GENTLEMEN: I am grateful for the magnificent reception which you have given me today in this great city of New York. I know that it is given to me only as the representative of the gallant men and women of our naval forces, and on their behalf, as well as my own, I thank you.

New York joins the rest of the Nation in paying honor and tribute to the 4 million fighting Americans of the Navy, Marine Corps, and Coast Guard—and to the ships which carried them to victory.

On opposite sides of the world, across two oceans, our Navy opened a highway for the armies and air forces of the United States. They landed our gallant men, millions of them, on the beach-heads of final triumph. Fighting from Murmansk, the English Channel, and the Tyrrhenian Sea, to Midway, Guadalcanal, Leyte Gulf, and Okinawa—they won the greatest naval victories in history. Together with their brothers in arms in the Army and Air Force, and with the men of the Merchant Marine, they have helped to win for mankind all over the world a new opportunity to live in peace and dignity—and, we hope, in security.

In the harbor and rivers of New York City and in other ports along the coasts and rivers of the country, ships of that mighty United States Navy are at anchor. I hope that you and the people everywhere will visit them and their crews, seeing for yourselves what your sons and daughters, your labor and your money, have fashioned into an invincible weapon of liberty.

The fleet, on V-J Day, consisted of 1,200 warships, more than 50,000 supporting and landing craft, and over 40,000 navy planes. By that day, ours was a sea power never before equaled in the history of the world. There were great carrier task forces capable of tracking down and sinking the enemy's fleets, beating down his airpower, and pouring destruction on his war-making industries. There were submarines which roamed the seas, invading the enemy's own ports, and destroying his shipping in all the oceans. There were amphibious forces capable of landing soldiers on beaches from Normandy to the Philippines. There were great battleships and cruisers which swept enemy ships from the seas and bombarded his shore defense almost at will.

And history will never forget that great leader who, from his first day in office, fought to reestablish a strong American Navy—who watched that Navy and all the other might of this Nation grow into an invincible force for victory—who sought to make that force an instrument for a just and lasting peace—and who gave his life in the effort— Franklin D. Roosevelt.

The roll call of the battles of this fleet reads like signposts circling the globe—on the road to final victory. North Africa, Sicily, Italy, Normandy, and southern France; Coral Sea, Midway, Guadalcanal, and the Solomons; Tarawa, Saipan, Guam, the Philippine Sea, Leyte Gulf; Iwo Jima, and Okinawa. Nothing which the enemy held on any coast was safe from its attack.

Now we are in the process of demobilizing our naval force. We are laying up ships, We are breaking up aircraft squadrons. We are rolling up bases and releasing officers and men. But when our demobilization is all finished as planned, the United States will still be the greatest naval power on earth.

In addition to that naval power, we shall still have one of the most powerful air forces in the world. And just the other day, so that on short notice we could mobilize a powerful and well-equipped land, sea, and air force, I asked the Congress to adopt universal training.

Why do we seek to preserve this powerful naval and air force, and establish this strong Army reserve? Why do we need them?

We have assured the world time and again—and I repeat it now—that we do not seek for ourselves one inch of territory in any place in the world. Outside of the right to establish necessary bases for our own protection, we look for nothing which belongs to any other power.

We do need this kind of armed might however, and for four principal tasks:

First, our Army, Navy, and Air Force, in collaboration with our Allies, must enforce the terms of peace imposed upon our defeated enemies.

Second, we must fulfil the military obligations which we are undertaking as a member of the United Nations Organization—to support a lasting peace, by force if necessary.

Third, we must cooperate with other American nations to preserve the territorial integrity and the political independence of the nations of the Western Hemisphere.

Fourth, in this troubled and uncertain world, our military forces must be adequate to discharge the fundamental mission laid upon them by the Constitution of the United States—to "provide for the common defense" of the United States.

These four military tasks are directed not toward war—not toward conquest—but toward peace.

We seek to use our military strength solely to preserve the peace of the world. For we now know that that is the only sure way to make our own freedom secure.

That is the basis of the foreign policy of the people of the United States.

The foreign policy of the United States is based firmly on fundamental principles of righteousness and justice. In carrying out those principles we shall firmly adhere to what we believe to be right; and we shall not give our approval to any compromise with evil.

But we know that we cannot attain perfection in this world overnight. We shall not let our search for perfection obstruct our steady progress toward international cooperation. We must be prepared to fulfil our responsibilities as best we can, within the framework of our fundamental principles, even though we recognize that we have to operate in an imperfect world.

Let me restate the fundamentals of that foreign policy of the United States:

1. We seek no territorial expansion or selfish advantage. We have no plans for aggression against any other state, large or small. We have no objective which need clash with the peaceful aims of any other nation.

2. We believe in the eventual return of sovereign rights and self government to all peoples who have been deprived of them by force.

3. We shall approve no territorial changes in any friendly part of the world unless they accord with the freely expressed wishes of the people concerned.

4. We believe that all peoples who are prepared for self-government should be permitted to choose their own form of government by their own freely expressed choice, without interference from any foreign source. That is true in Europe, in Asia, in Africa, as well as in the Western Hemisphere.

5. By the combined and cooperative action of our war Allies, we shall help the defeated enemy states establish peaceful, democratic governments of their own free choice. And we shall try to attain a world in which Nazism, Fascism, and military aggression cannot exist.

6. We shall refuse to recognize any government imposed upon any nation by the force of any foreign power. In some cases it may be impossible to prevent forceful impostion of such a government. But the United States will not recognize any such government.

7. We believe that all nations should have the freedom of the seas and equal rights to the navigation of boundary rivers and waterways and of rivers and waterways which pass through more than one country.

8. We believe that all states which are accepted in the society of nations should have access on equal terms to the trade and the raw materials of the world.

9. We believe that the sovereign states of the Western Hemisphere, without interference from outside the Western Hemisphere, must work together as good neighbors in the solution of their common problems.

10. We believe that full economic collaboration between all nations, great and small, is essential to the improvement of living conditions all over the world, and to the establishment of freedom from fear and freedom from want.

11. We shall continue to strive to promote freedom of expression and freedom of religion throughout the peace-loving areas of the world.

12. We are convinced that the preservation of peace between nations requires a

United Nations Organization composed of all the peace-loving nations of the world who are willing jointly to use force if necessary to insure peace.

That is the foreign policy which guides the United States now. That is the foreign policy with which it confidently faces the future.

It may not be put into effect tomorrow or the next day. But none the less, it is our policy; and we shall seek to achieve it. It may take a long time, but it is worth waiting for, and it is worth striving to attain.

The Ten Commandments themselves have not yet been universally achieved over these thousands of years. Yet we struggle constantly to achieve them, and in many ways we come closer to them each year. Though we may meet set-backs from time to time, we shall not relent in our efforts to bring the Golden Rule into the international affairs of the world.

We are now passing through a difficult phase of international relations. Unfortunately it has always been true after past wars that the unity among Allies, forged by their common peril, has tended to wear out as the danger passed.

The world can not afford any let-down in the united determination of the Allies in this war to accomplish a lasting peace. The world can not afford to let the cooperative spirit of the Allies in this war disintegrate. The world simply cannot allow this to happen. The people in the United States, in Russia and Britain, in France and China, in collaboration with all other peace-loving people, must take the course of current history into their own hands and mould it in a new direction—the direction of continued cooperation. It was a common danger which united us before victory. Let it be a common hope which continues to draw us together in the years to come.

The atomic bombs that fell on Hiroshima and Nagasaki must be made a signal, not for the old process of falling apart but for a new era—an era of ever closer unity and ever closer friendship among peaceful nations.

Building a peace requires as much moral stamina as waging a war. Perhaps it requires even more, because it is so laborious and painstaking and undramatic. It requires undying patience and continuous application. But it can give us, if we stay with it, the greatest reward that there is in the whole field of human effort.

Differences of the kind that exist today among the nations that fought together so long and so valiantly for victory are not hopeless or irreconcilable. There are no conflicts of interest among the victorious powers so deeply rooted that they can not be resolved. But their solution will require a combination of forbearance and firmness. It will require a steadfast adherence to the high principles we have enunciated. It will also require a willingness to find a common ground as to the methods of applying these principles.

Our American policy is a policy of friendly partnership with all peaceful nations, and of full support for the United Nations Organization. It is a policy that has the strong backing of the American people. It is a policy around which we can rally without fear or misgiving.

The more widely and clearly that policy is understood abroad, the better and surer will be the peace. For our own part, we must seek to understand the special problems of other nations. We must seek to understand their own legitimate urge toward security as they see it.

The immediate, the greatest threat to us is the threat of disillusionment, the danger of an insidious skepticism—a loss of faith in the effectiveness of international cooperation. Such a loss of faith would be dangerous at any time. In an atomic age it would be nothing short of disastrous.

There has been talk about the atomic bomb scrapping all navies, armies, and air forces. For the present, I think that such talk is 100 percent wrong. Today control of the seas rests in the fleets of the United States and her Allies. There is no substitute for them. We have learned the bitter lesson that the weakness of this great Republic invites men of ill-will to shake the very foundations of civilization all over the world.

What the distant future of atomic research will bring to the fleet which we honor today, no one can foretell. But the fundamental mission of the Navy has not changed. Control of our sea approaches and of the skies above them is still the key to our freedom and to our ability to help enforce the peace of the world. No enemy will ever strike us directly except across the sea. We cannot reach out to help stop and defeat an aggressor without crossing the sea. Therefore, the Navy, armed with whatever weapons science brings forth, is still dedicated to its historic task: control of the ocean approaches to our country and of the skies above them.

The atomic bomb does not alter the basic foreign policy of the United States. It makes the development and application of our policy more urgent than we could have dreamed six months ago. It means that we must be prepared to approach international problems with greater speed, with greater determination, and with greater ingenuity, in order to meet a situation for which there is no precedent.

We must find the answer to the problems created by the release of atomic energy—as we must find the answers to the many other problems of peace—in partnership with all the peoples of the United Nations. For their stake in world peace is as great as our own.

As I said in my message to the Congress, discussion of the atomic bomb with Great Britain and Canada and later with other nations cannot wait upon the formal organization of the United Nations. These discussions, looking toward a free exchange of fundamental scientific information, will be begun in the near future. But I emphasize again, as I have before, that these discussions will not be concerned with the processes of manufacturing the atomic bomb or any other instruments of war.

In our possession of this weapon, as in our possession of other new weapons, there is no threat to any nation. The world, which has seen the United States in two great recent wars, knows that full well. The possession in our hands of this new power of destruction we regard as a sacred trust. Because of our love of peace, the thoughtful people of the world know that that trust will not be violated, that it will be faithfully executed.

Indeed the highest hope of the American people is that world cooperation for peace will soon reach such a state of perfection that atomic methods of destruction can be definitely and effectively outlawed forever.

We have sought, and we will continue to seek, the attainment of that objective. We shall pursue that course with all the wisdom, patience, and determination that the God of Peace can bestow upon a people who are trying to follow in His path.

33   Eleventh hour efforts to accommodate Soviet fears

The following two readings—which among other things surprisingly suggest the relative fluidity of America's Russian policy as late as November 1945—indicate the extent to which the Truman Administration was prepared to accommodate the Soviet leadership's national security fears. In the first address, delivered before the *Herald Tribune* Forum in New York on October 31, 1945, Secretary of State Byrnes candidly recognized the USSR's 'special security interests' in the nations along her borderlands. Moreover, he went on to record the impression that the United States appreciated, in his words, 'the determination of the people of the Soviet Union that never again will they tolerate the pursuit of policies in those countries deliberately directed against the Soviet Union's security and way of life.' Several weeks later, in a speech delivered at a rally in New York sponsored by the National Council of American-Soviet Friendship, Under-Secretary of State Dean Acheson reinforced Byrne's remarks in pointing out that the pursuit of different ways of life had not in the past barred American-Russian cooperation. 'For nearly a century and a half' observed the soon-to-be quintessential Cold Warrior, 'we have gotten along well— remarkably well, when you consider that our forms of government, our economic systems, and our social habits have never been similar.' Acheson also went to great lengths to sympathize with the problems and security fears that stemmed from the recent German invasion of Russia, even asking his audience to imagine for a moment what the United States would have looked like in 1945 if it had been their country rather than the Soviet Union that had been invaded by the German Wehrmacht.

33(a)Byrnes on 'Neighboring Nations in One World', October 31, 1945.
'Far from opposing, we have sympathized with ... the efforts of the Soviet Union to draw into closer and more friendly association with her central and eastern European neighbors.'

Source: ibid, XIII (November 14, 1945), 709-11.

THE SUBJECT about which I wish to speak briefly this evening is "Neighboring Nations in One World."

It was no accident that President Roosevelt, who did so much to develop our inter-American system, did even more to develop the world community of the United Nations. For today all nations are neighbors, and although we may have special relations with our nearer neighbors in the Americas, we must remember that we and they are parts of a single, interdependent world.

When we consider the principles which govern our inter-American system as it has been worked out in recent years, it is well to remember that these principles were not always recognized by us in our relations with our neighbors. There were times, not so far distant, when we tried "dollar diplomacy" and intervention and were accused of "Yankee imperialism."

But we have learned by experience that to have good neighbors we must be a good neighbor.

We have discovered that understanding and good-will cannot be bought and cannot be forced. They must spring spontaneously from the people. We have learned also that there can be no lasting friendship between governments unless there is understanding and good-will between their peoples.

In the inter-American system the members do not interfere in the internal affairs of their neighbors nor do they brook interference in those internal affairs by others. Freedom means more than freedom to act as we would like them to act.

But we do want other people to know what our people are thinking and doing. And we want to know what other people are thinking and doing. Only with such knowledge can each people determine for itself its way of life.

We believe other nations have a right to know of our own deep attachment to the principles of democracy and human rights; our profound belief that governments must rest upon the free consent of the governed; and our firm conviction that peace and understanding among nations can best be furthered by the free exchange of ideas.

While we adhere to the policy of non-intervention, we assert that knowledge of what other people are thinking and doing brings understanding; and understanding brings tolerance and a willingness to cooperate in the adjustment of differences.

Censorship and blackouts, on the other hand, breed suspicion and distrust. And all too often this suspicion and distrust are justified. For censorship and blackouts are the handmaidens of oppression.

The policy of non-intervention in internal affairs does not mean the approval of local tyranny. Our policy is intended to protect the right of our neighbors to develop their own freedom in their own way. It is not intended to give them free rein to plot against the freedom of others.

We have learned by bitter experience in the past ten years that Nazi and Fascist plans for external aggression started with tyrannies at home which were falsely defended as matters of purely local concern. We have learned that tyranny anywhere must be watched, for it may come to threaten the security of neighboring nations and soon become the concern of all nations.

If, therefore, there are developments in any country within the inter-American system which, realistically viewed, threaten our security, we consult with other members in an effort to agree upon common policies for our mutual protection.

We Americans can take genuine pride in the evolution of the good-neighbor policy from what, in a way were its beginnings in the Monroe Doctrine. We surely cannot and will not deny to other nations the right to develop such a policy.

Far from opposing, we have sympathized with, for example, the effort of the Soviet Union to draw into closer and more friendly association with her central and eastern European neighbors. We are fully aware of her special security interests in those countries, and we have recognized those interests in the arrangements made for the occupation and control of the former enemy states.

We can appreciate the determination of the people of the Soviet Union that never again will they tolerate the pursuit of policies in those countries deliberately directed against the Soviet Union's security and way of life. And America will never join any groups in those countries in hostile intrigue against the Soviet Union. We are also confident that the Soviet Union would not join in hostile intrigue against us in this hemisphere.

We are concerned to promote friendship, not strife, among neighbors everywhere. For twice in our generation strife among neighbors has led to world conflict. Lasting peace among neighbors has its roots in spontaneous and genuine friendship. And that kind of friendship among nations depends upon mutual respect for one another.

It is our belief that all peoples should be free to choose their own form of government, a government based upon the consent of the governed and adapted to their way of life.

We have put that belief into practice in our relations with our neighbors. The Soviet Union has also declared that it does not wish to force the Soviet system on its neighbors. The whole-hearted acceptance of this principle by all the United Nations will greatly strengthen the bonds of friendship among nations everywhere.

But the point I wish to emphasize is that the policy of the good neighbor, unlike the institution of marriage, is not an exclusive arrangement. The best neighbors do not deny their neighbors the right to be friends with others.

We have learned that our security interests in this hemisphere do not require its isolation from economic and cultural relations with the rest of the world.

We have freely accepted the Charter of the United Nations, and we recognize the paramount authority of the world community. The Charter, while reserving to us and other nations the inherent right of individual and collective self-defense in case of armed attack, requires that enforcement action taken under regional arrangements be sanctioned by the Security Council of the United Nations Organization.

Moreover, we adhere strictly to the policy that cooperation among the American republics does not justify discrimination against non-American states. The American republics have practiced the policy of equal treatment for all states which respect the sovereignty and integrity of their fellow states.

Inter-American cooperation is not inconsistent with world-wide cooperation among the nations. Regional arrangements, like the inter-American system, which respect the rights and interests of other states and fit into the world system can become strong pillars in the structure of world peace.

But we cannot recognize regional arrangements as a substitute for a world system. To do so would not promote the common and paramount interests of all nations, large and small, in world peace.

We live in one world; and in this atomic age regional isolationism is even more dangerous than is national isolationism.

We cannot have the kind of cooperation necessary for peace in a world divided into spheres of exclusive influence and special privilege.

This was the great significance of the Moscow Declaration of 1943. That joint statement of policy pledged the world's most powerful nations to mutual cooperation in winning the war and maintaining the peace. It was a landmark in our efforts to create a world community of nations and to abandon the discredited system of international relations based upon exclusive spheres of influence.

Out of the Moscow Declaration have come the Dumbarton Oaks, Tehran, Crimea, San Francisco, and Potsdam conferences. And the United Nations Organization and the

London Council of Foreign Ministers were created in the spirit of that Declaration.

International cooperation must—as I emphasized in my recent report on the London Council—depend upon intelligent compromise. It does not require us or any other nation to neglect its special relations with its nearer neighbors. But it does require that all neighborly relations be fitted into an organized system of international relations world-wide in scope.

The world system which we seek to create must be based on the principle of the sovereign equality of nations.

That does not mean that all nations are equal in power and in influence any more than all men are equal in power and influence. But it does mean equal respect for the individuality and sovereignty of nations, large and small. Nations, like individuals, should be equal before the law.

That principle is the cornerstone of our inter-American system as it is the cornerstone of the United Nations.

Adherence to that principle in the making of the peace is necessary if we are to achieve enduring peace. For enduring peace is indivisible. It is not the exclusive concern of a few large states or a few large groups of states. It is the concern of all peoples.

Believing this, the position of the United States will continue to be that the nations, large and small, which have borne the burdens of the war must participate in making the peace.

In centuries past powerful nations have for various purposes tried to divide the world among themselves. They failed, and in failing left a trail of blood through the centuries. Such efforts have even less chance of success in the modern world where all nations have become neighbors.

Today the world must make its choice. There must be one world for all of us or there will be no world for any of us.

33(b) Dean Acheson on problems of security and understanding in American-Soviet friendship: November 14, 1945: *'There is the fact. . . that never, in the past, has there been any place on the globe where the vital interests of the American and Russian people have clashed . . .'*

Source: ibid, XIII (November 18, 1945), 787-89.

Friendship between nations, as between individuals—genuine friendship—is something that grows spontaneously. It isn't easy to promote. It never can be forced. Governments can set the tone of international relations, but in the long run it's the people who call the tune.

The word *friendship* has been applied so liberally and so loosely to international relations that it has lost much of its meaning. On this important occasion I shall try to use the word with all the care and respect that it deserves.

What are the factors that encourage close and friendly relations between the American and Soviet peoples? What are the obstacles in the way of a satisfactory friendship between us?

To say that there are overwhelming reasons why we should be friends is not to say that we are friends. To describe the bonds that unite us for better or for worse, on this miniature and crowded planet, is not to prove that we are happily united.

Now I don't propose to enter tonight into a philosophic discussion of the anatomy of friendship. But there are certain conditions that usually exist between friends, and where they don't exist you are almost certain to find something less than complete friendship.

One of those conditions might be described as an absence of tension. Friends may argue, disagree, and even quarrel, but they are relaxed with each other, in spite of their differences. They accept their disagreements as a normal part of the give and take of friendship.

To put it another way, friends are not forever taking each other apart—until each becomes obsessed and exasperated with the contradictions of the other's personality. They have accepted the terms of friendship, and they are not impelled to dig up the roots of friendship daily to see how the plant is growing.

To do this seems to me both silly and futile. Certainly it's not the way personal or international friendships are made or preserved. But in all honesty it must be admitted that there is a good deal of this sort of thing going on in both countries.

Judging from the way our national temperatures rise and fall in relation to day-to-day events, you would think we had had no experience of living together in the same world. As a matter of fact, we have had a long and close experience, dating from the time when President Jefferson and Czar Alexander the First carried on a warm and friendly correspondence.

For nearly a century and a half we have gotten along well—remarkably well, when you consider that our forms of government, our economic systems, and our social habits have never been similar.

Certainly the contrast between our ways of life and our political institutions is no greater today, with a Communist Russia, than it was in the time of Jefferson and Czar Alexander the First, or during the period of the Civil War, when Abraham Lincoln and Czar Alexander the Second guided our respective nations in a friendly collaboration of vital importance to us in our time of trial.

In perspective, the long history of amicable relations between the American and Russian peoples compares favorably with the history of our relations with the other great nations—not excluding France and Great Britain. By any standards of international relations, the record is good.

When I say this I am not for a moment forgetting or underestimating the tremendous events of 1917 and 1918 which eliminated Russia from the ranks of our allies at a crucial moment of the first World War, or the 16-year period of blackout between our two peoples, during which we withheld diplomatic recognition of each other's existence and suspended the normal contacts without which friendship cannot flourish.

But however great the loss to both our peoples from that gap in our relations, we need not regard it as irretrievable. Already a substantial part of it has been offset by our working partnership of World War II and the start toward peaceful cooperation that was made at the Moscow, Tehran, Crimea and San Francisco conferences, and by our joint membership in the United Nations Organization.

Taken as a whole, I repeat, the long record of common interest and common action is good. Can we put it down to chance? Can we ascribe it to all-wise governments or impeccable diplomacy? I don't think so. Forgetting governments and diplomats for the moment, let's look at more immutable facts of history and geography.

There is the fact, for example, that never, in the past, has there been any place on the globe where the vital interests of the American and Russian people have clashed or even been antagonistic—and there is no objective reason to suppose that there should, now or in the future, ever be such a place. There is an obvious reason for this. We are both continental peoples with adequate living space—interested in developing and enjoying the living space we have. Our ambition is to achieve the highest possible standards of living among our own peoples, and we have the wherewithal to achieve high standards of living without conquest, through peaceful development and trade.

We have that opportunity, moreover, only to the extent that we can create conditions of peace and prevent war. Thus the paramount interest, the only conceivable hope of both nations, lies in the cooperative enterprise of peace.

What, then, are the difficulties which lie across the path of this cooperative enterprise?

I believe the problem is capable of rational examination. I believe also that it is capable of solution. The hard core of the problem has two major aspects: first, the problem of security; and, second, the problem of understanding.

Both countries have been wantonly attacked. Both have suffered grievously but differently. Both are determined that aggression shall have no such opportunity in the future.

The attack upon the Soviet Union came from just beyond her western borders. There was grave danger of attack from just beyond her eastern border. We can get some idea of the consequences of this attack—the second of its kind in a quarter of a century—if we imagine the United States invaded by the German Wehrmacht, and an area roughly comparable to the New England and Middle Atlantic States almost completely devastated. If we imagine this area as including not only the industrial centers of New York, Boston, and Pittsburgh but a large part of the Middle Western bread basket and a third of our population as well, we can learn what aggression means to the Soviet people. We can understand also the measure of their determination to prevent it.

We understand and agree with them that to have friendly governments along her borders is essential both for the security of the Soviet Union and for the peace of the world. Secretary Byrnes made this clear beyond doubt in his speech of October thirty-first.

But it seems equally clear to us that the interest in security must take into account and respect other basic interests of nations and men, such as the interest of other peoples to choose the general surroundings of their own lives and of all men to be secure in their persons. We believe that that adjustment of interests should take place short of the point where persuasion and firmness become coercion, where a knock on the door at night strikes terror into men and women.

In this area where the room for adjustment is broad and where the necessity for extreme measures is absent, the problem seems wholly possible of friendly solution.

We, too, have our problem of security. The attack upon us came not from close at hand but from an aggressor, on two occasions, many thousands of miles away. The attacks were made upon a nation patently undesirous of and unprepared for war and solely because of our refusal supinely to acquiesce in conduct which outraged every sense of decency and right. This has led us to look for security through bases and methods which will keep danger far from us and stop the aggressor before he can again develop the power of his attack.

Our friends do not object to this but point out to us that we, too, must adjust our interest in security to the general interest in security and with the principles and organizations which have been agreed upon to insure it.

In the case of both the Soviet Union and ourselves the necessity to seek security by extreme measures or unilateral action is absent. Mr. Molotov has truly said:

"We have lived through difficult years and now each one of us can say: 'We have won and from now on we can consider our motherland rid from the menace of German invasion from the west and from the menace of Japanese invasion from the east.' The long awaited peace has come for the peoples of the whole world."

With the menaces to the security of both countries removed it would seem that there is both time and area within which to solve all questions arising out of the need of our two countries for security. The path to solution is both through the United Nations Organization, which we have joined in establishing, and in following in our dealings with other nations the principles upon which we have agreed in the Charter.

One of these is "To develop friendly relations among nations based on respect for the principle of equal rights and self-determination of peoples". Another is "to take . . . collective measures for the prevention and removal of threats to the peace".

These are principles of restraint and moderation and patience and respect for the dignity and integrity of nations and individuals. They furnish the best and surest foundations of friendship.

Then there is the second aspect of our problem of friendship—the second essential ingredient of friendship. I refer to the necessity for understanding and communication between the American and Soviet people.

Enduring friendship must be based on understanding and trust, not only between governments but between peoples. But we are faced with an immediate and practical question: How are we to know one another? Here are two peoples of strong convictions and different backgrounds. Each is committed to its way of life. Neither has the least desire to change the other. Yet each has an overwhelming desire to know and understand the other.

I confess I see no way to draw our peoples into closer understanding except by persistent efforts, on both sides, to free the lines of communication through the press and the radio, through books and magazines, through the exchange of knowledge and culture, and through travel and personal acquaintance. What we and the Soviet people need from each other and what we are entitled to ask was summed up by Marshal Stalin in a talk with Senator Pepper. "Just judge the Soviet Union objectively", said Marshal Stalin. "Do not either praise us or scold us. Just know us and judge us as we are, and base your estimate of us upon facts and not rumors."

We have so much to learn and, what is more difficult, to understand about each other that we cannot hope to succeed except in the spacious atmosphere of honesty, candor, and knowledge. Only in that atmosphere can we keep our minds and emotions on an even keel and avoid the pitfalls of over-optimism on the one side and despair on the other. Both are equally dangerous and equally unjustified.

34   The State Department gets tough with the Soviets: December 1, 1945.
      *'In pursuing the policy of collaboration [with the Soviet Union],
      however, we should always be prepared to stand firm against Soviet
      demands when acceptance of these demands would mean that we
      would have to compromise any of our fundamental principles.'*

Despite late efforts to assuage Soviet fears, and in a manner that foreshadowed the Administration's hardening attitude toward Stalin in the wake of the fruitless second meeting of the Conference of Foreign Ministers held at Moscow in December 1945, Department of State policy makers vigorously continued to object to the Soviet establishment of totalitarian political regimes and economic control over the countries of Eastern and Central Europe. In conformity with the American position of political self-determination and equality of commercial opportunities, which in New Left revisionist literature has taken on sinister overtones, State planners argued that 'we should use our full influence to break down the firm hold the Soviet Government is endeavouring to fasten on Eastern and Central Europe.' The method chosen to resist the Soviets lay principally in the economic sphere—not unnaturally, given the preponderance of the American economy at that time. Specifically, through the granting of credits, the United States government hoped to encourage nations behind the Iron Curtain that made sincere efforts at democratization; at the same time, through the withholding of credits, the United States hoped to persuade the Kremlin to relinquish some of its control over the same nations. Finally, it is interesting to note that in contrast with a number of accounts of early Cold War thinking, the Truman Administration showed, at least in this document, an unusual sensitivity to the 'non-communist left' as distinguished from the totalitarian left.

Source: Department of State, *Foreign Relations of the United States, Diplomatic Papers: 1946* (Wash. 1972), I,1136-39.

. . . Our policy toward the Soviet Union should be to continue our efforts to convince the Soviet authorities that it is to our mutual advantage to collaborate in all decisions in the international relations field. In order to attain this end, we should not hesitate to make clear to the Soviet authorities and, if necessary, to the American public that we cannot continue collaboration with the Soviet Union if it insists on making unilateral decisions and taking unilateral action in its dealings with other nations of the world. In pursuing the policy of collaboration, however, we should always be prepared to stand firm against Soviet demands when acceptance of these demands would mean that we would have to compromise any of our fundamental principles. The most effective way of following this policy is for us to use our full influence in backing the United Nations Organization in order to strengthen it and make it in fact an effective organization for the maintenance of peace. We should not hesitate to resist to the full any effort to weaken the organization and should be prepared to go along with all other nations who wish to make it an effective organization.

While considerable progress has been made in reaching a satisfactory relationship with the Soviet Union, it is just the beginning and there are still a number of very fundamental unsolved questions, many of which have been brought about by the unilateral action taken by the Soviet authorities. Some of these are:

1. The fact that totalitarian political regimes have been established under direct Soviet control in certain countries of Southeastern and Central Europe. We should continue to maintain that events in these countries are the responsibility of the three nations signatory to the Yalta Declaration on Liberated Europe. The fact that we have been unable to bring the Soviet Government to live up to the principles of this Declaration does not mean we should cease our efforts directed toward its implementation. We should, under all circumstances, avoid any action which would appear to accept any "democratic" incipient totalitarian regimes in these countries without on the other hand making it clear that we renounce any responsibility for these areas because of the unacceptable character of the political regimes which are in the process of being established. While we should not withdraw formal diplomatic recognition from regimes, such as Yugoslavia, which have not permitted the holding of democratic elections, we should make it clear that the maintenance of diplomatic relations with such regimes does not imply in any way our approval of the policies of such regimes, their methods of assuming control, or their failure to implement the guarantees of personal freedoms. We should refrain from according diplomatic recognition to the governments of Rumania and Bulgaria as now constituted but, on the other hand, should accord recognition to countries, such as we have done in the case of Hungary, where free elections have been held.

2. The establishment of almost complete Soviet economic control over the countries of Eastern and Central Europe through war booty and reparation deliveries, by bilateral barter trade agreements, and in certain cases by "agreements for economic collaboration", all of which in effect mean an economic blackout in these areas for all other nations. In conformity with our announced policies of favoring access to all raw materials by all nations and of equal economic opportunity in all areas, we should use our full influence to break down the firm hold which the Soviet Government is endeavoring to fasten on Eastern and Central Europe. We should be prepared to grant credits on an approved transaction basis to those countries in Eastern and South-eastern Europe in which sincere efforts are being made to establish representative democratic regimes. In granting such credits, however, we should be sure that the credits are not used as an indirect method for the payment of reparations to the Soviet Union. In connection with the economic developments in Eastern Europe, we should insist upon protecting all legitimate American interests and property in that area and demand compensation for the value of the American interests involved in the event that property owned directly or indirectly by United States nationals cannot be retained.

We should not accord credits to the Soviet Union until we have received concrete and tangible assurances and supporting evidence that its economic policies are in general accord with our announced international economic policies. In order to protect the basic interests of the United States we should not accord global credits but should grant credits only on an approved transaction basis, thus permitting a review of the situation each time an application is made for an advance for a specific purpose. Because of the comparatively limited facilities the Soviet Government has for obtaining foreign exchange, the total amount of credit granted should be limited to a sum for which there are reasonable assurances that repayment can be made in the normal processes of international trade.

3. The Soviet policy of endeavoring to prevent full news reports from being sent to the outside world from areas under Soviet domination makes it difficult for the American public to evaluate developments in these areas. Now that we have obtained permission for American correspondents to enter these areas, we should continue our efforts to see that they are permitted freely to send factual reports on developments.

4. The indications of the adoption of a policy by the Soviet Government in the Far East of giving indirect support to communist elements in that area. While we have primary responsibility for the control of Japan and therefore the establishment of normal conditions in the Far East, we should nevertheless, as far as circumstances permit, make a full effort to consult with the Soviet Government in all matters affecting this area. As is the case in Europe, we should use our full influence, however, to assure that democratic regimes are established in the area, rather than Soviet-sponsored totalitarian governments.

In our policy in dealing with countries under Soviet domination we should, when possible, work out a concrete program, both political and economic, designed to support all the democratic elements in these countries but should not take any action which would strengthen the totalitarian left. On the other hand, since in general the non-communist left appears to have the broadest basis of popular support in this area, we should be prepared to assist these groups whenever possible. Present indications point to the possibility that the Soviet Government may realize that its efforts completely to control the areas under Soviet domination are not meeting with success and are in fact proving to be a liability. This development appears to be taking place because of the growing resistance to Soviet methods and the disrupting influence which contact with these countries is having on Soviet occupation troops. Since the Soviet Union itself has many internal problems to solve in the next few years, it is possible that because of the difficulties encountered in Eastern and Central Europe and because it needs to exert its maximum efforts internally, the Soviet Government may decide to abandon its policy of full control in these areas. We should adapt our policy to encourage them in this direction without loss of face, if circumstances permit.

In the conduct of our relations with the Soviet Government we must always bear in mind that because of the differences between the economic and political systems of our two countries, the conduct of our relations requires more patience and diligence than with other countries. We should be prepared to overlook minor grievances, explain carefully and in detail our reasons for all of our actions or requests, and if it is deemed advisable to take a firm position regarding the Soviet Union, we should always be as careful as possible to assure that our facts are correct. The adoption of a firm and friendly attitude in our dealings with the Soviet Government when our interests are involved will put our relations on a much more satisfactory basis than yielding in the hope of securing greater consideration in the future, or the adoption of half-way measures, or failure to make our position clear in each case. On the other hand, in order to minimize Soviet suspicions of our motives we should avoid even the appearance of taking unilateral action ourselves.

CHAPTER SEVEN

The War of Ideas

35   Molotov and Stalin prepare the Russian people for the Cold War
       ahead

The Truman Administration began to abandon hope of accommodating Russian
fears and plans of expansion—President Truman was alleged to have said to
Secretary of State Byrnes in early January 1946, 'I'm tired of babying the Soviets'. At
the same time, Soviet leaders began the difficult task of preparing the Russian
people for the struggle ahead, for the continued sacrifices they would have to make
in the name of rebuilding their war-torn economy, and for the inevitable
postponement of the production of consumer goods for the sake of heavy industry.
To achieve this goal Molotov and Stalin appealed to the heightened sense of
Russian nationalism that accompanied the Red Army's victory over Germany and
Japan and to the Marxist theme of capitalist antagonism to industrial socialism. The
first of the addresses below enunciated, in Adam B. Ulam's words, 'This simple
nationalistic creed'; Molotov outlined for the voters of the electoral district in which
he was the only candidate for the Supreme Soviet the great achievement of the
USSR in smashing the armies of fascist aggression. So decisive was that victory,
observed the Foreign Minister, that 'The USSR ranks today among the most
authoritative of the world powers.' Several days later, on February 9, 1946, Stalin
also delivered a speech before the voters of his own electoral district. Molotov's
speech had been followed with some interest in the West, but Stalin's was regarded
as the single most important Soviet pronouncement of the postwar period. With its
particular emphasis on Marxist-Leninist ideology, Stalin's speech generated a high
degree of interest and comment within the Department of State. In a characteristic
reaction, H. Freeman Matthews, Director of the Office of European Affairs, noted on
February 11, 1946 that 'Stalin's speech of February 9 constitutes the most important
and authoritative guide to postwar Soviet policy .... It should be given great
weight in any plans which may be under consideration for extending credits or
other forms of economic assistance to the Soviet Union.' Or, as then Under-

Secretary of State Dean Acheson recalled in his memoirs *Present at the Creation* (1969): 'This was the start of the "cold war", and was [together with the events of 1945 to 1950] to condition the rest of my official life.'

35(a) Speech at a meeting of voters of the Molotov electoral area of Moscow: February 6 1946. *'The time has come to take up the work interrupted by the war.'*

Source: *Molotov Speeches*, 26-36.

Comrades,

You and the voters you represent have nominated me as a candidate to the Supreme Soviet, and the Election Commission of the Molotov Electoral Area of Moscow has registered my candidacy. Permit me to express my deep gratitude for the confidence you have thereby accorded to the Communist Party, for the confidence and honour you have accorded me personally as a representative of the Party. *(Loud applause. All rise.)* I thank you for the kind words you have said here about me and my work. *(Applause.)*

On my part I wish to assure you and all the voters that I remember well what Comrade Stalin said about a deputy's prime duty: to have the great image of the great Lenin always before him and to emulate Lenin in everything. *(Prolonged applause.)* To emulate Lenin means at the same time to emulate the great Stalin, the continuer of Lenin's cause. *(Prolonged applause.)* There can be no nobler task for a deputy than to emulate Lenin and Stalin and to be really worthy of this. Rest assured, comrades, that I have always striven with all my heart for this. *(Applause.)*

We are on the eve of new general elections. The entire adult population of the country is taking part in these elections. The attitude of all the many millions in the Soviet Union towards the leadership of the Communist Party and towards the policy of the Soviet Government is now being tested. Well, we have reason to look confidently ahead. One confirmation of this is the fact that the communist and non-party bloc has become still stronger and is working in great harmony. There may be people abroad who still dream that it would be a good thing if some party other than the Communist Party were to assume the leadership of our country. To these people one might reply in the simple words of the proverb: "If ifs and ands were pots and pans. . ." *(Laughter and applause.)* There is no need to say much about such people, people, so to speak, "from the other world." *(Laughter and applause.)* As for our people, they have their own opinion on the subject. What's to be done, when the Soviet people have formed bonds of close kinship and have identified themselves with their Communist Party? *(Loud and prolonged applause.)* And if there are people abroad who still do not like this, we can console them with the thought that nowadays in other countries, too, it is no rare thing to find the Communists, as leaders, enjoying the confidence of the broad mass of the people. *(Applause.)* This only goes to show that the lessons of life are not wasted. In short, the earth is not only revolving, but, one might say, is not revolving in vain *(laughter, applause)*, and is pursuing a forward course towards a better future. *(Applause.)*

The four-year war with Germany, and then with Japan, was a supreme test for the young Soviet State. This war, which strained all the spiritual and material forces of the people, was an exceptionally severe test of the policy of the Bolshevik Party. More, it was a test of the stability of the very political system of the Soviet Republic. Now no one can deny that the Soviet State has passed this test with flying colours.

Compare Russia as she was before the October Revolution with what she has become today. We know that the Russo-Japanese War of 1904-05 caused upheaval in tsarist Russia. Everyone knows about the first Russian revolution, when the first thunderstorm burst over the tsarist regime. The war with Germany of 1914-17 snapped tsarism at its roots and ended with the abolition of the bourgeois landlord system in Russia. At the time of the war with Japan, the tsarist government admitted its defeat and hastened to end the war. But tsarist Russia was unable to survive the war with Germany, thus demonstrating how utterly rotten and moribund the old regime had become.

Compare this with the present state of our country, after a most gruelling war with Germany and then the war with Japan. Both aggressors, together with their satellites, have been smashed, thanks chiefly to our Red Army. *(Applause.)* The Soviet Union achieved victory in the West and then in the East, which, as you see, is quite unlike the old pre-Soviet times. Having stood these supreme tests, the Soviet Union has advanced still further to the fore as a major factor in international life. The U.S.S.R. ranks today among the most authoritative of the world powers. *(Applause.)* Important problems of international relations cannot nowadays be settled without the participation of the Soviet Union or without heeding the voice of our country. The participation of Comrade Stalin is regarded as the best guarantee of a successful solution of complicated international problems. *(Prolonged applause.)* Without indulging in self-complacency, and always remembering how tenacious of life the reactionary forces in the capitalist countries still are, we must, nevertheless, recognize that the new position the Soviet Union now occupies in international affairs is not the result of fortuitous circumstances, that it corresponds with the interests of all peace-loving nations as well as with the interests of all countries that are following the road of democratic development and assertion of their national independence.

The credit for all this belongs primarily to the heroic Red Army. *(Applause.)* Our Red Army men and Red Navy men, officers and commanders of all arms, have served devotedly, to the glory of our country. Our generals and marshals, with Generalissimo Stalin at their head, have brought fame and renown to the Soviet Union. The enemy was halted at the gates of Moscow, and this marked the turn of the tide on the Soviet-German front. The enemy surrounded Leningrad, but proved powerless to carry out his plan of capturing the city. The enemy was beaten at Stalingrad, and that marked the beginning of the utter rout of the German army on our front. These tasks were accomplished according to the strategic plan, and under the direct leadership of our great captain, Comrade Stalin. *(Loud and prolonged applause.)*

The defeat of the enemy came as a result of the efforts of the entire Soviet people, who ensured the victory. We had to lengthen the working day. Millions of women replaced men on collective farms and at mills and factories. Young people self-sacrificingly did the work of adults. We had to reconcile ourselves to serious restrictions of the most vital necessities, to a grave housing shortage, to evacuation to distant parts, and to other wartime hardships. And in spite of this our national economy coped with its main tasks. The needs of the front were satisfied unfailingly and uninterruptedly. The urgent needs of the rear were also met, although with great restrictions. Comrade Stalin's call, "Everything for the front!" was responded to with unanimity by the entire Soviet people, and this ensured victory. *(Applause.)*

Overcoming all difficulties at the front and in the rear, we achieved victory. We were able to do so because not only during the war, but in the years preceding the war, we pursued a correct course. We swept the internal enemies out of our way, all those saboteurs and subversive elements who in the end turned into a gang of spies and wreckers in the employ of foreign masters. We also know that the Soviet people had long dampened all ardour for direct foreign interference in our internal affairs. In spite of all who tried to put spokes in our wheel, our people transformed their country and created a mighty Socialist State. *(Applause.)* The foundations of our victory were laid by the creation of the Red Army, the industrialization of the country, the reconstruction of agriculture on the basis of collective farming, the intensive work to raise the cultural level of the people, and the persistent training of engineering and other skilled personnel. And now we are able to review the glorious results: we have smashed a most dangerous enemy, scored a glorious victory, welded the family of Soviet nations still closer together, and raised the international prestige of the Soviet Union to unprecedented heights. Is any better test required of the correctness of the policy of the Bolshevik Party? *(Applause.)* After this, it is not difficult to understand why confidence in our Party has grown so immensely, why confidence in Comrade Stalin's leadership is so unshakable. *(Prolonged applause.)*

The termination of the war confronted us with new tasks, and this also lays new obligations upon us.

The time has come to take up the work interrupted by the war. We shall need some time to raise socialist industry to the level it had reached before the war. But a couple of years will pass and we shall have accomplished it, which is more than any capitalist country could do. *(Applause.)* This task will be an integral part of the new five-year plan, which we are launching this year and which in many respects will enable us to surpass the prewar level of our national economy. *(Applause.)* We are again developing the branches of industry which will provide agriculture with the necessary quantity of tractors, farm machinery and fertilizer, and also those which will furnish locomotives, rolling stock and everything else needed by the railways and other important branches of transportation— sea, river and automobile. Another task on the order of the day is an all-round improvement in the supply of consumer goods to the population of town and country. For that a number of our industries will have to be expanded. The housing problem to be coped with has become particularly acute in view of the aftermath of destruction left by the war with the German invader. The construction of schools and hospitals, colleges and laboratories, cinemas and theatres and many other cultural and social institutions must be duly expanded, bearing in mind the shortcomings of the past and the need to draw more extensively on the experience of other countries. The people of Moscow will again address themselves to plans for the reconstruction of the capital, and we shall all actively participate in this work of major state importance. *(Applause.)*

You will remember that shortly before the war the Party and the Government had recognized that the time had come to practically tackle and accomplish the cardinal economic task of the U.S.S.R. This cardinal task was formulated as follows: to overtake and outstrip economically the most highly developed capitalist European countries and the United States of America, and definitely to accomplish this task in the nearest future. Our country was to produce no less industrial goods per head of population than the most developed capitalist country—that was the task. *(Applause.)*

We made a good start in this work. But Germany's attack interrupted the great effort. Now we shall tackle the job again, and with a deeper realization of its importance, and we shall try to make the pace of our work commensurate with the grandeur of the task. The crises, the industrial slumps, characteristic of the capitalist countries are unknown, and will be unknown, to us. We do not know and shall not know unemployment, for we have long discarded the fetters of capitalism and the rule of private property. It is conscious endeavour and socialist emulation in our mills and factories, on collective and state farms, on railways and in offices that are the mainsprings of our economic progress. *(Applause.)*

We must especially strive to make the labour of all more productive, for that is not only in the personal interest of every working man and woman, but in the common interest of the state. The time has passed when work was done to the strains of "Dubinushka." "Dubinushka," of course, is a good song; so is the Volga Boatmen's song. But there is a time for everything. In our age, the age of machinery and high technique—and especially when we are out to "overtake and outstrip"—new machinery must be introduced more extensively and effectively in all branches of our economy, so that the latest achievements of technology and science may play an ever greater part in the development of our industry and of our national economy generally. Then we shall accomplish our task—the task of overtaking and outstripping economically the most developed capitalist countries with that success which is required by the interests of our country and the interests of Communism. *(Applause.)*

Naturally, in order definitely to accomplish this colossal task, we need a lengthy period of peace and security for our country. The peaceable policy of the Soviet Union is not something transient; it springs from the fundamental interests and vital needs of our people, from their desire to raise their living standards as speedily as possible, from the tremendous urge felt by Soviet men and women to fashion their own way of life—the new cultural socialist way of life—and from our people's profound conviction that the Soviet Union will successfully accomplish all these tasks, provided the hounds of aggression are kept on the leash. That is why the Soviet people are so vigilant with regard to possible seats of disturbance of peace and international security or to any intrigues along these lines.

Our people spring to the alert today, too, when circumstances require it. Can we, for example, close our eyes to such facts as, say, the preservation in one form or another of hundreds of thousands of German troops of Hitler's defeated army in an area administered by our ally? It cannot but be regarded as a good sign that our ally has admitted that this state of affairs must be ended.

Or take another fact. To this day tens of thousands of troops of the Polish fascist General Anders, who is notorious for his enmity to the Soviet Union and who is ready for any adventurous gamble against the new democratic Poland, are being maintained in

Italy at the expense of the Allies. Facts like these certainly cannot be explained by concern for the peace and security of nations. Or take this instance. There still exists on Austrian territory, outside the Soviet zone, Colonel Rogozhin's Russian Whiteguard infantry corps, which during the war was in Hitler's pay and service. We have naturally demanded that this gang of degenerates be disbanded, again in the interest of peace and friendly relations among the Allies.

The Soviet Union has done no little to promote the building of a new and more effective organization to safeguard the peace and security of nations. The United Nations organization has already begun to function, and we wish it success in its important tasks. Our participation in this organization is aimed at making it effective in preventing fresh wars and in curbing all and every imperialist aggressor and violator of the will of other nations. The Soviet Union is always prepared in the interest of general peace to work in concord and harmony with peace-loving countries, big and small. There are no bellicose adventurist groups in the Soviet Union, as there are among the ruling classes of certain other countries where rather dangerous talk is already being encouraged by insatiable imperialists about a "third world war." True friends of the peace and security of nations will continue to find the Soviet Union a faithful ally and a reliable bulwark. *(Prolonged applause.)*

This does not mean that we are not concerned for the might of the Red Army and our Navy. No, concern for our armed forces is unrelaxing. Our army has accumulated fighting experience, has grown strong and steeled as never before. In the course of the war it underwent a great reorganization and geared itself to the demands of modern warfare. The fighting spirit and Soviet patriotism of our troops are well known. The government and the leadership of the Red Army are doing everything to ensure that as regards the very latest types of armaments, too, our army may be in no way inferior to the army of any other country. It is enough to say that all these years the armed forces of the Soviet Union have been headed by the great soldier and farsighted leader of our country, Generalissimo Stalin. *(Stormy cheers.)*

All this determines our new, postwar tasks.

These include both major problems, domestic and foreign, decisive for the future of our country and of our cause, and current tasks that demand urgent solution. The Bolshevik Party teaches us the art of combining these tasks. Unless we concentrate the necessary forces and means on the fundamental tasks of the state, we cannot look ahead with confidence, not to mention the fact that the war has borne out with tremendous cogency the correctness of this Bolshevik policy, which throughout the past has been pursued in the building of our state. *(Applause.)* One of the major achievements of our Party is the indisputable fact that our people have long grasped the profound import of this general line of Bolshevik policy. *(Applause.)* But the Party has always demanded that the available opportunities, and we have no few of them, should be used more widely and persistently to satisfy urgent needs connected with raising the standard of living of our population. The Party has always fought ruthlessly against bureaucratic disdain for what are called "minor" problems and has urged not only Bolshevik self-criticism, but active public criticism of the work of inefficient executives. And now that the war has left a whole crop of these "minor" problems, this is a fitting time to remind the executives of our organizations and institutions of this.

Much depends, of course, on ability to work, and still more on a genuine desire to learn how to work. It is never too late to learn, as you know. This applies both to local and to central executive officials. Comrade Stalin has told us more than once how useful it is for people in authority to take daily stock of their work, to sudy more frequently and more deeply the results of their activity. After all, nowadays, a good deal depends in every sphere of activity on the executives. The same factory, the same collective farm, the same organization or institution yields certain results under one manager, and much better results under another, more efficient manager. The factory worker, as you know, takes stock of his or her work every day. Factory workers want to know, and do know, how much they have produced in the course of the day, what they have to show for their work. The same thing may be said of the men and women of the countryside. The results of their work find expression in the number of collective-farm workday units; and we know what good care our collective farmers take to have as many of these units to their credit as they can, and how deeply rooted this now is in the life of the collective farms. Executives, too, must develop the habit of taking stock of their work every day, and must learn to be properly self-critical of the results of their activity. Then there will be fewer shortcomings in the work of many of our respected comrades, and we shall achieve the modern Bolshevik tempo we need in the solution of all urgent problems.

The Party, in its policy, gives us the correct line to work on. And we in authority in local and central organizations must prove by our deeds that we know how to work. We must prove our Bolshevik desire to work better, more productively, with maximum benefit for the people. You will probably agree that this is the thing which all our voters want.

We have every ground to expect that at the elections to the Supreme Soviet our people will again demonstrate their confidence in the Bolshevik Party and will unanimously support the candidates of the Stalin communist and non-party bloc of workers, peasants and intellectuals. This only enhances the responsibility devolving on the deputies: they must prove themselves worthy of the confidence of our great people and must justify the confidence of their electors. *(Applause.)* So let the new elections serve to weld our people together still more strongly, and to promote our further advance under the tried leadership of the Bolshevik Party and of our great and beloved Stalin. *(Stormy and prolonged cheers. All rise. Cries of: "Long live our great Stalin!" "Long live Stalin's faithful colleague, Comrade Molotov!")*

35(b) Speech at a meeting of voters of the Stalin electoral area of Moscow: February 9, 1946. *'Marxists have stated more than once that the capitalist system of world economy conceals in itself the elements of general crisis and military clashes . . .'*

Source: Embassy of the USSR, *Speech Delivered by J. V. Stalin at a Meeting of Voters of the Stalin Electoral Area of Moscow* (Wash. 1946).

Eight years have elapsed since the last elections to the Supreme Soviet. This was a period rich in events of a decisive nature.

The first four years passed in the intense work of the Soviet people for carrying out the Third Five-Year Plan. The following four years comprise the events of the war against the German and Japanese aggressors—the events of the Second World War. The war undoubtedly was the principal event of the past period.

It would be wrong to believe that the Second World War broke out accidentally or as a result of the mistakes of some or other statesmen, though mistakes certainly were made. In reality, the war broke out as an inevitable result of the development of world economic and political forces on the basis of modern monopoly capitalism.

Marxists have stated more than once that the capitalist system of world economy conceals in itself the elements of general crisis and military clashes, that in view of this in our time the development of world capitalism takes place not as a smooth and even advance but through crises and war catastrophies.

The reason is that the unevenness of the development of capitalist countries usually results, as time passes, in an abrupt disruption of the equilibrium within the world system of capitalism and that a group of capitalist countries which believes itself to be less supplied with raw materials and markets usually attempts to alter the situation and re-divide the 'spheres of influence" in its own favour by means of armed force.

This results in the splitting of the capitalist world into two hostile camps and in war between them.

Perhaps the catastrophies of war could be avoided if there existed the possibility of re-distributing periodically raw materials and markets among the countries in accordance with their economic weight—by means of adopting co-ordinated and peaceful decisions. This, however, cannot be accomplished under present capitalist conditions of the development of world economy.

Thus the first crisis of the capitalist system of world economy resulted in the First World War, and the second crisis resulted in the Second World War.

This does not mean, of course, that the Second World War was an exact replica of the first. On the contrary, the Second World War substantially differs in its nature from the first.

One should bear in mind that the principal fascist States, Germany, Japan, Italy—before attacking the Allied countries, had destroyed the last remnants of bourgeois-democratic liberties at home, established a brutal terroristic regime within their countries, trampled underfoot the principle of the sovereignty and free development of small countries, proclaimed that their policy was one of seizure of foreign lands, and declared, for all to hear, that their aim was world domination and the extension of the fascist regime to the whole world; while by the seizure of Czechoslovakia and the central provinces of China, the axis states demonstrated that they were ready to carry out their threat concerning the enslavement of all freedom-loving nations.

In view of this, as distinct from the First World War, the Second World War against the axis states from the very outset assumed the nature of an anti-fascist war, a war of liberation, one of the tasks of which was also to re-establish democratic liberties. The entry of the Soviet Union into the war against the axis states could only strengthen—and actually did strengthen—the anti-fascist and liberating character of the Second World War.

It was on this basis that the anti-fascist coalition of the Soviet Union, the United States of America, Great Britain and other freedom-loving States took shape, a coalition which later played a decisive part in routing the armed forces of the axis states. This is how matters stand with regard to the question of the origin and nature of the Second World War.

Now probably everyone agrees that the war indeed was not, and could not have been, an accident in the life of the nations, that it actually turned into a war of the nations for their existence, and that, for this very reason, it could not be a fleeting, lightning war.

As to our country, for her the war was the severest and hardest of all the wars our Motherland has ever experienced in her history.

But the war was not only a curse. It was at the same time a great school in which all the forces of the people were tried and tested. The war laid bare all the facts and events in the rear and at the front, it mercilessly tore off all the veils and covers which had concealed the true faces of States, governments, and parties, and placed them on the stage without masks, without embellishments, with all their shortcomings and virtues. . . .

And so, what are the results of the war?

There is one main result which served as a basis for all other results. This result is that at the end of the war the enemies suffered defeat and we, together with our Allies, emerged as victors. We ended the war in complete victory over the enemy—this is the principal result of the war. But this is too general a result, and we cannot stop at that.

Of course, to defeat the enemy in a war such as the Second World War, the like of which had never occurred in the history of mankind, means to attain an epoch-making victory. All this is true. Still, all this is a general result, and we cannot rest content with this. To realise the great historical significance of our victory, we must go into this matter more concretely. And so, how should we understand our victory over the enemies, what can this victory mean from the viewpoint of the condition and development of the internal forces of our country?

Our victory means, in the first place, that our Soviet social system has won, that the Soviet social system successfully withstood the trial in the flames of war and proved its perfect viability.

It is well known that the foreign press more than once asserted that the Soviet social system is a "risky experiment" doomed to failure, that the Soviet system is a "house of cards," without any roots in life, imposed upon the people by the organs of the "Cheka," that a slight push from outside would be enough to blow this "house of cards" to smithereens.

Now we can say that the war swept away all these assertions of the foreign press as groundless. The war has shown that the Soviet social system is a truly popular system, which has grown from the people and enjoys its powerful support, that the Soviet social system is a perfectly viable and stable from of organisation of society.

More than that, the point is now not whether the Soviet social system is viable or not, since after the objective lessons of the war no single sceptic now ventures to come out with doubts concerning the viability of the Soviet social system. The point now is that the Soviet social system has proved more viable and stable than a non-Soviet social system, that the Soviet social system is a better form of organisation of society than any non-Soviet social system.

Secondly, our victory means that out Soviet State system has won, that our multi national Soviet State withstood all the trials of war and proved its viability.

It is well known that prominent foreign journalists more than once made statements to the effect that the Soviet multi-national State is an "artificial and non-viable structure," that in the event of any complications collapse of the Soviet Union would be inevitable, that the Soviet Union would share the fate of Austro-Hungary.

Now we can say that the war refuted these statements of the foreign press as being utterly groundless. The war has shown that the Soviet multi-national State system successfully passed the test, grew even stronger during the war, and proved to be a perfectly viable State system.

Those gentlemen failed to understand that the comparison with Austro-Hungary is fallacious because our multi-national State has grown not on a bourgeois foundation which stimulates feelings of national distrust and national enmity, but on a Soviet foundation which, on the contrary, cultivates feelings of friendship and fraternal cooperation among the peoples of our State.

However, after the lessons of the war, those gentlemen no longer venture to deny the viability of the Soviet State system. The point now is not whether the Soviet State system is viable, for its viability is not to be doubted.

The point now is that the Soviet State system proved to be a model of the multi-national State, that the Soviet State system is such a system of State organisation in which the national problem and the problem of co-operation among nations have been solved better than in any other multi-national State.

Thirdly, our victory means that the Soviet armed forces have won, that our Red Army has won, that the Red Army heroically withstood all the adversities of war, utterly routed the armies of our enemies and emerged from the war as victor.

(Shout from the audience: "Under Comrade Stalin's leadership!" All rise. Stormy, continuous applause turning into an ovation).

Now everyone, both friends and enemies, admit that the Red Army was equal to its great tasks. But the situation was different some six years ago, in the pre-war period.

It is well known that prominent representatives of the foreign press and many recognised military authorities abroad repeatedly stated that the condition of the Red Army inspired grave doubts, that the Red Army was poorly armed and had no real commanding personnel, that its morale was beneath criticism, that it might perhaps prove useful in defence but was not fit for an offensive, that in the event of a blow by German troops the Red Army must fall apart like a "colossus with feet of clay."

Such assertions were made not in Germany alone but also in France, Britain and America.

Now we can say that the war swept away all these assertions as being groundless and laughable. The war has demonstrated that the Red Army is no "colossus with feet of clay" but a first-rate Army of our times, possessing quite modern armament, a most experienced commanding personnel and high moral and fighting qualities. One should not forget that the Red Army is that very army which utterly routed the German Army that but yesterday struck terror into the armies of European states. . . .

These are the main results of the war.

It would be erroneous to think that such an historic victory could have been achieved without preliminary preparation of the entire country for active defence. It would be no less erroneous to believe that such preparations could have been carried out within a short time, within some three or four years. Still more erroneous would it be to assert that we achieved victory owing solely to the gallantry of our troops.

Naturally, without gallantry, it is impossible to achieve victory. But gallantry alone is not sufficient to overpower an enemy possessing a big army, first-rate armament, a well-trained officer corps and a fairly well-organised supply. To meet the blow of such an enemy, to rebuff him and then utterly to defeat him, it was necessary to have, besides the unexampled gallantry of our troops, quite modern armament, and in sufficient quantity at that, and a well-organised supply, also in sufficient quantity.

But for this purpose it was necessary to have, and in sufficient quantities at that, such elementary things as metal for the production of armaments, equipment, industrial machinery; fuel for the maintenance of the work of factories and transport; cotton for the production of army clothing; bread to supply the army.

Is it possible to assert that before joining the Second World War our country already had at its disposal the necessary minimum of material possibilities in order to satisfy these needs in the main? I believe that we can assert this.

To prepare this colossal accomplishment it was necessary to carry out the three Five-Year Plans of development of the national economy. It was these three Five-Year Plans that helped us to create these material possibilities. In any case, the position of our country in this respect before the Second World War in 1940 was several times better than it had been before the First World War in 1913.

What material possibilities were at the disposal of our country before the Second World War?

To help you to get at the truth in this matter, I shall have to give here a short account of the activities of the Communist Party in preparing our country for active defence.

If we take the figures for 1940—the eve of the Second World War—and compare them with the figures for 1913—the eve of the First World War—we get the following picture:

In 1913 our country produced 4,220,000 tons of pig iron, 4,230,000 tons of steel, 29,000,000 tons of coal, 9,000,000 tons of oil, 21,600,000 tons of marketable grain, 740,000 tons of raw cotton.

Such were the material potentialities with which our country entered the First World War. This was the economic basis of the old Russia which could be used for waging war.

As to 1940, in that year our country produced: 15,000,000 tons of pig iron, that is, nearly four times as much as in 1913: 18,300,000 tons of steel, that is, four and a-half times as much as in 1913; 166,000,000 tons of coal, that is, five and a-half times as much as in 1913; 31,000,000 tons of oil, that is, three and a-half times as much as in 1913; 38,300,000 tons of marketable grain, that is, 17,000,000 tons more than in 1913; 2,700,000 tons of raw cotton, that is, three and a-half times as much as in 1913.

Such were the material potentialities with which our country entered the Second World War. Such was the economic basis of the Soviet Union which could be used for waging the war.

The difference is tremendous, as you see. Such an unexampled growth of production cannot be regarded as a simple and ordinary development of a country from backwardness to progress. This was a leap by means of which our Motherland turned from a backward into an advanced country, from an agrarian into an industrial country.

This historic transformation was carried out within the three Five Year Plans beginning with 1928—the first year of the First Five-Year Plan. Until that time we had had to engage in the restoration of destroyed industry and in healing the wounds received as a result of the First World War and the Civil War. If we consider besides, that the First Five-Year Plan was carried out in four years, and that the work on the Third Five-Year Plan was interrupted by the war in the fourth year of its execution, we shall see that it took only about 13 years to convert our country from an agrarian into an industrial country.

One cannot help admitting that 13 years is an unbelievably short time for accomplishing such a tremendous task.

It is this that essentially explains why the publication of these figures at the time evoked a storm of contradictory comment in the foreign press. Friends decided that a "miracle" had taken place. As to ill wishers, they declared that the Five-Year Plans were "Bolshevik propaganda" and "tricks of the Cheka." But since miracles do not happen and the Cheka is not strong enough to abolish the laws of the development of society, "public opinion" abroad had to reconcile itself to the facts.

What was the policy which enabled the Communist Party to secure these material possibilities in the country within such a short time?

In the first place, it was the Soviet policy of industrialisation of the country. The Soviet method of industrialisation of the country differs radically from the capitalist method of industrialisation. In capitalist countries, industrialisation usually begins with light industry. Since light industry requires smaller investments, since the turnover of capital is quicker and the profits are made more easily than in heavy industry, it is light industry that becomes there the first object of industrialisation.

Only after a long period during which light industry accumulates profits and concentrates them in banks, only then comes the turn of heavy industry and there begins a gradual transfer of accumulated profits into heavy industry in order to create the conditions for its development. But this is a lengthy process, requiring a long period of several decades, during which it is necessary to wait until light industry develops and to vegetate without heavy industry.

Naturally, the Communist Party could not adopt this path. The Party knew that the war was coming, that it was impossible to defend the country without heavy industry, that it was necessary as quickly as possible to tackle the development of heavy industry, that to be late in this matter meant to lose. The Party remembered Lenin's words that without heavy industry it is impossible to uphold the country's independence, that without it the Soviet system may fall.

Therefore, the Communist Party of our country rejected the "usual" way of industrialisation and began the industrialisation of the country with the development of heavy industry. This was very difficult but feasible. Of great help in this matter was the nationalisation of industry and the banks which permitted the quick gathering and transfer of funds into heavy industry.

It is beyond doubt that without this it would have been impossible to achieve the transformation of our country into an industrial country within such a short time.

Secondly, it was the policy of collectivisation of agriculture.

In order to put an end to the backwardness of our agriculture and give the country more marketable grain, more cotton, etc., it was necessary to pass from small peasant farming to large-scale farming, because only a large farm is able to use new machinery, to take advantage of all the achievements of agronomic science and to yield more marketable produce.

There are, however, two kinds of large-scale farming—capitalist and collective. The Communist Party could not adopt the capitalist path of development of agriculture, and not as a matter of principle alone but also because it implies too prolonged a development and involves preliminary ruination of the peasants and their transformation into farm hands. Therefore, the Communist Party took the path of the collectivisation of agriculture, the path of creating large-scale farming by uniting peasant farms into collective farms.

The method of collectivisation proved a highly progressive method not only because it did not involve the ruination of the peasants but especially because it permitted, within a few years, the covering of the entire country with large collective farms which are able to use new machinery, take advantage of all the achievements of agronomic science and give the country greater quantities of marketable produce.

There is no doubt that without the policy of collectivisation we would not have been able to put an end to the age-old backwardness of our agriculture within such a short time.

One cannot say that the Party's policy did not encounter resistance. Not only backward people, who always shun everything new, but also many prominent Party members systematically pulled the Party back and in every way tried to drag it on to the "usual" capitalist path of development. All the anti-Party machinations of Trotskyites and the Right, all their "work" in sabotaging the measures of our Government pursued a single aim: to thwart the Party's policy and to retard the cause of industrialisation and collectivisation.

But the Party did not succumb either to the threats of some or to the howling of others, and confidently marched forward despite everything. It is to the Party's credit that it did not adapt itself to the backward elements, was not afraid of swimming against the stream and always preserved its position of the leading force. There can be no doubt that without this staunchness and perseverance the Communist Party would not have been able to uphold the policy of the industrialisation of the country and the collectivisation of agriculture.

Did the Communist Party succeed in utilising correctly the material possibilities thus created in order to develop war production and supply the Red Army with the necessary armament?

I believe it succeeded in accomplishing that, and accomplished it with the utmost success.

Leaving out of account the first year of the war when the evacuation of industry to the East retarded the development of war production, in the remaining three years of the war the Party succeeded in rising to such achievements as enabled it not only to supply the front with sufficient quantities of ordnance, machine-guns, rifles, aircraft, tanks, ammunition, but also to build up reserves.

And it is known that our armaments, far from being inferior to German arms, even surpassed them in quality. It is known that during the last three years of the war our tank-building industry annually built on an average more than 30,000 tanks, self-propelled guns and armoured cars.

It is also known that our aircraft industry in the same period produced annually up to 40,000 planes.

It is also known that in the same period our ordnance industry built annually up to 120,000 guns of all calibres, up to 450,000 light and heavy machine-guns, more than 3,000,000 rifles and nearly 2,000,000 tommy-guns.

Lastly, it is known that in the period of 1942-44 our mortar industry manufactured annually on an average up to 100,000 mortars.

Naturally, corresponding quantities of artillery shells, mines of various kinds, aircraft bombs, rifle and machine-gun cartridges were produced simultaneously.

It is known, for instance, that in 1944 alone more than 240,000,000 shells, bombs and mines, and 7,400,000,000 cartridges were manufactured.

Such is the general picture of the supply of the Red Army with arms and ammunition.

As you see, it does not resemble the picture of the supply of our Army during the First World War when the front experienced a chronic shortage of artillery and shells, when the Army fought without tanks and aircraft, when one rifle was issued for every three soldiers.

As to the supply of the Red Army with provisions and clothing, it is universally known that, far from suffering any shortages in this respect, the front even had the necessary reserves on the spot.

This is how matters stand as regards the work of the Communist Party of our country in the period before the war and during the war.

Now a few words concerning the plans for the work of the Communist Party in the near future. As is well known, these plans are set forth in the new Five-Year Plan, which is to be approved shortly. The main tasks of the new Five-Year Plan are to restore the afflicted districts of the country, to restore industry and agriculture to their pre-war level and then to exceed this level to a more or less considerable degree. Not to mention the fact that the ration card system will be abolished in the near future, special attention will be given to the extension of production of consumer goods, to raising the standard of living of the working people by means of the steady reduction of the prices of all commodities and to extensive construction of scientific research institutions of all kinds which will enable science to deploy its forces.

I do not doubt that if we render proper assistance to our scientists they will be able not only to come level with, but even to surpass, in the near future, the achievements of science beyond the boundaries of our country.

As to plans for a longer period, our Party intends to organise a new powerful upsurge of the national economy which would enable us, for instance, to raise the level of our industry three-fold as compared with the pre-war level. We must achieve a situation wherein our industry is able to produce annually up to 50,000,000 tons of pig iron, up to 60,000,000 tons of steel, up to 500,000,000 tons of coal, up to 60,000,000 tons of oil.

Only under such conditions can we regard our country as guaranteed against any accidents. This will require perhaps three new Five-Year Plans, if not more. But this task can be accomplished, and we must accomplish it.

Such is my brief account of the activities of the Communist Party in the recent past and of its plans for work in the future. It is for you to judge how correctly the Party worked, and is working now, and whether it could not have worked better.

They say that victors may not be judged, that they should not be criticised or controlled. This is wrong. Victors may and must be judged, they may and must be criticised and controlled. This is useful not only for the work but for the victors themselves, there will be less presumption, there will be more modesty.

I consider that in the election campaign, the electors are sitting in judgment on the Communist Party as the ruling party. And the result of the elections will signify the verdict returned by the electors. The Communist Party of our country would be worth little were it afraid of criticism, of a check-up. The Communist Party is ready to accept the electors verdict.

The Communist Party does not march alone in the election struggle. It goes to the elections in a bloc with the non-Party people. In past times the Communists treated non-Party people and being non-Party with a certain distrust. This was due to the fact that the non-Party banner was not infrequently used as a cover by various bourgeois groups which found it to their disadvantage to appear before the electors without a mask.

Thus it was in the past. But now we are living in different times. Non-Party people are now separated from the bourgeoisie by a barrier called the Soviet social system. The same barrier has united non-Party people with Communists in one common team of Soviet citizens.

Living in a common team, they struggled together to enhance the might of our country, they fought and shed blood together at the fronts in the name of the freedom and greatness of our country, they were forging and forged together victory over the enemies of our country.

The only difference between them is that some belong to the Party while others do not. But this is a formal difference. What is important is that both are working for the same common cause. Therefore, the bloc of Communists and non-Party people is a natural and vital thing.

In conclusion, allow me to thank you for the trust you have extended to me by nominating me a candidate to the Supreme Soviet. You need not doubt that I shall try to justify your trust.

36   An interpretative analysis of future Soviet policy—Kennan's Long
      Telegram: February 22, 1946. '. . . we have here a political force
      committed fanatically to the belief that with US there can be no
      permanent modus vivendi . . .'

In the so-called 'Long Telegram' of February 22, 1946 (which was initially a response
to the State Department's request for an interpretative analysis of the significance
and meaning of Stalin's and other Soviet officials' pre-election speeches to the
Supreme Soviet), the then American chargé George F. Kennan formulated an
assessment of Soviet foreign policy that uniquely captured the mood of the Truman
Administration's determination to resist the perceived threat of Stalinist Russia to
world peace. For, as Kennan wrote in his Memoirs, 1925-1950 (1967), 'The effect
produced in Washington by this elaborate pedagogical effort was nothing less than
sensational. It was one that changed my career and my life in very basic ways.'
Among Kennan's conclusions, which in retrospect tell us almost as much about the
state of Kennan's mind as they do about a contemporary American view of the
springs of Soviet policy, is the judgment that ' . . . we have here [the Soviet Union] a
political force committed fanatically to the belief that with the US there can be no
permanent modus vivendi, that it is desirable and necessary that the internal
harmony of our society be disrupted, our traditional way of life be destroyed, the
international authority of our state be broken, if Soviet power is to be secure.' Given
the rigidity of such a statement, it is not hard to imagine Kennan writing in the late
1960's that 'I read it over today with a horrified amusement.' Amusement or not,
Kennan's characterization of the motives of Soviet leadership became the
centerpiece of the emerging Cold War paradigm in Washington, and one that was to
last for a generation of Americans.

Source: Department of State, Foreign Relations of the United States, Diplomatic Papers: 1946 (Wash. 1969), VI,
696-709.

[The State Department's request] involves questions so intricate, so delicate, so strange to
our form of thought, and so important to analysis of our international environment that I
cannot compress answers into single brief message without yielding to what I feel would
be dangerous degree of over-simplification. I hope, therefore, Dept will bear with me if I
submit in answer to this question five parts, subjects of which will be roughly as follows:

(1)   Basic features of post-war Soviet outlook.
(2)   Background of this outlook.
(3)   Its projection in practical policy on official level.
(4)   Its projection on unofficial level.
(5)   Practical deductions from standpoint of US policy.

I apologize in advance for this burdening of telegraphic channel; but questions
involved are of such urgent importance, particularly in view of recent events, that our

answers to them, if they deserve attention at all, seem to me to deserve it at once. There follows

Part 1: Basic Features of Post War Soviet Outlook, as Put Forward by Official Propaganda Machine, Are as Follows:

(a) USSR still lives in antagonistic "capitalist encirclement" with which in the long run there can be no permanent peaceful coexistence. As stated by Stalin in 1927 to a delegation of American workers:

> "In course of further development of international revolution there will emerge two centers of world significance: a socialist center, drawing to itself the countries which tend toward socialism, and a capitalist center, drawing to itself the countries that incline toward capitalism. Battle between these two centers for command of world economy will decide fate of capitalism and of communism in entire world."

(b) Capitalist world is beset with internal conflicts, inherent in nature of capitalist society. These conflicts are insoluble by means of peaceful compromise. Greatest of them is that between England and US.

(c) Internal conflicts of capitalism inevitably generate wars. Wars thus generated may be of two kinds: intra-capitalist wars between two capitalist states, and wars of intervention against socialist world. Smart capitalists, vainly seeking escape from inner conflicts of capitalism, incline toward latter.

(d) Intervention against USSR, while it would be disastrous to those who undertook it, would cause renewed delay in progress of Soviet socialism and must therefore be forestalled at all costs.

(e) Conflicts between capitalist states, though likewise fraught with danger for USSR, nevertheless hold out great possibilities for advancement of socialist cause, particularly if USSR remains militarily powerful, ideologically monolithic and faithful to its present brilliant leadership.

(f) It must be borne in mind that capitalist world is not all bad. In addition to hopelessly reactionary and bourgeois elements, it includes (1) certain wholly enlightened and positive elements united in acceptable communistic parties and (2) certain other elements (now described for tactical reasons as progressive or democratic) whose reactions, aspirations and activities happen to be "objectively" favorable to interests of USSR. These last must be encouraged and utilized for Soviet purposes.

(g) Among negative elements of bourgeois-capitalist society, most dangerous of all are those whom Lenin called false friends of the people, namely moderate-socialist or social-democratic leaders (in other words, non-Communist left-wing). These are more dangerous than out-and-out reactionaries, for latter at least march under their true colors, whereas moderate left-wing leaders confuse people by employing devices of socialism to serve interests of reactionary capital.

So much for premises. To what deductions do they lead from standpoint of Soviet policy? To following:

(a) Everything must be done to advance relative strength of USSR as factor in international society. Conversely, no opportunity must be missed to reduce strength and influence, collectively as well as individually, of capitalist powers.

(b) Soviet efforts, and those of Russia's friends abroad, must be directed toward deepening and exploiting of differences and conflicts between capitalist powers. If these eventually deepen into an "imperialist" war, this war must be turned into revolutionary upheavals within the various capitalist countries.

(c) "Democratic-progressive" elements abroad are to be utilized to maximum to bring pressure to bear on capitalist governments along lines agreeable to Soviet interests.

(d) Relentless battle must be waged against socialist and social-democratic leaders abroad.

Part 2: Background of Outlook

Before examining ramifications of this party line in practice there are certain aspects of it to which I wish to draw attention.

First, it does not represent natural outlook of Russian people. Latter are, by and large, friendly to outside world, eager for experience of it, eager to measure against it talents they are conscious of possessing, eager above all to live in peace and enjoy fruits of their own labor. Party line only represents thesis which official propaganda machine puts forward with great skill and persistence to a public often remarkably resistant in the stronghold of its innermost thoughts. But party line is binding for outlook and conduct of people who make up apparatus of power—party, secret police and Government—and it is exclusively with these that we have to deal.

Second, please note that premises on which this party line is based are for most part simply not true. Experience has shown that peaceful and mutually profitable coexistence of capitalist and socialist states is entirely possible. Basic internal conflicts in advanced countries are no longer primarily those arising out of capitalist ownership of means of production, but are ones arising from advanced urbanism and industrialism as such, which Russia has thus far been spared not by socialism but only by her own backwardness. Internal rivalries of capitalism do not always generate wars; and not all wars are attributable to this cause. To speak of possibility of intervention against USSR today, after elimination of Germany and Japan and after example of recent war, is sheerest nonsense. If not provoked by forces of intolerance and subversion "capitalist" world of today is quite capable of living at peace with itself and with Russia. Finally, no sane person has reason to doubt sincerity of moderate socialist leaders in Western countries. Nor is it fair to deny success of their efforts to improve conditions for working population whenever, as in Scandinavia, they have been given chance to show what they could do.

Falseness of these premises, every one of which pre-dates recent war, was amply demonstrated by that conflict itself. Anglo-American differences did not turn out to be major differences of Western World. Capitalist countries, other than those of Axis, showed no disposition to solve their differences by joining in crusade against USSR. Instead of imperialist war turning into civil wars and revolution, USSR found itself obliged to fight side by side with capitalist powers for an avowed community of aims.

Nevertheless, all these theses, however baseless and disproven, are being boldly put forward again today. What does this indicate? It indicates that Soviet party line is not based on any objective analysis of situation beyond Russia's borders; that it has, indeed, little to do with conditions outside of Russia; that it arises mainly from basic inner-

Russian necessities which existed before recent war and exist today.

At bottom of Kremlin's neurotic view of world affairs is traditional and instinctive Russian sense of insecurity. Originally, this was insecurity of a peaceful agricultural people trying to live on vast exposed plain in neighborhood of fierce nomadic peoples. To this was added, as Russia came into contact with economically advanced West, fear of more competent, more powerful, more highly organized societies in that area. But this latter type of insecurity was one which afflicted rather Russian rulers than Russian people; for Russian rulers have invariably sensed that their rule was relatively archaic in form, fragile and artificial in its psychological foundation, unable to stand comparison or contact with political systems of Western countries. For this reason they have always feared foreign penetration, feared direct contact between Western world and their own, feared what would happen if Russians learned truth about world without or if foreigners learned truth about world within. And they have learned to seek security only in patient but deadly struggle for total destruction of rival power, never in compacts and compromises with it.

It was no coincidence that Marxism, which had smouldered ineffectively for half a century in Western Europe, caught hold and blazed for first time in Russia. Only in this land which had never known a friendly neighbor or indeed any tolerant equilibrium of separate powers, either internal or international, could a doctrine thrive which viewed economic conflicts of society as insoluble by peaceful means. After establishment of Bolshevist regime, Marxist dogma, rendered even more truculent and intolerant by Lenin's interpretation, became a perfect vehicle for sense of insecurity with which Bolsheviks, even more than previous Russian rulers, were afflicted. In this dogma, with its basic altruism of purpose, they found justification for their instinctive fear of outside world, for the dictatorship without which they did not know how to rule, for cruelties they did not dare not to inflict, for sacrifices they felt bound to demand. In the name of Marxism they sacrificed every single ethical value in their methods and tactics. Today they cannot dispense with it. It is fig leaf of their moral and intellectual respectability. Without it they would stand before history, at best, as only the last of that long succession of cruel and wasteful Russian rulers who have relentlessly forced country on to ever new heights of military power in order to guarantee external security of their internally weak regimes. This is why Soviet purposes must always be solemnly clothed in trappings of Marxism, and why no one should underrate importance of dogma in Soviet affairs. Thus Soviet leaders are driven [by?] necessities of their own past and present position to put forward a dogma which [apparent omission] outside world as evil, hostile and menacing, but as bearing within itself germs of creeping disease and destined to be wracked with growing internal convulsions until it is given final *coup de grace* by rising power of socialism and yields to new and better world. This thesis provides justification for that increase of military and police power of Russian state, for that isolation of Russian population from outside world, and for that fluid and constant pressure to extend limits of Russian police power which are together the natural and instinctive urges of Russian rulers. Basically this is only the steady advance of uneasy Russian nationalism, a centuries old movement in which conceptions of offense and defense are inextricably confused. But in new guise of international Marxism, with its honeyed promises to a desperate and war torn outside world, it is more dangerous and insidious than ever before.

It should not be thought from above that Soviet party line is necessarily disingenuous and insincere on part of all those who put it forward. Many of them are too ignorant of outside world and mentally too dependent to question [apparent omission] self-hypnotism, and who have no difficulty making themselves believe what they find it comforting and convenient to believe. Finally we have the unsolved mystery as to who, if anyone, in this great land actually receives accurate and unbiased information about outside world. In atmosphere of oriental secretiveness and conspiracy which pervades this Government, possibilities for distorting or poisoning sources and currents of information are infinite. The very disrespect of Russians for objective truth—indeed, their disbelief in its existence—leads them to view all stated facts as instruments for furtherance of one ulterior purpose or another. There is good reason to suspect that this Government is actually a conspiracy within a conspiracy; and I for one am reluctant to believe that Stalin himself receives anything like an objective picture of outside world. Here there is ample scope for the type of subtle intrigue at which Russians are past masters. Inability of foreign governments to place their case squarely before Russian policy makers—extent to which they are delivered up in their relations with Russia to good graces of obscure and unknown advisers whom they never see and cannot influence—this to my mind is most disquieting feature of diplomacy in Moscow, and one which Western statesmen would do well to keep in mind if they would understand nature of difficulties encountered here.

Part 3: Projection of Soviet Outlook in Practical Policy on Official Level

We have now seen nature and background of Soviet program. What may we expect by way of its practical implementation?

Soviet policy, as Department implies in its query under reference, is conducted on two planes: (1)   official plane represented by actions undertaken officially in name of Soviet Government; and (2)   subterranean plane of actions undertaken by agencies for which Soviet Government does not admit responsibility.

Policy promulgated on both planes will be calculated to serve basic policies *(a)* to *(d)* outlined in part 1. Actions taken on different planes will differ considerably, but will dovetail into each other in purpose, timing and effect.

On official plane we must look for following:

(a)   Internal policy devoted to increasing in every way strength and prestige of Soviet state: intensive military-industrialization; maximum development of armed forces; great displays to impress outsiders; continued secretiveness about internal matters, designed to conceal weaknesses and to keep opponents in dark.

(b)   Wherever it is considered timely and promising, efforts will be made to advance official limits of Soviet power. For the moment, these efforts are restricted to certain neighboring points conceived of here as being of immediate strategic necessity, such as Northern Iran, Turkey, possibly Bornholm. However, other points may at any time come into question, if and as concealed Soviet political power is extended to new areas. Thus a "friendly" Persian Government might be asked to grant Russia a port on Persian Gulf. Should Spain fall under Communist control, question of Soviet base at Gibraltar Strait might be activated. But such claims will appear on official level only when unofficial preparation is complete.

(c)   Russians will participate officially in international organizations where they see opportunity of extending Soviet power or of inhibiting or diluting power of others. Moscow sees in UNO not the mechanism for a permanent and stable world society founded on mutual interest and aims of all nations, but an arena in which aims just mentioned can be favorably pursued. As long as UNO is considered here to serve this purpose, Soviets will remain with it. But if at any time they come to conclusion that it is serving to embarrass or frustrate their aims for power expansion and if they see better prospects for pursuit of these aims along other lines, they will not hesitate to abandon UNO. This would imply, however, that they felt themselves strong enough to split unity of other nations by their withdrawal, to render UNO ineffective as a threat to their aims or security, and to replace it with an international weapon more effective from their viewpoint. Thus Soviet attitude toward UNO will depend largely on loyalty of other nations to it, and on degree of vigor, decisiveness and cohesion with which these nations defend in UNO the peaceful and hopeful concept of international life, which that organization represents to our way of thinking. I reiterate, Moscow has no abstract devotion to UNO ideals. Its attitude to that organization will remain essentially pragmatic and tactical.

(d)   Toward colonial areas and backward or dependent peoples, Soviet policy, even on official plane, will be directed toward weakening of power and influence and contacts of advanced Western nations, on theory that in so far as this policy is successful, there will be created a vacuum which will favor Communist-Soviet penetration. Soviet pressure for participation in trusteeship arrangements thus represents, in my opinion, a desire to be in a postion to complicate and inhibit exertion of Western influence at such points rather than to provide major channel for exerting of Soviet power. Latter motive is not lacking, but for this Soviets prefer to rely on other channels than official trusteeship arrangements. Thus we may expect to find Soviets asking for admission everywhere to trusteeship or similar arrangements and using levers thus acquired to weaken Western influence among such peoples.

(e)   Russians will strive energetically to develop Soviet representation in, and official ties with, countries in which they sense strong possibilities of opposition to Western centers of power. This applies to such widely separated points as Germany, Argentina, Middle Eastern countries, etc.

(f)   In international economic matters, Soviet policy will really be dominated by pursuit of autarchy for Soviet Union and Soviet-dominated adjacent areas taken together. That, however, will be underlying policy. As far as official line is concerned, position is not yet clear. Soviet Government has shown strange reticence since termination hostilities on subject foreign trade. If large scale long term credits should be forthcoming, I believe Soviet Government may eventually again do lip service, as it did in 1930's to desirability of building up interntional economic exchanges in general. Otherwise I think it possible Soviet foreign trade may be restricted largely to Soviet's own security sphere, including occupied areas in Germany, and that a cold official shoulder may be turned to principle of general economic collaboration among nations.

(g)   With respect to cultural collaboration, lip service will likewise be rendered to desirability.of deepening cultural contacts between peoples, but this will not in practice be interpreted in any way which could weaken security position of Soviet peoples. Actual

manifestations of Soviet policy in this respect will be restricted to arid channels of closely shepherded official visits and functions, with super-abundance of vodka and speeches and dearth of permanent effects.

(h) Beyond this, Soviet official relations will take what might be called "correct" course with individual foreign governments, with great stress being laid on prestige of Soviet Union and its representatives and with punctilious attention to protocol, as distinct from good manners.

Part 4: Following May Be Said as to What We May Expect by Way of Implementation of Basic Soviet Policies on Unofficial, or Subterranean Plane, i.e. on Plane for Which Soviet Government Accepts no Responsibility

Agencies utilized for promulgation of policies on this plane are following:

1. Inner central core of Communist Parties in other countries. While many of persons who compose this category may also appear and act in unrelated public capacities, they are in reality working closely together as an underground operating directorate of world communism, a concealed Comintern[1] tightly coordinated and directed by Moscow. It is important to remember that this inner core is actually working on underground lines, despite legality of parties with which it is associated.

2. Rank and file of Communist Parties. Note distinction is drawn between these and persons defined in paragraph 1. This distinction has become much sharper in recent years. Whereas formerly foreign Communist Parties represented a curious (and from Moscow's standpoint often inconvenient) mixture of conspiracy and legitimate activity, now the conspiratorial element has been neatly concentrated in inner circle and ordered underground, while rank and file—no longer even taken into confidence about realities of movement—are thrust forward as bona fide internal partisans of certain political tendencies within their respective countries, genuinely innocent of conspiratorial connection with foreign states. Only in certain countries where communists are numerically strong do they now regularly appear and act as a body. As a rule they are used to penetrate, and to influence or dominate, as case may be, other organizations less likely to be suspected of being tools of Soviet Government, with a view to accomplishing their purposes through [apparent omission] organizations, rather than by direct action as a separate political party.

3. A wide variety of national associations or bodies which can be dominated or influenced by such penetration. These include: labor unions, youth leagues, women's organizations, racial societies, religious societies, social organizations, cultural groups, liberal magazines, publishing houses, etc.

4. International organizations which can be similarly penetrated through influence over various national components. Labor, youth and women's organizations are prominent among them. Particular, almost vital, importance is attached in the connection to international labor movement. In this, Moscow sees possibility of sidetracking western governments in world affairs and building up international lobby capable of compelling governments to take actions favorable to Soviet interests in various countries and of paralyzing actions disagreeable to USSR.

5. Russian Orthodox Church, with its foreign branches, and through it the Eastern Orthodox Church in general.

6. Pan-Slav movement and other movements (Azerbaijan, Armenian, Turcoman, etc.) based on racial groups within Soviet Union.

7. Governments or governing groups willing to lend themselves to Soviet purposes in one degree or another, such as present Bulgarian and Yugoslav Governments, North Persian regime, Chinese Communists, etc. Not only propaganda machines but actual policies of these regimes can be placed extensively at disposal of USSR.

It may be expected that component parts of this far-flung apparatus will be utilized, in accordance with their individual suitability, as follows:

(a) To undermine general political and strategic potential of major western powers. Efforts will be made in such countries to disrupt national self confidence, to hamstring measures of national defense, to increase social and industrial unrest, to stimulate all forms of disunity. All persons with grievances, whether economic or racial, will be urged to seek redress not in mediation and compromise, but in defiant violent struggle for destruction of other elements of society. Here poor will be set against rich, black against white, young against old, newcomers against established residents, etc.

(b) On unofficial plane particularly violent efforts will be made to weaken power and influence of Western Powers of [*on*] colonial backward, or dependent peoples. On this level, no holds will be barred. Mistakes and weaknesses of western colonial administration will be mercilessly exposed and exploited. Liberal opinion in Western countries will be mobilized to weaken colonial policies. Resentment among dependent peoples will be stimulated. And while latter are being encouraged to seek independence of Western Powers, Soviet dominated puppet political machines will be undergoing preparation to take over domestic power in respective colonial areas when independence is achieved.

(c) Where individual governments stand in path of Soviet purposes pressure will be brought for their removal from office. This can happen where governments directly oppose Soviet foreign policy aims (Turkey, Iran), where they seal their territories off against Communist penetration (Switzerland, Portugal), or where they compete too strongly, like Labor Government in England, for moral domination among elements which it is important for Communists to dominate. (Sometimes, two of these elements are present in a single case. Then Communist opposition becomes particularly shrill and savage.[)]

(d) In foreign countries Communists will, as a rule, work toward destruction of all forms of personal independence, economic, political or moral. Their system can handle only individuals who have been brought into complete dependence on higher power. Thus, persons who are financially independent—such as individual businessmen, estate owners, successful farmers, artisans and all those who exercise local leadership or have local prestige, such as popular local clergymen or political figures, are anathema. It is not by chance that even in USSR local officials are kept constantly on move from one job to another, to prevent their taking root.

(e) Everything possible will be done to set major Western Powers against each other. Anti-British talk will be plugged among Americans, anti-American talk among British. Continentals, including Germans, will be taught to abhor both Anglo-Saxon powers. Where suspicions exist, they will be fanned; where not, ignited. No effort will be spared to discredit and combat all efforts which threaten to lead to any sort of unity or cohesion

among other [apparent omission] from which Russia might be excluded. Thus, all forms of international organization not amenable to Communist penetration and control, whether it be the Catholic [apparent omission] international economic concerns, or the international fraternity of royalty and aristocracy, must expect to find themselves under fire from many, and often [apparent omission].

(f)   In general, all Soviet efforts on unofficial international plane will be negative and destructive in character, designed to tear down sources of strength beyond reach of Soviet control. This is only in line with basic Soviet instinct that there can be no compromise with rival power and that constructive work can start only when Communist power is dominant. But behind all this will be applied insistent, unceasing pressure for penetration and command of key positions in administration and especially in police apparatus of foreign countries. The Soviet regime is a police regime par excellence, reared in the dim half world of Tsarist police intrigue, accustomed to think primarily in terms of police power. This should never be lost sight of in gauging Soviet motives.

Part 5: [Practical Deductions From Standpoint of US Policy]

In summary, we have here a political force committed fanatically to the belief that with US there can be no permanent *modus vivendi,* that it is desirable and necessary that the internal harmony of our society be disrupted, our traditional way of life be destroyed, the international authority of our state be broken, if Soviet power is to be secure. This political force has complete power of disposition over energies of one of world's greatest peoples and resources of world's richest national territory, and is borne along by deep and powerful currents of Russian nationalism. In addition, it has an elaborate and far flung apparatus for exertion of its influence in other countries, an apparatus of amazing flexibility and versatility, managed by people whose experience and skill in underground methods are presumably without parallel in history. Finally, it is seemingly inaccessible to considerations of reality in its basic reactions. For it, the vast fund of objective fact about human society is not, as with us, the measure against which outlook is constantly being tested and re-formed, but a grab bag from which individual items are selected arbitrarily and tendenciously to bolster an outlook already preconceived. This is admittedly not a pleasant picture. Problem of how to cope with this force in [*is*] undoubtedly greatest task our diplomacy has ever faced and probably greatest it will ever have to face. It should be point of departure from which our political general staff work at present juncture should proceed. It should be approached with same thoroughness and care as solution of major strategic problem in war, and if necessary, with no smaller outlay in planning effort. I cannot attempt to suggest all answers here. But I would like to record my conviction that problem is within our power to solve—and that without recourse to any general military conflict. And in support of this conviction there are certain observations of a more encouraging nature I should like to make:

(1)   Soviet power, unlike that of Hitlerite Germany, is neither schematic nor adventuristic. It does not work by fixed plans. It does not take unnecessary risks. Impervious to logic of reason, and it is highly sensitive to logic of force. For this reason it can easily withdraw—and usually does—when strong resistance is encountered at any point. Thus, if the adversary has sufficient force and makes clear his readiness to use it, he

rarely has to do so. If situations are properly handled there need be no prestige-engaging showdowns.

(2)   Gauged against Western World as a whole, Soviets are still by far the weaker force. Thus, their success will really depend on degree of cohesion, firmness and vigor which Western World can muster. And this is factor which it is within our power to influence.

(3)   Success of Soviet system, as form of internal power, is not yet finally proven. It has yet to be demonstrated that it can survive supreme test of successive transfer of power from one individual or group to another. Lenin's death was first such transfer, and its effects wracked Soviet state for 15 years. After Stalin's death or retirement will be second. But even this will not be final test. Soviet internal system will now be subjected, by virtue of recent territorial expansions, to series of additional strains which once proved severe tax on Tsardom. We here are convinced that never since termination of civil war have mass of Russian people been emotionally farther removed from doctrines of Communist Party than they are today. In Russia, party has now become a great and—for the moment—highly successful apparatus of dictatorial administration, but it has ceased to be a source of emotional inspiration. Thus, internal soundness and permanence of movement need not yet be regarded as assured.

(4)   All Soviet propaganda beyond Soviet security sphere is basically negative and destructive. It should therefore be relatively easy to combat it by any intelligent and really constructive program.

For these reasons I think we may approach calmly and with good heart problem of how to deal with Russia. As to how this approach should be made, I only wish to advance, by way of conclusion, following comments:

(1)   Our first step must be to apprehend, and recognize for what it is, the nature of the movement with which we are dealing. We must study it with same courage, detachment, objectivity, and same determination not to be emotionally provoked or unseated by it, with which doctor studies unruly and unreasonable individual.

(2)   We must see that our public is educated to realities of Russian situation. I cannot over-emphasize importance of this. Press cannot do this alone. It must be done mainly by Government, which is necessarily more experienced and better informed on practical problems involved. In this we need not be deterred by [ugliness?] of picture. I am convinced that there would be far less hysterical anti-Sovietism in our country today if realities of this situation were better understood by our people. There is nothing as dangerous or as terrifying as the unknown. It may also be argued that to reveal more information on our difficulties with Russia would reflect unfavorably on Russian-American relations. I feel that if there is any real risk here involved, it is one which we should have courage to face, and sooner the better. But I cannot see what we would be risking. Our stake in this country, even coming on heels of tremendous demonstrations of our friendship for Russian people, is remarkably small. We have here no investments to guard, no actual trade to lose, virtually no citizens to protect, few cultural contacts to preserve. Our only stake lies in what we hope rather than what we have; and I am convinced we have better chance of realizing those hopes if our public is enlightened and if our dealings with Russians are placed entirely on realistic and matter-of-fact basis.

(3)   Much depends on health and vigor of our own society. World communism is like malignant parasite which feeds only on diseased tissue. This is point at which domestic

and foreign policies meet. Every courageous and incisive measure to solve internal problems of our own society, to improve self-confidence, discipline, morale and community spirit of our own people, is a diplomatic victory over Moscow, worth a thousand diplomatic notes and joint communiques. If we cannot abandon fatalism and indifference in face of deficiencies of our own society, Moscow will profit—Moscow cannot help profiting by them in its foreign policies.

(4)   We must formulate and put forward for other nations a much more positive and constructive picture of sort of world we would like to see than we have put forward in past. It is not enough to urge people to develop political processes similar to our own. Many foreign peoples, in Europe at least, are tired and frightened by experiences of past, and are less interested in abstract freedom than in security. They are seeking guidance rather than responsibilities. We should be better able than Russians to give them this. And unless we do, Russians certainly will.

(5)   Finally we must have courage and self-confidence to cling to our own methods and conceptions of human society. After all, the greatest danger that can befall us in coping with this problem of Soviet communism, is that we shall allow ourselves to become like those with whom we are coping.

[1]   The Third (Communist) International, founded by the Bolsheviks at Moscow in March 1919, announced as having been dissolved in May 1943.

37   Senator Vandenberg and the Soviet challenge: February 27, 1946. '*It would be entirely futile to blink the fact that two great rival ideologies — democracy in the west and communism in the east — here, find themselves face to face with the desperate need for mutual understanding in finding common ground upon which to strive for peace for both.*'

On February 27, 1946, Senator Vandenberg, the leading Republican spokesman on foreign policy in the Senate and one of the early supporters of a bipartisan approach to postwar international relations, put the Truman Administration on notice that the G.O.P. was fast losing patience with Secretary of State Byrnes's presumably conciliatory attitude toward the Soviet Union. In particular, Vandenberg believed that up to now the United States had been less than forceful in stating its own position on various issues. 'I assert my own belief that we can live together in reasonable harmony', declared the Senator from Michigan on the Senate floor, 'if the United States speaks as plainly upon all occasions as Russia does; if the United States just as vigorously sustains its own purposes and its ideals upon all occasions as Russia does. . . .' In this sense, then, wrote the editor of the *Private Papers of Senator Vandenberg* (1952), 'above all the speech was a call for a new firm philosophy meeting the Russian postwar challenge, a forerunner of what observers—but not Vandenberg—called the "get-tough" with Russia policy.' And so it was.

Source: *Vital Speeches of the Day*, XX (March 15, 1946), 322-26.

. . . I say frankly, at the outset, that I return from London with mixed emotions. I return with no illusion that atuomatic peace awaits the world just because the machinery of the United Nations is now in gear. But I return also with an over-riding conviction, even more emphatic than before, that the world's only hope of organized peace and security is inseverably linked with the evolution and the destiny of this United Nations Organization. I return in the convinced belief that the more complex or ominous the world's international relations may become, in that same degree the greater becomes the critical need that the peace loving peoples of the earth shall strive to make this enterprise succeed. I return in the belief that it can succeed unless Russia, Britain, and the United States, individually or collectively, make it impossible.

I can share you disappointments over some phases of the London record. I can share your anxieties over some of the disturbing trends. I can share your desires that the San Francisco Charter should be improved in certain aspects. I intend to speak frankly about some of these things. But I cannot—and do not—share the melancholy pessimism heard in some quarters, that the United Nations, as a result of this experience, will be unable to cope with world realities as disclosed in current history. It would be silly to ignore the hazards. It would be sillier to ignore vindicated hopes. The amazing thing is not that at London there were vast areas of disagreement but that the areas of agreement were so vast and so significant . . .

This Charter clearly has its imperfections. We must be constantly alert to opportunities for its improvement. It is helpful that the earnest friends of peace should press these discussions. But it seems clear to me that we must first learn to live with what we have. It seems clear to me that our challenge is to make the United Nations work. It is particularly a challenge to the so-called five great powers. More particularly it is a challenge to three of them. Still more particularly, it is an individual challenge to the Union of Soviet Socialist Republics, upon the one hand, and to our own United States, upon the other . . .

It would be entirely futile to blink the fact that two great rival ideologies—democracy in the west and communism in the east—here, find themselves face to face with the desperate need for mutual understanding in finding common ground upon which to strive for peace for both. In the final analysis this means that the two great spokesmen for these rival ideologies—Soviet Russia and the United States—find themselves face to face with the same need for mutual understanding, both in and out of the United Nations. Indeed, if this does not oversimplify the problem, it might even be said that the future of the United Nations itself is wrapped up in this equation.

If this be so, Mr. President, I assert my own belief that we can live together in reasonable harmony if the United States speaks as plainly upon all occasions as Russia does; if the United States just as vigorously sustains its own purposes and its ideals upon all occasions as Russia does; if we abandon the miserable fiction, often encouraged by our own fellow travelers, that we somehow jeopardize the peace if our candor is as firm as Russia's always is; and if we assume a moral leadership which we have too frequently allowed to lapse. The situation calls for patience and good will; it does not call for vacillation.

Let me make it wholly clear that I do not complain because Russia speaks—indeed, Mr. Vishinsky probably spoke in this Security Council more than the spokesmen of all the other powers combined. I am glad she speaks. She ought to speak. That is what this forum is for. But it is for others, too, Mr. President—just as Mr. Bevin used it upon more than one eloquent and courageous occasion. It is, I repeat, for others, too. All should feel an equal freedom, an equal duty, and an equivalent responsibility. The governments of the world suddenly find themselves in the presence of a new technique in international relations. It is in this forum of the United Nations where the most dominant of all debates and decisions are hereafter calculated to occur. It would be impossible to over-emphasize the importance of our own role and our own performance in such epochal events, and the need for positive foreign policies as our consistent guide therein.

Speaking in New York last week at a celebration in honor of the great Red Army which Marshal Stalin certifies will be kept at a progressive peak, our new American Ambassador-designate to Moscow, Lt. Gen. Walter Bedell Smith, said; "It is imperative that our national temperatures remain normal." I agree. He said that "both nations want nothing so much as peace and security." I not only agree; but, in addition, if what still bothers Russia is really a security fear against resurgent aggression, I would renew my offer of 1 year ago for a direct treaty of mutual defense, under the United Nations, in the event an aggressor axis ever rises again.

General Smith said that "the United States is willing to go a long way in meeting its international associates, but that it must be watchful of its own vital interests and hold to the line beyond which compromise cannot go." Again I heartily concur. There is a line beyond which compromise cannot go: even if we have previously crossed that line under the pressures of the exigencies of war, we cannot cross it again. But how can we expect our alien friends to know where that line is unless we reestablish the habit of saying only what we mean and meaning every word we say? I have the deep conviction that this way is the dependable way to permanent peace and concord between us, with its inevitable effect upon the United Nations. Indeed, I have the feeling it is the only way. I have the feeling it is the best way to win Soviet respect and Soviet trust. Respect must precede trust; and both are indispensable to peace.

General Smith said that "America and the Union of Soviet Socialist Republics, given honesty and frankness on both sides, can get along together in the future just as well as they have for almost 150 years, in spite of the fact that our Governments and our economic systems have been quite different." Again I associate myself with that sentiment. But the honesty and frankness must be mutual.

Sometimes it is a useful, albeit painful, thing to search our own souls in critical hours like these. Was Sumner Welles, the late President Roosevelt's long-time Under Secretary of State, right in a recent statement from which I quote:

If the United States is to exercise any potent influence in promoting world peace and in establishing a better international order, other nations must be confident that this Government will abide by our professions. American foreign policy must possess the all-important quality of dependability . . . The United States continues to possess the influence in world affairs which is derived from its potential military might and from its material resources. But the moral influence which it possessed during the war years . . . is rapidly vanishing . . . It would be better far to refrain from giving assurances, however noble they may be, than to fail to carry them out. For the United States cannot exercise any effective leadership until all nations know that it means what it says.

Mr. President, this sort of an analysis does not detract for an instant from the notably loyal and richly helpful record which the United States has made to the foundations of the United Nations . . . The startling fact at London—I cannot repeat too often—is not that it sometimes trembled in the gale but rather that it so staunchly weathered all the storms. But, sir, we would be dubious mariners if we did not look back upon this pioneering journey to assess the dangers that developed and to put up warning signals for journeys yet to come.

Therefore, in addition to what I have already said, I must add two further admonitions.

I confess that in this first meeting of the United Nations I missed the uplifting and sustaining zeals for a great, crusading, moral cause which seemed to imbue the earlier Charter sessions at San Francisco. Perhaps it was because the agenda was so largely confined to the humdrum routine of organizational details. Perhaps it was the burden of anxiety over the misgivings that are inevitable in launching a peace project which never yet has succeeded in the history of civilization; or, on the other hand, perhaps it was the accumulated tiredness which dampens ardor and easily surrenders to the expedient notion that "all's well." Perhaps it was because, in the aftermath of war, we confront too many grim realities that are utterly at odds with precepts of justice which we presume to defend. In any event, and whatever the cause, we are on notice that the peoples of the earth must never cease to evangelize this struggle for peace if it shall reach full flower.

Again, Mr. President, I sensed at London what seemed to be too great a tendency to relapse into power politics, in greater or less degree, and, as some-one has said, to use the United Nations as a self-serving tribune rather than as a tribunal. It will require constant, consistent, courageous guidance to keep the United Nations within the main channel of its obligations—and here again is a clear call to America always to act in its traditional character for liberty and justice, and not to lapse, as I fear we may have done on some occasions.

38   The first public expression of the Truman Administration's new Soviet policy: February 28, 1946. '. . . we cannot allow agression to be accomplished by coercion or pressure or by subterfuges such as political infiltration.'

In a speech delivered on February 28, 1946, to the Overseas Press Club in New York and broadcast on radio to the American people, Secretary of State Byrnes clearly indicated a shift in the Truman Administration's Russian policy. According to John Lewis Gaddis's scholarly *The United States and the Origins of the Cold War, 1941-1947* (1972), 'This was the first open manifestation of the tougher Russian policy toward which the Truman Administration had been moving since the Moscow Conference.' Among other things, Byrnes warned the Soviet leadership that the United States had a distinct moral obligation both as a great power and as a permanent member of the Security Council to uphold the United Nations Charter. Given the choice of the Secretary's words, Senator Vandenberg need not have overly concerned himself with the apparent failure of the nation's policy makers to spell out America's vital interests.

Source: Department of State, *Bulletin*, XIV (March 10, 1946), 355-58.

We are beginning to realize that the war is over. It is good to have sons, husbands, and fathers home again. It is good to open a newspaper without fear of finding in the casualty lists the name of one near and dear to us.

But this is not wholly a time of celebration and rejoicing. As families in their homes on the farms and in the cities settle back from the dinner table to hear the boys tell of Normandy and Iwo Jima; there is an unspoken question in every mind. The question is what we can do to make certain that there will never be another war.

During the war our goal was clear. Our goal was victory. The problems of industrial and military mobilization, it is true, were problems of the first magnitude. Production bottlenecks often seemed unbreakable, transportation difficulties and manpower shortages insurmountable. On the fighting front the combined land, sea, and air operations were heartbreaking in complexity.

These were hard tasks. Yet we were able to apply a yardstick to each proposal by asking a simple question: "Will it help to win the war?" The common goal of victory served to unite us and to give purpose and direction to our efforts.

Now that we have come into calmer waters, our relief and gratitude are mixed with uncertainty. Our goal now is permanent peace, and surely we seek it even more anxiously than we sought victory.

The difficulty is that the path to permanent peace is not so easy to see and to follow as was the path to victory.

When an issue is presented, we ask, "Will it help to win the peace?" When the answer is slow to come or does not come at all, we grow uneasy and apprehensive.

While we may be in doubt about many things, there are certain basic propositions on which we are clear.

One is that a just and lasting peace is not the inevitable result of victory. Rather, victory has given us the opportunity to build such a peace. And our lives depend upon whether we make the most of this opportunity.

Another thing of which we are certain is that we Americans alone cannot determine whether the world will live in peace or perish in war. Peace depends quite as much upon others as it does upon us. No nation is the complete master of its fate. We are all bound together for better or for worse.

Because we know this, we have pinned our hopes to the banner of the United Nations. And we are not content simply to take our place in that Organization. We realize that, although the dreams of the world are lodged in it, the United Nations will fail unless its members give it life by their confidence and by their determination to make it work in concrete cases and in everyday affairs.

And so I wish to talk to you about the first meetings of the United Nations. What has been said in these meetings has been said as plainly and bluntly as anything I have heard said by responsible statesmen in any private conference.

These first meetings were intended only to establish the various organs of the United

Nations. But so pressing were some of the problems presented to the Security Council that they had to be dealt with before there was a chance for the Council to adopt even provisional rules of procedure.

All was not calm and peaceful at the meetings in London. There was effort to use the United Nations to advance selfish national aims. But the clash of national interests and purposes which were neglected in the debates in London was very much like the clash of local and special interests which are reflected in our national and state legislatures.

We may deprecate some of these clashes of interest. But when they exist, it is better that they should be publicly revealed. If these conflicts of interest did not appear in the forums of the United Nations, these forums would be detached from reality and in the long run turn out to be purposeless and futile.

A most significant precedent was established when the Security Council finished its discussions of the complaint of the Syrian and Lebanese Governments requesting the withdrawal of French and British troops from their territories.

The Council did not take formal action because of a difference among the permanent members as to the form of the resolution. But no one questioned the general proposition that no state has the right to maintain its troops on the territory of another independent state without its consent, nor the application of this proposition to the pending case.

The particular form of resolution to this general effect which was presented by the United States representative, Mr. Stettinius, was supported by most of the members of the Council. It failed of acceptance, however, because the Soviet Union vetoed it on the ground that it was not definite enough.

But the British and French Governments immediately announced that, notwithstanding the technical veto of the Soviet Union, they would act in accordance with the American resolution as it clearly represented the views of the Council.

This indicates that the mere legal veto by one of the permanent members of the Council does not in fact relieve any state, large or small, of its moral obligation to act in accordance with the purposes and principles of the Charter.

The United Nations got off to a good start. However, that does not mean it is an assured success. It simply means that the Charter will work if the peoples of the United Nations are determined to make it work. At times our Congress may make serious errors of omission and commission. Such errors are not the fault of the Congress as an institution. They are the fault of its members or of their constituents who fail to measure up to their responsibilities.

So it is with the United Nations. It will succeed only as we, the peoples of the United Nations, measure up to our responsibilities.

I should be lacking in candor if I said to you that world conditions today are sound or reassuring. All around us there is suspicion and distrust which in turn breeds suspicion and distrust.

Some suspicions are unfounded and unreasonable. Of some others that cannot be said. That requires frank discussion between great powers of the things that give rise to suspicion. At the Moscow conference there was such frank discussion. It was helpful. But the basis of some suspicions persists and prompts me to make some comments as to our position.

We have joined with our allies in the United Nations to put an end to war. We have covenanted not to use force except in the defense of law as embodied in the purposes and principles of the Charter. We intend to live up to that covenant.

But as a great power and as a permanent member of the Security Council we have a responsibility to use our influence to see that others powers live up to their covenant. And that responsibility we also intend to meet.

Unless the great powers are prepared to act in the defense of law, the United Nations cannot prevent war. We must make it clear in advance that we do intend to act to prevent aggression, making it clear at the same time that we will not use force for any other purpose.

The great powers are given special responsibilities because they have the strength to maintain peace, if they have the will to maintain peace. Their strength in relation to one another is such that no one of them can safely break the peace if the others stand united in defense of the Charter.

The present power relationships of the great states preclude the domination of the world by any one of them. Those power relationships cannot be substantially altered by the unilateral action of any one great state without profoundly disturbing the whole structure of the United Nations.

Therefore, if we are going to do our part to maintain peace in the world we must maintain our power to do so; and we must make it clear that we will stand united with other great states in defense of the Charter.

If we are to be a great power we must act as a great power, not only in order to ensure our own security but in order to preserve the peace of the world.

Much as we desire general disarmament and much as we are prepared to participate in a general reduction of armaments, we cannot be faithful to our obligations to ourselves and to the world if we alone disarm.

While it is not in accord with our traditions to maintain a large professional standing army, we must be able and ready to provide armed contingents that may be required on short notice. We must also have a trained citizenry able and ready to supplement those armed contingents without unnecessarily prolonged training.

That is why in the interest of peace we cannot allow our military establishment to be reduced below the point required to maintain a position commensurate with our responsibilities; and that is why we must have some form of universal military training.

Our power thus maintained cannot and will not be used for aggressive purposes. Our tradition as a peace-loving, law-abiding, democratic people should be an assurance that our force will not be used except in the defense of law. Our armed forces, except as they may be called into action by the Security Council, cannot be employed in war without the consent of the Congress. We need not fear their misuse unless we distrust the representatives of the people.

I am convinced that there is no reason for war between any of the great powers. Their present power relationships and interests are such that none need or should feel insecure in relation to the others, as long as each faithfully observes the purposes and principles of the Charter.

It is not enough for nations to declare they do not want to make war. Hitler said that. In a sense he meant it. He wanted the world to accept the domination of a totalitarian government under his direction. He wanted that without war if possible. He was determined to get it with war if necessary.

To banish war, nations must refrain from doing the things that lead to war.

It has never been the policy of the United States in its internal affairs or in its foreign relations to regard the *status quo* as sacrosanct. The essence of our democracy is our belief in life and growth and in the right of the people to shape and mould their own destiny.

It is not in our tradition to defend the dead hand of reaction or the tyranny of privilege. We did not fight against the Nazis and Fascists who turned back the clock of civilization in order that we might stop the clock of progress.

Our diplomacy must not be negative and inert. It must be capable of adjustment and development in response to constantly changing circumstances. It must be marked by creative ideas, constructive proposals, practical and forward-looking suggestions.

Though the *status quo* is not sacred and unchangeable, we cannot overlook unilateral gnawing away at the *status quo*. The Charter forbids aggression, and we cannot allow aggression to be accomplished by coercion or pressure or by subterfuges such as political infiltration.

When adjustments between states, large or small, are called for, we will frankly and fairly consider those adjustments on their merits and in the light of the common interests of all states, large and small, to maintain peace and security in a world based on the unity of all great powers and the dominance of none.

There are undoubtedly vitally important adjustments which will require our consideration. Some of these situations are delicate to deal with. I am convinced, however, that satisfactory solutions can be found if there is a stop to this maneuvering for strategic advantage all over the world and to the use of one adjustment as an entering wedge for further and undisclosed penetrations of power.

We must face the fact that to preserve the United Nations we cannot be indifferent— veto or no veto—to serious controversies between any of the great powers, because such controversies could affect the whole power relationship between all of the great powers.

The United States wishes to maintain friendly relations with all nations and exclusive arrangements with no nation. Naturally there are some problems which concern some nations much more than other nations. That is true in regard to many problems related to inter-American affairs. That is true in regard to the control of Germany and Japan.

In our relations with the other great powers there are many problems which concern two or three of us much more than the others of us. I see no objection to conferences between the big three or the big four or the big five.

Even conferences between ourselves and the Soviet Union alone, conferences between ourselves and Britain alone, or conferences between ourselves and France or China alone, can all help to further general accord among the great powers and peace with the smaller powers.

But in such conferences, so far as the United States is concerned, we will gang up against no state. We will do nothing to break the world into exclusive blocs or spheres of influence. In this atomic age we will not seek to divide a world which is one and indivisible.

We have openly, gladly and whole-heartedly welcomed our Soviet Ally as a great power, second to none in the family of the United Nations. We have approved many adjustments in her favor and, in the process, resolved many serious doubts in her favor.

Only an inexcusable tragedy of errors could cause serious conflict between us in the future. Despite the differences in our way of life, our people admire and respect our Allies and wish to continue to be friends and partners in a world of expanding freedom and rising standards of living.

But in the interest of world peace and in the interest of our common and traditional friendship we must make plain that the United States intends to defend the Charter.

Great powers as well as small powers have agreed under the United Nations Charter not to use force or the threat of force except in defense of law and the purposes and principles of the Charter.

We will not and we cannot stand aloof if force or the threat of force is used contrary to the purposes and principles of the Charter.

We have no right to hold our troops in the territories of other sovereign states without their approval and consent freely given.

We must not unduly prolong the making of peace and continue to impose our troops upon small and impoverished states.

No power has a right to help itself to alleged enemy properties in liberated or ex-satellite countries before a reparation settlement has been agreed upon by the Allies. We have not and will not agree to any one power deciding for itself what it will take from these countries.

We must not conduct a war of nerves to achieve strategic ends.

We do not want to stumble and stagger into situations where no power intends war but no power will be able to avert war.

We must not regard the drawing of attention to situations which might endanger the peace, as an affront to the nation or nations responsible for those situations.

It is quite possible that any nation may in good faith embark on a course of conduct without fully appreciating the effects of its conduct. We must all be willing to review our actions to preserve our common interest in the peace, which are so much more important to all of us than the differences which might divide us.

We must get back to conditions of peace. We must liquidate the terrible legacy which the war has left us. We must return our armies to their homelands. We must eliminate the breeding grounds of suspicion and fear. We must not deceive ourselves or mislead our Allies. To avoid trouble we must not allow situations to develop into incidents from which there is not retreat.

We must live by the Charter. That is the only road to peace.

To live by the Charter requires good-will and understanding on the part of all of us. We who had patience and gave confidence to one another in the most trying days of the war must have patience and give confidence to one another now.

No nation has a monopoly of virtue or of wisdom, and no nation has a right to act as if it had. Friendly nations should act as friendly nations.

Loose talk of the inevitability of war casts doubt on our own loyalty to the Charter and jeopardizes our most cherished freedoms, both at home and abroad.

There are ideological differences in the world. There always have been. But in this world there is room for many people with varying views and many governments with varying systems. None of us can foresee the far-distant future and the ultimate shape of things to come. But we are bound together as part of a common civilization.

As we view the wreckage of the war, we must realize that the urgent tasks of reconstruction, the challenging tasks of creating higher standards of living for our people, should absorb all our constructive energies.

Great states and small states must work together to build a friendlier and happier world. If we fail to work together there can be no peace, no comfort, and little hope for any of us.

39   Winston Churchill's 'Iron Curtain' speech at Fulton, Missouri: March 5, 1946. *'From Stettin in the Baltic to Trieste in the Adriatic, an iron curtain has descended across the Continent.'*

At the request of President Truman and in the capacity of a private citizen, Winston Churchill travelled to Fulton, Missouri, in March 1946 to deliver an address at Westminster College. Calling on the inspired rhetoric of his wartime experience, Churchill calmly observed that 'From Stettin in the Baltic to Trieste in the Adriatic, an iron curtain has descended across the Continent.' For Churchill, the only threat to world peace was Soviet Russia, although he made it clear that she preferred the fruits of war rather than war itself. Furthermore, he went on to say, all Russia respected was military strength, strong and ever-present. The significance of Churchill's address lay in the fact that its tough-sounding tones and emphasis on military preparedness readily lent itself to President Truman's purposes of stiffening his opposition to the Soviets and, equally important, educating American public opinion to the dangers ahead. And although at the time he denied foreknowledge of the speech's contents, there can be little doubt that the President had been fully informed of its message.

Source: *Vital Speeches of the Day,* XII (March 15, 1946), 329-32.

. . . The United States stands at this time at the pinnacle of world power. It is a solemn moment for the American democracy. With primacy in power is also joined an awe-inspiring accountability to the future. As you look around you, you must feel not only the sense of duty done but also feel anxiety lest you fall below the level of achievement. Opportunity is here now, clear and shining, for both our countries. To reject it or ignore it or fritter it away will bring upon us all the long reproaches of the aftertime. It is necessary that constancy of mind, persistency of purpose and the grand simplicity of decision shall guide and rule the conduct of the English-speaking peoples in peace as they did in war. We must and I believe we shall prove ourselves equal to this severe requirement.

When American military men approach some serious situation they are wont to write at the head of their directive the words, "over-all strategic concept." There is wisdom in this as it leads to clarity of thought. What, then, is the over-all strategic concept which we should inscribe today? It is nothing less than the safety and welfare, the freedom and progress of all the homes and families of all the men and women in all the lands . . .

To give security to these countless homes they must be shielded from the two gaunt marauders—war and tyranny. We all know the frightful disturbance in which the ordinary family is plunged when the curse of war swoops down upon the bread winner and those for whom he works and contrives. The awful ruin of Europe, with all its vanished glories, and of large parts of Asia, glares in our eyes. When the designs of wicked men or the aggressive urge of mighty states dissolve, over large areas, the frame of civilized society, humble folk are confronted with difficulties with which they cannot cope. For them all is distorted, broken or even ground to pulp . . . Our supreme task and duty is to guard the homes of the common people from the horrors and miseries of another war . . .

I now come to the second danger which threatens the cottage home and ordinary people, namely tyranny . . . It is not our duty at this time, when difficulties are so numerous, to interfere forcibly in the internal affairs of countries whom we have not conquered in war, but we must never cease to proclaim in fearless tones the great principles of freedom and the rights of man, which are the joint inheritance of the English-speaking world and which, through Magna Carta, the Bill of Rights, the habeas corpus, trial by jury and the English common law, find their most famous expression in the Declaration of Indepenence.

All this means that the people of any country have the right and should have the power by constitutional action, by free, unfettered elections, with secret ballot, to choose or change the character or form of government under which they dwell, that freedom of speech and thought should reign, that courts of justice independent of the executive, unbiased by any party, should administer laws which have received the broad assent of large majorities or are consecrated by time and custom. Here are the title deeds of freedom, which should lie in every cottage home. Here is the message of the British and American peoples to mankind. Let us preach what we practice and practice what we preach . . .

Neither the sure prevention of war, nor the continuous rise of world organization will be gained without what I have called the fraternal association of the English-speaking peoples. This means a special relationship between the British Commonwealth and Empire and the United States. This is no time for generalities. I will venture to be precise. Fraternal association requires not only the growing friendship and mutual understanding between our two vast but kindred systems of society but the continuance of the intimate relationships between our military advisers, leading to common study of potential dangers, similarity of weapons and manuals of instruction and inter-change of officers and cadets at colleges. It should carry with it the continuance of the present facilities for mutual security by the joint use of all naval and air force bases in the possession of either country all over the world. This would perhaps double the mobility of the American Navy and Air Force . . .

A shadow has fallen upon the scenes so lately lighted by the Allied victory. Nobody knows what Soviet Russia and its Communist international organization intends to do in the immediate future, or what are the limits, if any, to their expansive and proselytizing tendencies. I have a strong admiration and regard for the valiant Russian people and for my war-time comrade, Marshal Stalin. . . . We understand the Russians need to be secure on her western frontiers from all renewal of German aggression. We welcome her to her rightful place among the leading nations of the world. Above all we welcome constant, frequent and growing contacts between the Russian people and our own people on both sides of the Atlantic . . .

From Stettin in the Baltic to Trieste in the Adriatic, an iron curtain has descended across the Continent. Behind that line lie all the capitals of the ancient states of central and eastern Europe, Warsaw, Berlin, Prague, Vienna, Budapest, Belgrade, Bucharest, and Sofia, all these famous cities and the populations around them lie in the Soviet sphere and all are subject in one form or another, not only to Soviet influence but to a very high and increasing measure of control from Moscow . . .

In front of the iron curtain which lies across Europe are other causes for anxiety. In Italy the Communist party is seriously hampered by having to support the Communist trained Marshal Tito's claims to former Italian territory at the head of the Adriatic. Nevertheless the future of Italy hangs in the balance. Again one cannot imagine a regenerated Europe without a strong France. All my public life I have worked for a strong France and I never lost faith in her destiny, even in the darkest hours. I will not lose faith now. However, in a great number of countries, far from the Russian frontiers and throughout the world, Communist fifth columns are established and work in complete unity and absolute obedience to the directions they receive from the Communist center. Except in the British Commonwealth and in this United States, where Communism is in its infancy, the Communist parties or fifth columns constitute a growing challenge and peril to Christian civilization . . .

The outlook is also anxious in the Far East and especially in Manchuria. The agreement which was made at Yalta, to which I was a party, was extremely favorable to Soviet Russia, but it was made at a time when no one could say that the German war might not extend all through the summer and autumn of 1945 and when the Japanese war was expected to last for a further eighteen months from the end of the German war . . .

On the other hand I repulse the idea that a new war is inevitable; still more that it is imminent. It is because I am so sure that our fortunes are in our own hands and that we hold the power to save the future, that I feel the duty to speak out now that I have an occasion to do so. I do not believe that Soviet Russia desires war. What they desire is the fruits of war and the indefinite expansion of their power and doctrines. But what we have to consider here today while time remains, is the permanent prevention of war the establishment of conditions of freedom and democracy as rapidly as possible in all countries. Our difficulties and dangers will not be removed by closing our eyes to them. They will not be removed by mere waiting to see what happens; nor will they be relieved by a policy of appeasement. What is needed is a settlement and the longer this is delayed the more difficult it will be and the greater our dangers will become. From what I have seen of our Russian friends and allies during the war, I am convinced that there is nothing they admire so much as strength, and there is nothing for which they have less respect than for military weakness. For that reason the old doctrine of a balance of power is unsound. We cannot afford, if we can help it, to work on narrow margins, offering temptations to a trial of strength. If the western democracies stand together in strict adherence to the principles of the United Nations Charter, their influence for furthering these principles will be immense and no one is likely to molest them. If, however, they become divided or falter in their duty, and if these all-important years are allowed to slip away, then indeed catastrophe may overwhelm us all . . .

If the population of the English-speaking commonwealth be added to that of the

United States, with all that such co-operation implies in the air, on the sea and in science and industry, there will be no quivering, precarious balance of power to offer its temptation to ambition or adventure. On the contrary, there will be an overwhelming assurance of security . . .

40   Henry A. Wallace on·reconsidering American-Soviet relations: September 12, 1946. '*The tougher we get, the tougher the Russians will get.*'

Cast in the role of Cold War critic though no pacifist himself, as his recently published diary amply attests, Secretary of Commerce Henry A. Wallace delivered in September 1946 before an overflow political rally in Madison Square Garden one of the most controversial addresses of his mostly controversial career. In a speech that was originally intended to criticize the failure of both the United States and the Soviet Union to reach mutual settlement on the major problems of the day, and in a speech that was supposed to have been personally cleared by the President, the Secretary of Commerce lashed out at what he regarded as the uncompromising get-tough critics of Russia working within the State Department. Such a policy, for Wallace, was futile and self-defeating. For, as he declared to an audience surprisingly filled with some of his detractors,·'The tougher we get, the tougher the Russians will get.' Wallace's speech, which seems in retrospect a model of moderation, caused much consternation within the State Department and aroused the ire of such diverse policy makers as Byrnes and Kennan. Shortly afterwards Wallace was asked for his resignation.

Source: ibid, XII (October 1, 1946), 738-41.

. . . Tonight I want to talk about peace—and how to get peace. Never have the common people of all lands so longed for peace. Yet, never in a time of comparative peace have they feared war so much.

Up till now peace has been negative and unexciting. War has been positive and exciting. Far too often, hatred and fear, intolerance and deceit have had the upper hand over love and confidence, trust and joy. Far too often, the law of nations has been the law of the jungle; and the constructive spiritual forces of the Lord have bowed to the destructive forces of Satan.

During the past year or so, the significance of peace has been increased immeasurably by the atom bomb, guided missiles and airplanes which soon will travel as fast as sound. Make no mistake about it—another war would hurt the United States many times as much as the last war. We cannot rest in the assurance that we invented the atom bomb— and therefore that this agent of destruction will work best for us. He who trusts in the atom bomb will sooner or later perish by the atom bomb—or something worse.

I say this as one who steadfastly backed preparedness throughout the Thirties. We have no use for namby-pamby pacifism. But we must realize that modern inventions have now made peace the most exciting thing in the world—and we should be willing to pay a just price for peace. If modern war can cost us $400 billion, we should be willing and happy to pay much more for peace. But certainly, the cost of peace is to be measured not in dollars but in the hearts and minds of men . . .

I plead for an America vigorously dedicated to peace—just as I plead for opportunities for the next generation throughout the world to enjoy the abundance which now, more than ever before, is the birthright of man.

To achieve lasting peace, we must study in detail just how the Russian character was formed—by invasions of Tartars, Mongols, Germans, Poles, Swedes, and French; by the czarist rule based on ignorance, fear and force; by the intervention of the British, French and Americans in Russian affairs from 1919 to 1921; by the geography of the huge Russian land mass situated strategically between Europe and Asia; and by the vitality derived from the rich Russian soil and the strenuous Russian climate. Add to all this the tremendous emotional powers which Marxism and Leninism gives to the Russian leaders—and then we can realize that we are reckoning with a force which cannot be handled successfully by a "Get tough with Russia" policy. "Getting tough" never bought anything real and lasting—whether for schoolyard bullies or businessmen or world powers. The tougher we get, the tougher the Russians will get.

Throughout the world there are numerous reactionary elements which had hoped for Axis victory—and now profess great friendship for the United States. Yet these enemies of yesterday and false friends of today continually try to provoke war between the United States and Russia. They have no real love of the United States. They only long for the day when the United States and Russia will destroy each other.

We must not let our Russian policy be guided or influenced by those inside or outside the United States who want war with Russia. This does not mean appeasement.

We must earnestly want peace with Russia—but we want to be met half way. We want cooperation. And I believe that we can get cooperation once Russia understands that our primary objective is neither saving the British Empire nor purchasing oil in the Near East with the lives of American soldiers. We cannot allow national oil rivalries to force us into war. All of the nations producing oil, whether inside or outside of their own boundaries, must fulfill the provisions of the United Nations Charter and encourage the development of world petroleum reserves so as to make the maximum amount of oil available to all nations of the world on an equitable peaceful basis—and not on the basis of fighting the next war.

For her part, Russia can retain our respect by cooperating with the United Nations in a spirit of openminded and flexible give-and-take.

The real peace treaty we now need is between the United States and Russia. On our part, we should recognize that we have no more business in the *political* affairs of Eastern Europe than Russia has in the *political* affairs of Latin America, Western Europe and the United States. We may not like what Russia does in Eastern Europe. Her type of land reform, industrial expropriation, and suppression of basic liberties offends the great majority of the people of the United States. But whether we like it or not the Russians will try to socialize their sphere of influence just as we try to democratize our sphere of influence. This applies also to Germany and Japan. We are striving to democratize Japan and our area of control in Germany, while Russia strives to socialize eastern Germany.

As for Germany, we all must recognize that an equitable settlement, based on a unified

German nation, is absolutely essential to any lasting European settlement. This means that Russia must be assured that never again can German industry be converted into military might to be used against her—and Britain, Western Europe and the United States must be certain that Russia's German policy will not become a tool of Russian design against Western Europe.

The Russians have no more business in stirring up native communists to political activity in Western Europe, Latin America and the United States than we have in interfering in the politics of Eastern Europe and Russia. We know what Russia is up to in Eastern Europe, for example, and Russia knows what we are up to. We cannot permit the door to be closed against our trade in Eastern Europe any more than we can in China. But at the same time we have to recognize that the Balkans are closer to Russia than to us— and that Russia cannot permit either England or the United States to dominate the politics of that area.

China is a special case and although she holds the longest frontier in the world with Russia, the interests of world peace demand that China remain free from any sphere of influence, either politically or economically. We insist that the door to trade and economic development opportunities be left wide open in China as in all the world. However, the open door to trade and opportunities for economic development in China are meaningless unless there is a unified and peaceful China—built on the cooperation of the various groups in that country and based on a hands-off policy of the outside powers.

We are still arming to the hilt. Our excessive expenses for military purposes are the chief cause for our unbalanced budget. If taxes are to be lightened we must have the basis of a real peace with Russia—a peace that cannot be broken by extremist propagandists. We do not want our course determined for us by master minds operating out of London, Moscow or Nanking.

Russian ideas of social economic justice are going to govern nearly a third of the world. Our ideas of free enterprise democracy will govern much of the rest. The two ideas will endeavor to prove which can deliver the most satisfaction to the common man in their respective areas of political dominance. But by mutual agreement, this competition should be put on a friendly basis and the Russians should stop conniving against us in certain areas of the world just as we should stop scheming against them in other parts of the world. Let the results of the two systems speak for themselves.

Meanwhile, the Russians should stop teaching that their form of communism must, by force if necessary, ultimately triumph over democratic capitalism—while we should close our ears to those among us who would have us believe that Russian communism and our free enterprise system cannot live, one with another; in a profitable and productive peace.

Under friendly peaceful competition the Russian world and the American world will gradually become more alike. The Russians will be forced to grant more and more of the personal freedoms; and we shall become more and more absorbed with the problems of social-economic justice.

Russia must be convinced that we are not planning for war against her and we must be certain that Russia is not carrying on territorial expansion or world domination through native communists faithfully following every twist and turn in the Moscow party line. But in the competition, we must insist on an open door for trade throughout the world. There will always be an ideological conflict—but that is no reason why diplomats cannot work out a basis for both systems to live safely in the world side by side.

Once the fears of Russia and the United States Senate have been allayed by practical regional political reservations, I am sure that concern over the veto power would be greatly diminished. Then the United Nations would have a really great power in those areas which are truly international and not regional. In the world-wide, as distinguished from the regional field, the armed might of the United Nations should be so great as to make opposition useless. Only the United Nations should have atomic bombs and its military establishment should give special emphasis to air power. It should have control of the strategically located air bases with which the United States and Britain have encircled the world. And not only should individual nations be prohibited from manufacturing atomic bombs, guided missiles and military aircraft for bombing purposes, but no nation should be allowed to spend on its military establishement more than perhaps 15 per cent of its budget . . .

In brief, as I see it today, the World Order is bankrupt—and the United States, Russia and England are the receivers. These are the hard facts of power politics on which we have to build a functioning, powerful United Nations and a body of international law. And as we build, we must develop fully the doctrine of the rights of small peoples as contained in the United Nations Charter. This law should ideally apply as much to Indonesians and Greeks as to Bulgarians and Poles—but practically, the application may be delayed until both British and Russians discover the futility of the methods.

In the full development of the rights of small nations, the British and Russians can learn a lesson from the Good Neighbor policy of Franklin Roosevelt. For under Roosevelt, we in the Western Hemisphere built a workable system of regional internationalism that fully protected the sovereign rights of every nation—a system of multilateral action that immeasurably strengthened the whole of world order.

In the United States an informed public opinion will be all-powerful. Our people are peace-minded. But they often express themselves too late—for events today move much faster than public opinion. The people here, as everywhere in the world, must be convinced that another war is not inevitable. And through mass meetings such as this, and through persistent pamphleteering, the people can be organized for peace—even though a large segment of our press is propagandizing our people for war in the hope of scaring Russia. And we who look on this war-with-Russia talk as criminal foolishness must carry our message direct to the people—even though we may be called communists because we dare to speak out.

I believe that peace—the kind of peace I have outlined tonight—is the basic issue, both in the Congressional campaign this fall and right on through the Presidential election in 1948. How we meet this issue will determine whether we live not in "one world" or "two worlds"—but whether we live at all.

41   Some last thoughts in Moscow

In his replies to a series of questions put to him in September 1946 by *London Sunday Times* correspondent Alexander Werth, Stalin, for reasons known only to himself, suggested a shift away from the ideological rigidity of his pre-election speech of February 9. Specifically, the Soviet leader went on record as unqualifiedly believing in the 'possibility of friendly and lasting cooperation between Soviet Union and Western democracies despite the existence of ideological divergences of view. . . .' The official American assessment of Stalin's remarks, which in any case were seen as a tactical maneuver, was at best skeptical. Elbridge Durbrow, then counselor of the embassy at Moscow and former Chief of the Division of Eastern European Affairs, judged that the immediate aim of Stalin's statement was twofold: first, 'To strengthen elements in USA advocating appeasement of USSR'; and second, 'To tempt British Government elements with prospect of collaboration with USSR in hope that this might develop rift between USA and British which according to Stalinist doctrine must culminate in conflict between two last strongholds of capitalism.' Such an analysis, with its reference to 'appeasement' and 'Stalinist doctrine' indicate both the hold of the past on policy makers and the closing down of options in dealing with Soviet Russia. Given the political climate of this time in the West, it is not hard to imagine the 'credibility gap' that followed Stalin's pronouncements.

41(a) Stalin answers *Sunday Times* correspondent Alexander Werth, September 20, 1946. '*I do not think that ruling circles of Great Britain could create "capitalist encirclement" of Soviet Union, even if they wanted to . . .*'

Source: Department of State, *Foreign Relations of the United States, Diplomatic Papers: 1946* (Wash. 1969), VI, 784-86.

Translation follows Stalin's answers in Soviet press September 24 to questions by *Sunday Times* correspondent Alexander Werth in his note to Stalin of September 17:

Question: Do you believe in real danger of "new war" about which there is so much irresponsible talk throughout world at present time? What steps should be taken for prevention of war if such danger exists?
Answer: I do not believe in real danger of "new war".
The furor about "new war" is being raised now mainly by military political reconnoiterers and their numerous supporters from ranks of civilian officials. They need this furor if only to: *(a)*   frighten with spectre of war certain naive politicians from among their partners and thus assist their governments in wrestling greater concessions from these partners; *(b)*   hinder for certain length of time reduction of military budgets in their countries; *(c)*   put brake on demobilization of troops and thus prevent rapid growth of unemployment in their countries.

It is necessary to make strict distinction between furor about "new war", which is being raised at present time, and real danger of "new war" which does not exist at present time.

Question: Do you consider that Great Britain and USA are deliberately creating "capitalist encirclement" of Soviet Union?

Answer: I do not think that ruling circles of Great Britain and USA could create "capitalist encirclement" of Soviet Union, even if they wanted to, which, however, I cannot assert.

Question: Speaking in words of Mr. Wallace's recent speech, can Great Britain, Western Europe and US be assured that Soviet policy in Germany will not be turned into weapon for Russian designs directed against Western Europe?

Answer: I consider use of Germany by Soviet Union against Western Europe and USA out of question. I consider it out of question not only because Soviet Union is bound by treaty mutual aid against German aggression with Great Britain and France, and by decisions of Potsdam Conference of three Great Powers with USA, but also because a policy of utilizing Germany against Western Europe and USA would signify departure of Soviet Union from its fundamental national interests.

In short, policy of Soviet Union on German question amounts to demilitarization and democratization of Germany. I think that demilitarization and democratization of Germany are one of the most important guarantees for establishment of firm and lasting peace.

Question: What is your opinion with regard to accusations that policy of Communist Parties of Western Europe "is dictated by Moscow"?

Answer: This accusation I consider absurd—borrowed from the bankrupt arsenal of Hitler and Goebbels.

Question: Do you believe in possibility of friendly and lasting cooperation between Soviet Union and Western democracies despite existence of ideological divergencies of view, and in "friendly competition" between two systems about which Wallace spoke in his speech?

Answer: I unqualifiedly believe this.

Question: During visit of Labor Party delegation here, you, as I understand, expressed confidence in possibility of friendly relations between Soviet Union and Great Britain. What would assist establishment of these relations which are so earnestly desired by wide masses British people?

Answer: I am really confident of possibility of friendly relations between Soviet Union and Great Britain. Establishment of such relations would be greatly assisted by strengthening of political, trade and cultural ties between these countries.

Question: Do you consider that the speediest withdrawal of all American troops from China is a vital necessity for future peace?

Answer: Yes, I do.

Question: Do you believe that virtual monopolistic possession by USA of atom bomb is one of main threats to peace?

Answer: I do not believe atom bomb to be such a serious force as certain politicians are inclined to consider it. Atom bombs are designed to frighten the weak-nerved, but they cannot determine the outcome of war since for this atom bombs are utterly insufficient. Of course, the monopolistic possession of the secret of atom bomb creates a threat, but there exist at least two remedies against it: *(a)*   monopolistic possession of atom bomb cannot long continue: *(b)*   use of atom bomb will be prohibited.

Question: Do you suppose that with further advance of Soviet Union towards communism possibilities of peaceful cooperation with outside world will not be diminished, so far as Soviet Union is concerned? Is "communism in one country" possible?

Answer: I do not doubt that possibilities of peaceful cooperation not only will not diminish but may even increase. "Communism in one country" is entirely possible, especially in such country as Soviet Union.

41(b) The American Chargé responds: September 25, 1946. *'Stalin's answers . . . represent in our opinion tactical maneuver rather than pronouncement of strategic policy.*

Source: ibid, 786-87.

Stalin's answers to questions posed by Alec Werth represent in our opinion tactical maneuver rather than pronouncement of strategic policy.

Stalin's statements seem to have two immediate tactical aims:

(1)   To strengthen elements in USA advocating appeasement of USSR. Stalin's release of his exchange with Werth is timed to capitalize on Wallace affair.

(2)   To tempt British Government elements with prospect of collaboration with USSR in hope that this might develop rift between USA and British which according to Stalinist doctrine must culminate in conflict between two last strongholds of capitalism. This move is a follow up on overtures made to Labor Party representatives who visited USSR some weeks ago.

At the same time Stalin's comments may have wider connotations. We say this because several of Stalin's statements, conspiciously his denial of capitalist encirclement, seem to contradict ideoligical line vigorously plugged since February. We shall not know for some time to come whether Stalin's replies to Werth signify a broad departure to a new tactical line. We would suggest however possibility of following parallel:

Early this year Soviet policy in Iran utilized tactics of open military intervention and intimidation. Kremlin apparently counted on post-war demoralization of Western democracies to render UNO ineffective. Early in March it became evident that policy of saber rattling and bluff in Iran was not going to work against aroused conscience and determination of Western Powers. Stalin's reply to questions posed by AP correspondent Gilmore regarding Soviet attitude towards UNO was one of symptoms of Soviet change of tactics in Iran from overt intimidation to covert political machination.

During past several months USSR has been talking and acting tough to Western democracies. These tactics have failed to intimidate USA and Britain. Rather they have resulted in increased firmness in American and British policy. Final demonstration of resolute American policy was showdown on Wallace. Stalin may now estimate that he had best change his truculent tune. He may feel that his bluff had been called and from now on he would do well to follow a somewhat more circumspect policy. If this is so his replies to Werth are probably indicative of the new line.

There are valid domestic reasons, as well as foreign ones, for possible revision of foreign policy pursued heretofore. Overall reason may be that Stalin is not able to back up, excepting in most immediate terms and only in certain ares, truculent foreign policy. Soviet industry is in comparatively bad shape. Rate of reconstruction and new construction is by American standards unbelievably slow. Difficulties have grown up in collective farm system which is now being radically overhauled. There are symptoms of uneasiness and discontent in armed forces. Intelligentsia, which should be a source of enthusiasm and spiritual vitality, has been considerably demoralized as result of dragooning by Communist Party. This unhealthy situation has been aggravated by anxiety of Soviet public over constant hammering by Soviet propaganda of possibility of new world war. This anxiety, as we have pointed out, has not contributed to Soviet morale.

Whether foregoing foreign and domestic reasons for tactical change in line will be acted upon remains, as stated above, to be seen. Stalin may choose to allow apparent contradiction between his replies to Werth and recent published party line to remain unresolved. Or he may feel that Soviet propaganda should adopt somewhat more conciliatory tone. There are precedents in past Soviet policy for either course.

Whatever tactical course he follows there is no reason to believe that it involves any change in basic long term strategy. . . .

CHAPTER EIGHT

The Truman Doctrine and the Marshall Plan:
The Completion of the American Diplomatic Revolution

42   Acheson to Byrnes on the significance of defending Turkey against Soviet aggression—early warnings: August 15, 1946. *'If the Soviet Union succeeds in its objective obtaining control over Turkey it will be extremely difficult, if not impossible, to prevent the Soviet Union from obtaining control over Greece and over the whole Near and Middle East.'*

Against the background of the American embroilment in the British-Venezuelan boundary dispute of 1895 and in defence of the 'two-spheres' concept (the view that held the problems of Europe as distinct and separate from those of the Western Hemisphere), Secretary of State Richard Olney declaimed to his English counterpart that 'If all Europe were to suddenly fly to arms over the fate of Turkey, would it not be preposterous that any American state should find itself inextricably involved in the miseries and burdens of the contest?' That the United States 'should find itself inextricably involved in the miseries and burdens' of just such a contest—at this time in connection with Soviet Russia's unilateral attempt to revise the Montreux Straits Convention with Turkey in 1946—suggests the nature and character of the American diplomatic revolution that occurred in the aftermath of World War II. For in the years since the Japanese attack on Pearl Harbor, in a sense the midwife of the triumph of American internationalism, the United States had moved from its post-Versailles posture of political noninterference in the endless and time-honored struggle of Europe (this posture itself being a fiction supposedly enshrined in the neutrality legislation of the 1930's) to a posture of standard bearer of international collective security. In a top secret memorandum on Turkey formulated by the highest levels of government in late 1946 and which Acting Secretary of State Dean Acheson transmitted to Byrnes (then in Paris), the major components of what came to be the predominant Cold War paradigm were clearly identified. Among the telegram's more interesting themes is the early enunciation of the so-called 'domino theory' of chain reaction collapse—a theory as old as history itself, despite the supposed revelations of the Pentagon Papers many years later.

Source: Department of State, *Foreign Relations of the United States, Diplomatic Papers: 1946* (Wash. 1969), VII, 840-42.

. . . For Secretary Byrnes only. State War Navy Depts at highest levels, after series of meetings, agreed upon a memorandum re Turkey and the Soviet Union. This memo was presented to President in person today by Secretaries of War and Navy and myself. Also present were top ranking officers of army and navy.

President approved policy recommended in the memo and stated he was prepared to pursue it "to the end". President specifically asked for any comments which you may care to make.

It was agreed with President that draft reply to Turkish Govt's inquiry as to our attitude toward Soviet proposals re the Straits should be prepared at once and sent to you for comment and to him for approval before despatch to Ankara.

Draft reply will follow in subsequent telegram. President planning leave Washington Aug 16—2:30 PM so any comment re memo should reach him before that hour.

Memo reads as follows:

"In our opinion, the primary objective of the Soviet Union is to obtain control of Turkey.

We believe that if the Soviet Union succeeds in introducing into Turkey armed forces with the ostensible purpose of enforcing the joint control of the Straits, the Soviet Union will use these forces in order to obtain control over Turkey.

If the Soviet Union succeeds in its objective obtaining control over Turkey it will be extremely difficult, if not impossible, to prevent the Soviet Union from obtaining control over Greece and over the whole Near and Middle East.

It is our experience that when the Soviet Union obtains predominance in an area, American and, in fact all Western influences and contacts are gradually eliminated from that area. In our opinion, therefore, the establishment by the Soviet Union of bases in the Dardanelles or the introduction of Soviet armed forces into Turkey on some other pretext would, in the natural course of events, results in Greece and the whole Near and Middle East, including the Eastern Mediterranean, falling under Soviet control and in those areas being cut off from the Western world.

When we refer to the Near and Middle East, we have in mind the territory lying between the Mediterranean and India. When the Soviet Union has once obtained full mastery of this territory, which is strategically important from the point of view of resources, including oil, and from the point of view of communications, it will be in a much stronger position to obtain its objectives in India and China.

We, therefore, feel that it is in the vital interests of the United States that the Soviet Union should not by force or through threat of force succeed in its unilateral plans with regard to the Dardanelles and Turkey. If Turkey under pressure should agree to the Soviet proposals, any case which we might later present in opposition to the Soviet plan before the United Nations or to the world public would be materially weakened; but the Turkish Government insists that it has faith in the United Nations system and that it will resist by force Soviet efforts to secure bases in Turkish territory even if Turkey has to fight alone. While this may be the present Turkish position, we are frankly doubtful whether Turkey will continue to adhere to this determination without assurance of support from the United States.

It is unfortunate that the Soviet Union, ignoring the United Nations and Montreux concept of Straits control, has made a formal proposal to Turkey for bilateral agreement regarding the joint defense of the Straits because it is always extremely difficult to persuade the Soviet Union, once formally committed on a subject, to retreat. Experience has shown such a retreat cannot be brought about by skillful argument or the appeal to reason. The only thing which will deter the Russians will be the conviction that the United States is prepared, if necessary, to meet aggression with force of arms. There is a strong possibility that if the Soviet Union is given clearly and unequivocally to understand that the United States will firmly and with determination support Turkey in case Turkey is made the object of Soviet measures threatening the independence, sovereignty or territorial interests of Turkey the Soviet Union will pause and will not push the matter further at this time.

In our opinion therefore the time has come when we must decide that we shall resist with all means at our disposal any Soviet aggression and in particular, because the case of Turkey would be so clear, any Soviet aggression against Turkey. In carrying out this policy our words and acts will only carry conviction to the Soviet Union if they are· formulated against the background of an inner conviction and determination on our part that we cannot permit Turkey to become the object of Soviet aggression. Threats or provocations should have no part in the implementation of this policy which will require in the first instance frank discussions with the principal nations involved and strong support of Turkey in the United Nations, should that become necessary.

In our judgment the best hope of preserving peace is that the conviction should be carried to the U.S.S.R., Turkey and all other powers that in case the United Nations is unsuccessful in stopping Soviet aggression, the United States would not hesitate to join other nations in meeting armed aggression by the force of American arms."

43   The traditional British role in Greece and Turkey comes to an end: a
       frank plea for US aid

In the light of the Russian experience in Eastern Europe and Iran, the Truman Administration was determined to resist what it regarded as Soviet aggression the next time it reared its head, although the actual form and timing of that resistance were much in doubt. In this sense the immediate background of the pronouncement of the Truman Doctrine was the official disclosure in February 1947 that the British Government would shortly be terminating its military and economic support of the existing Greek and Turkish regimes. By this act, according to State Department official Joseph M. Jones in *The Fifteen Weeks* (1955), 'Great Britain had within the hour handed the job of world leadership, with all its burdens and all its glory, to the United States.' Whether or not Jones exaggerated the importance of the British notes, which themselves indicate American foreknowledge of British plans in the region, they have assumed a high degree of historical significance.

43(a) Top secret British *aide-mémoire* on Greece: February 21, 1947. '. . . *His Majesty's Government take the view that it is most urgent that the United States Government should be able to decide what economic help they will give to Greece and what form it will take.'*

Source: Department of State, *Foreign Relations of the United States, Diplomatic Papers: 1947* (Wash. 1971), V, 32-35.

His Majesty's Government are giving most earnest and anxious consideration to the important problem that on strategic and political grounds Greece and Turkey should not be allowed to fall under Soviet influence.[1]

2. It will be remembered that at the Paris Peace Conference Mr. Byrnes expressed full realisation of the great importance of this question and proposed that the United States Government should give active help in sustaining the economic and military position in those two countries, the United States Government in particular taking care of the economic side.

3. On various occasions subsequent to the meeting referred to above the United States Government have exchanged views with His Majesty's Government, indicating the acute interest of the United States Government in the future of Greece, and from these exchanges His Majesty's Government have understood that the United States Government does not exclude the possibility of helping Greece on the military side as well as the economic.

4. The State Department will recollect the conversation between Mr. Byrnes and the Minister of Defence which took place on the 15th October, 1946, subsequent to which the whole question of British military and economic help for Greece has been carefully examined by His Majesty's Government. On the economic side, the reports received by His Majesty's Government from their representatives in Greece show that the Greek economic situation is on the point of collapse, owing to the virtual exhaustion of Greece's foreign exchange reserves and the low level of industrial activity resulting from political instability. In this connection His Majesty's Embassy attach to this *Aide-Mémoire* Appendix "A"[2] which is a report dated the 5th February, from His Majesty's Representative in Athens, on the acute economic and financial situation in Greece.

5. The United States Government are as well aware as His Majesty's Government that unless Greece can obtain help from outside there is certain to be widespread starvation and consequent political disturbances during the present year. The Experts Committee of the United Nations have estimated Greek relief needs in 1947 at £21 million. This figure is based on the maintenance of the present subnormal standard of industrial activity and will, in the view of His Majesty's Government, be wholly inadequate to achieve our political objective of maintaining stability. His Majesty's Government

estimate the actual needs of Greece, excluding the foreign exchange cost of the armed forces, at a minimum of £40 million in 1947. However, the serious economic plight of Greece as outlined above is already well known to the United States Government from the reports of their representatives in Greece and is no doubt being supplemented at the present time by preliminary reports from the Porter Mission.

6. In view of the position outlined in the above paragraph, His Majesty's Government take the view that it is most urgent that the United States Government should be able to decide what economic help they will give to Greece and what form it will take.

7. In the event of the United States Government being able to offer economic aid to Greece, it would no doubt consider the despatch of a United States economic mission. If this should be done, the future of the British Economic Mission in Greece would have to be considered.

8. On the military side, Greek needs have been very carefully considered by the British military authorities during the last few months, and the position has been investigated personally by the Chief of the Imperial General Staff during his recent visit to Greece. His Majesty's Government have agreed to pay the foreign exchange cost of the Greek armed forces, both in regard to maintenance and initial equipment, until the 31st March next. This is likely to cost H.M.G. during 1946 and the first 3 months of 1947 approximately £18 million for maintenance, together with £11 million for initial equipment. This, in view of H.M.G.'s financial difficulties, can be regarded as a very generous measure of assistance to Greek reconstruction. Hitherto the Greek armed forces have been built up on an establishment which allows for an army of 100,000 men, the total foreign exchange cost of which is estimated at about £16 million a year. In order to meet the present emergency caused by the bandits, the British service authorities consider that the Greek armed forces should now be reorganised to enable them to make an all-out assault on the bandits in the Spring. The reasons why this reorganisation has become necessary are set out in papers which are now in the possession of the British Joint Staff Mission in Washington, who also have full details of the present organisation of the Greek armed forces and of the reorganisation proposed by the British military authorities. These details are available for study by the State Department and the United States Chiefs of Staff. The Joint Staff Mission are also in a position to provide the United States Government with a list of the equipment required by the Greek armed forces which cannot be supplied from British sources.

9. His Majesty's Government suggest that, if the United States Government agree, the various military questions involved should be taken over for urgent consideration by the combined Chiefs of Staff.

10. In view of the extreme urgency of taking some immediate action to enable the reorganisation proposals to be undertaken, His Majesty's Government have agreed to make available additional equipment to the value of £2 million free of charge to the Greek Government. This, supplemented by American supplies of equipment which is not available to H.M.G., will enable the Greek armed forces to be put in a position to undertake operations in the Spring against the bandits, provided that means can be found to meet the rest of the foreign exchange cost of such operations. On the assumption that operations will last six months, the foreign exchange cost of this reorganisation, together

with the foreign exchange cost of the operations themselves, will over this period amount to £20 million. (The foreign exchange cost after the end of the operations will be smaller but will remain considerable.)

11.   His Majesty's Government had hoped that part of the foreign exchange cost of the Greek armed forces after 31st March, 1947 could be met out of the money due to Greece by His Majesty's Government for the supply of currency and local services to the British forces in Greece. But £5 million out of the amount so due was recently placed at the disposal of the Greek Government for the purchase of food and is therefore no longer available to cover part of the cost of the armed forces.

12.   Thus the total amount of assistance for civilian and military needs which Greece requires during 1947 appears to be between £60 million and £70 million. His Majesty's Government have already strained their resources to the utmost to help Greece and have granted, or undertaken to grant, assistance up to 31st March, 1947 to the amount of £40 million. The United States Government will readily understand that His Majesty's Government, in view of their own situation, find it impossible to grant further financial assistance to Greece. Since, however, the United States Government have indicated the very great importance which they attach to helping Greece, His Majesty's Government trust that the United States Government may find it possible to afford financial assistance to Greece on a scale sufficient to meet her minimum needs, both civil and military.

13.   His Majesty's Ambassador is instructed to express the earnest hope of His Majesty's Government that, if a joint policy of effective and practical support for Greece is to be maintained, the United States Government will agree to bear, as from the 1st April, 1947, the financial burden, of which the major part has hitherto been borne by His Majesty's Government. In view of the extreme urgency, both on economic and military grounds, that the Greek Government should know what financial help is going to be available in the present year, His Majesty's Government express the hope that the United States Government will indicate their position at the earliest possible moment.

[1]   This *aide-mémoire* and the one *infra* were handed informally to Mr. Loy Henderson, Director of the Office of Near Eastern and African Affairs by Herbert M. Sichel, First Secretary of the British Embassy, on February 21. They were formally delivered to the Secretary of State by the British Ambassador on February 24.
[2]   Not printed.

43(b)   Top secret British *aide-mémoire* on Turkey: February 21, 1947. '. . . *His Majesty's Government wish now to suggest that the strategic and military position of Turkey should be considered by the Combined Chiefs of Staff . . .'*

Source: ibid, 35-37.

In the course of his conversations with the Minister of Defence on October 15, 1946, Mr. Byrnes emphasized that the United States Government was as interested in developments in Turkey as in Greece, and stated that the United States Government was prepared to do everything possible to help Turkey economically, expressing the hope that His Majesty's Government on their side would be able to provide the military equipment required to bring the Turkish forces into a sufficient state of readiness.

2.   His Majesty's Government subsequently undertook a fresh study of the Turkish military and economic situation, the latter being carried out jointly by the British and American Commercial Counsellors in Turkey, in accordance with arrangements made with the United States Government.

3.   On the military side, the Chiefs of Staff have examined the strategic importance of Turkey, the state of the Turkish Armed Forces, and the assistance necessary to bring these forces into a reasonable state of preparedness. The conclusions of the British Chiefs of Staff, which are available at the British Joint Staff Mission in Washington, are briefly as follows:—

(a)   that it is of the greatest importance that Turkish independence should be maintained;

(b)   that the Turkish Armed Forces as they exist at present would not be able to offer effective resistance to aggression by a first-class power;

(c)   that in their present state of efficiency the mere provision of modern weapons would do little to increase the Turkish Armed Forces' power of resistance. The first requirement is to strengthen Service requirement in Turkey with a view to advising the Turks how best to improve the organisation and raise the general standard of training of all three Services;

(d)   that when this has been done it would be possible to estimate more clearly what amount of material assistance would be required. As at present advised, the Chiefs of Staff consider that the Turkish Army will require a very large measure of re-equipment and they do not consider that this task could be undertaken by the United Kingdom owing to shortage of manpower and productive capacity. Consequently the task would have to be undertaken by the United States. His Majesty's Government could probably look after the needs of the Navy and Air Force, provided satisfactory financial arrangements can be made.

4.   The economic situation has been exhaustively discussed locally between the British and American Commercial Counsellors, and His Majesty's Government understand that a very full report was sent to Washington by the United States Commercial Counsellor on December 23, 1946. His Majesty's Government have no reason to dissent from the main conclusions of the American representative's report, and the following appear to be the salient features of the Turkish economic situation:—

5.   Turkey can finance her current foreign exchange requirements out of the proceeds of her exports; she can also maintain her existing industry without further foreign financial assistance. On the other hand, she would not be able to finance any extensive programme of industrial development, such as the Turkish Government have in mind, or meet any substantial foreign exchange demands for armaments without either drawing on her gold resources or borrowing from abroad. As regards foreign exchange, current income and liabilities roughly cancel out over a period of twelve months. On the other hand, the last available Central Bank statement shows gold reserves of approximately pounds sterling 59 million. It is understood that the Finance Minister insists that he must hold at least half of this amount as cover for the note issue if confidence in the currency is to be maintained. The balance could reasonably be used either for a programme of economic and industrial development, transport, ports, agricultural, coal-mining etc., or for the purchase of armaments. There is clearly not

enough for both. If, therefore, Turkey is to be able to carry out any plan of extensive military reorganisation and also a plan of economic development, which in itself would be desirable in order to increase the military preparedness of the country, Turkey must look for financial assistance from abroad. In their existing financial situation His Majesty's Government could not, as the United States Government will readily appreciate, contemplate themselves making any further credits available to Turkey. Consequently, Turkey would have to look either to the United States Government or to one of its lending agencies, such as the Import-Export Bank, or to the International Bank or the International Monetary Fund.

6. In view of the great interest shown by the United States Government in the situation in Turkey, His Majesty's Government wish now to suggest that the strategic and military position of Turkey should be considered by the Combined Chiefs of Staff in the light of the conclusions reached by the British Chiefs of Staff in their recent studies, with a view to making recommendations to the United States Government and His Majesty's Government regarding the measures which should be taken to bring the Turkish Armed Forces up to a reasonable state of preparedness. For their part, His Majesty's Government would be ready, if the Combined Chiefs of Staff agree that this would be useful, to send to Turkey additional Military, Naval and Air Advisers amounting to some 60 officers, for whom the Turkish Government asked some months ago.[1] On the economic side, His Majesty's Government would be glad to know whether the United States Government have any suggestions to make as to how a programme of military reorganisation thay may be recommended by the Combined Chiefs of Staff should be financed.

[1] The British Embassy corrected this sentence in an *aide-mémoire* of March 6, which stated: 'While His Majesty's Government in the United Kingdom are prepared to provide sixty British officers in all, the reference in the *aide-mémoire* [of February 21] should have been to only thirty additional officers as thirty are already there.'

44   The Truman Doctrine: March 15, 1947. *'I believe that it must be the policy of the United States to support free peoples who are resisting attempted subjugation by armed minorities or by outside pressures.'*

President Truman's response both to the plight of the British and to the deteriorating situation in Greece and Turkey was swift and unequivocal. Within the context of requesting urgent economic and financial assistance for the relief of these countries, the President boldly declared to a joint session of Congress on March 12, 1947: 'I believe that it must be the policy of the United States to support free peoples who are resisting attempted subjugation by armed minorities or by outside pressures. I believe that we must assist free peoples to work out their own destinies in their own way.' The exact meaning of these words, although Truman specifically qualified them to mean 'that our help should be primarily through economic and financial aid', has been the subject of much historical debate; their significance is still obvious in the post-Viet-Nam world in which United States foreign policy is now being conducted. Early Realist critiques, such as Hans J. Morgenthau's *In Defense of National Interest* (1952), were especially hostile to Truman's use of universal moral principles to defend the nation's traditional defence of the European balance of power. Others, writing later with the benefit of perspective, have argued that the Truman Doctrine was, in the words of John Lewis Gaddis in an important article in *Foreign Affairs,* 'very much in line with previously established precedents for dealing with shifts in the European balance of power; ... and that the real commitment to contain communism everywhere originated in the events surrounding the Korean War, not the crisis in Greece and Turkey.' Still others have regarded the President's remarks as 'the characteristic American phenomenon of building ideological castles to house pragmatic kitchens.' Whatever Truman meant, there can be little doubt that his speech was a turning point in American foreign policy.

Source: *Presidential Papers: Harry S. Truman, 1947* (Wash. 1963), 176-80.

The gravity of the situation which confronts the world today necessitates my appearance before a joint session of the Congress.

The foreign policy and the national security of this country are involved.

One aspect of the present situation, which I present to you at this time for your consideration and decision, concerns Greece and Turkey.

The United States has received from the Greek Government an urgent appeal for financial and economic assistance. Preliminary reports from the American Economic Mission now in Greece and reports from the American Ambassador in Greece corroborate the statement of the Greek Government that assistance is imperative if Greece is to survive as a free nation.

I do not believe that the American people and the Congress wish to turn a deaf ear to the appeal of the Greek Government.

Greece is not a rich country. Lack of sufficient natural resources has always forced the Greek people to work hard to make both ends meet. Since 1940, this industrious, peace loving country has suffered invasion, four years of cruel enemy occupation, and bitter internal strife.

When forces of liberation entered Greece they found that the retreating Germans had destroyed virtually all the railways, roads, port facilities, communications, and merchant marine. More than a thousand villages had been burned. Eighty-five percent of the children were tubercular. Livestock, poultry, and draft animals had almost disappeared. Inflation had wiped out practically all savings.

As a result of these tragic conditions, a militant minority, exploiting human want and misery, was able to create political chaos which, until now, has made economic recovery impossible.

Greece is today without funds to finance the importation of those goods which are essential to bare subsistence. Under these circumstances the people of Greece cannot make progress in solving their problems of reconstruction. Greece is in desperate need of financial and economic assistance to enable it to resume purchases of food, clothing, fuel and seeds. These are indispensable for the subsistence of its people and are obtainable only from abroad. Greece must have help to import the goods necessary to restore internal order and security so essential for economic and political recovery.

The Greek Government has also asked for the assistance of experienced American administrators, economists and technicians to insure that the financial and other aid given to Greece shall be used effectively in creating a stable and self-sustaining economy and in improving its public administration.

The very existence of the Greek state is today threatened by the terrorist activities of several thousand armed men, led by Communists, who defy the government's authority at a number of points, particularly along the northern boundaries. A Commision appointed by the United Nations Security Council is at present investigating disturbed conditions in northern Greece and alleged border violations along the frontier between Greece on the one hand and Albania, Bulgaria, and Yugoslavia on the other.

Meanwhile, the Greek Government is unable to cope with the situation. The Greek army is small and poorly equipped. It needs supplies and equipment if it is to restore authority to the government throughout Greek territory.

Greece must have assistance if it is to become a self-supporting and self-respecting democracy.

The United States must supply this assistance. We have already extended to Greece certain types of relief and economic aid but these are inadequate.

There is no other country to which democratic Greece can turn.

No other nation is willing and able to provide the necessary support for a democratic Greek government.

The British Government, which has been helping Greece, can give no further financial or economic aid after March 31. Great Britain finds itself under the necessity of reducing or liquidating its commitments in several parts of the world, including Greece.

We have considered how the United Nations might assist in this crisis. But the situation is an urgent one requiring immediate action, and the United Nations and its related organizations are not in a position to extend help of the kind that is required.

It is important to note that the Greek Government has asked for our aid in ulitizing effectively the financial and other assistance we may give to Greece, and in improving its public administration. It is of the utmost importance that we supervise the use of any funds made available to Greece, in such a manner that each dollar spent will count toward making Greece self-supporting, and will help to build an economy in which a healthy democracy can flourish.

No government is perfect. One of the chief virtues of a democracy, however, is that its defects are always visible and under democratic processes can be pointed out and corrected. The government of Greece is not perfect. Nevertheless it represents 85 percent of the members of the Greek Parliament who were chosen in an election last year. Foreign observers, including 692 Americans, considered this election to be a fair expression of the views of the Greek people.

The Greek Government has been operating in an atmosphere of chaos and extremism. It has made mistakes. The extension of aid by this country does not mean that the United States condones everything that the Greek Government has done or will do. We have condemned in the past, and we condemn now, extremist measures of the right or the left. We have in the past advised tolerance, and we advise tolerance now.

Greece's neighbor, Turkey, also deserves our attention.

The future of Turkey as an independent and economically sound state is clearly no less important to the freedom-loving peoples of the world than the future of Greece. The circumstances in which Turkey finds itself today are considerably different from those of Greece. Turkey has been spared the disasters that have beset Greece. And during the war, the United States and Great Britain furnished Turkey with material aid.

Nevertheless, Turkey now needs our support.

Since the war Turkey has sought additional financial assistance from Great Britain and the United States for the purpose of effecting that modernization necessary for the maintenance of its national integrity.

That integrity is essential to the preservation of order in the Middle East.

The British Government has informed us that, owing to its own difficulties, it can no longer extend financial or economic aid to Turkey.

As in the case of Greece, if Turkey is to have the assistance it needs, the United States must supply it. We are the only country able to provide that help.

I am fully aware of the broad implications involved if the United States extends assistance to Greece and Turkey, and I shall discuss these implications with you at this time.

One of the primary objectives of the foreign policy of the United States is the creation of conditions in which we and other nations will be able to work out a way of life free from coercion. This was a fundamental issue in the war with Germany and Japan. Our victory was won over countries which sought to impose their will, and their way of life, upon other nations.

To ensure the peaceful development of nations, free from coercion, the United States has taken a leading part in establishing the United Nations. The United Nations is designed to make possible lasting freedom and independence for all its members. We shall not realize our objectives, however, unless we are willing to help free peoples to maintain their free institutions and their national integrity against aggressive movements that seek to impose upon them totalitarian regimes. This is no more than a frank recognition that totalitarian regimes imposed upon free peoples, by direct or indirect aggression, undermine the foundations of international peace and hence the security of the United States.

The peoples of a number of countries of the world have recently had totalitarian regimes forced upon them against their will. The Government of the United States has made frequent protests against coercion and intimidation, in violation of the Yalta agreement, in Poland, Rumania, and Bulgaria. I must also state that in a number of other countries there have been similar developments.

At the present moment in world history nearly every nation must choose between alternative ways of life. The choice is too often not a free one.

One way of life is based upon the will of the majority, and is distinguished by free institutions, representative government, free elections, guarantees of individual liberty, freedom of speech and religion, and freedom from political oppression.

The second way of life is based upon the will of a minority forcibly imposed upon the majority. It relies upon terror and oppression, a controlled press and radio, fixed elections, and the suppression of personal freedoms.

I believe that it must be the policy of the United States to support free peoples who are resisting attempted subjugation by armed minorities or by outside pressures.

I believe that we must assist free peoples to work out their own destinies in their own way.

I believe that our help should be primarily through economic and financial aid which is essential to economic stability and orderly political processes.

The world is not static, and the *status quo* is not sacred. But we cannot allow changes in the *status quo* in violation of the Charter of the United Nations by such methods as coercion, or by such subterfuges as political infiltration. In helping free and independent nations to maintain their freedom, the United States will be giving effect to the principles of the Charter of the United Nations.

It is necessary only to glance at a map to realize that the survival and integrity of the Greek nation are of grave importance in a much wider situation. If Greece should fall under the control of an armed minority, the effect upon its neighbor, Turkey, would be immediate and serious. Confusion and disorder might well spread throughout the entire Middle East.

Moreover, the disappearance of Greece as an independent state would have a profound effect upon those countries in Europe whose peoples are struggling against great difficulties to maintain their freedoms and their independence while they repair the damages of war.

It would be an unspeakable tragedy if these countries, which have struggled so long against overwhelming odds, should lose that victory for which they sacrificed so much. Collapse of free institutions and loss of independence would be disastrous not only for them but for the world. Discouragement and possibly failure would quickly be the lot of neighboring peoples striving to maintain their freedom and independence.

Should we fail to aid Greece and Turkey in this fateful hour, the effect will be far reaching to the West as well as to the East.

We must take immediate and resolute action.

I therefore ask the Congress to provide authority for assistance to Greece and Turkey in the amount of $400,000,000 for the period ending June 30, 1948. In requesting these funds, I have taken into consideration the maximum amount of relief assistance which would be furnished to Greece out of the $350,000,000 which I recently requested that the Congress authorize for the prevention of starvation and suffering in countries devastated by the war.

In addition to funds, I ask the Congress to authorize the detail of American civilian and military personnel to Greece and Turkey, at the request of these countries, to assist in the tasks of reconstruction, and for the purpose of supervising the use of such financial and material assistance as may be furnished. I recommend that authority also be provided for the instruction and training of selected Greek and Turkish personnel.

Finally, I ask that the Congress provide authority which will permit the speediest and most effective use, in terms of needed commodities, supplies, and equipment, of such funds as may be authorized.

If further funds, or further authority, should be needed for the purposes indicated in this message, I shall not hesitate to bring the situation before the Congress. On this subject the Executive and Legislative branches of the Government must work together.

This is a serious course upon which we embark.

I would not recommend it except that the alternative is much more serious.

The United States contributed $341,000,000,000 toward winning World War II. This is an investment in world freedom and world peace.

The assistance that I am recommending for Greece and Turkey amounts to little more than 1/10 of 1 percent of this investment. It is only common sense that we should safeguard this investment and make sure that it was not in vain.

The seeds of totalitarian regimes are nurtured by misery and want. They spread and grow in the evil soil of poverty and strife. They reach their full growth when the hope of a people for a better life has died.

We must keep that hope alive.

The free peoples of the world look to us for support in maintaining their freedoms.

If we falter in our leadership, we may endanger the peace of the world—and we shall surely endanger the welfare of this Nation.

Great responsibilities have been placed upon us by the swift movement of events. I am confident that the Congress will face these responsibilities squarely.

45   Legislative origins of the Truman Doctrine

The decision of the Truman Administration to come to the rescue of the Greeks and Turks was only half the problem; the second, and in many ways more important, half was persuading the American people, through their representatives in Congress, of the necessity of such a task. To bring home the critical nature of the situation Lincoln MacVeagh, American Ambassador to Greece, and Edwin C. Wilson, American Ambassador to Turkey, were called back to Washington to brief, among others, the Senate Foreign Relations Committee. Due to the courtesy of the Office of Senator J.W. Fulbright, the following two readings include the testimony of MacVeagh and Wilson in hearings held in executive session before the Senate Foreign Relations during March and April 1947. These hearings were only made public in January 1973.

45(a) Testimony of Lincoln MacVeagh, American Ambassador to Greece: March 28, 1947. '*At the present moment, the situation in Greece is exceedingly grave and critical . . .*'

Source: *Hearings Held in Executive Session before the Committee on Foreign Relations*, United States Senate, 80th Congress, First Session (Wash. 1973), 32-47.

Ambassador MacVeagh. Of course, I have been over there a good long time, and I have seen Greece under different conditions from the conditions that exist now, and perhaps the best thing I can do in the course of my talk is to emphasize the great difference that exists at the present time from what existed before, and the reasons for it.

At the present moment, the situation in Greece is exceedingly grave and critical, actually critical. Any delay, if we are going to do anything about it, is very dangerous if we are going to avoid a total collapse of the country, both economically and socially, which will bring the country into the satellite orbit of the Russian Empire. The situation has been growing for a long time until it has got to a point where there seems to be very little chance of doing anything about it unless somebody from the outside takes a hand.

Now, when I was in Greece in the old days we used to have plenty of revolutions. I have seen every kind of revolution.

Senator CONNALLY. What do you mean by "old days"?

Ambassador MacVEAGH. I mean from 1933 to 1940. But that period was a period which was very similar to what took place from 1917 on. It was just a continuation of Greek history in a normal way between the two world wars. It is a highly unstable political country, and they are very, very fond of changing their Government and chasing it out and putting in another one.

Senator CONNALLY. We have that fever here now.

Ambassador MacVEAGH. They did that quite regularly. I have been in Greece under every kind of government—when it was a republic, when it was a regency, a monarchy, a dictatorship, a monarchy, and then another regency.

The CHAIRMAN. I understand there are 46 political parties in Greece.

Ambassador MacVEAGH. Almost everybody can be a political party. I have had a man come in and talk to me and say, "I have a party." He had a man with him.

"Who is this man?"

"This man is going to run my newspaper."

"That is very interesting."

Then he tells me all his ideas and finally gets so excited that he rises and, with a typical Greek gesture, says, "I represent the people of Greece," and the only people in his party are himself and his newspaperman, and they have their newspapers. It is politically a very lively society. But those revolutions never made very much difference to the people in the whole. They took place and there was a little shooting in the streets, some bystander would be hit, they would have a section of the army on the side of the revolution that would walk in and take over the Prime Minister's office and the revolution was over, and they would all go in and talk about it in the cafes. Now it is a very different thing.

BACKGROUND FOR CURRENT POLITICAL SITUATION

The European situation has changed. Greece has become a part of a larger area in Europe which is involved in social strains and stresses. Since the Communist Revolution in Russia, Russia has become the only great power on the European Continent. Great Britain has no possibility any more of forming the old coalitions against the dominant European power. Russia's influence is getting stronger and stronger, and she has, owing to the fact that during the World War the Russians liberated the northern part of the Balkan Peninsula and the British liberated the tip end of the peninsula in Greece, there has come about a frontier between the Western World and the expanding eastern Communist-dominated world along the frontiers of Greece, where you have a situation like oil and water, where they do not mix.

That creates these strains and stresses in Greece which have greatly increased the power of the Communist Party within Greece itself, which has become today a very powerful fifth column movement.

Before the war there was very little Communist activity in Greece. Senator Connally has been in Greece. He knows what it looks like in that country. It was largely an agricultural country. There were a few places in the country where there was some industry, around Salonika and in the tobacco region in the north, and around Athens, where there were small industries that rose up to take care of the refugees that came in from Turkey in 1935. But the great majority of the population are land-owning peasants. There is no agrarian problem there. The peasants have been given their land years ago; they are highly individualistic, highly democratic.

The Communist Party in Greece got its start after the last World War in Macedonia, and I was a witness to its first attempt to do something in the way of controlling the Government.

Senator CONNALLY. When you speak of Macedonia, do you speak of the part of it in Greece?

GREEK TOBACCO INDUSTRY

Ambassador MacVEAGH. I am using that in a broad sense, Senator, the northern part, eastern and western Macedonia, in Greece. I am using the phrase a little bit to mean the northern provinces of Greece. The tobacco business extends into Thrace, which is the eastern continuation of the Macedonian strip. That is where the principal growing of tobacco is done in Greece and where most of our tobacco companies get their oriental tobacco from to mix into our Chesterfields, Camels, Old Golds, Lucky Strikes, and so forth. There is in all those cigarettes widely sold over here about 12 to 13 percent of oriental tobacco. A good deal of it comes from Turkey, but a good deal also comes from Greece.

We have out there companies who operate in a very specialized way, and with that specialized industrial business of the tobacco which was the first thing to attract Communist organization, and it was done under the presidency of old Mr. Venizelos, the great democratic liberal leader of Greece, who was faced with the problem of settling the refugees who came from Turkey in 1925 in the exchange of populations and settling there those people and giving them something to do. At the time there came into Greece, whose population was 6 million, about 1 million refugees with nothing to do. It was a tremendous problem. Mr. Morgenthau headed the Refugee Settlement Commission of the League of Nations and went over there, and the problem was finally solved by settling these little fellows in every village and town of Greece, to do what they could in little business that they understood, little manufacturing business they understood from Turkey, like weaving rugs and making little clay pots and any little thing that they could do.

They were also given some land to cultivate, with the understanding that after 20 years or within 20 years or so they would repay the fund.

But there were quite a lot of them left over after all that had been done, and Mr. Venizelos said, "Here is a great idea." In the tobacco business of the North they run it this way. The farmer grows his tobacco and the buyers, who are all foreigners except for a few agents in Greece, come in and they establish highly paid and very expert staffs in the towns of Kavalla, Drama, Serrai, Xanthe, Alexandroupolis, and Salonika. Those fellows live there and learn the language and get to know every farmer personally. Then they go out in their little cars and they visit these farmers living in the farm houses and buy the tobacco for the big companies like R. J. Reynolds, Liggett & Myers, and so on, right there on the ground.

Then the farmer packs the things up and sends them into the central towns, where these companies have big magazines. Those magazines are the property of the companies. The tobacco is spilled on the floor in vast barnlike structures, and Greeks are hired to come in and sit on the ground, cross-legged, in great long rows and do what they call pick the tobacco. They pick the leaves over for quality, and then the thing is supervised by the American staff, and this stuff is packed up in bales and again kept for a long time, turned over from time to time, its temperature taken, and after about a year of storage the bales are put in ships and sent across the ocean, and then they are mixed with Virginia tobacco over here.

Venizelos said, "Here is a thing that is going on where you are using the same people to do two jobs." The farmers' daughters and their wives would come in and do the tobacco picking, and they also were connected with the fellow who was picking the tobacco in these warehouses. He said, "We will put the refugees in to do the tobacco picking," and large settlements of them were formed around all these little towns that I told you about, and they did the tobacco picking. But they did not think of the fact that this was a seasonal occupation, and for many months during the year the tobacco pickers had nothing to do. The farmer, of course, and his wife, got pretty well paid for the tobacco, lived on the farm, and grew their own things. These industrial workers were occupied for a few months of the year, and the rest of the time had nothing to do.

ORIGINS OF COMMUNIST INFLUENCE

That is where the first Communist organizers came into Greece. They organized the tobacco pickers of those towns in the early thirties, with agents that came down, the head men trained in Moscow, and it got to such a point that in 1936, in the spring, there was a strike in Salonika of small workmen and so on who had not been very well treated, and the tobacco people declared a general sympathetic strike throughout the whole of Macedonia and Thrace.

I happened to arrive in Salonika the morning the strike was called. It was a very bad thing. There was a great deal of shooting; there were many bodies carried around the streets; the Governor General sent word to me to stay in the hotel, he could not guarantee me my safety. I got hold of the consul and we got hold of a car and we drove through the whole northern region. The strike had to be quelled by the Government, who sent an army corps from Thessaly into that region, and also moved up some destroyers from Athens, and they broke the strike. Three months later the man who broke the strike, who was then a Prime Minister, declared to the King that he had information that a similar strike was going to take place in the Athens region. That was the beginning of the dictatorship, because, when the King signed the document giving him full powers, he assumed, he said, temporary dictatorial powers in order to quell the Communist movement, and later on he changed that into a perpetual dictatorship. That was Metaxas. He was given a mandate for 3 or 4 months, until elections could be held, but during that time he organized his own system of secret police, got his hands on everything, and took over what he thought was going to be a perpetual dictatorship.

Senator SMITH. How many years did Metaxas cover?

Ambassador MACVEAGH. From the fall of 1936 until the time the Germans came in. That was the first sign of what was coming up. That was your storm cloud, your connection of international communism with Greece.

During the dictatorship the Communist Party in Greece went underground. Nothing more was heard of it.

The CHAIRMAN. Were these imported agitators who organized?

Ambassador MACVEAGH. Some of them were. The chief men were. They were men who had been trained there and in other places in Europe.

Kavalla became a little center like Barcelona in Spain. It was a soft spot being developed like a soft spot on your lung that gives you pneumonia. Metaxas was a strong organizer and he didn't stand for any opposition, so they went underground. All the other political parites were abolished by decree. If any people got together and began talking politics, they were either allowed to sit on a block of ice for a while or they were sent into what they call exile in Greece. You put them on one of the islands and let them live there. It is not exile, because they do not go out of the country, but they go to an island and are told to stay on that island. The politicians were all handled that way and the records of the parties were destroyed, the party headquarters were broken up, and everything was dispersed. The ballot boxes were put into a museum and the new civilization in Greece had started along the lines of Metaxas.

The Communist Party was not destroyed. The Communist Party itself just dispersed and the people connected with it took on another aspect—tended to be something else, and said they had given up their communism, and they just went underground.

DEMORALIZATION OF WORLD WAR II

When the World War came along Metaxas died, the Germans came in, and the whole thing was overlaid with a domination of Germans and Italians, and the government fled. During that occupation a very terrific amount of destruction in the country took place, and a great deterioration in the morale of the Greek people took place.

I must say they are a very gallant people and have stood up pretty well, but under the enemy occupation, which operates the SS and Gestapo and those things, you get natually a deterioration of morality all over the country. Everybody who lived had to live by his wits and fighting against the other fellow, looking after No. 1 first of all, and the morale and the morality of Greece at the present time is far below what it used to be. It is a demoralized country at the present time, demoralized by this occupation, partly inadvertently by the Germans pressing down on them, partly on purpose. They tried to demoralise the Greek people. They wanted to destroy them.

So you had a country when we came back into Greece which was destroyed physically and also destroyed morally, and the country today is a country that is full of people who have not got any sense of responsibility or any sense of corporate activities. They care only about themselves, and thievery and murder and everything of that kind has gone up tremendously. It used to be a very moral little town, was Athens in the old days. It was a safer town to walk around in at 2 or 3 o'clock in the morning than any American city of which I knew. Practically crime was nonexistent. The only murders you had that took place in Greece were in the Port of Piraeus, among the Levantine sailors, and the crime of murder was nearly entirely restricted to the question of adultery, because in Greece, according to their old custom, if a wife commits adultery she has to be killed as well as the man, so you get that kind of thing. But it also kept the morality of the people pretty high, too, that kind of system. But that was practically what crime was. There was practically no stealing or anything of that kind.

Now it is universal. It is an awful mess. You cannot leave a car for a minute on the street. You just turn around and it is gone. They are expert thieves. They learned all these things under the occupation.

We have a demoralized country, we have a country the population of which goes around in fear of each other, because under the occupation some people collaborated, some people did not. The fellows who collaborated told on the others, the others have to get revenge, and you have revenge and vendetta going on all through the countryside.

Meanwhile the Communist Party is lying dormant. You come back with a government that has been chased out and that tries to establish itself in a vacant country where there is no government whatsoever. It has no control over anything. What takes the place of that government? The government itself has no means, no civil service, nothing to work with, no judges anywhere, no gendarmerie in the district, nothing with which to keep order. It is just a Cabinet that sits in Athens when it first comes in.

RESISTANCE MOVEMENT DIRECTED BY COMMUNISTS

What happens there? During the occupation the Allies, in order to fight the Germans, gave their assistance and support, money and arms, to what they called the resistance movement in Greece, which was made up of chaps, partly fellows who had resisted the Germans to such a degree that they did not dare live at home so they went into the mountains and others who had committed crimes and were afraid to stay in their homes and who went to the mountains, and others, adventurers, and others who went up there and said, "We are going to carry on the war against the Germans."

That looked fine. We said, "Here is a chance to sabotage this German effort."

At that time Greece was a strategic country. Rommel was in Egypt, trying to capture Egypt, and a line of supply was established by the Germans down through the Greek peninsula, and then by ship and plane across to Rommel in Egypt. It was an important place. They got a tremendous amount of supplies, so this sabotage work for which we hired these fellows was tremendously important—the British Force 133, MO-4, and later our OSS joined in with them. They helped to build up the resistance movement. It was a valuable movement. We sent in adventurous young men, dropped them in by airplane, and they tried to organize these rather disorganized bands of resistance forces into effective sabotage groups, and they naturally looked around to find the best people that they could get among the Greeks to assist them and to be the leaders of these groups.

Senator SMITH. Is that the EAM?

Ambassador MACVEAGH. This is the beginning of the EAM. It had not yet formed itself. EAM means the national resistance movement, and it gradually became, with our help, a unified movement with a name and a program to sabotage the German war effort. It was rather successful, and it had, up to a certain point, a good result. That is, it would occasionally blow up a bridge, and the Germans had to lose several days repairing the bridge.

But, in order to find fellows to do this work effeciently, the men they got were men trained in that thing. They were the men who used to be the old Communist saboteurs, you see—certain fellows from the Balkans and the north of Greece. The men they picked out were the men expert in sabotaging anything, you see, and the leadership became Communist leadership in the groups, and little by little the Communist Party in Greece, which had gone underground, came out that way and became the leaders of the national resistance movement, with our help.

Then the next stage was that Greece was no longer a strategic country. Rommel was chased out of Egypt, the Germans had nothing more to do with Greece, they were fighting for their lives up north, yet the order went on: "You must go on and sabotage everything you can in Greece."

What happened? Every time you did that the Germans took revenge, and they would burn a village for any effort made by the national resistance movement against them. Village after village—some 1,500 villages during that period were erased, largely in the mountains of Greece, the Central Pindus Range where, of course, fellows who took refuge would have the best chance to go. It was up among the mountain villages that these fellows hid. It was the villages in those regions that were destroyed, and that is where the greatest hunger and misery is today.

Senator CONNALLY. You say they destroyed 1,500 villages?

Ambassador MACVEAGH. 1,500 villages in Greece were destroyed, which created a homeless population which gradually began to drift more and more into the resistance movement, and that resistance movement became very large. Thirty or forty thousand men were involved, directed by the Communist movement. They organized themselves into battalions, companies, regiments, and divisions, as they call them on paper, and in each of the organizations there was a Communist who was under the orders of the headman, who was a member of the Communist Party.

That was the picture of the resistance movement at the time we came into Greece, and they first showed, during the war period, what they had done, how the Communists had come up to take charge of the resistance when we were in Egypt, and they fomented mutinies in the Greek forces in Cairo and Alexandria which caused great difficulty for the British in Egypt, and that movement was, on the face of it, a good old Greek political revolution, but it was instigated from below by the Communist organizers, and the reason why it was so hard to put down and why the mutiny in the ships was so bad, and in the army also, was that the fellows who were really running it were in the rank and file and were agents of the Communist movement, and were not just old Greek democrats or royalists.

LIBERATION OF GREECE

We saw that. We knew what was going on. We knew the makeup of this movement. But the British were still hoping that they could get through liberating Greece by just bringing in the government and waving the flag and not putting very much effort into it so far as the military was concerned. They came into Greece and were told they ought to have 20,000 men come in there and nothing would happen, because there would be no effort to oppose them by this movement. But they went in with about 3,000 men.

Senator CONNALLY. Who went in?

Ambassador MacVEAGH. The British. They liberated Greece. The Russians had liberated the rest. They came in and liberated Greece with about 3,000 men, in the face of a movement in the country which was strongly led, organized, and used by the Communists. And that brought about the trouble, because when the British scattered the troops around and said, "Now we have liberated Greece" and took it easy, these fellows moved into Athens, and in December 1944, a very determined effort was made to seize the Government, and then the idea was that that Government would then be put into the hands of the Communists or fellow travelers.

Senator CONNALLY. Was that 1944 or 1945?

Ambassador MacVEAGH. December 1944 I saw this thing go on. It was obviously a little social revolution. It was just like living through what you read of the French Revolution in the old days. The jails were opened; people went around liquidating people on all sides and carrying off anybody who happened to have a little money or something, or ladies in their evening slippers were taken and marched off as hostages to the hills. Many of them never came back. They were judged by people's courts. The whole thing was a social revolution, and not one of the nice old revolutions we used to have in the old days.

There is your difference. You are coming up to something that is entirely new, and the efforts made, the measures taken to combat this and to foresee it were not sufficient. The British were just able to help this Government that they had brought back in, that had no strength of its own, and to save the three or four blocks around the main hotel in Athens, and they held on there until they brought in reinforcements, and then they pushed the thing back, and after a month and a half the resistance movement head said, "Well, let's call it a day. Let's make an agreement." And they made an agreement, then, with the Greek Government, supported by the British, to call the whole thing off, to surrender their arms, and everything was going to be fine and dandy after that. They were going to have elections, and Greece was going right back to her old basis again.

DECEPTION OF RESISTANCE MOVEMENT

The nigger in the woodpile was still there, which was still not being recognized by the British. We recognized it. We had nothing to say about it. The men who signed this agreement for the resistance movement were the actual heads of the Communist Party of Greece. They were not democrats, as they were represented to be. They were not fellows looking to put Greece back on its old basis with the Democratic Party or the Royalist Party fighting it out at the polls. They were men dedicated to the revolutionary idea, men who were running cells of the Commununist Party throughout Greece, who were a revolutionary outfit designed in one way or other to get the power and to turn Greece into a totalitarian state.

Senator WILEY. They are Greeks?

Ambassador MacVEAGH. They were Greeks. The head man, Zachariades, is a trainee of the Moscow School for International Communism. Those fellows knew perfectly well what they were doing in signing this thing. They were getting themselves a breathing spell. They signed the agreement and warfare was off and everybody went back ostensibly to ordinary life and so on. But they went on preparing for the second round. They did not turn in by any means all the arms that they had in Greece, which had been pumped in by Force 133, OSS, and the rest and were hidden up in the hills. They proceeded to organize the second round.

Between the two rounds we made a lot of progress in Greece. UNRRA[1] came in right after this war. Before that there was what they called ML, the military liaison, that tried to bring in supplies to the Greek people. The UNRRA came in, and UNRRA did by and large an excellent job. There has been an awful lot of criticism of UNRRA, but it is all on details here and there. They kept hundreds of thousands of people alive, and I think they missed a point in not giving themselves a little bit more credit than they have got. They did a fine job.

The peasants did a fine job. They went back to work, and today, in most of Greece, if you go around the country, you will be surprised to see how beautifully cultivated every inch of ground is. And a certain amount of progress was made.

On the other hand the other fellows worked too, and our second round started last fall. What they decided to do then was to give up the idea of taking Athens and to concentrate themselves where their friends are across the border.

Bulgaria is under the command of Mr. Demitrev, the present Prime Minister, one of the original Communist organizers in Southeastern Europe. Tito runs Yugoslavia, and Enderhovia runs Albania—three Communist-dominated states. Across from those borders little control can be exercised. You can always take a path; you do not take the road, and supplies and ammunition can come very easily into that northern territory. Then it becomes more difficult as you get down, because you have to go through the government territory of Greece for a long way down to Athens.

REAPPEARANCE OF COMMUNISTS AND THE GREEK REACTION

So they began to build themselves up again up there. A lot of their best fighters, who had been engaged in the fight with the British in Athens, went back into Yugoslavia and were trained by the Yugoslavs and indoctrinated plenty in regard to communism, and equipped and sent back into Greece to recreate this subversive movement in Greece. And they began coming back in.

Naturally they ran across a lot of trouble when the Greeks found this thing out, and there came a situation which the Department described to me in a telegram as a "deteriorating situation along the Greek frontier," and wanted to know what was the reason for the deteriorating situation along the Greek frontier. Well, there was the reason for it. They wanted to know who was to blame, and I could not say anything else and tell the truth except that the fellow to blame was the fellow who controls the little countries to the north of Greece, the fellow who is backing them, right square back to the Moscow Government.

The Greeks have tried to repel that. They have got going to such a degree that they have found it very difficult to put it down. The Greeks have their army, such as it is, modeled after the British. It is a sort of streamlined army with trucks and all their mechanical equipment, and they march up there to try to quell these bands that have been organized by these fellows from across the border, and then when they get up there they find that it is not the kind of warfare they had been trained to do. They hear a village has been attacked by a band of 200 or 300 of these very well equipped bandits. They rush a column up to the village. Before it gets to the village they run across a bridge that has been blown out, and their nice streamlined army cannot get across a ravine. By the time they fix the bridge up and get across the bandits have disappeared. They are very mobile in the country, moving around here and there and attacking the places where the army isn't, and the army is practically powerless to get them to grips.

So it became perfectly clear that if they were going to do anything to stop that situation they have to reorganize the Government's forces so that it can fight these fellows on their own basis. They have to get thousands of mules: they have to get light mountain guns and more light automatic weapons, and a great deal of equipment in the way of walkie-talkie radio equipment and that kind of thing, so that they can know where they are to be found and each will know what the other fellow is doing.

COMMUNIST GUERRILLA MOVEMENT AND ITS ORGANIZATION

You know the country in Greece, Senator. You know how rocky it is. Guerrilla fighting in that place takes a special kind of organization, and heretofore, up to now, the Greek Army has been an army of 100,000 men completely brought to a stand-still in controlling the situation through this fluid fighting by about 12,000 well-organized bandits.

Who are these bandits? Colonel Miller, if he could have been here, could have given you personally his account of going to their headquarters. He was attached to the Ethridge mission, and the Ethridge mission in Salonika or the U.N. Commission on which Ethridge is our representative were pushed by the Russians up there to contact and take the testimony of the democratic general of this army, so-called, which is the bandits. So they did not think his testimony would be worth hearing, because they knew it would be biased, but they finally sent an echelon of the Commission to go down and contact him. They had prepared, meanwhile, a dossier on this man. His name is Markov. He calls himself a democratic general. They were going to ask him a whole lot of very unhappy questions about his past.

He happens to be—and here I can tie this little discourse up—one of the original Communist organizers of the tobacco business. He had a long record of being in jail for various crimes he has committed, and he now has been put at the head of this army and calls himself a general of the democratic army. That is the picture of what the thing is.

Miller got up to this place and he saw his staff and headquarters. Those people are all, in the headquarters of this general, youngsters, fanatical Communists who hold schools and meetings 2 hours in the morning and 2 hours in the afternoon to study the works of Marx and Lenin, and they go out from there to the heads of these bandit groups and spread that doctrine to them and give them the orders that are issued by General Markov.

Many of these poor bandits are just bandits, that is all, just out to loot, but they are gradually becoming unified by this continual pressure of propaganda and that control that is being exercised over them into a subversive army for the destruction of the Greek state.

Senator SMITH. Are those successors of EAM?

Ambassador MACVEAGH. EAM has sort of adopted them. The fighting men that went into Yugoslavia and came back are members of the old Elas, which was the fighting army of the EAM. The EAM is headed by the head of the Communist Party. It is an interlocking affair, see. The EAM is a democratic movement, ostensibly, for the freedom of Greece. It is headed up by the Communist Party. It has a subversive army called the Elas. That army was defeated and scattered. It now reforms and comes back into northern Macedonia, and is being helped by the satellite countries on the other side, which they did not have before when they made their abortive attempt on Athens.

Senator SMITH. Is that the crowd that refrained from voting in this recent election of the King?

Ambassador MACVEAGH. That is the crowd that refrained from the election, the only group in Greece that did.

Senator SMITH. Is it a strong minority?

Ambassador MACVEAGH. It is a strong minority. They would not have been a strong minority in the old days. They are a strong minority now because of the help that they have, the backing that they have.

Senator CONNALLY. Is it pretty well substantiated that Yugoslavia and Bulgaria are actively assisting them?

(Discussion was off the record.)

PRESSURE FROM THE NORTH

Ambassador MACVEAGH. There is the danger behind the whole thing. While in Greece the fellows are looking at themselves, behind it all is this big world movement. The Greeks themselves are sensitive, of course, to that big thing. They know that. They see the shadow of this immense thing. They may not think it all out, but that is why in this country today you find it practically impossible to get any reaction out of the Greeks themselves to any economic assistance.

Our help must be double; it cannot be just single. If you go in there to a frightened and demoralized people and try to get them to work again, you can go in so long as you like and give them food to eat. That is one thing. If we are going to stop and give aid to the Greeks you have to get them into the state of mind where they can react to this kind of treatment. It will be of no use to furnish economic help to Greece unless we relieve them of this overmastering fear in which they are all living today of this pressure from the north. They do not know whether they are going to be free or under the yoke of somebody like Tito in a short time, hence why go out to work? If they have some money outside the country, why bring it back into the country? It may belong to the Soviets in a short time.

The CHAIRMAN. Are these powerful minorities that you describe just going to sit idly by and watch us come in and checkmate this entire prospectus?

Ambassador MACVEAGH. They are already on the run, Senator, with just the statement by the President. It has shocked those fellows so much that they are already beginning to show weakness.

Senator WILEY. That army of 15,000 is composed of Greeks?

Ambassador MACVEAGH. It is not a powerful army. It is powerful on account of the situation. That is the internal trouble.

Senator CONNALLY. You mean the 12,000 under arms. Of course they have a large following.

Ambassador MacVEAGH. Oh, they have a following, but a following that would desert them if they get pushed.

The CHAIRMAN. You said this was the most lawless country on earth.

Ambassador MacVEAGH. I did not say that. I said it was demoralized and unhappy, where the old sense of law and order do not exist as existed before the war.

The CHAIRMAN. I thought you said you could get yourself shot very easily.

Ambassador MacVEAGH. I said you could lose your ear very easily, and that is true.

The CHAIRMAN. I was wondering about the minority group, trained as they are in subversion and its tactics. What are they going to do when our engineers appear up there to build a bridge? Are they just going to let them build it?

SUBVERSION EASILY NEUTRALIZED

Ambassador MacVEAGH. Oh, yes. You get this thing quieted down, this kind of fifth column movement in Greece. It is beaten at the top. I think that the organizers, these fellows who are organizing the unfortunates in Greece, and that is what it amounts to—the unfortunates and miserable have gone into the mountains and are organized and tightened up and being formed into a weapon by an international Communist group. You break down their organization and you chase out or capture the fellows who are organizing them, and you will have a certain amount of banditry in Greece for a great many years, but it will not be an organized subversive political movement. It will be just fellows in the hills like Robin Hood, who occasionally come down and carry off somebody for ransom.

This is what happened after the Greek war of independence. The situation is very similar to what happened in the 1820's. The Turks devastated the entire country and when the great powers finally intervened on the side of the Greeks and Greece was recognized as a sovereign nation in 1832, what was left was a lot of destroyed villages and a lot of fellows who had gone to the mountains fleeing the Turks and afterward stayed on in the mountains preying on the Greek inhabitants. They were cleared out, finally, in 1935. It lasted 100 years. But they were not an organized political movement for this subversive state. It was sort of good clean fun compared with this type of bandit. . . .

AID VALUELESS IF CONTINUED PRESSURE FROM NORTH

If we can get tranquility back there, we can remove, through this United Nations thing which I have a hope will gradually cut the infiltration and make these fellows cease pressing in on Greece, that fear, and also break up this bandit movement so it is no longer a coordinated and powerful assault against the state. Then you will get the Greek people to go back to work a little bit, relieved of this fear, and our economic help can be of value. Otherwise it will not be of value, and will just be lost.

Senator SMITH. What percentage of the whole Greek population would this Communist group be? They refrained from voting. If that percentage was very large, it might have had a different effect.

Ambassador MacVEAGH. It was not very large. It was about 9.3 percent of the electorate that abstained. Suppose that is low; suppose you allowed it to be 15 percent. They would have had a voting strength in the Parliament of about 25 deputies out of

342. But it is so well organized.

Let me tell you that the best organizers in Greece, and the best men, are the heads of the Communist movement, the most vital fellows in the country. That is the sad part of it. These fellows over there now are trying to make bricks without straw, but you have to go ahead and make the bricks or you are going to lose the country.

The CHAIRMAN. What do these men do when we move in?

DISSOLUTION OF COMMUNIST ORGANIZATION

Ambassador MacVEAGH. I think the head men will go back across the border. The weaker members, the chaps who have been organized by them, the general rank and file of the bandits, will come in and say, "Oh, we give it up." But hundreds of them, perhaps, will still remain bandits in the inaccessible mountains of Greece for a good many years to come, but you can turn them over to the gendarmerie and the country police.

Senator CONNALLY. Has there been any perceptible change since this Commission went over there? Have any of these fellows taken to the woods and gotten out of the way?

Ambassador MacVEAGH. No. They are so well organized and so well equipped now that there is no particular change in the actual operations of the fellows in the mountains, but there has been a considerable change in their mode of supply. When the Commission went up to Salonika and began looking around, you see, our information is that the supply routes and traffic back and forth between Yugoslavia and Greece ceased. It was practically gone. But it has moved away over to the end of the Bulgarian border, away over next to the Turkish border.

On Miller's map, which he showed me, this is the place here. The infiltration of this area, while these fellows have been there, has ceased, and this one has become much stronger, and this is where there has been far less observation than over here, and this is where the stuff is coming in now.

Senator SMITH. That is Thrace, that area?

Ambassador MacVEAGH. Yes, that little hook on the Turkish-Bulgarian border. The main pressure comes from here and around through Bulgaria, which allows it to pass through, and then it infiltrates in this direction. That was a change of tactics they had to make, and they did that. If the Commission arrives at the kind of solution we hope, there will be, naturally, observers all along the border as a regular thing. There should be that between states of that kind, to report any violation that comes up and bring it into the open. The only thing you can do is to have it public, and if it is public you have a chance of beating it. So long as you let it go on secretly it will go on more and more.

The CHAIRMAN. If the Border Commission's report is clean-cut and the United Nations takes action on it, I suppose with the opposition in the United Nations and in the Commission of the Soviet and its satellites, is it possible, in your opinion, that enough can be done to substantially immunize this border?

COMMUNIST PRESSURE MAY BE APPLIED ELSEWHERE

Ambassador MacVEAGH. Yes, I think so. I think so. I think one of the things that will happen on this thing is that the orders will be changed from above. If the orders are changed from Moscow as to where their efforts are to be made along their frontiers, that is all that is necessary for these boys down here. The say, "Well, this hasn't worked; just let up on this. There is no use in our carrying on because it is costly. It is not going to get anywhere." They will drop it and put their pressure somewhere else.

The CHAIRMAN. Where do you mean by "somewhere else"?

Ambassador MacVEAGH. The thing that I used to tell President Roosevelt about when I was in Cairo was the "critical crescent." It went from Afghanistan to Finland, and along that crescent the Soviet has bulged and bulged and bulged. All the Balkan states are gone and a large part of Poland is gone. Rumania is gone. They tried Azerbaijan; they may try Afghanistan. Who knows? There is an expansionist movement there, undoubtedly. Any empire that bases itself on revolution always has expansionist tendencies.

THE CHAIRMAN. Then one might infer from your analysis that all we succeed in doing is transferring the point of trouble.

Ambassador MacVEAGH. I think very likely. I have no doubt. But then there are different ways of answering the troubles. A firm show that this is not a soft spot, that this is a place where you can not go and ingest every bit of contiguous territory that you see—"This is finished; you can't do this," then you try some other places. But the cure in another place may not be the same cure as it is here. I think you have to take a firm stand everywhere. It will not necessarily mean that you will have to step in and put billions of dollars into India or anything like that. There are other means of convincing them that we are serious.

Senator CONNALLY. If we do not do this, and they are successful in Greece, they will be more successful as they go on.

Ambassador MacVEAGH. The appetite grows with eating.

The CHAIRMAN. We are confronted, ourselves, with the fundamental fact that if we desert the President of the United States at the moment we cease to have any influence in the world forever.

Ambassador MacVEAGH. I am afraid that is true. It is awfully serious.

Senator CONNALLY. Do you regard this election as having been a fairly decent election?

Ambassador MacVEAGH. There was a plebiscite for the King and there was the election for the political parties, which came first, and we observed both of them, and then both of them came out about the same way. As I was saying, you can not compare this country here with a Near Eastern country like Greece. It was a pretty good election.

The CHAIRMAN. Suppose we hear Mr. Wilson now, for a little while; if the committe is willing, I suggest that we sit until 1 o'clock today. I will go up and get permission, and then, after we have heard from Ambassador Wilson, we can put the two stories under examination.

Senator CONNALLY. Mr. MacVeagh, who is the strong man in Greece?

Ambassador MacVEAGH. Mr. Zachariades, head of the Communist Party.

Senator CONNALLY. I mean on our side.

DEARTH OF STRONG GREEK LEADERSHIP

Ambassador MacVEAGH. I wish there were some, but they are all fellows who have come back heading these destroyed parties, trying to build up the political life of Greece.

That was one of the troubles, sir. The dictatorship allowed no young men to come up as leaders—5 years of war and 4 years of dictation, so you have no young men coming up. The old fellows are going out.

Senator CONNALLY. What happened to John Stefanopoulos? He was the old Premier.

Ambassador MacVEAGH. Stefanopoulos, who has been over here? He was not Prime Minister. He was Foreign Minister. He is playing quite an ambitious game. He sort of figured that the Communist-controlled EAM movement was bound to win, and he has more and more put himself on their side. I think it is largely from ambition and he jumped on the wrong horse. He is very much of a lightweight in politics. He has no party.

The CHAIRMAN. He came to see me, and his plea was for a coalition government that took everybody in, which of course would mean destruction from within.

Ambassador MacVEAGH. That is what they want. They want to get the fellows in and get the key ministries in their hands. He has no political following whatsoever, so he has allied himself hoping to ride in on the victory of this movement.

¹ United Nations Relief and Rehabilitation Administration.

45(b) Testimony of Edwin C. Wilson, American Ambassador to Turkey: March 28, 1947. '. . . I believe that if we can keep the Turkish situation healthy, maintain them in their independence, . . . if we can convince the Russians that we mean business in that area and are not going to permit the expansion of the Soviets beyond where they have gone now, that is the surest way of preventing a world conflict.'

Source: ibid, 47-63.

TURKISH INDEPENDENCE VITAL TO U.S. INTEREST

Ambassador WILSON. Mr. Chairman, in the nearly 2 years that I have been in Turkey I have come to the conviction that the maintenance of an independent position by Turkey is a question of vital interest to our own country, and I will tell you why I think so.

Turkey is the only independent country on the borders of the Soviet Union from the Baltic to the Black Sea. If Turkey should be allowed to fall under Soviet domination, either through breaking down the regime through outside pressure or through an act of overt aggression against the country, you then have the Soviet borders running through Syria to Iraq and coming well along the western frontiers of Iran. You have the Soviet Union then in a position where it seems to me it would be more than you could ask human nature, certainly Soviet human nature, to resist the temptation to push on. There is nothing between them, then, and the Persian Gulf, Suez Canal, on out to the East—Afghanistan, India, and China.

So for that reason it seems to me that it is vitally important from our point of view to give assistance to the Turks to maintain their independent position there.

COUNTRY INTERNALLY STABLE

Turkey is a good risk today. They have been in this business a long time, standing up against Russian designs on their territory. Since the time of Peter the Great, say about 1699-1700, they have fought 10 wars against Russia, one about every 25 years. They have lost, most of the time. They have given up territory frequently as a result of losing the wars. But never once have they voluntarily ceded territory, and they do not intend to today.

There is very little communism in Turkey. They are keenly aware of the danger. They are united. I say united; today there is an opposition party in Turkey. There has been a very interesting movement toward the western type of liberal democracy in Turkey which I would like to tell you about a little later, and the opposition party in Turkey is just as firm in its attitude as the People's Party, the majority party in the country, in its opposition to the Soviet demands.

The CHAIRMAN. Have you any underground movement comparable to the thing the Ambassador described in Greece?

Ambassador WILSON. Fortunately not. Turkey has a clean situation that way. They have not allowed these fellows to come in and mess up inside the house. They have kept it clean.

Of the Turkish population, about 80 percent is peasant. The live on the land. Communism does not appeal to them. And the people in power, the governing elements in the country, know communism for what it is, because at the close of the First World War, when Turkey was trying to save something out of the debacle of the Ottoman Empire, Turkey and Russia at that time were the pariahs of the world. They were both outcasts, so they worked together for some little while, so the Turks came to know the Russians and what the aims of the Russians are very well, so they are on the alert.

In Turkey the financial position of the country is quite good. You might ask, Why should we aid Turkey? Turkey has a gold reserve of something over 660 million lira. That is, roughly, about $230 million or $235 million. That provides a cover of about 70 percent for their note issue. They, of course, do not need that much. But the Finance Minister in Turkey believes they need a cover of about 35 percent. That would be about half of this gold reserve. The balance the Turks feel is required for any emergency that may come up, as a war chest.

They have built up that favorable financial position at the cost of the general economy of the country. Instead of plowing back into the country their reserves for needed economic development they have saved it, and they have done it because Turkey has been mobilized ever since 1939.

TURKISH EXPERIENCE IN WORLD WAR II

First, Turkey was under German pressure to allow German troops to come through Turkey, first to help Rommel in North Africa and later, after the Nazis attacked Russia in June 1941, under German pressure to permit their troops to come through Turkey

and take the Russians in the back in the Caucasus. The Turks resisted the pressure.
Senator CONNALLY. They refused the privilege?
Ambassador WILSON. They refused absolutely. I have been up into Turkey and
Thrace, along the Bulgarian border. The road there, the one highway, still has
roadblocks along it, zigzags with concrete fortifications put up to prevent tanks from
coming through. They blew up the bridge over the Maritsa River at one stage when they
felt the Germans were coming in. They were fully prepared to defend themselves
against the Germans coming in.

After the Nazi attack on the Soviets in June 1941, when the Turks resisted the further
Nazi pressure to be allowed to go through and get the Russians from the rear, Soviet
Russia was very grateful to the Turks for their attitude, for their position at that time. In
fact, early in 1943 the Soviet Ambassador in Ankara, under the instructions of his
Government, expressed very warm gratitude to the Turkish Government for the
neutrality they had maintained.

As soon, however, as the pressure on the Soviets began to lessen and the Germans
were being driven back, the attitude of Soviet Russia toward Turkey changed
immediately and changed fundamentally. There were again indications of Soviet
displeasure with Turkey, particularly because Turkey had at the outset of the war, in
October 1939, made a treaty of alliance with Britain and France. Indications of Soviet
displeasure became apparent, so when the war ended the Turks found it impossible to
demobilize. They found themselves under pressure from the Russians, and in their own
interest they felt it necessary to keep a very large standing army in being.

PRESSURE FROM SOVIET UNION

That situation has gone on. Soviet pressure is becoming intensified. The latest phase
of it began in 1945. In March of 1945 the Soviet Government denounced its treaty of
friendship with Turkey, which had been in effect since 1925. I might say parenthetically
that the Turks realize perfectly well that in the long run if they are to be relieved of this
pressure and have any hope of an opportunity of developing their country in peaceable
stability they have got to have good relations with Russia. They then sought means to
negotiate a new treaty of friendship with Russia. They had their Ambassador in Moscow
in June of 1945 inquire of Molotove what could be done to negotiate a new treaty of
friendship, and to get their relations with Russia on a proper basis.

Molotov replied in effect, as understood by the Turks, that there were two conditions
precedent to any new treaty of friendship between the two countries. Those were, first,
the cession of Turkish territory in eastern Anatolia; and secondly, the granting of
military bases to Russia in the Straits area.

The Turks refused that flatly and declined to carry on any conversations on that basis
at all, because they understood that as meaning the end of Turkish independence if they
grant any such demands.

Since that time the Soviets have maintained their pressure on Turkey by a constant
bombarding of official radio, Moscow radio, to Turkey, which has criticized Turkey for
a number of things. Recently the theme has been that Turkey is betraying the principles
of Attaturk, one of the principal ones of which was to free Turkey of the foreign
domination and control that had been in effect during the latter half of the 19th century

under the Ottoman Empire of Abdul Hamid; that the Turkish Government was selling the country and the people out to imperialistic capitalistic United States and Great Britain.

I get the transcript of those broadcasts. I get them in translation. I see a great many of them. It is a constant incitement to the people of Turkey to rise up against their government and overthrow it, and to come to an understanding with their great friends in Soviet Russia.

In addition to that sort of pressure there have at different intervals been efforts to keep the Turks' nerves on edge by troop movements along the border in Bulgaria, by troop movements in Caucasus, by rumors that are planted in the coffee houses in Istanbul that the United States and Great Britain do not mean what they say; they will never come to Turkey's aid; that suddenly an air attack may come from the Russian side, and things of that sort. The last time when that sort of campaign was put on in force was last October, when there were troop movements along the Bulgarian frontier and the Turkish general staff at that time was very seriously concerned, and felt they might really have to face a movement over the border.

(Discussion was off the record.)

COST OF STANDING ARMY HIGH

Ambassador WILSON. The necessity of maintaining what is for Turkey a very large standing army is proving a very serious burden on the economy of the country. The cost of living in Turkey today is about 400 percent of what it was in 1938 or 1939. I noticed in one of the documents that is in this binder that the figures give it about 300 or a little above. Those are taken from official indices in Turkey. They are not very complete, and I think they are slightly unreal, because there is rent control in Turkey and they figure house rents at 100, the same as they were in 1938. As a matter of fact, they are four or five times as high now. New people coming out to live cannot get an apartment without paying a certain amount on the side, and they have to pay a great deal more than the official list says. That is the only way you can get a lease there.

That simply means the actual cost of living runs up to about 400 percent as well. That affects the Turks as well. Their salaries and wages have gone up very little. The Government recently increased the wages of Government employees, but they can not do it very much if they do not want to get their budget out of balance. So increasingly you have this strain on the Turkish economy.

I, of course, am not in the secrets of the Kremlin. I do not know what Russian long term policy against Turkey is, but for whatever it is worth, here is the way I dope the thing out.

U.S. SUPPORT WOULD OFFSET SOVIET STRATEGY

In June 1945, the Soviets put on this pressure on Turkey. They tried to break them down. They tried to get them to give way so that they could change their government, get a government in Turkey that would be friendly to the Soviets, set up a stooge type of government there. They did not get anywhere with it. They tried that periodically since, again and again. It has failed. So that the Russians turned their attention to Greece. There they have an easier operation. They have friends in the country, as Ambassador

MacVeagh has just been explaining. They have people along the borders; they have elements to work with which they lack in Turkey.

I should think that their plan for Turkey would be to keep up this pressure, oblige the Turks to maintain a very large standing army, neglect the economic development of their country, hoping that in the long run the pressure would be so great and the people would become so discouraged that they would finally say, "Hell, what's the use? Let's come to the best terms we can with these fellows."

For that reason it seems to me the Turks, recognizing that the maintenance of that situation out there is of direct interest to us, have need, morally and materially, of getting some definite indication of support by the United States for their position, and getting aid that is going to enable them to carry this situation on.

I might say again, expressing my personal view in this, that I believe that if we can keep the Turkish situation healthy, maintain them in their independence, in their position as they are today, if we can convince the Russians that we mean business in that area and are not going to permit the expansion of the Soviets beyond where they have gone now, that is the surest way of preventing a world conflict. . . .

IMMEDIACY OF U.S. AID

Senator LODGE. Mr. Chairman, I would like to get clear in my mind what it is that gives this Turkish situation its emergency, immediate character. Why do we have it now rather than last year. Is there something that has happened in the last 3 months. In the case of Greece we realize that the British are pulling out and that gives it its timeliness. What is it that gives Turkey its timeliness now?

Ambassador WILSON. I should say, Senator, that it was the notification by the British that they will no longer be able to take care of furnishing military equipment to Turkey. In the past, Britain has been doing that. Britain has been extending very considerable armament loans to Turkey. Britain has now informed us that she will not be able to do that any longer. The Turks have a program where they hope to be able to improve and strengthen their army, and where else can they turn for it?

Senator LODGE. Although their economic situation is not so desperate as it is in Greece or in lots of other countries, this is a form of economic aid, is it not? It will relieve them of some military expenditures that they would have to assume otherwise if they were to maintain their army at its present size.

Ambassador WILSON. That is correct, Senator. The dangerous element in the situation would be that they would then go into their gold reserves and get their financial situation into a bad position, because they would feel it essential to use those funds to do it themselves.

Senator LODGE. The British have announced that they were not going to help Greece and they were not going to help Turkey, but apparently they are going to go on with certain activities in other parts of the world. Do you have any theories as to why the British have decided to give up in one place and not to give up in another place?

Ambassador WILSON. I might say that so far as Turkey is concerned, they have a mission of military, air, and naval advisers there.

(Discussion was had off the record.)

Ambassador WILSON. They are prepared, I believe, to continue that mission there.

Senator LODGE. For what purpose?

Ambassador WILSON. Instruction in material that has been furnished by them. They have men there—naval officers, air, artillery, and radar experts.

Senator LODGE. But there has been no military development on the part of the Soviet Union in the last 3 or 4 months that has been particularly startling or different?

Ambassador WILSON. Of course, troops remain along the border. There has been nothing as startling as the situation last October.

Senator CONNALLY. Senator Lodge made the distinction between Turkey and Greece, but on account of the fact that they both occupy a strategical position in that area, according to my view we have to deal with them both. If we simply dealt with Greece it would probably stimulate their pressure on Turkey—it would stimulate the Russian pressure on Turkey—and since the President has come out openly before the world as to the both of them, we could not very well split them up and simply aid Greece and leave Turkey out on a limb. What do you have to say about that?

Ambassador WILSON. Senator, of those three countries that occupy pretty vital postions there—Greece, Turkey, and Iran—Turkey is right in the center. Turkey is in the soundest and healthiest position of any of the three in its resistance to the spread of Soviet Communism. If Turkey should be allowed to go by default and get a Communist regime established within it, and be broken down, I do not see how in God's world you could hold the two countries on the flanks.

Also, here is another aspect of it that strikes me. This program for aid to Greece and Turkey has attracted, of course, tremendous interest throughout the world. There have been reactions, noticeable reactions, in many countries. It has been enthusiastically welcomed in Turkey. If now this should be split up, if Turkey should be put out and aid given to Greece alone, the Turks brought to feel that we believed that they were either a bad risk or that they did not merit support or that we did not care whether they fell under Soviet domination or not, I feel it would have a disastrous effect in that country. . . .

STATEMENT OF U.S. SELF-INTEREST

[The CHAIRMAN] Now we are down to the question, what reason can you give the American people publicly to identify our self-interest in this program?

Ambassador WILSON. The first thing that would come into my mind, Senator, would be that we are pledged to the support of the principles of the United Nations, to support of the independence of small countries and of their right then to choose their own way of life. And here we have a case where a small country has been subjected to considerable pressure, and we feel that in accordance with our obligations it is incumbent upon us to give encouragement and support to these countries to maintain their independence against any efforts from outside to destroy or weaken or break down that independent position. . . .

CONSEQUENCES OF U.S. REFUSAL TO ASSIST

Senator BARKLEY. Let me ask you this in connection with that very thing. I would like to have your personal view as to the reaction that would result. Suppose that the United Nations were equipped now with the authority and with the funds to do what we are proposing and that it was brought to the Security Council, and that after debate, deliberation and controversy the Soviet delegation would veto it. That would probably be several months hence. In the meantime the situation might have grown worse, both in Greece and Turkey.

Then, because of the veto or our inability to get the United Nations to take action, or its unwillingness or its impotence to take action we were then forced to do what we are now. What would be the reaction in the Mediterranean region and in the world to our position as it would then exist, having gone in a roundabout way to avoid this responsibility by putting it upon the shoulders of the United Nations, which could not accept it for any reason, whether the veto or otherwise? Where would we be then in the estimation not only of the Mediterranean region but of the world at large, in your mind? Would it strengthen or weaken our position?

Ambassador WILSON. It seems to me that we would be doing a dis-service to the United Nations. We would be going in and then doing something which the United Nations was not in agreement should be done. We would be doing it unilaterally.

Senator BARKLEY. And we would be doing it against the verdict of the United Nations, which had passed upon it, no matter whether their verdict came about through impotence or failure to act or inability to act by unanimous vote. That phase of it is important, as affecting the moral standards and the standing that we will necessarily occupy in the opinion of the world in this whole enterprise.

It is not anything we want to do; it is not anything we will relish. It is not anything we go out to seek. But it is a situation that has been brought to our attention by these governments.

46   George F. Kennan, the Policy Planning Staff, and the origins of the Marshall Plan: May 16, 1947. *'The Policy Planning Staff does not see communistic activities as the root of the difficulties of western Europe. It believes that present crisis results in large part from the disruptive effect of the war on the economic, political, and social structure of Europe and from a profound exhaustion of physical plant and of spiritual vigor.'*

The Department of State's Policy Planning Staff was established in early May 1947 to deal with the development of long-range foreign policies of the government. As a reward for his services and because of the reputation for profundity he had earned for his assessment of the springs of Soviet foreign policy, George F. Kennan was asked to head the Policy Planning Staff. Anxious that the United States should contribute in a positive way to the rebuilding of Europe, which in its weakened condition in 1947 made it 'vulnerable to exploitation by any and all totalitarian movements', Kennan encouraged his superiors to persuade Europe, in his words, 'to undertake to draw up unilaterally and to promulgate formally on its own initiative a program designed to place western Europe on its own feet economically. This is the business of the Europeans.' In one of the ironies of history, Kennan, whose name became almost solely identified with containment, has failed to receive due credit for his part in laying the ground work for the Marshall Plan.

Source: Department of State, *Foreign Relations of the United States, Diplomatic Papers: 1947* (Wash. 1972), III, 224-28.

1.   The Policy Planning Staff has selected the question of American aid to western Europe as the first subject of its attention. This does not mean that the Staff is unmindful of the importance or urgency of problems in other areas or of its mission to coordinate long-term policy on a global basis. It means simply that western Europe appears to be the area for which long-term planning might most advantageously begin.

2.   The Policy Planning Staff does not see communist activities as the root of the difficulties of western Europe. It believes that the present crisis results in large part from the disruptive effect of the war on the economic, political, and social structure of Europe and from a profound exhaustion of physical plant and of spiritual vigor. This situation has been aggravated and rendered far more difficult of remedy by the division of the continent into east and west. The Planning Staff recognizes that the communists are exploiting the European crisis and that further communist successes would create serious danger to American security. It considers, however, that American effort in aid to Europe should be directed not to the combatting of communism as such but to the restoration of the economic health and vigor of European society. It should aim, in other words, to combat not communism, but the economic maladjustment which makes European society vulnerable to exploitation by any and all totalitarian movements and which Russian communism is now exploiting. The Planning Staff believes that American plans should be drawn to this purpose and that this should be frankly stated to the American public.

3.   The Policy Planning Staff sees in this general question of American aid to western Europe two problems: a long-term one and a short-term one. The long-term problem is that of how the economic health of the area is to be restored and of the degree and form of American aid for such restoration. The short-term problem is to determine what effective and dramatic action should be taken in the immediate future to halt the economic disintegration of western Europe and to create confidence that the overall problem can be solved and that the United States can and will play its proper part in the solution.

4.   The Policy Planning Staff feels that there is some misconception in the mind of the American people as to the objectives of the Truman Doctrine and of our aid to foreign countries and recommends that immediate action be taken to correct this misunderstanding.

II. THE SHORT-TERM PROBLEM

5.   With respect to the short-term problem, the Planning Staff feels that we should select some particular bottleneck or bottlenecks in the economic pattern of western Europe and institute immediate action which would bring to bear the full weight of this Government on the breaking of those bottlenecks. The purpose of this action would be on the one hand psychological—to put us on the offensive instead of the defensive, to convince the European peoples that we mean business, to serve as a catalyst for their hope and confidence, and to dramatize for our people the nature of Europe's problems and the importance of American assistance. On the other hand, this action would be designed to make a real contribution to the solution of Europe's economic difficulties.

The Planning Staff attaches great importance to this project and considers it almost essential to the success of the general scheme. It fears that unless something of this sort is done at once the result may be a further deterioration of morale in Europe which will seriously jeopardize the long-term program. For this reason it recommends that most careful and intensive consideration be given at once to this project.

The production of coal in the Rhine Valley and its movement to the places of consumption in Europe has suggested itself as the most suitable object of such an action. The Planning Staff has this question under consideration and expects to come up with more detailed suggestions in the near future.

It may be necessary as a matter of short time urgency to take certain other measures with respect to Italy supplementary to such aid as may be given to that country out of the $350,000,000 appropriation. Since this question is already under advisement in operational sections of the Department the Planning Staff is not including it in this survey.

III. THE LONG-TERM PROBLEM

6.   The Policy Planning Staff recognizes that the long-term problem is one of enormous complexity and difficulty. It should be the subject of a careful study which must of necessity extend over a period of at least several weeks. The Staff proposes to occupy itself with that study at once. In the belief, however, that this Government cannot afford to delay the adoption of some overall approach to the solution of the problem, the following tentative views are set forth:

a.   It is necessary to distinguish clearly between a program for the economic revitalization of Europe on the one hand, and a program of American support of such revitalization on the other. It would be neither fitting nor efficacious for this Government to undertake to draw up unilaterally and to promulgate formally on its own initiative a program designed to place western Europe on its feet economically. This is the business of the Europeans. The formal initiative must come from Europe; the program must be evolved in Europe; and the Europeans must bear the basic responsibility for it. The role of this country should consist of friendly aid in the drafting of a European program and of the later support of such a program, by financial and other means, at European request.

b.   The program which this country is asked to support must be a joint one, agreed to by several European nations. While it may be linked to individual national programs, such as the Monnet plan in France, it must, for psychological and political as well as economic reasons, be an internationally agreed program. The request for our support must come as a joint request from a group of friendly nations, not as a series of isolated and individual appeals.

c.   This European program must envisage bringing western Europe to a point where it will be able to maintain a tolerable standard of living on a financially self-supporting basis. It must give promise of doing the whole job. The program must contain reasonable assurance that if we support it, this will be the last such program we shall be asked to support in the foreseeable future.

d.   The overall European program must embrace, or be linked to, some sort of plan for dealing with the economic plight of Britain. The plan must be formally a British one, worked out on British initiative and British responsibility, and the role of the United States, again, must be to give friendly support.

e. This does not mean that the United States need stand aside or remain aloof from the elaboration of the overall European program. As a member of the United Nations and particularly of the Economic Commission for Europe, and as a power occupying certain European territories, it is entitled and obliged to participate in working out the program. Our position as an occupying power also makes it incumbent upon us to cooperate whole-heartedly in the execution of any program that may be evolved. For this reason, and because we must know as soon as possible to what extent such a program is technically feasible, we must undertake an independent and realistic study of the entire problem of European rehabilitation. But we must insist, for the sake of clarity, for the sake of soundness of concept, and for the sake of the self-respect of European peoples, that the initiative be taken in Europe and that the main burden be borne by the governments of that area. With the best of will, the American people cannot really help those who are not willing to help themselves. And if the requested initiative and readiness to bear public responsibility are not forthcoming from the European governments, then that will mean that *rigor mortis* has already set in on the body politic of Europe as we have known it and that it may be already too late for us to change decisively the course of events.

f. While this program must necessarily center in the European area, it will admittedly have widespread ramifications in other areas. It will also have important connotations for the UN, and we should bear constantly in mind the need for maximum utilization of UN machinery.

g. American support for such a program need not be confined to financial assistance. It may involve considerable practical American cooperation in the solution of specific problems.

h. With respect to any program which this Government may eventually be asked to support, it will be necessary for it to insist on safeguards to assure

first, that everything possible be done to whittle down the cost of such support in dollars;

secondly, that the European Governments use the full force of their authority to see that our aid is employed in a purposeful and effective way; and

thirdly, that maximum reimbursement be made to this country in any forms found to be economically feasible and in United States interest.

i. The problem of where and in what form the initiative for the formulation of a European program should be taken is admittedly a tremendously difficult and delicate one. It cannot be definitely predetermined by us. Presumably an effort would first be made to advance the project in the Economic Commission for Europe, and probably as a proposal for general European (not just western European) cooperation; but then it would be essential that this be done in such a form that the Russian satellite countries would either exclude themselves by unwillingness to accept the proposed conditions or agree to abandon the exclusive orientation of their economies. If the Russians prove able to block any such scheme in the Economic Commission for Europe, it may be necessary for the key countries of western Europe to find means of conferring together without the presence of the Russians and Russian satellites. In general, however, the question of where and how this initiative should be taken is primarily one for the European nations, and we should be careful not to seek unduly to influence their decision.

47   Memorandum by the Under Secretary of State for Economic Affairs
      on the impending European crisis: May 27, 1947. *'Europe is steadily
      deteriorating.'*

The following memorandum by the Under Secretary of State, William L. Clayton, who had just returned from Western Europe and had observed the deteriorating economic conditions at first hand, accurately captures the sense of urgency of the time. Clayton, often the target of New Left criticism, contended that in the absence of maintaining the even low European standard of living 'there will be revolution'. In this regard Clayton's views coincided with Kennan's; but unlike Kennan, who repeatedly cautioned against giving the impression of America initiating Europe's rehabilitation, Clayton insisted that *'The United States must run this show.'* (Clayton's italics.)

Source: ibid, 230-32

1. It is now obvious that we grossly underestimated the destruction to the European economy by the war. We understood the physical destruction, but we failed to take fully into account the effects of economic dislocation on production—nationalization of industries, drastic land reform, severance of long-standing commercial ties, disappearance of private commercial firms through death or loss of capital, etc., etc.

2. Europe is steadily deteriorating. The political position reflects the economic. One political crisis after another merely denotes the existence of grave economic distress. Millions of people in the cities are slowly starving. More consumer's goods and restored confidence in the local currency are absolutely essential if the peasant is again to supply food in normal quantities to the cities. (French grain acreage running 20-25% under prewar, collection of production very unsatisfactory—much of the grain is fed to cattle. The modern system of division of labor has almost broken down in Europe.)

3. Europe's current annual balance of payments deficit:

UK	$2¼ billions
France	1¾ "
Italy	½ "
US-UK Zone Germany	½ "
	$5 billions

not to mention the smaller countries.

The above represents an absolute minimum standard of living. If it should be lowered, there will be revolution.

Only until the end of this year can England and France meet the above deficits out of their fast dwindling reserves of gold and dollars. Italy can't go that long.

4.   Some of the principal items in these deficits:

From the U.S.:	Coal, 30 million tons	\$ 600 million
,, ,, ,,	Bread grains, 12 million tons	1,400 ,,
,, ,, ,,	Shipping services at very high rates on imports and exports..................... xxxxx ,,

Before the war, Europe was self-sufficient in coal and imported very little bread grains from the United States.

Europe must again become self-sufficient in coal (the U.S. must take over management of Ruhr coal production) and her agricultural production must be restored to normal levels. (Note: No inefficient or forced production through exorbitant tariffs, subsidies, étc., is here contemplated).

Europe must again be equipped to perform her own shipping services. The United States should sell surplus ships to France, Italy and other maritime nations to restore their merchant marine to at least prewar levels. (To do it, we will have to lick the shipping lobby, fattening as it is off the U.S. Treasury).

5.   Without further prompt and substantial aid from the United States, economic, social and political disintegration will overwhelm Europe.

Aside from the awful implications which this would have for the future peace and security of the world, the immediate effects on our domestic economy would be disastrous: markets for our surplus production gone, unemployment, depression, a heavily unbalanced budget on the background of a mountainous war debt.

These things must not happen?

6.   Mr. Baruch[1] asks for the appointment of a Commission to study and report on our national assets and liabilities in order to determine our ability to assist Europe.

This is wholly unnecessary.

The facts are well known

Our resources and our productive capacity are ample to provide all the help necessary.

The problem is to organize our fiscal policy and our own consumption so that sufficient surpluses of the necessary goods are made available out of our enormous production, and so that these surpluses are paid for out of taxation and not by addition to debt.

This problem can be met only if the American people are taken into the complete confidence of the Administration and told all the facts and only if a sound and workable plan is presented.

7.   It will be necessary for the President and the Secretary of State to make a strong spiritual appeal to the American people to sacrifice a little themselves, to draw in their own belts just a little in order to save Europe from starvation and chaos (*not* from the Russians) and, at the same time, to preserve for ourselves and our children the glorious heritage of a free America.

8.   Europe must have from us, as a grant, 6 or 7 billion dollars worth of goods a year for three years. With this help, the operations of the International Bank and Fund

should enable European reconstruction to get under way at a rapid pace. Our grant could take the form principally of coal, food, cotton, tobacco, shipping services and similar things—all now produced in the United States in surplus, except cotton. The probabilities are that cotton will be surplus in another one or two years. Food shipments should be stepped up despite the enormous total (15 million tons) of bread grains exported from the United States during the present crop year. We are wasting and over-consuming food in the United States to such an extent that a reasonable measure of conservation would make at least another million tons available for export with no harm whatsoever to the health and efficiency of the American people.

9.   This three-year grant to Europe should be based on a European plan which the principal European nations, headed by the UK, France and Italy, should work out. Such a plan should be based on a European economic federation on the order of the Belgium-Netherlands-Luxembourg Customs Union. Europe cannot recover from this war and again become independent if her economy continues to be divided into many small watertight compartments as it is today.

10.   Obviously, the above is only the broad outline of a problem which will require much study and preparation before any move can be made.

Canada, Argentina, Brazil, Australia, New Zealand, Union of South Africa could all help with their surplus food and raw materials, but we must avoid getting into another UNNRA. *The United States must run this show.*

[1] Bernard M. Baruch had served as Chairman of the War Industries Board in 1918, as an adviser to the Director of War Mobilization, 1943-1945, and as U.S. Representative on the U.N. Atomic Energy Commission in 1946.

48   The Marshal Plan: June 5, 1947. *'Our policy is directed not against any country or doctrine but against hunger, poverty, desperation, and chaos.'*

On the occasion of commencement exercises held at Harvard University on June 5, 1947, the eminent soldier and Secretary of State George C. Marshall observed that in the name of enlightened self-interest, 'It is logical that the United States should do whatever it is able to do to assist in the return of normal economic health in the world, without which there can be no political stability and no assured peace.' Reflecting the recommendations of the Policy Planning Staff, even to the point of adopting Kennan's phraseology, Marshall called for the reconstruction of Europe by Europeans. And so was born the Marshall Plan—or, more accurately the European Recovery Act, which was signed into law by President Truman on April 3, 1948, and which pumped thirteen billion dollars into the economy of Western Europe over the next four years. Thus, the American diplomatic revolution was completed.

Source: Department of State, *Bulletin*, XVI (June 15, 1947), 1159-60.

I need not tell you gentlemen that the world situation is very serious. That must be apparent to all intelligent people. I think one difficulty is that the problem is one of such enormous complexity that the very mass of facts presented to the public by press and radio make it exceedingly difficult for the man in the street to reach a clear appraisement of the situation. Furthermore, the people of this country are distant from the troubled areas of the earth and it is hard for them to comprehend the plight and consequent reactions of the long-suffering peoples, and the effect of those reactions on their governments in connection with our efforts to promote peace in the world.

In considering the requirements for the rehabilitation of Europe, the physical loss of life, the visible destruction of cities, factories, mines, and railroads was correctly estimated, but it has become obvious during recent months that this visible destruction was probably less serious than the dislocation of the entire fabric of European economy. For the past 10 years conditions have been highly abnormal. The feverish preparation for war and the more feverish maintenance of the war effort engulfed all aspects of national economies. Machinery has fallen into disrepair or is entirely obsolete. Under the arbitrary and destructive Nazi rule, virtually every possible enterprise was geared into the German war machine. Long-standing commercial ties, private institutions, banks, insurance companies, and shipping companies disappeared, through loss of capital, absorption through nationalization, or by simple destruction. In many countries, confidence in the local currency has been severely shaken. The breakdown of the business structure of Europe during the war was complete. Recovery has been seriously retarded by the fact that two years after the close of hostilities a peace settlement with Germany and Austria has not been agreed upon. But even given a more prompt solution of these difficult problems, the rehabilitiation of the economic structure of Europe quite evidently will require a much longer time and greater effort than had been foreseen.

There is a phase of this matter which is both interesting and serious. The farmer has always produced the foodstuffs to exchange with the city dweller for the other necessities of life. This division of labor is the basis of modern civilization. At the present time it is threatened with breakdown. The town and city industries are not producing adequate goods to exchange with the food-producing farmer. Raw materials and fuel are in short supply. Machinery is lacking or worn out. The farmer or the peasant cannot find the goods for sale which he desires to purchase. So the sale of his farm produce for money which he cannot use seems to him an unprofitable transaction. He, therefore, has withdrawn many fields from crop cultivation and is using them for grazing. He feeds more grain to stock and finds for himself and his family an ample supply of food, however short he may be on clothing and the other ordinary gadgets of civilization. Meanwhile people in the cities are short of food and fuel. So the governments are forced to use their foreign money and credits to procure these necessities abroad. This process exhausts funds which are urgently needed for reconstruction. Thus a very serious situation is rapidly developing which bodes no good for the world. The modern system of the division of labor upon which the exchange of products is based is in danger of breaking down.

The truth of the matter is that Europe's requirements for the next three or four years of foreign food and other essential products—principally from America—are so much greater than her present ability to pay that she must have substantial additional help or face economic, social, and political deterioration of a very grave character.

The remedy lies in breaking the vicious circle and restoring the confidence of the

European people in the economic future of their own countries and of Europe as a whole. The manufacturer and the farmer throughout wide areas must be able and willing to exchange their products for currencies the continuing value of which is not open to question.

Aside from the demoralizing effect on the world at large and the possibilities of disturbances arising as a result of the desperation of the people concerned, the consequences to the economy of the United States should be apparent to all. It is logical that the United States should do whatever it is able to do to assist in the return of normal economic health in the world, without which there can be no political stability and no assured peace. Our policy is directed not against any country or doctrine but against hunger, poverty, desperation, and chaos. Its purpose should be the revival of a working economy in the world so as to permit the emergence of political and social conditions in which free institutions can exist. Such assistance, I am convinced, must not be on a piecemeal basis as various crises develop. Any assistance that this Government may render in the future should provide a cure rather than a mere palliative. Any government that is willing to assist in the task of recovery will find full cooperation, I am sure, on the part of the United States Government. Any government which maneuvers to block the recovery of other countries cannot expect help from us. Furthermore, governments, political parties, or groups which seek to perpetuate human misery in order to profit therefrom politically or otherwise will encounter the opposition of the United States.

It is already evident that, before the United States Government can proceed much further in its efforts to alleviate the situation and help start the European world on its way to recovery, there must be some agreement among the countries of Europe as to the requirements of the situation and the part those countries themselves will take in order to give proper effect to whatever action might be undertaken by this Government. It would be neither fitting nor efficacious for this Government to undertake to draw up unilaterally a program designed to place Europe on its feet economically. This is the business of the Europeans. The initiative, I think, must come from Europe. The role of this country should consist of friendly aid in the drafting of a European program and of later support of such a program so far as it may be practical for us to do so. The program should be a joint one, agreed to by a number, if not all, European nations.

An essential part of any successful action on the part of the United States is an understanding on the part of the people of America of the character of the problem and the remedies to be applied. Political passion and prejudice should have no part. With foresight, and a willingness on the part of our people to face up to the vast responsibility which history has clearly placed upon our country, the difficulties I have outlined can and will be overcome.

Epilogue

As part of a well-orchestrated propaganda effort both to denigrate the Marshall Plan and to justify Soviet Russia's rejection of it, Politburo member Zhdanov warned communist delegates attending the founding conference of the Cominform in September 1947 that the world had been divided into two hostile camps with rival headquarters in Washington and Moscow. The twin objectives of the West, continued Zhdanov, were nothing less than preventive war against the USSR and the destruction of the newly constructed People's Democracies in Eastern Europe as well as of national revolutions in such places as Viet-Nam.[1] The seedtime of the Cold War was over, while the reality of a 'hot war' was increasingly on the horizon. In this sense, then, and in a manner that should not be underestimated, the outspoken and unrelieved hostility of Soviet Russia towards the West coincided with the conclusion of the first phase of what W.W. Rostow once referred to as 'the American diplomatic revolution'.[2] From this time forward, events such as the communist purges in Czechoslovakia, the Berlin Blockade, the triumph of Mao in China and the North Korean invasion of South Korea all confirmed basic American policy formulated in the period from 1945 to 1947. In the words of Ernest R. May: 'Truman and his associates did not just become antipathetic toward the Soviet Union; they adopted the position that communist Russia represented a threat which the United States had to resist, if necessary by war.'[3] On the other side, to complete the 'mirror image' of the Cold War emerging in Moscow, Soviet policy makers saw in the American decision to toughen out over Berlin, the creation of North Atlantic Treaty Organisation, and President Truman's swiftness in committing troops to Korea as confirmation of what they came to regard as a threat to their own East European and Far Eastern empire. The Cold War was thus joined at this juncture.

Who was to blame? And which side contributed most to the *way* in which the Cold

War developed? Such questions and attempts to answer them have informed much of the Cold War literature during the past thirty years. Realists, who deplore what George Kennan called the 'moralistic-legalistic' approach of the United States to international affairs, argued that had the United States conceded the Soviets their own sphere of influence and recognized its own limitations in influencing events outside its own sphere of interest, the worst episodes of the Cold War could have been avoided. More idealistic commentators in turn condemned the Realists for presumably betraying the nation's traditional commitment to the equality of all states, as well as adherence to the right of national self-determination. New Left revisionists found both schools of thought on the subject wanting, and suggested alternatively that not enough attention had been paid to the role of economics—an incontrovertible fact. The difficulty here, of course, is that the dynamics of American diplomacy are not easily susceptible to Marxist analysis; for in a nation devoid, on balance, of class conflict and proletariats in search of revolution, the New Left data often produced strange and strained historical scenarios with little general appeal. To say this, however, is not to say that policy formulation did not result from clashing interests. It frequently did, but the interests clashing were usually interdepartmental and bureaucratic in character, not the forces of light and darkness. Focussing on responsibility and moral conduct, writers of the Cold War have turned the history of postwar American-Soviet relations into an endless and meaningless theological debate. Fortunately, more recent, serious scholars have desisted in attempting to assign responsibility to this or that side. Instead, they have turned to the more important question of *why* the Cold War took the shape it did, a question much more suitable to the training and true interests of historians and students of history.

[1]For a discussion of the formulation of America's early Cold War policy in Viet-Nam, see Joseph M. Siracusa, 'The United States, Viet-Nam, and the Cold War: A Reappraisal', *Journal of Southeast Asian Studies*, V (March/ 1974), 82-101.

[2]W.W. Rostow, *The American Diplomatic Revolution* (Oxford/ 1946), 6.

[3]Ernest R. May, *'Lessons' of the Past: The Use and Misuse of History in American Foreign Policy* (N.Y./ 1973), 31.

Suggestions for Additional Reading

The best, most scholarly, and most recent introduction to American diplomacy in the years from 1941 to 1947 is John Lewis Gaddis's *The United States and the Origins of the Cold War, 1941-1947* (N.Y. 1972).Traditionalist works that emphasize the protracted nature of Soviet aggressiveness include: John W. Spanier, *American Foreign Policy since World War II* (N.Y. 1960); Herbert Druks, *Harry S. Truman and the Russians 1945-1953* (N.Y. 1966); Dexter Perkins, *The Diplomacy of a New Age: Major Issues in U.S. Policy Since 1945*, (Bloomington, Indiana, 1967); David Rees, *The Age of Containment: The Cold War, 1945-1965* (London 1967); and Charles Burton Marshall, *The Cold War: A Concise History* (N.Y. 1965). For the so-called 'realist' interpretation of the Cold War, which underscores the role of power politics and tends to find fault with the execution of US foreign policy, one should begin with W. H. McNeil, *America, Britain and Russia: Their Co-operation and Conflict, 1941-1946* (London 1953); the incomparable studies by Herbert Feis, *Churchill, Roosevelt, Stalin: The War They Waged and the Peace They Sought* (Princeton N.J., 1957); *Between War and Peace: The Potsdam Conference* (Princeton, N.J., 1960); and *From Trust to Terror: The Onset of the Cold War, 1945-1950* (N.Y. 1970); the dated but still useful Norman A. Graebner, *Cold War Diplomacy, 1945-1960* (Princeton, N.J. 1962); Martin F. Hertz, *Beginnings of the Cold War* (Bloomington, Indiana, 1966); and Louis B. Halle, *The Cold War as History* (N.Y. 1967).

Other more critical works include Walter Lippmann, *The Cold War: A Study in U.S. Foreign Policy* (N.Y. 1947); K. Zilliacus, *I Choose Peace* (N.Y. 1949); Kenneth Ingram, *History and the Cold War* (London 1955); J.P. Morray, *From Yalta to Disarmament: Cold War Debate* (N.Y. 1961); Hans J. Morgenthau, *In Defense of National Interest* (N.Y. 1961); John Lukacs, *A New History of the Cold War* (3rd ed. expanded of *A History of the Cold War*, Garden City, N.Y., 1966); Marshall D. Shulman, *Beyond the*

Cold War (New Haven, Conn., 1966); Charles O. Lerche, Jr., *The Cold War and After* (Englewood, N.J., 1965); Wilfrid Knapp, *A History of War and Peace, 1939-1965* (London 1967); and Paul Seabury, *Rise and Decline of the Cold War* (N.Y.1967)

For the antecedents of the New Left revisionism of the 1960s and 1970s, see D.F. Fleming, *The Cold War and Its Origins, 1917-1960* (2 vols., Garden City, N.Y., 1961); Frederick L. Schuman, *The Cold War: Retrospect and Prospect* (Baton Rouge, La., 1962); and the seminal works of William A. Williams, *American-Russian Relations, 1781-1947* (N.Y. 1952); and *The Tragedy of American Diplomacy* (rev. and enlarged, N.Y. 1962). The classic New Left study of the Cold War with its emphasis on the foreign policy necessities of an 'Open-Door empire' is Walter LaFeber's *America, Russia, and the Cold War* (N.Y. 1967). For other revisionist works of merit consult Lloyd C. Gardner's *Economic Aspects of New Deal Diplomacy* (Madison, Wis., 1965); *Architects of Illusion: Men and Ideas in American Foreign Policy, 1941-1949* (Chicago 1970); and Diane Shaver Clemens's *Yalta* (N.Y. 1970). For New Left diplomatic history at its most tendentious, one need look no further than Gabriel Kolko, *The Politics of War: The World and United States Foreign Policy, 1945-1954* (N.Y. 1972); Joyce and Gabriel Kolko, *The Limits of Power: The World and United States Foreign Policy, 1945-1954* (N.Y. 1972); and David Horowitz, *The Free World Colossus: A Critique of American Foreign Policy in the Cold War* (N.Y. 1965).

An examination of the impact and significance of New Left scholarship in terms of its contribution to political science, American diplomatic historiography, and historical methodology is found, respectively, in Robert W. Tucker, *The Radical Left and American Foreign Policy* (Baltimore 1971); Joseph M. Siracusa, *New Left Diplomatic Histories and Historians: The American Revisionists* (Port Washington, N.Y., 1973); and Robert James Maddox, *The New Left and the Origins of the Cold War* (Princeton, N.J., 1972). Other important and valuable comments on this subject include the following articles: Irwin Unger, 'The "New Left" and American History: Some Recent Trends in United States Historiography', *American Historical Review*, LXXII (July 1967), 1237-63; Arthur Schlesinger, Jr., 'Origins of the Cold War', *Foreign Affairs*, XLVI (October 1967), 22-52; Norman A. Graebner, 'Cold War Origins and the Continuing Debate', *Journal of Conflict Resolution*, XIII (March 1969), 123-32; Charles S. Maier, 'Revisionism and the Interpretation of Cold War Origins', *Perspectives in American History*, VI (1970), 313-47; Daniel M. Smith, 'The New Left and the Cold War', review of *Empire and Revolution: A Radical Interpretation of Contemporary World History*, by David Horowitz, in *the Denver Quarterly*, IV (Winter 1970), 78-88; J.L. Richardson, 'Cold War Revisionism: A Critique', *World Politics*, XXIV (1972), 579-612; and Ole R. Holsti, 'The Study of International Politics Makes Strange Bedfellows: Theories of the Radical Right and the Radical Left', *American Political Science Review*, LXVIII (March 1974), 217-42.

Background in American perceptions of Soviet Russia is contained in Christopher Lasch, *The American Liberals and the Russian Revolution* (N.Y. 1972); Peter G. Filene, *Americans and the Soviet Experiment, 1917-1933* (Cambridge, Mass., 1967); Robert P. Browder, *The Origins of Soviet-American Diplomacy* (Princeton, N.J., 1953); and , more recently, William Welch, *American Images of Soviet Foreign Policy: An Inquiry into Recent Appraisals from the Academic Community* (New Haven, Conn., 1970). For a discussion of the American 'discovery' of totalitarianism in the 1930s with suggestive implications for the 1940s refer to Robert Allen Skotheim's *Totalitarianism and American Social Thought* (N.Y. 1971).

Of the other other works dealing with the intellectual history of the period under consideration the most relevant are Cushing Strout, *The American Image of the Old World* (N.Y. 1963), especially chapters 11 and 12; Charles Alexander, *Nationalism in American Thought, 1930-1945* (N.Y. 1969); Reinhold Niebuhr, *The Children of Light and the Children of Darkness* (N.Y. 1944); *The Irony of American History* (N.Y. 1952); and Arthur Schlesinger, Jr., *The Vital Center* (Boston 1949). A model of its kind and one of the essential works for understanding the transformation of American foreign policy attitudes toward collective security is Robert A. Divine's *Second Chance: The Triumph of Internationalism in America during World War II* (N.Y. 1967).

With regard to the springs of Soviet foreign policy in general and Soviet perceptions of the United States in particular, one should begin with the following: Frederick C. Barghoorn, *The Soviet Image of the United States: A Study in Distortion* (N.Y. 1950); Louis Fischer, *The Road to Yalta: Soviet Foreign Relations, 1941-1945* (N.Y. 1972); Alexander Dallin, ed., *Soviet Conduct in World Affairs* (N.Y. 1960); George F. Kennan, *Russia and the West under Lenin and Stalin* (London 1961); Marshall D. Schulman, *Stalin's Foreign Policy Reappraised* (Cambridge, Mass., 1963); and Adam B. Ulam's two superb studies, *Expansion and Coexistence: The History of Soviet Foreign Policy, 1917-67* (N.Y. 1968); and *The Rivals: America and Russia since World War II* (N.Y. 1972). Also see Isaac Deutscher, *Ironies of History: Essays on Contemporary Communism* (London 1966); and Bernard P. Kiernan, 'Ideology and Foreign Policy: A Reconsideration', *Virginia Quarterly Review*, L (Winter 1974), 22-38.

For an analysis of Stalin's leadership, consult the older but still useful Leon Trotsky, *Stalin: An Appraisal of the Man and His Influence* (N.Y. 1946); and Isaac Deutscher's classic *Stalin: A Political Biography* (N.Y. 1967). Other efforts to come to grips with Stalin include among others Adam B. Ulam, *Stalin: The Man and his Era* (N.Y. 1973) Robert C. Tucker, *Stalin and the Uses of Psychology* (Santa Monica, California, 1955); *The Soviet Political Mind: Studies in Stalinism and Post-Stalin Change* (N.Y. 1963); and *Stalin as Revolutionary, 1879-1929* (N.Y. 1973).

An earlier and apparently influential critique of 'atomic diplomacy' is P.M.S. Blackett's *Military and Political Consequences of Atomic Energy* (London 1948). The New Left argument is found in Gar Alperovitz, *Atomic Diplomacy: Hiroshima and Potsdam, The Use of the Atomic Bomb and the American Confrontation with Soviet Power* (N.Y. 1965); and more briefly in *Cold War Essays* (Garden City, N.Y., 1970). In conjunction with Alperovitz's work also see Robert J. Maddox's persuasive critique, 'Atomic Diplomacy: A Study in Creative Writing', *Journal of American History*, LIX (March 1973), 925-34, a chapter in the above-mentioned Maddox book. The official position that the atomic bomb was used primarily to shock the Japanese into surrendering is found in Herbert Feis, *The Atomic Bomb and the End of World War II* (rev. ed., Princeton, N.J., 1966). On this point refer also to Lisle A. Rose, *After Yalta* (N.Y. 1973), and the Gaddis study. For a discussion and two revisionist critiques of America's early atomic energy policies, consult, respectively, Richard G. Hewlett and Oscar E. Henderson, Jr., *The New World 1939-1946, Vol I of A History of the United States Atomic Energy Commission* (University Park, Pa., 1962); Martin J. Sherwin, 'The Atomic Bomb and the Origins of the Cold War: U.S. Atomic — Energy Policy and

Diplomacy, 1941-1945', *American Historical Review*, LXXVIII (October 1973), 945-68; and Barton J. Bernstein, 'The Quest for Security: American Foreign Policy and International Control of Atomic Energy, 1942-1946', *Journal of American History*, LX (March 1974), 1003-44.

A convenient survey of American memoir literature is Robert W. Sellen, 'Origins of the Cold War: An Historiographical Survey', *Studies in the Social Sciences*, IX (June 1970), 57-97. Memoirs of especial importance for American-Soviet relations during the 1940s include among others Henry L. Stimson and McGeorge Bundy, *On Active Service in Peace and War* (N.Y. 1948); James MacGregor Burns, *Roosevelt: The Soldier of Freedom* (N.Y. 1970); Robert E. Sherwood, *Roosevelt and Hopkins: An Intimate History* (rev. ed., N.Y., 1950); Cordell Hull, *The Memoirs of Cordell Hull* 2 vols. (N.Y. 1948); Arthur H. Vandenberg Jr., ed., *The Private Papers of Senator Vandenberg* (Boston 1952); Harry S. Truman, *Memoirs* 2 vols. (Garden City, N.Y., 1955-56); Walter Millis, ed., *The Forrestal Diaries* (N.Y. 1951); Dean G. Acheson, *Present at the Creation: My Ten Years in the State Department* (N.Y. 1969); George F. Kennan, *Memoirs: 1925-1950* (Boston 1967); Charles E. Bohlen, *Witness to History, 1929-1969* (N.Y. 1973); W. Averell Harriman, *America and Russia in a Changing World: A Half Century of Personal Observation* (Garden City, N.Y., 1971); and John Morton Blum, ed., *From the Morgenthau Diaries: Years of War, 1941-1945* (Boston 1967); and *The Price of Vision: The Diary of Henry A. Wallace, 1942-1946* (Boston 1973).

The origins of the Truman Doctrine and the Marshall Plan are examined at length in most of the Cold War histories cited. In addition to those works one will find much of interest in John L. Gaddis's 'Was the Truman Doctrine a Real Turning Point', *Foreign Affairs*, LII (January 1974), 386-402; Geoffrey Warner's 'The Truman Doctrine and the Marshall Plan', *International Affairs*, L (January 1974), 82-92; and Henry Butterfield Ryan's 'The American Intellectual Tradition Reflected in the Truman Doctrine', *American Scholar*, XLII (Spring 1973), 294-307. Other important books and articles include Harry B. Price, *The Marshall Plan and Its Meaning* (Ithaca, N.Y., 1955); Hadly Arkes, *Bureaucracy, The Marshall Plan, and the National Interest* (Princeton, N.J., 1972); Joseph M. Jones, *The Fifteen Weeks* (N.Y. 1955); and George F. Kennan, 'The Sources of Soviet Conduct', *Foreign Affairs*, XXV (July 1947), 566-82.

Representative examples of primary source materials in English are cited throughout the text. The most important of these are US Department of State, *Foreign Relations of the United States, Diplomatic Papers;* US Department of State, *Bulletin;* and *Public Papers of the Presidents of the United States.* Excellent guides to the contents of recent publications in the *Foreign Relations* series for the Cold War period are three review articles by Geoffrey Warner, 'From Teheran to Yalta: Reflections on F.D.R.'s Foreign Policy', *International Affairs*, XLIII (July 1967), 530-36; 'The United States and the Cold War', *ibid*, XLVI (July 1970), 529-44; and his above-cited Truman article. Another superb piece along these same lines is Richard W. Leopold's 'The *Foreign Relations* Series Revisited: One Hundred Plus Ten', *Journal of American History*, LIX (March 1973), 935-57). Finally, and of indispensable use to students of Truman foreign policy is Richard S. Kerkendall's, *The Truman Period as a Research Field: A Reappraisal, 1972* (rev., Columbia, Mo., 1974). Of the articles contained in this collection, the most noteworthy are those by Robert H. Ferrell and Alonzo L. Hamby.

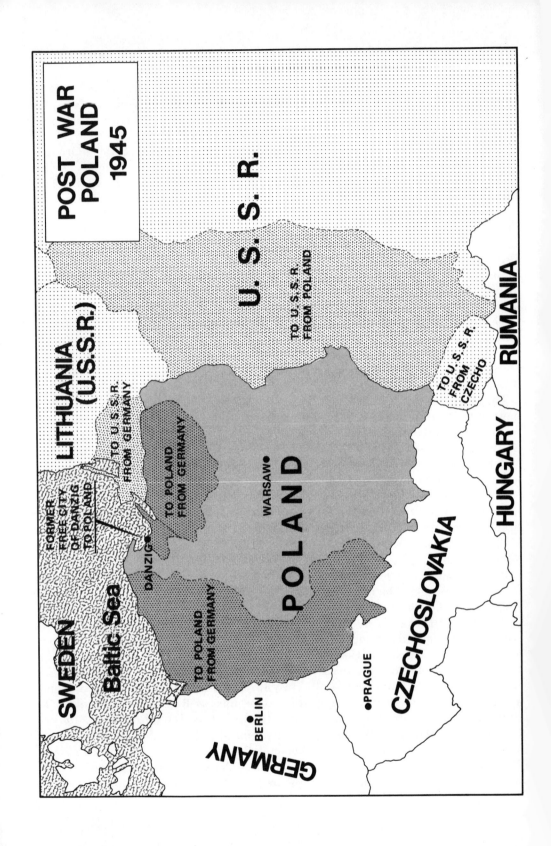

POST WAR
POLAND
1945

SWEDEN

Baltic Sea

LITHUANIA
(U.S.S.R.)

FORMER
FREE CITY
OF DANZIG
TO POLAND

TO U.S.S.R.
FROM GERMANY

U. S. S. R.

TO U.S.S.R.
FROM POLAND

DANZIG

TO POLAND
FROM GERMANY

WARSAW

POLAND

BERLIN

GERMANY

TO POLAND
FROM GERMANY

TO U.S.S.R.
FROM
CZECHO

PRAGUE

CZECHOSLOVAKIA

HUNGARY

RUMANIA

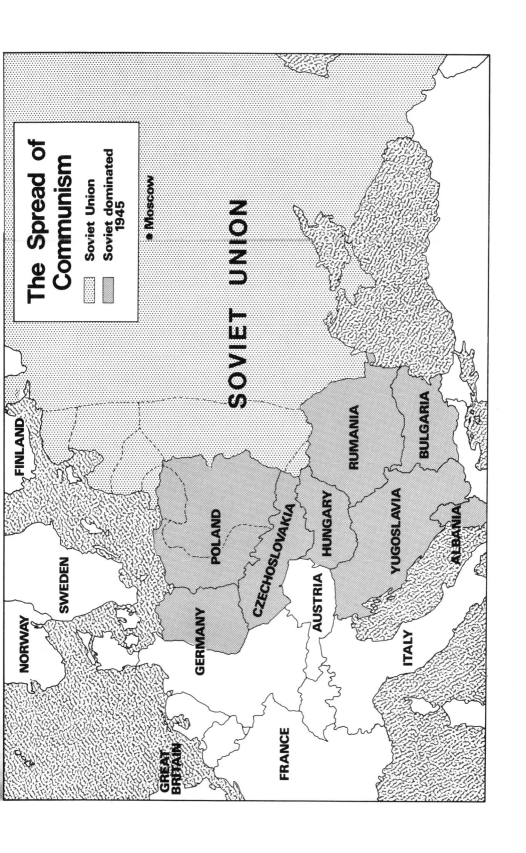

The Spread of Communism

Soviet Union

Soviet dominated
1945

● Moscow

SOVIET UNION

NORWAY

SWEDEN

FINLAND

GREAT
BRITAIN

GERMANY

POLAND

CZECHOSLOVAKIA

AUSTRIA

HUNGARY

RUMANIA

BULGARIA

YUGOSLAVIA

ALBANIA

FRANCE

ITALY

The Editor

A native of Chicago, Illinois, Dr. Joseph M. Siracusa has studied and taught in America, Europe, and Australia where he is presently a Senior Lecturer in American Diplomatic History at the University of Queensland and Acting Editor of *The Australian Journal of Politics and History*. In regard to his work on the Cold War, Dr. Siracusa has been the recipient of the Australian Government Research Grants Committee Award and a Harry S. Truman Library Institute for National and International Affairs Grant-in-Aid. Dr. Siracusa's publications include *New Left Diplomatic Histories and Historians* (1973) and (co-authored) *The Impact of the Cold War* (1977) and *Australian-American Relations Since 1945* (1976).